International Technical Support

Enterprise Security Architecture using IBM Tivoli Security Solutions

April 2002

SG24-6014-00

First Edition (April 2002)

This edition applies to the following Tivoli products: Access Manager for e-business 3.9, Access Manager for MQSeries 3.7.1, Risk Manager 3.8, PKI 3.7, User Administration 3.8, Security Manager 3.8, and Identity Manager 1.1. Various other related IBM, Tivoli and Lotus products are mentioned in this book.

Comments may be addressed to:
IBM Corporation, International Technical Support Organization
Dept. JN9B Building 003 Internal Zip 2834
11400 Burnet Road
Austin, Texas 78758-3493

When you send information to IBM, you grant IBM a non-exclusive right to use or distribute the information in any way it believes appropriate without incurring any obligation to you.

Contents

Figures xi

Tables xv

Notices xvii
Trademarks xviii

Preface xix
The team that wrote this redbook xix
Special notices xxii
Comments welcome xxiii

Part 1. Terminology 1

Chapter 1. Introduction 3
1.1 The BS7799 security standard 4
1.2 Mitigate risk 6
1.3 Corporate policy 8
    1.3.1 Standards, practices, and procedures 10
    1.3.2 Practical example 10
1.4 Other considerations 12
    1.4.1 The human factor impact 12
1.5 Closing remarks 14

Chapter 2. Method for Architecting Secure Solutions 15
2.1 Problem statement 18
2.2 Analysis 18
    2.2.1 Security-specific taxonomies, models, and methods 19
    2.2.2 Common Criteria 20
    2.2.3 Summary of analysis 21
2.3 System model for security 22
    2.3.1 Security subsystems 24
2.4 Developing security architectures 34
    2.4.1 Business process model 35
    2.4.2 Security design objectives 35
    2.4.3 Selection and enumeration of subsystems 36
    2.4.4 Documenting conceptual security architecture 37
2.5 Integration into the overall solution architecture 40
    2.5.1 Solution models 40

2.5.2 Documenting architectural decisions 40
2.5.3 Use cases 41
2.5.4 Refining the functional design. 44
2.5.5 Integrating requirements into component architectures 46
2.5.6 Summary of the design process 46
2.6 Conclusions 47
2.6.1 Actions and further study 48

Chapter 3. IT infrastructure topologies and components 49
3.1 The network becomes mission critical 50
3.1.1 Evolution 50
3.2 Connectivity framework 50
3.2.1 A local global vision with MASS 52
3.2.2 E-business security requirement and MASS. 55
3.3 Practical designs 55
3.4 Additional components 58
3.5 WebSphere Application Server. 59
3.5.1 WebSphere Application Server overview 60
3.6 WebSphere Edge Server 64
3.6.1 What Edge means. 64
3.6.2 Edge Server product features 66
3.6.3 Benefits of integrating Edge Server and Access Manager 70
3.7 Domino Application Server 71
3.7.1 Using two IBM application server products 72
3.8 IBM SecureWay Firewall 72
3.9 Public Key Infrastructure 74
3.9.1 Tivoli Public Key Infrastructure (TPKI) 75
3.10 Conclusions 76

Part 2. Managing access control 77

Chapter 4. Introduction to Access Manager components. 79
4.1 Base components. 80
4.1.1 Overview 80
4.1.2 User registry 81
4.1.3 Authorization database 84
4.1.4 Authorization Service 85
4.1.5 Policy Server. 86
4.1.6 The pdadmin utility 86
4.1.7 Web Portal Manager 86
4.2 Blades 91
4.2.1 WebSEAL 91
4.2.2 Plug-In for Edge Server. 97
4.2.3 Plug-in for Web Servers 98

    4.2.4 Access Manager for Business Integration. 101
    4.2.5 Other blades 103
  4.3 Interfaces. 106
    4.3.1 aznAPI. 106
    4.3.2 Java API for AM-based authorization 106
    4.3.3 Management API 106
    4.3.4 External Authorization Service 107
    4.3.5 Cross Domain Authentication Service. 108
    4.3.6 Cross Domain Mapping Framework 109

Chapter 5. Access Manager Web-based architecture 111
  5.1 Typical Internet Web server security characteristics. 112
  5.2 Access control of Web content and applications. 114
  5.3 Access control subsystem 115
  5.4 WebSEAL requirement issues 117
    5.4.1 Typical business requirements 117
    5.4.2 Typical design objectives (technical requirements). 118
  5.5 WebSEAL architectural principles. 118
    5.5.1 Principle 1 119
    5.5.2 Principle 2 119
    5.5.3 Principle 3 119
  5.6 Basic WebSEAL component interactions 120
  5.7 Component configuration and placement 123
    5.7.1 Network zones 123
    5.7.2 Secure communication issues 126
    5.7.3 Specific Access Manager component placement guidelines 126
    5.7.4 Summarizing Access Manager component placement issues 137
  5.8 Physical architecture considerations. 138
    5.8.1 Access Manager components. 138
    5.8.2 Other infrastructural components 139
    5.8.3 General host "hardening" considerations 141
  5.9 WebSEAL in an overall security solution 142

Chapter 6. A basic WebSEAL scenario 143
  6.1 Company profile 144
    6.1.1 Technology background 144
    6.1.2 IT infrastructure. 145
    6.1.3 Business requirements 147
    6.1.4 Security design objectives. 148
    6.1.5 Requirements analysis 148
    6.1.6 Access control architecture. 149
    6.1.7 Building the physical architecture 155
    6.1.8 Architectural summary 156

Chapter 7. Increasing availability and scalability 157
7.1 Further evolution 158
 7.1.1 Business requirements 158
 7.1.2 Security design objectives. 158
7.2 Availability 159
 7.2.1 Failure situations 159
 7.2.2 Providing high availability 162
7.3 Adding scalability 170

Chapter 8. Authentication and delegation with Access Manager 173
8.1 Typical business requirements 175
8.2 Typical security design objectives 175
8.3 Solution architecture with WebSEAL 176
 8.3.1 Authentication and delegation mechanisms 178
 8.3.2 Trust 180
 8.3.3 Generic authentication mechanism with WebSEAL 181
 8.3.4 Generic delegation mechanism with WebSEAL 183
8.4 Supported WebSEAL authentication mechanisms 184
 8.4.1 Basic authentication with user ID/password 185
 8.4.2 Forms-based login with user ID/password 185
 8.4.3 Authentication with X.509 client certificates 185
 8.4.4 Authentication with RSA SecurID token 186
 8.4.5 Custom authentication using CDAS 186
 8.4.6 Authentication using customized HTTP headers 188
 8.4.7 Authentication based on IP address 188
 8.4.8 No authentication 188
 8.4.9 MPA authentication. 189
8.5 WebSEAL delegation mechanisms. 190
 8.5.1 Tivoli Global Sign-On (TGSO)-lockbox 191
 8.5.2 Integrating applications requiring forms-based login. 195
 8.5.3 Passing an unchanged Basic Authentication header 196
 8.5.4 Junction without authentication. 196
 8.5.5 Providing a generic password. 196
 8.5.6 Supplying user and group information 197
 8.5.7 Using LTPA authentication with WebSEAL. 198

Chapter 9. WebSphere application integration. 201
9.1 Business requirements. 202
9.2 Security design objectives 203
9.3 WebSphere Application Server Version 4.0 security. 206
9.4 Access Manager and WebSphere integration. 210
 9.4.1 Shared user registry 211
 9.4.2 Single sign-on 212

9.4.3 Application integration. 219

Chapter 10. Access control in a distributed environment. 227
10.1 Cross-site distribution of a single security domain 228
    10.1.1 Business requirements 228
    10.1.2 Technical requirements. 229
    10.1.3 Access Manager architecture discussion 232
    10.1.4 Communication between distributed components 238
    10.1.5 Stocks-4u.com distributed architecture. 241
10.2 Distributed security domains 242
    10.2.1 CDSSO. 243
    10.2.2 e-Community single sign-on 246
    10.2.3 Comparing CDSSO and e-Community single sign-on 251
10.3 Distributed messaging applications 252
    10.3.1 An MQSeries distributed application at Stocks-4u.com 252
10.4 Conclusion 255

Part 3. Managing identities and credentials 257

Chapter 11. Basic management for identities. 259
11.1 The weak link. 260
11.2 Efficient managing of an IT environment. 260
11.3 Company profile. 261
    11.3.1 Security related problems 262
    11.3.2 Business requirements 263
    11.3.3 Security design objectives. 264
    11.3.4 Summary. 265
11.4 Planned architecture overview 265
11.5 Detailed architecture (solution design) 269
    11.5.1 Security policies 271
    11.5.2 Account management. 272
    11.5.3 Endpoint 272
    11.5.4 Logical network view. 272
11.6 Tivoli User Administration. 274
    11.6.1 Default and validation policies. 275
    11.6.2 OnePassword 276
    11.6.3 Integration with the existing infrastructure. 276
    11.6.4 Tivoli Management Framework. 278
    11.6.5 Tivoli Global Sign-On 278

Chapter 12. Advanced management for identities and credentials . . . 283
12.1 Company profile. 285
12.2 Business requirements. 287
12.3 Security design objectives 288

12.4 Planned architecture overview 289
 12.4.1 Initial security risk assessment 293
12.5 Detailed architecture (solution design) 294
 12.5.1 Tivoli Management Framework 297
 12.5.2 Identity Manager Web Interface 300
 12.5.3 Identity Manager Management Server 307
 12.5.4 Tivoli Security Manager 310

Part 4. Managing a security audit 329

Chapter 13. Risk Manager topology and infrastructure 331
13.1 From the front door to the backyard 332
13.2 Overview of components 333
 13.2.1 Web server environment 333
 13.2.2 Back-end data 334
 13.2.3 Firewall 335
 13.2.4 Router 336
 13.2.5 Intrusion Detection System 336
 13.2.6 Antivirus 337
 13.2.7 Mail infrastructure 337
13.3 Tivoli Framework architecture 337
 13.3.1 Tivoli Management Server 339
 13.3.2 Tivoli Management Desktop 339
 13.3.3 Managed Node 339
 13.3.4 Tivoli Endpoint 339
 13.3.5 Gateway 340
 13.3.6 Tivoli Management Desktop 340
 13.3.7 Policies and policy regions 341
 13.3.8 Centrally Managed Policies 341
 13.3.9 Tivoli Enterprise Console 342
 13.3.10 Availability Intermediate Manager (AIM) 345
13.4 Risk Manager architecture 347
 13.4.1 Adapters 348
 13.4.2 Adapters and managed technologies 349
 13.4.3 Event management platform architecture 349
 13.4.4 Correlation for enterprise risk management 350
 13.4.5 Decision Support for enterprise risk management 351
13.5 The benefits of enterprise risk management 352
 13.5.1 Firewall management 352
 13.5.2 Intrusion detection 353
 13.5.3 Application intrusion detection management 355
 13.5.4 Managing host intrusions using Tivoli Host IDS 356
 13.5.5 Risk assessment 357

13.5.6 Tasks for enterprise risk management 358
13.5.7 The value of enterprise risk management. 358

Chapter 14. Building a centralized security audit subsystem 363
14.1 Company profile. 364
14.1.1 Security related problem 365
14.1.2 Business requirements 365
14.1.3 Business design 366
14.1.4 Security design objectives. 366
14.2 Security audit subsystem 367
14.2.1 Audit subsystem at Nuts & Bolts, Inc.. 368
14.2.2 Risk Manager in the audit subsystem 369
14.2.3 Integration of Risk Manager 372
14.3 Expanding security monitoring 375
14.3.1 Tools supported 376
14.4 Mapping the solution to the organization 377
14.5 Intrusion Manager 378
14.6 Summary 379

Chapter 15. Extending the centralized security audit subsystem 381
15.1 Company profile. 382
15.1.1 Business requirements 383
15.1.2 Business design 384
15.1.3 Security design objectives. 384
15.1.4 Security audit subsystem 385
15.2 Risk Manager. 385
15.2.1 The distributed environment 385
15.3 Tivoli Decision Support. 387
15.3.1 TDS and Risk Manager. 388
15.3.2 TDS in the company architecture 389
15.3.3 Mapping the solution to the organization 392
15.4 Summary 394

Part 5. Using MASS in business scenarios. 395

Chapter 16. Global MASS - an example. 397
16.1 Business view 398
16.2 Logical view 399
16.3 Detailed view 400
16.4 Full architectural view. 402

Part 6. Appendixes 405

Appendix A. Additional product information 407

Firewall packages. 408
    Cisco PIX 408
    Symantec Enterprise Firewall 408
    Check Point Software's Check Point FireWall-1 409
PKI 410
    iPlanet/Netscape Certificate Management System. 410
    RSA Keon 411
    VeriSign. 411
Antivirus software. 412
    Norton AntiVirus by Symantec 412
    Panda Software Global Virus Insurance 414
    Trend Antivirus Solutions 415
    Additional resources and information 415

Appendix B. Single Sign-On - a contrarian view 417
Introduction 418
The problem 419
The Proxy-SSO "Solution" 419
The solution is difficult, expensive, and incomplete 420
The Web. 421
An alternative approach 423
Conclusion 426

Related publications 427
IBM Redbooks 427
    Other resources 427
Referenced Web sites 428
How to get IBM Redbooks 430
    IBM Redbooks collections. 430

Glossary 431

Abbreviations and acronyms 435

Index 439

Figures

1-1   Risk categorization. 7
1-2   Dynamics for policy, standards, practices, and procedures. 9
1-3   The five steps in defining your IT security 11
1-4   Principal threat sources 13
2-1   IT security processes and subsystems 25
2-2   Security audit subsystem processes 27
2-3   Integrity subsystem processes. 28
2-4   Access control subsystem processes 30
2-5   Information flow control subsystem processes 31
2-6   Credential subsystem processes. 33
2-7   Networked information system environment 34
2-8   The normal and imperiled IT business process flow 35
2-9   Defending against attacks 38
2-10 Ensuring correct and reliable operation 39
2-11 Boundary flow control with security subsystems 41
2-12 Three-tier client/server input flow with security subsystems 43
2-13 Sample PKI digital certificate enrollment process flow 45
3-1   High level architectural model including all network components 51
3-2   How security fits into the enterprise 52
3-3   Applying MASS domain concepts 54
3-4   Basic DMZ design 56
3-5   Segregating the intranet client 57
3-6   Management zone, high availability, and load balancing. 58
3-7   WebSphere family of products. 60
3-8   Basic Edge Server placement 65
4-1   Relationship between the protected object space, ACLs, and POPs . . 85
4-2   Access Manager delegation model example 88
4-3   Web Portal Manager architecture 90
4-4   WebSEAL architecture. 96
4-5   Plug-in for Edge Server architecture 98
4-6   Access Manager Web server plug-in architecture 100
4-7   Access Manager for Business Integration architecture 103
4-8   WebSEAL EAS architecture 108
4-9   CDAS architecture 109
5-1   A typical basic Internet Web architecture. 112
5-2   Typical advanced Web application architecture. 113
5-3   Access control subsystem 116
5-4   WebSEAL interaction with other Access Manager components 120

5-5   Direct serving of Web content from WebSEAL 121
5-6   Basic WebSEAL proxy functionality 122
5-7   Network zones 125
5-8   Policy Server placement guidelines 127
5-9   User Registry placement guidelines 128
5-10   Restricting network access to User Registry 129
5-11   Separating User Registry read and write functions 130
5-12   Web Portal Manager placement guidelines 131
5-13   Restricting HTTP/HTTPS network traffic paths 132
5-14   WebSEAL placement guidelines 134
5-15   Web server placement guidelines 135
5-16   Limiting network access to Web servers 136
5-17   An example Access Manager WebSEAL architecture 137
5-18   An example physical component layout 139
6-1   Stocks-4u.com data network 146
6-2   Current Stocks-4u.com architecture 150
6-3   Initial WebSEAL architecture 151
6-4   WebSEAL security architecture with internal WebSEAL 152
6-5   Detailed WebSEAL security architecture with internal WebSEAL 154
6-6   WebSEAL physical architecture 156
7-1   Initial Web architecture 160
7-2   Server replication to increase availability 162
7-3   WebSEAL availability overview 163
7-4   WebSEAL availability configuration 164
7-5   Authorization Server scenario for Stocks-4U.com 166
7-6   Authorization Server scenario with high availability 167
8-1   Reverse proxy flow for authentication, delegation, and authorization . 177
8-2   Access Manager authentication methods with WebSEAL 179
8-3   Overview of Web server products protected with WebSEAL 181
8-4   Generic WebSEAL authentication model 182
8-5   WebSEAL authentication model with CDAS 187
8-6   LDAP shared by Access Manager and other applications 193
8-7   Shared LDAP with separate user entries 194
8-8   SSO servlet 195
8-9   WebSEAL LTPA token delegation 200
9-1   Category 1 systems 203
9-2   Category 2 systems 204
9-3   Category 3 systems 205
9-4   Policy Enforcement based on consistent decision making 206
9-5   Role based security 209
9-6   TAI using a junction with the -b supply option 214
9-7   TAI using a junction without the -b supply option 215
9-8   TAI using a mutually authenticated SSL junction 216

9-9   WebSEAL creates LTPA cookies for authenticated users. 218
9-10 Access Manager integration with WebSphere Application Server. . . . 222
9-11 Access Manager utility to map roles to principals and groups 223
9-12 Central administration for multiple WebSphere servers. 225
10-1 Stocks-4u.com security domain 230
10-2 Stocks-4u.com updated data network 231
10-3 IT center network zones. 232
10-4 Distributed WebSEALs - replicated Web servers 234
10-5 Stocks-4u.com production network distributed server configuration . . 237
10-6 Cross-site SSL communication 239
10-7 Cross-site VPN communication 240
10-8 Bridged cross-site communication 241
10-9 Stocks-4u.com distributed WebSEAL architecture summary 242
10-10 CDSSO identity determination process 244
10-11 Stocks-4u.com CDSSO scenario. 246
10-12 The e-Community model 247
10-13 e-Community initial identity determination process 248
10-14 e-Community subsequent identity determination process 249
10-15 Stocks-4u.com e-Community scenario 251
10-16 A Stocks-4u.com MQSeries application. 253
10-17 AM/BI architecture 254
10-18 A Stocks-4u.com AM/BI scenario 255
11-1 Enterprise layout 262
11-2 Planned architecture 266
11-3 TUA interactions 270
11-4 TUA policy example 271
11-5 Mixed UNIX environment. 273
11-6 User and server groups installed 274
11-7 Functional TUA solution diagram. 277
11-8 Tivoli Global Sign-On (TGSO) infrastructure 279
12-1 Intranet environment of our virtual company 285
12-2 Components for advanced security management solution 290
12-3 Tivoli Identity Manager overview 296
12-4 Solution design with Tivoli Identity Manager 297
12-5 Supported platforms for Tivoli Identity Manager 300
12-6 Delegated user and security administration. 303
12-7 New user registration workflow 305
12-8 Technical workflow implementation with BPs and BPOs. 306
12-9 Web access to Identity Manager using WebSEAL 309
12-10 Role-based authorization model 311
12-11 Role-based policy information for TUA and TSM. 317
12-12 Logical AMOS architecture on UNIX systems 319
13-1 e-business topology 332

13-2 Tivoli management architecture. 338
13-3 Tivoli Management Desktop 340
13-4 TEC console all open events 343
13-5 TEC console situation overview. 343
13-6 TEC console individual event details 344
13-7 AIM topology 346
13-8 Tivoli Enterprise Console AIM 347
13-9 Risk Manager architecture. 348
13-10 Adapters convert events and alerts into IDEF 349
14-1 Initial IT architecture for Nuts & Bolts, Inc. 365
14-2 Audit flow structure 366
14-3 Audit subsystem. 367
14-4 Audit functions 369
14-5 Logic view with Risk Manager components 370
14-6 Risk Manager flows 373
14-7 Local summarization engine 376
14-8 Organization flows 378
15-1 Network integration architecture 383
15-2 Enhanced audit flow structure 384
15-3 RM and TEC architecture 386
15-4 TDS architecture 389
15-5 TDS Sensors report 390
15-6 TDS Top 100 Intruders 391
15-7 TDS antivirus report. 392
15-8 Organization flow 393
16-1 Business view 398
16-2 Logical view 400
16-3 Detailed view 401
16-4 The full architectural view 403

Tables

2-1   Placing Common Criteria classes in functional categories 23
2-2   Mapping design objectives to security subsystems 36
2-3   Determining the security subsystems in a design 37
4-1   Delegated administration roles in Access Manager. 89
4-2   Plug-in for Web servers functionalities. 98
9-1   LDAP directories supported by WebSphere and Access Manager . . . 211
12-1   System resources and corresponding AMOS resource types 321
12-2   AMOS permissions defined in the [OSSEAL] action group 323

Notices

This information was developed for products and services offered in the U.S.A.

IBM may not offer the products, services, or features discussed in this document in other countries. Consult your local IBM representative for information on the products and services currently available in your area. Any reference to an IBM product, program, or service is not intended to state or imply that only that IBM product, program, or service may be used. Any functionally equivalent product, program, or service that does not infringe any IBM intellectual property right may be used instead. However, it is the user's responsibility to evaluate and verify the operation of any non-IBM product, program, or service.

IBM may have patents or pending patent applications covering subject matter described in this document. The furnishing of this document does not give you any license to these patents. You can send license inquiries, in writing, to:
IBM Director of Licensing, IBM Corporation, North Castle Drive Armonk, NY 10504-1785 U.S.A.

The following paragraph does not apply to the United Kingdom or any other country where such provisions are inconsistent with local law: INTERNATIONAL BUSINESS MACHINES CORPORATION PROVIDES THIS PUBLICATION "AS IS" WITHOUT WARRANTY OF ANY KIND, EITHER EXPRESS OR IMPLIED, INCLUDING, BUT NOT LIMITED TO, THE IMPLIED WARRANTIES OF NON-INFRINGEMENT, MERCHANTABILITY OR FITNESS FOR A PARTICULAR PURPOSE. Some states do not allow disclaimer of express or implied warranties in certain transactions, therefore, this statement may not apply to you.

This information could include technical inaccuracies or typographical errors. Changes are periodically made to the information herein; these changes will be incorporated in new editions of the publication. IBM may make improvements and/or changes in the product(s) and/or the program(s) described in this publication at any time without notice.

Any references in this information to non-IBM Web sites are provided for convenience only and do not in any manner serve as an endorsement of those Web sites. The materials at those Web sites are not part of the materials for this IBM product and use of those Web sites is at your own risk.

IBM may use or distribute any of the information you supply in any way it believes appropriate without incurring any obligation to you.

Information concerning non-IBM products was obtained from the suppliers of those products, their published announcements or other publicly available sources. IBM has not tested those products and cannot confirm the accuracy of performance, compatibility or any other claims related to non-IBM products. Questions on the capabilities of non-IBM products should be addressed to the suppliers of those products.

This information contains examples of data and reports used in daily business operations. To illustrate them as completely as possible, the examples include the names of individuals, companies, brands, and products. All of these names are fictitious and any similarity to the names and addresses used by an actual business enterprise is entirely coincidental.

COPYRIGHT LICENSE:
This information contains sample application programs in source language, which illustrates programming techniques on various operating platforms. You may copy, modify, and distribute these sample programs in any form without payment to IBM, for the purposes of developing, using, marketing or distributing application programs conforming to the application programming interface for the operating platform for which the sample programs are written. These examples have not been thoroughly tested under all conditions. IBM, therefore, cannot guarantee or imply reliability, serviceability, or function of these programs. You may copy, modify, and distribute these sample programs in any form without payment to IBM for the purposes of developing, using, marketing, or distributing application programs conforming to IBM's application programming interfaces.

Trademarks

The following terms are trademarks of the International Business Machines Corporation in the United States, other countries, or both:

3090™	IBM®	Redbooks™	Tivoli Enterprise
AIX®	Informix™	Redbooks(logo)™	Console®
AS/400®	MQSeries®	S/390®	TME®
Balance®	NetView®	SecureWay®	TXSeries™
CICS®	OS/2®	SP™	VisualAge®
Cross-Site®	OS/390®	SP2®	WebSphere®
DB2®	OS/400®	TCS®	z/OS™
e (logo)®	Perform™	Tivoli®	zSeries™
Everyplace™	RACF®	Tivoli Enterprise™	

The following terms are trademarks of International Business Machines Corporation and Lotus Development Corporation in the United States, other countries, or both:

cc:Mail®	Lotus®	Notes®
Domino™	Lotus Notes®	

ActionMedia, LANDesk, MMX, Pentium and ProShare are trademarks of Intel Corporation in the United States, other countries, or both.

Microsoft, Windows, Windows NT, and the Windows logo are trademarks of Microsoft Corporation in the United States, other countries, or both.

Java and all Java-based trademarks and logos are trademarks or registered trademarks of Sun Microsystems, Inc. in the United States, other countries, or both.

C-bus is a trademark of Corollary, Inc. in the United States, other countries, or both.

UNIX is a registered trademark of The Open Group in the United States and other countries.

SET, SET Secure Electronic Transaction, and the SET Logo are trademarks owned by SET Secure Electronic Transaction LLC.

Other company, product, and service names may be trademarks or service marks of others.

Preface

This redbook will look at Tivoli's overall Enterprise Security Architecture, focusing on the integration of authentication, authorization, encryption, and risk management throughout extensive e-business enterprise implementations. The available security product diversity in the marketplace challenges everybody in charge of designing single secure solutions or an overall enterprise security architecture. With Access Manager, Privacy Manager, Risk Manager, PKI, User Admin, Security Manager, and Identity Director, Tivoli offers a complete set of products designed to address these challenges.

This redbook will depict several e-business scenarios with different security challenges and requirements. It will use the IBM Method for Architecting Secure Solutions (MASS) to describe necessary architectural building blocks and components. By matching the desired Tivoli SecureWay product criteria, it will describe appropriate security implementations that will meet the targeted requirements.

This book is a valuable resource for security officers, administrators, and architects who wish to understand and implement enterprise security following architectural guidelines.

The team that wrote this redbook

This redbook was produced by a team of specialists from around the world working at the International Technical Support Organization, Austin Center.

The team that wrote this book is shown in the picture above. They are, from left to right: Jim, Mari, Guy, Stefan, Cynthia, Oleg, Rick, Axel, and Julien

Axel Bücker is a Certified Consulting Software I/T Specialist at the International Technical Support Organization, Austin Center. He writes extensively and teaches IBM classes worldwide on areas of Software Security Architecture and Network Computing Technologies. He holds a degree in computer science from the University of Bremen, Germany. He has 15 years of experience in a variety of areas related to Workstation and Systems Management, Network Computing, and e-business solutions. Before joining the ITSO in March 2000, Axel was working for IBM in Germany as a Senior IT Specialist in Software Security Architecture.

Oleg Bascurov is a Systems Engineer at Tivoli/IBM, Germany. He has two years experience in the systems management field. His areas of expertise include Tivoli security products for Web and classical enterprise environments as well as security aspects of Java-based web application server technologies.

Cynthia Davis is a Technical Specialist in the IBM Software Group Briefing Center in Austin, Texas. She focuses on Tivoli Security products. She has 23 years of experience in the technical sales field with IBM. She has worked as a Systems Engineer and Hospital Industry Specialist. Her areas of expertise include security management, storage management, and health care applications. She has written documentation for several IBM program offerings.

Stefan Fassbender is a Certified IT Security Consultant with IBM Germany. He holds a degree in computer science from the University of Bonn, Germany. Before he joined IBM in 1993 he worked three years at a national research organization in Germany (GMD) building and managing Internet infrastructure. During the last few years, he worked on various customer projects performing security assessments, ethical hacking, and architecting secure E-business infrastructure.

Julien Montuelle is an IT Specialist in France. He has three years of experience in the security field. He holds a degree in computer science from CPE Lyon France. His areas of expertise include Tivoli SecureWay products and firewalls. He has written extensively on Risk Manager.

Mari Heiser is a senior IT Architect in the United States, specializing in networking and e-commerce. She has 17 years of experience in the IT industry related to E-business Solutions, Network Computing, and Enterprise Management. She holds a degree in Education from Cleveland State University as well as a degree in Electrical Engineering. Her areas of expertise include e-business and network architectures, and middleware integration into an environment. She has written and edited several books relating to the IT industry.

Rick McCarty is a senior security Architect and Practice Lead for Security with IBM Tivoli Services. Based in Austin, Texas, his current work focuses on Policy Director Architecture. In addition to security, Rick's background extends across a broad range of computing areas, including operating systems, artificial intelligence, TCP/IP networking, e-mail gateway systems, directory services, and high-availability. His software development experience spans approximately 17 years at IBM, Tandem Computers, and Texas Instruments. Rick received his Bachelor Degree from the University of Texas at Austin in 1979.

Guy Moins is a Security Architect in Belgium. He has eight years of experience in the security areas field, coming from a UNIX and networking background. He holds a degree in Computer Science from the ATC. His areas of expertise include the deployment of security architecture for corporations and e-business architecture, as well as awareness and global security improvement programs. Guy has written several courses or white papers in the security area and extensively on the policies of Tivoli User Administration and the advanced Identity Directory and Methodology for Architecting Secure Solutions.

Jim Whitmore is a certified Senior Consulting Information Technology Architect currently working in IBM Global Services. He holds a Bachelor of Science in Electrical Engineering and Master of Science Degree in Telecommunications Management from the University of Maryland, and has more than 18 years experience in the technical disciplines of data communications, networking, and security. Jim's recent responsibilities include methodology development and practitioner mentoring associated with IT Security Architectures and related solutions.

Thanks to the following people for their contributions to this project:

International Technical Support Organization, Austin Center
Wade Wallace

IBM US
Paul Ashley, Sadu Bajekal, Keys Botzum, Michael Campbell, Rich Caponigro, Luis Casco-Arias, Rick Cohen, Daniel Craun, Mike Garrison, David Hemsath, Greg Hess, Heather Hinton, Christopher Lapoint, Luca Loiodice, Ivan Milman, Sridhar Muppidi, Ray Neucom, Venkat Raghavan, Neil Readshaw, Max Rodriguez, Mark Simpson, Roseanne Swart, Brian Turner, Mark Vandenwauver, Ron Williams

IBM US Security Architectures
David K. Jackson and Larry Shick

IBM Germany Security Architectures
Klaus Oberhammer

IBM Switzerland
Daniel Kipfer

IBM UK Security Architectures
Phil Billin

IBM UK
Jon Harry and Avery Salmon (for their outstanding deliverables and class material on Policy Director), Vincent Cassidy, Imran Tyabji

Special notices

This publication is intended to help security officers, administrators, and architects understand the overall Tivoli security architecture. It will provide information on the integration with different e-business patterns in order to better design security aspects in heterogeneous IT environments. The information in this publication is not intended as the specification of any programming interfaces that are provided by any Tivoli branded security product. See the individual product documentation section of the Tivoli security applications for a more detailed description.

Comments welcome

Your comments are important to us!

We want our IBM Redbooks to be as helpful as possible. Send us your comments about this or other Redbooks in one of the following ways:

► Use the online **Contact us** review redbook form found at:

  `ibm.com`/redbooks

► Send your comments in an Internet note to:

  redbook@us.ibm.com

► Mail your comments to the address on page ii.

Part 1

Terminology

In this part, we introduce the approach we are following in this redbook and we describe the different Tivoli product areas we are taking a closer look at. We also give you an introduction to the IBM Method for Architecting Secure Solutions (MASS) that will be used to develop customer security architectures.

Introduction

Addressing an overall enterprise security architecture is a somewhat complex undertaking because it involves many areas. There are different approaches that are used throughout the industries, but there are some security textbooks that can be considered a standard. The most popular of these guides is the British Standard 7799, or BS7799. Although there might be other ways of addressing enterprise security, we will take a little closer look at BS7799 to present the enormous scope of this task.

1.1 The BS7799 security standard[1]

The British Standard 7799 is the most widely recognized security standard in the world. The last major publication was in May 1999, an edition that included many enhancements and improvements on previous versions. In December 2000, it was republished again, and evolved into International Organization for Standardization 17799 (ISO 17799).

BS7799 (ISO17799) is comprehensive in its coverage of security issues. It contains a significant number of control requirements, some extremely complex. Compliance with BS7799 is, consequently, a far from trivial task, even for the most security conscious of organizations. Full certification can be even more daunting.

It is therefore recommended that BS7799 is approached in a step-by-step manner. The best starting point is usually an assessment of the current position/situation, followed by an identification of what changes are needed for BS7799 compliance. From here, planning and implementing must be rigidly undertaken.

This section is intended to help you understand the ten different categories that have to be considered when applying an overall enterprise security approach. After the categories have been briefly described, we talk about the next step in the implementation of a security policy. The categories are:

1. Business continuity planning

   The objectives of this section are:

   a. To counteract interruptions to business activities and to critical business processes from the effects of major failures or disasters.

2. System access control

   The objectives of this section are:

   a. To control access to information.

   b. To prevent unauthorized access to information systems.

   c. To ensure the protection of network services.

   d. To prevent unauthorized computer access.

   e. To detect unauthorized activities.

   f. To ensure information security when using mobile computing and tele-networking facilities.

---

[1] RiskServer, Security Risk Analysis, ISO17799, Information Security Policies and Business Continuity

3. System development and maintenance

   The objectives of this section are:

   a. To ensure security is built into operational systems.

   b. To prevent loss, modification, or misuse of user data in application systems.

   c. To protect the confidentiality, authenticity, and integrity of information.

   d. To ensure IT projects and support activities are conducted in a secure manner.

   e. To maintain the security of application system software and data.

4. Physical and environmental security

   The objectives of this section are:

   a. To prevent unauthorized access, damage, and interference to business premises and information.

   b. To prevent loss, damage, or compromise of assets and interruption to business activities.

   c. To prevent compromise or theft of information and information processing facilities.

5. Compliance

   The objectives of this section are:

   a. To avoid breaches of any criminal or civil law, statutory, regulatory, or contractual obligations and of any security requirements.

   b. To ensure compliance of systems with organizational security policies and standards.

   c. To maximize the effectiveness of and to minimize interference to/from the system audit process.

6. Personnel security

   The objectives of this section are:

   a. To reduce risks of human error, theft, fraud, or misuse of facilities.

   b. To ensure that users are aware of information security threats and concerns, and are equipped to support the corporate security policy in the course of their normal work.

   c. To minimize the damage from security incidents and malfunctions and learn from such incidents.

7. Security organization

   The objectives of this section are:

   a. To manage information security within the company.

   b. To maintain the security of organizational information processing facilities and information assets accessed by third parties.

   c. To maintain the security of information when the responsibility for information processing has been outsourced to another organization.

8. Computer and network management

   The objectives of this section are:

   a. To ensure the correct and secure operation of information processing facilities.

   b. To minimize the risk of systems failures.

   c. To protect the integrity of software and information.

   d. To maintain the integrity and availability of information processing and communication.

   e. To ensure the safeguarding of information in networks and the protection of the supporting infrastructure.

   f. To prevent damage to assets and interruptions to business activities.

   g. To prevent loss, modification or misuse of information exchanged between organizations.

9. Asset classification and control

   The objectives of this section are to maintain appropriate protection of corporate assets and to ensure that information assets receive an appropriate level of protection.

10. Security Policy

   The objectives of this section are to provide management direction and support for information security.

1.2 Mitigate risk

As you have seen in the last section, most of the categories are addressing different sorts of risks for an organization. It basically does not matter what kind of organization we are looking at; everybody is facing certain risks and everybody is striving for a maximum of security.

That is why it is of immense importance that the overall enterprise security policy is the responsibility of the top business management. They have to decide where the major security risks for that type of business lie and how to proceed from there. A security policy has to define how to deal with the different categories of risks, as depicted in Figure 1-1.

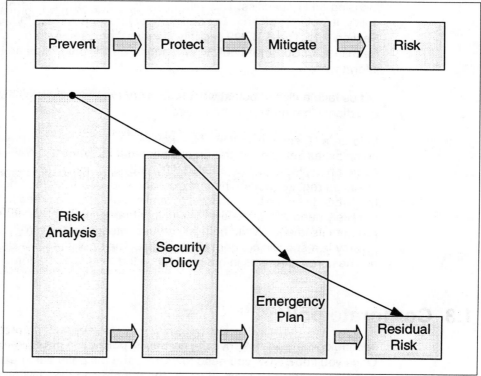

Figure 1-1   Risk categorization

1. First, you have to analyze where the major risks for your enterprise are in order to define procedures that will help prevent these risks from happening.

2. The next step is to define a security policy to deal with assets where you cannot prevent malicious actions without putting protective measures into place.

3. In case protective measures are overcome, you need to have an emergency plan that tells you what to do in those cases.

4. Because all those problems are not solved just by defining a security policy, but only by investing money for certain activities and countermeasures, it is the final call of the senior management on what residual risk can be accepted.

For this final risk, there are always insurance carriers who are happy to provide coverage for these residual risks.

However, the depicted rate on how the risk can be reduced by defining and applying a security policy can vary in different cases.

Until now, we have purely discussed general security policies and risks without focusing on IT specifics. This will still be the case for the enterprise security policy. It includes all areas as outlined, for example, in BS7799, described in Section 1.1, "The BS7799 security standard" on page 4. In our example in Section 1.3, "Corporate policy" on page 8, we will only focus on IT relevant information.

Let us take a closer look at what a *Security Policy* really is by asking the question: what protection do I need?

In today's IT, security is one of the key words. However, security can be quite complex, as complex as the organization needs or wants. While based on the same principles, it will be applied differently on each enterprise based on its business requirements. The first question should not be "do I need a firewall?" but "what do I have to protect?" or "what should I be protected from?". A bank will not likely need the same level of security than an enterprise using the Internet to promote its image. While both will require integrity of their Web site content, privacy is a specific concern for the bank. The right start is to understand the business requirements in order to derive the threats and address them.

1.3 Corporate policy

Technology should not drive the corporate policy, it is the other way around. Once you know what you need to protect and the potential threats and risks, you can start addressing them. First, all the threats and risks will be classified in a study based on elements such as:

- ► Direct financial loss
- ► Indirect financial loss (such as investigation, recovery, and so on)
- ► Loss of confidential information
- ► Liability
- ► Image impact
- ► Cost of mitigation
- ► Accepting residual risk

This study can process the same threats and risks, but conclude at a different severity, based on your particular business. Then the decision has to be made: accept or mitigate the risk. This process can be handled by external consultants such as IBM Global Services. The threat identification, as well as this severity study, is done in conjunction with the organization by applying a standard and a proven methodology.

It is tempting to directly translate the threat analysis into a technical solution. But first, it should lead to the corporate policy and standards. These documents will highlight the risks and present how they must be handled enterprise wide.

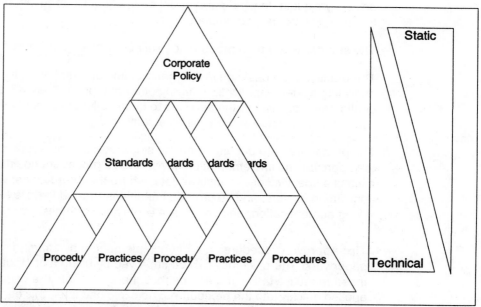

Figure 1-2   Dynamics for policy, standards, practices, and procedures

If it does not exist, the first document that will be written is the *corporate policy*. It must outline the high-level directions to be applied enterprise wide. It is absolutely not technical; it is derived from the business of the enterprise and should be as static as possible, as seen in Figure 1-2.

Attention: *Policies* is a very common term and in many products you will find specific *policies* sections. These are the product related policies that are covered in the practice or procedure documents. The corporate *policy* is not related to products and is a high level document.

1.3.1 Standards, practices, and procedures

Standards are derived from the corporate policy. They are documents explaining how to apply the policy details in terms of *authentication*, *access control*, and so on. They explain how the policy must be applied. Changes in threats or major technology changes can impact them.

The standards are then mapped to *practices* and/or *procedures*.

The practices are descriptions of practical implementation of the standard on an operating system, application, or any other end point. They will detail precise configurations, such as the services to be installed, the way to set-up user accounts, or how to securely install a software.

The procedures are documenting the single steps to be applied to requests and the approval and implementation flows. Such a procedure could be the request to access a specific set of sensitive data, where the approval path (system owner, application owners, and so on) and conditions (Virtual Private Network (VPN), strong authentication, and so on) are explained in details.

Tip: Approval procedures are often implemented by sending e-mails or paperwork. The efficiency can be improved by using a computer to handle these repetitive tasks and ensure that changes within the company are applied quickly into the procedures. As explained later, this can reduce human errors.

1.3.2 Practical example

Here is an example of how a policy is defined and implemented with procedures and practices.

The operations manager has reported an increased workload on the help desk due to problems caused by employees downloading non-business related programs onto their systems.

The problems range from the introduction of viruses to disruption of business processes, with a real financial impact. To address this problem, upper management incorporated in the corporate policy that "the corporate assets may be used only to perform enterprise related tasks".

First, the policy must be communicated to all employees in the enterprise.

The standards for the networking part explain which services may be allowed on the employee computer. The practice will then explain how to set-up the Windows or Linux clients accordingly to the standards and the procedures will explain how to perform a request, the requirements and the approval paths, to get special services installed on your computer.

The existing clients will be updated and controls will be performed to verify the compliance in addition to further audit of the environment.

The five steps we went through are summarized in Figure 1-3. It is a common approach adopted in many methodologies.

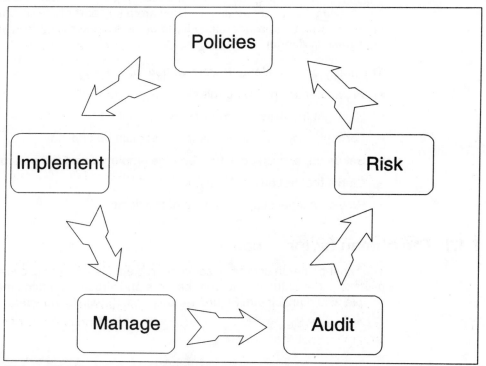

Figure 1-3   The five steps in defining your IT security

1.4 Other considerations

It is frustrating to work in an environment where you are constantly trying to discover what you can do or not. It is even more frustrating when services are blocked or you are being blamed without any plausible reason.

How can you accuse an employee of making unauthorized actions when it is not properly documented? Worse, if you need to take any legal action against an employee, how can you justify it without supporting documents?

As these documents will be used as rules within an enterprise, they must be clear and not subject to interpretation.

In addition, they must be publicly advertised and available. If a policy or a standard is written but not appropriately published, how can an employee be expected to follow it? It is not a loss of time to train the staff on these documents, especially when it is new and complex.

It is more efficient to get the staff enforcing a policy or standard they understand than having them fight against it. They are a key part of the global security level of the enterprise, and when they try to bypass some policy, they put your enterprise in danger.

The policy and the standards are written to:

► Provide enterprise wide rules

► Highlight the risks and the way to cope with it

► Formalize the security measures that must be applied

► Set up the expectations between the employee and the enterprise

► Clarify the procedures to follow

► Provide a legal support in case of problems

1.4.1 The human factor impact

The most common source of security problems is when employees are making mistakes. The actual threat from hackers and viruses is much smaller than most people would anticipate. Figure 1-4 on page 13 details the various sources.

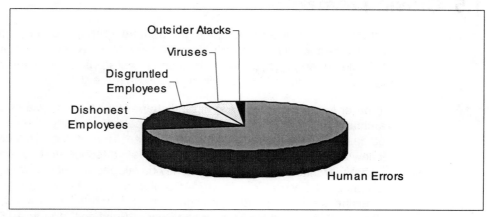

Figure 1-4   Principal threat sources

The biggest threat is inside. A total of 71 percent of the problems are directly related to employees, with 55 percent not intending to cause damage.

Having policies and procedures in place will help you address your risks. However, they will not directly cover the human factor errors.

Managing your security and auditing it will allow you to perform checks and discover some errors and correct them. However, if discovered, they could have already been the cause of a security breach.

Another important factor in managing and implementing your procedures is in using computer assistance with automatic verifications in order to reduce the possibility of human errors. A good example is the management of user accounts and access rights. Even today, communication about a new employee or one changing from one department to another is still being implemented using mail or paper. These steps, with a lot of human interaction, are the most error prone processes, easily leading to assigning too much access rights or the wrong ones, or even keeping an account alive for somebody who left the enterprise long time ago.

This risk in this example, introduced by the human factor, can be partially mitigated by using a workflow and/or a user management tool. It will be configured to apply the standards at all time. Some of these tools are using workflow systems that can even implement the procedures. This will not prevent all the errors, but will cover a lot of them. Using a central repository will also increase the global security by avoiding discrepancies between the various access control systems. The way your corporate policy and standards are applied has a direct impact to the quality and the level of security.

1.5 Closing remarks

After bringing a little more light to the general approach of developing an enterprise security architecture, and implementing a corporate policy that defines the rules of engagement when it comes to enterprise assets, we will now focus on discussing the next two building blocks in more detail.

In order to build a complex structural shape like an enterprise security architecture, you will need somebody capable of applying a set of rules and guides to the unique facts of your enterprise: an *architect*. This architect will follow a methodology that is designed to help describe and develop a complex security architecture. IBM has recently developed a *Methodology for Architecting Secure Solutions* (MASS) that reflects the current impact of thriving e-business environments. We explore this methodology in more detail in Chapter 2, "Method for Architecting Secure Solutions" on page 15. We also use this methodology in several sections throughout this book in order to proof the validity of our solutions.

Network topographies play an immensely important role for the enterprise security IT architecture, and without detailed knowledge of where to establish perimeter security components, one cannot succeed. Chapter 3, "IT infrastructure topologies and components" on page 49 talks about these aspects by laying a foundation of understanding about why the network becomes more and more critical to the overall IT infrastructure and security.

Method for Architecting Secure Solutions

This chapter introduces a new Method for Architecting Secure Solutions (MASS) that will be used by IBM Global Service employees in future security architecture engagements. It helps understand and categorize security related problems and discussions in today's e-business driven enterprise IT infrastructures. This discussion was originally posted in a special edition of the IBM Systems Journal on *End-to-End Security*, Vol. 40, No. 3[1].

The task of developing IT solutions that consistently and effectively apply security principles has many challenges, including the complexity of integrating the specified security functions within the several underlying component architectures found in computing systems, the difficulty in developing a comprehensive set of baseline requirements for security, and a lack of widely accepted security design methods. With the formalization of security evaluation criteria into an international standard known as Common Criteria, one of the barriers to a common approach for developing extensible IT security architectures has been lowered; however, more work remains. This chapter describes a systematic approach for defining, modeling, and documenting security functions within a structured design process in order to facilitate greater trust in the operation of resulting IT solutions.

---

[1] Copyright 2001 International Business Machines Corporation. Reprinted with permission from IBM Systems Journal, Vol. 40, No. 3.

Trust is the measure of confidence that can be placed on the predictable occurrence of an anticipated event, or an expected outcome of a process or activity.

For business activities that rely on IT, trust is dependent on both the nature of the agreement between the participants and the correct and reliable operation of the IT solution. The reliance on computerized processes for personal, business, governmental, and legal functions is evolving into a dependency and a presumption (not to be confused with trust) that the processes, and the IT systems within which they execute, will function without flaw. It is reasonable to expect that legal findings relative to the correct and reliable operation of IT solutions will be the basis for whether one party is liable for the damages suffered by another party as a result of a computerized operation.

Trustworthiness of IT solutions can be affected by many factors found throughout the life cycle of solution definition, design, deployment, and operation. The trustworthiness of design of IT solutions can be affected by the clarity and completeness with which the requirements are expressed by stakeholders and interpreted by solution designers. The trustworthiness of operation of IT solutions can be affected by the trustworthiness of the components and processes upon which they are built, the accuracy with which the design is implemented, and the way in which the resulting computing systems are operated and maintained. The trustworthiness of operational IT solutions can also be affected by the environments in which the solutions are positioned, by individuals who access them, and by events that occur during their operational lifetime.

Given that IT components will most likely continue to have flaws, that unexpected events will most likely occur, and that individuals will most likely continue to seek to interfere with the operation of computing solutions and the environmental infrastructure upon which the solutions rely, what can be done to instill a sufficient measure of confidence, that is, trust, in the correct and reliable operation of a given information technology solution?

One realistic expectation is that designers and integrators of IT solutions will enlist all reasonable measures to effect the correct and reliable operation of IT solutions throughout the design, development, and deployment phases of the solution life cycle.

While the responsibility for considering all reasonable measures is shared among all individuals involved in the design, development, and deployment of every IT solution, the role of anticipating the perils that the IT solution may face, and ensuring that the business risks of IT solution operation are mitigated, is generally the focus of IT security professionals.

Information technology security is a discipline that until recently was centered within the military, national security organizations, and the banking industry. With the growth of the Internet as a core networking and cooperative computing infrastructure, the need for, and the value of, IT security expertise has increased dramatically. The position of today's security architect closely parallels the role of the network manager or operator of the early 1980s. The similarities include the need to meet high expectations and service levels, a limited set of tools and techniques, low visibility of the electronic activities within the operational environment, plus the challenge of timely recognition and response to events and peril. In the mid-1980s, the development of a systems management discipline provided a focus, a method, and a tool set for standardized approaches to system-wide design, operation, and management.

To date, the application of IT security countermeasures is generally limited to addressing specific vulnerabilities, such as applying network and systems management processes, hardening operating systems for publicly available servers, applying and monitoring intrusion detection systems, configuring and operating digital certificate servers, and installing and configuring firewalls.

Based upon the evolution of destructive computer codes and viruses, the repeated breaches of sensitive computer systems, and recurring incidents of compromise of private information stored on networked computing systems, it is reasonable to conclude that the effectiveness of security measures in computing solutions needs to be improved. Recently, security experts from government and industry expressed the need for a more comprehensive approach to describing security requirements and designing secure solutions.

This chapter documents the findings and recommendations of a project for which the initial objective was to develop training materials for a recently defined technical discipline, within IBM Global Services, for security architects. During the project, early attempts to organize and present the "prior art" dealing with information technology security produced incomplete and unsatisfactory results, leading to the conclusion that a more fundamental analysis was needed. The refocused analysis produced a thought-provoking proposal for articulating, documenting, and synthesizing security within information technology solutions.

Although the project objectives were met, the by-products are different from those first envisioned. The observations and conclusions from the project are summarized within this chapter, including an examination of the basic motivations for implementing security, a review and recategorization of commonly invoked security standards, an analysis of the fundamental elements of security architecture and its design, and some first attempts to render architectural representations.

2.1 Problem statement

A systematic approach for applying security throughout information technology solutions is necessary in order to ensure that all reasonable measures are considered by designers, and that the resulting computing systems will function and can be operated in a correct and reliable manner.

In IBM Global Services, the requirement for a method for designing secure solutions is driven from several perspectives:

1. There is a need to "grow" the community of IT architects with a shared security focus.

2. There is a need to create synergy among the several technical disciplines within the IT architect profession relative to security issues.

3. There is a need to develop consistent designs, because many businesses and organizations have similar security and privacy compliance requirements based upon statute, regulation, and industry affiliation, and many enterprises are multinational, with geographically diverse installations operating under similar security policies and practices.

To be effective, the resulting method should use existing security paradigms, integrate with other information technology architectures, and work with today's technologies.

A logical and systematic technique for designing secure solutions has potential value beyond IBM Global Services:

► To individuals, by fostering trust within computing environments that would otherwise be suspect.

► To information technology professionals, by promoting rigor within an emerging discipline of computing science.

► To enterprises, by providing a technical standard with which the effectiveness of information technology designs, and designers, can be evaluated.

2.2 Analysis

Information technology architects rely on a wide range of techniques, tools, and reference materials in the solution design process. The results of a design activity may include an operational computing system or a set of documents that describe the system to be constructed from one or more viewpoints and at different levels of granularity. The documents provide a visualization of the system architecture.

To arrive at a system architecture, architects may use personal experience, or they may rely upon documented systematic procedures or methods. In addition to methods, architects refer to prioritize work and employ data collection techniques to define the problem space and the solution space. Reference materials can include a taxonomy of the problem space, a catalog of solution requirements, and documented models, patterns, or integrated solution frameworks. In general, as the definition of a given problem space matures, the taxonomy of the solution requirements stabilizes. This leads to well-defined reference models, proven solution frameworks, and mature solution design methods.

IT security architecture fits this model for limited problem spaces such as securing a network perimeter, where a set of solution requirements can be defined. A solution framework can be constructed for an enterprise firewall, and a solution architecture can be documented using known reference models for *demilitarized zones* (refer to Chapter 3, "IT infrastructure topologies and components" on page 49). IT security does not, in general, fit this model, because:

1. The security problem space has not stabilized in that the number and type of threats continue to grow and change.

2. Existing security solution frameworks take a limited view of the problem space, as with firewalls and network-level security.

3. Methods for creating security solution architectures are generally confined to the defined solution frameworks. For ill-defined problem spaces like IT security, the path to maturity of models and methods requires a different approach.

2.2.1 Security-specific taxonomies, models, and methods

ISO (International Organization for Standardization) 7498-2[6] is a widely referenced document associated with IT security solution design. Its purpose is to extend the applicability of the seven-layer OSI (Open Systems Interconnection) system model to cover secure communication between systems. Section 5 of this document describes a set of security services and mechanisms that could be invoked at the appropriate layer within the OSI system model, in appropriate combinations, to satisfy security policy requirements. Section 8 documents the need for ongoing management of OSI security services and mechanisms, to include management of cryptographic functions, network traffic padding, and event handling.

Many security practitioners use the OSI security services (authentication, access control, data confidentiality, data integrity, and nonrepudiation) as the complete taxonomy for the security requirements for IT solutions. However, the preamble of ISO 7498-2 specifically states that " ... OSI security is not concerned with security measures needed in end systems, installations, and organizations, except where these have implications on the choice and position of security services visible in OSI. These latter aspects of security may be standardized but not within the scope of OSI Recommendations."

Security evaluation criteria: Agencies and standards bodies within governments of several nations have developed evaluation criteria for security within computing technology. In the United States, the document has the designation "Trusted Computer System Evaluation Criteria," or TCSEC. The European Commission has published the Information Technology Security Evaluation Criteria, also known as ITSEC, and the Canadian government has published the Canadian Trusted Computer Product Evaluation Criteria, or CTCPEC. In 1996, these initiatives were officially combined into a document known as the Common Criteria, or CC. In 1999, this document was approved as a standard by the International Organization for Standardization. This initiative opens the way to worldwide mutual recognition of product evaluation results.

2.2.2 Common Criteria

Common Criteria provide a taxonomy for evaluating security functionality through a set of functional and assurance requirements. The Common Criteria include 11 functional classes of requirements:

► Security audit
► Communication
► Cryptographic support
► User data protection
► Identification and authentication
► Management of security functions
► Privacy
► Protection of security functions
► Resource utilization
► Component access
► Trusted path or channel.

These 11 functional classes are further divided into 66 families, each containing a number of component criteria. There are approximately 130 component criteria currently documented, with the recognition that designers may add additional component criteria to a specific design. There is a formal process for adopting component criteria through the Common Criteria administrative body, which can be found at:

http://www.commoncriteria.org

Governments and industry groups are developing functional descriptions for security hardware and software using the Common Criteria. These documents, known as protection profiles, describe groupings of security functions that are appropriate for a given security component or technology. The underlying motivations for developing protection profiles include incentives to vendors to deliver standard functionality within security products and reduction of risk in information technology procurement. In concert with the work to define protection profiles, manufacturers of security-related computer software and hardware components are creating documentation that explains the security functionality of their products in relation to accepted protection profiles. These documents are called "security targets." Manufacturers can submit their products and security targets to independently licensed testing facilities for evaluation in order to receive compliance certificates.

Common Criteria: a taxonomy for requirements and solutions

The security requirements defined within the Common Criteria have international support as "best practices." Common Criteria are intended as a standard for evaluation of security functionality in products. They have limitations in describing end-to-end security; because the functional requirements apply to individual products, their use in a complex IT solution is not intuitive. Protection profiles aid in the description of solution frameworks, although each protection profile is limited in scope to the specification of functions to be found in a single hardware or software product.

Common Criteria: a reference model

The Common Criteria introduce a few architectural constructs: the target of evaluation, or TOE, represents the component under design, and the TOE security functions document, or TSF, represents that portion of the TOE responsible for security. Under Common Criteria, the system or component under consideration is a "black box"; it exhibits some security functionality and some protection mechanisms for the embedded security functions.

2.2.3 Summary of analysis

For well-understood problem spaces, methods document the prior work and provide best practices for future analysis. For changing problem spaces such as IT security, methods can only postulate a consistent frame of reference for practitioners in order to encourage the development of future best practices. With time and experience, the methods and models associated with IT security will mature.

The Common Criteria document has important value to the security community, given its history and acceptance as a standard for security requirements definition, and its linkage to available security technologies through documented protection profiles and security targets. Common Criteria do not provide all of the guidance and reference materials needed for security design.

To develop an extensible method for designing secure solutions, additional work is required to develop:

1. A system model that is representative of the functional aspects of security within complex solutions.

2. A systematic approach for creating security architectures based on the Common Criteria requirements taxonomy and the corresponding security system model.

2.3 System model for security

Eberhardt Rechtin[2] suggests an approach for developing an architecture, differentiating between the "system" (what is built), the "model" (a description of the system to be built), the "system architecture" (the structure of the system), and the "overall architecture" (an inclusive set consisting of the system architecture, its function, the environment within which it will live, and the process used to build and operate it).

For the purposes of this project, the type of IT solutions addressed is consistent with a networked information system (NIS). Furthermore, the overall architecture is represented by the security architecture found within an NIS, and the security architecture is represented by the structure of a security system model. With a generalized system model for security in an NIS environment, architects could create instances of the system model, based upon detailed functional and risk management requirements.

Rechtin outlines the steps for creating a model as follows:

1. Aggregating closely related functions

2. Partitioning or reducing the model into its parts

3. Fitting or integrating components and subsystems together into a functioning system

---

[2] E. Rechtin, *Systems Architecting: Creating and Building Complex Systems*, Prentice Hall, 1991.

The security system model will be represented by the aggregation of security functions, expressed in terms of subsystems and how the subsystems interact. The security-related functions within an NIS can be described as a coordinated set of processes that are distributed throughout the computing environment. The notion of distributed security systems, coordinated by design and deployment, meets the intuitive expectation that security within an NIS should be considered pervasive. In an NIS environment, security subsystems must be considered as abstract constructs in order to follow Rechtin's definition.

For this project, Common Criteria were considered to be the description of the complete function of the security system model. The classes and families within the Common Criteria represent an aggregation of requirements; however, after careful review, it was determined that the class and family structures defined within Common Criteria do not lend themselves to be used as part of a taxonomy for pervasive security. The aggregation is more reflective of abstract security themes, such as cryptographic operations and data protection, rather than security in the context of IT operational function. To suit the objective of this project, the Common Criteria functional criteria were re-examined and reaggregated, removing the class and family structures. An analysis of the 130 component-level requirements in relation to their function within an NIS solution suggests a partitioning into five operational categories:

► Audit
► Access control
► Flow control
► Identity and credentials
► Solution integrity

A summary mapping of CC classes to functional categories is provided in Table 2-1.

Table 2-1 Placing Common Criteria classes in functional categories

Functional category	Common Criteria functional class
Audit	Audit, component protection, and resource utilization
Access control	Data protection, component protection, security management, component access, cryptographic support, identification and authentication, communication, and trusted path/channel
Flow control	Communication, cryptographic support, data protection, component protection, trusted path/channel, and privacy

Functional category	Common Criteria functional class
Identity/credentials	Cryptographic support, data protection, component protection, identification and authentication, component access, security management, and trusted path/channel
Solution integrity	Cryptographic support, data protection, component protection, resource utilization, and security management

While redundancy is apparent at the class level, there is only a small overlap at the family level of the hierarchy defined within Common Criteria and below. Much of the overlap represents the intersection of function and interdependency among the categories.

2.3.1 Security subsystems

The component-level guidance of Common Criteria documents rules, decision criteria, functions, actions, and mechanisms. This structure supports the assertion that the five categories described in Table 2-1 represent a set of interrelated processes, or subsystems, for security. The notion of a security subsystem has been proposed previously; the authors of *Trust in Cyberspace*[3] described functions within operating system access control components as belonging to a decision subsystem or an enforcement subsystem. The five interrelated security subsystems proposed here and depicted in Figure 2-1 on page 25 expand the operating system-based concept and suggest that function and interdependency of security-related functions, beyond centralized access control, can be modeled as well.

---

[3] Committee on Information Systems Trustworthiness, National Research Council, *Trust in Cyberspace*, National Academy Press, 1999.

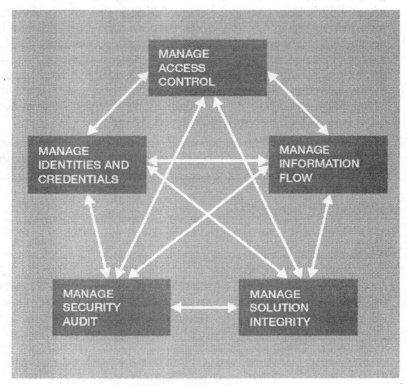

Figure 2-1   IT security processes and subsystems

A brief description of each of the five security subsystems, along with further detail of the aggregation of CC component-level criteria within each subsystem, is now provided. The subsystem diagrams are represented as parts of a closed-loop control system showing the internal processes that each performs, along with its external interfaces. In this representation, each subsystem consists of a managing process with a default idle state and several execution paths that can be invoked either by an asynchronous request signaled by another security subsystem or by a synchronized request from a nonsecurity process. Complementary representations composed of component views and interaction diagrams for the subsystems are being developed.

Security audit subsystem

The purpose of the security audit system in an IT solution is to address the data collection, analysis, and archival requirements of a computing solution in support of meeting the standards of proof required by the IT environment. A security audit subsystem is responsible for capturing, analyzing, reporting, archiving, and retrieving records of events and conditions within a computing solution. This subsystem can be a discrete set of components acting alone, or a coordinated set of mechanisms among the several components in the solution. Security audit analysis and reporting can include real-time review, as implemented in intrusion detection components, or after-the-fact review, as associated with forensic analysis in defense of repudiation claims. A security audit subsystem may rely upon other security subsystems in order to manage access to audit-related systems, processes, and data, control the integrity and flow of audit information, and manage the privacy of audit data. From Common Criteria, security requirements for an audit subsystem would include:

► Collection of security audit data, including capture of the appropriate data, trusted transfer of audit data, and synchronization of chronologies

► Protection of security audit data, including use of time stamps, signing events, and storage integrity to prevent loss of data

► Analysis of security audit data, including review, anomaly detection, violation analysis, and attack analysis using simple heuristics or complex heuristics

► Alarms for loss thresholds, warning conditions, and critical events

The closed loop process for a security audit subsystem is represented in Figure 2-2 on page 27.

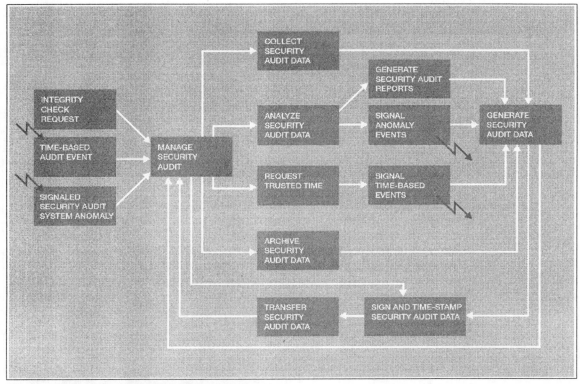

Figure 2-2   Security audit subsystem processes

Solution integrity subsystem

The purpose of the solution integrity subsystem in an IT solution is to address the requirement for reliable and correct operation of a computing solution in support of meeting the legal and technical standard for its processes. A solution integrity subsystem can be a discrete set of components or a coordinated set of mechanisms among the several components in the solution. The solution integrity subsystem may rely upon the audit subsystem to provide real-time review and alert of attacks, outages, or degraded operations, or after-the-fact reporting in support of capacity and performance analysis. The solution integrity subsystem may also rely upon the other subsystems to control access and flow. From Common Criteria, the focus of a solution integrity subsystem could include:

► Integrity and reliability of resources

► Physical protections for data objects, such as cryptographic keys, and physical components, such as cabling, hardware, and so on.

► Continued operations including fault tolerance, failure recovery, and self-testing

- ► Storage mechanisms: cryptography and hardware security modules
- ► Accurate time source for time measurement and time stamps
- ► Prioritization of service via resource allocation or quotas
- ► Functional isolation using domain separation or a reference monitor
- ► Alarms and actions when physical or passive attack is detected

The closed loop process for a solution integrity subsystem is represented in Figure 2-3.

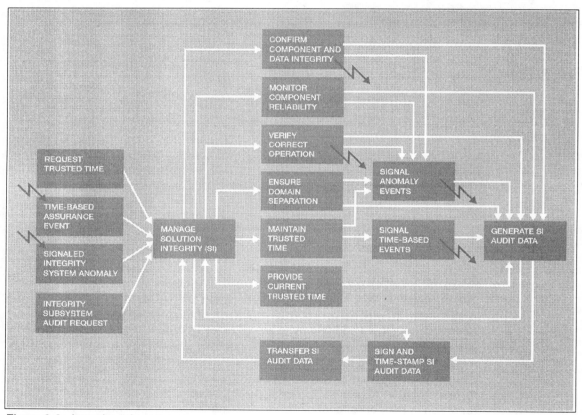

Figure 2-3   Integrity subsystem processes

Access control subsystem

The purpose of an access control subsystem in an IT solution is to enforce security policies by gating access to, and execution of, processes and services within a computing solution via identification, authentication, and authorization processes, along with security mechanisms that use credentials and attributes.

The credentials and attributes used by the access control subsystem along with the identification and authentication mechanisms are defined by a corresponding credential subsystem. The access control subsystem may feed event information to the audit subsystem, which may provide real-time or forensic analysis of events. The access control subsystem may take corrective action based upon alert notification from the security audit subsystem. From Common Criteria, the functional requirements for an access control subsystem should include:

► Access control enablement

► Access control monitoring and enforcement

► Identification and authentication mechanisms, including verification of secrets, cryptography (encryption and signing), and single- versus multiple-use authentication mechanisms

► Authorization mechanisms, to include attributes, privileges, and permissions

► Access control mechanisms, to include attribute-based access control on subjects and objects and user-subject binding

► Enforcement mechanisms, including failure handling, bypass prevention, banners, timing and timeout, event capture, and decision and logging components

The closed loop process for an access control subsystem is represented in Figure 2-4 on page 30.

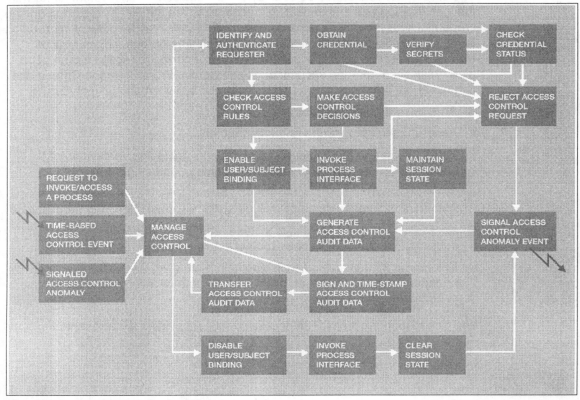

Figure 2-4   Access control subsystem processes

Information flow control subsystem

The purpose of an information flow control subsystem in an IT solution is to enforce security policies by gating the flow of information within a computing solution, affecting the visibility of information within a computing solution, and ensuring the integrity of information flowing within a computing solution. The information flow control subsystem may depend upon trusted credentials and access control mechanisms.

This subsystem may feed event information to the security audit subsystem, which may provide real-time or forensic analysis of events. The information flow control subsystem may take corrective action based upon alert notification from the security audit subsystem. From Common Criteria, an information flow control subsystem may include the following functional requirements:

► Flow permission or prevention

► Flow monitoring and enforcement

- ► Transfer services and environments: open or trusted channel, open or trusted path, media conversions, manual transfer, and import to or export between domains

- ► Mechanisms observability: to block cryptography (encryption)

- ► Storage mechanisms: cryptography and hardware security modules

- ► Enforcement mechanisms: asset and attribute binding, event capture, decision and logging components, stored data monitoring, rollback, and residual information protection and destruction

The closed loop process for an information flow control subsystem is represented in Figure 2-5.

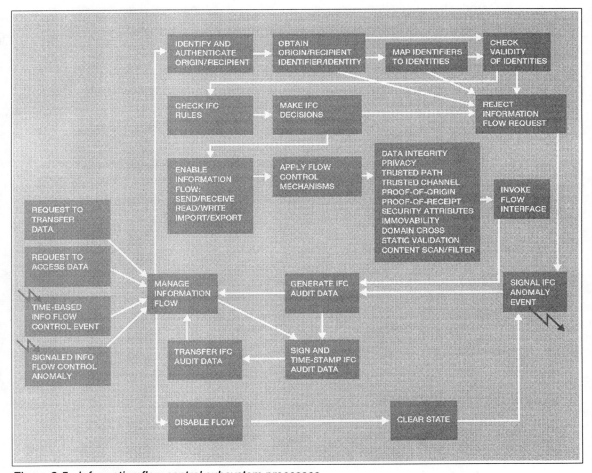

Figure 2-5   Information flow control subsystem processes

Identity or credential subsystem

The purpose of a credential subsystem in an IT solution is to generate, distribute, and manage the data objects that convey identity and permissions across networks and among the platforms, the processes, and the security subsystems within a computing solution. In some applications, credential systems may be required to adhere to legal criteria for creation and maintenance of trusted identity used within legally binding transactions.

A credential subsystem may rely on other subsystems in order to manage the distribution, integrity, and accuracy of credentials. A credential subsystem has, potentially, a more direct link to operational business activities than the other security subsystems, owing to the fact that enrollment and user support are integral parts of the control processes it contains. From Common Criteria, a credential subsystem may include the following functional requirements:

► Single-use vs. multiple-use mechanisms, either cryptographic or non-cryptographic

► Generation and verification of secrets

► Identities and credentials to be used to protect security flows or business process flows

► Identities and credentials to be used in protection of assets: integrity or non-observability

► Identities and credentials to be used in access control: identification, authentication, and access control for the purpose of user-subject binding

► Credentials to be used for purposes of identity in legally binding transactions

► Timing and duration of identification and authentication

► Life cycle of credentials

► Anonymity and pseudonymity mechanisms

The closed loop process for a credential subsystem is represented in Figure 2-6 on page 33.

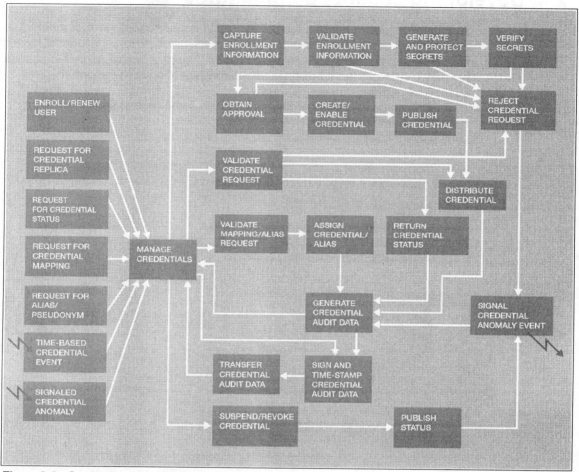

Figure 2-6   Credential subsystem processes

Summary of the security system model

This study postulates that the five security subsystems described here exist within every IT solution at the conceptual level, and that the design, integration, and interworking of the services and mechanisms associated with these subsystems represent the security functionality of the solution. This "security system model" needs to be combined with a method for developing the detailed security architecture for a given IT solution.

2.4 Developing security architectures

A system architecture has been defined as "the structure of the system to be built." In this study, the "system to be built" consists of the security control system found within a networked information system. Figure 2-7 represents the solution environment. Here, an e-business computing solution serves information or supports electronic commerce transactions via the Internet. The e-business computing solution is operated by an enterprise and provides services to one or more user communities.

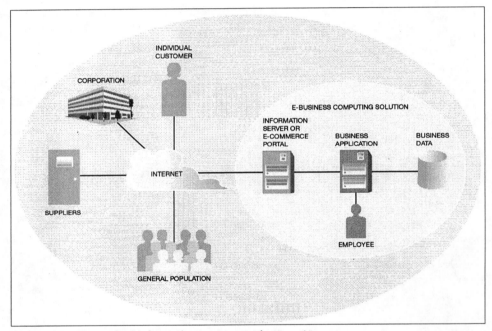

Figure 2-7   Networked information system environment

The e-business computing solution can be described as a set of automated business processes supporting the business context that requires security assurances and protections. The design goal is to infuse security into the computing solution and the related IT environment.

From a business perspective, there are two objectives:

1. To ensure that the desired IT business process flow yields correct and reliable results

2. To ensure that the potential vulnerabilities and exception conditions (that is, perils) within IT business process flows are addressed in ways that are consistent with the risk management objectives

These objectives show the duality of security design: to support and assure normal flows, as well as identify and account for all illicit flows and anomalous events.

2.4.1 Business process model

Figure 2-8 represents IT process flows for a generalized business system. The process flows reflect the events and conditions in which information assets are acted upon by processes that are invoked by users, or by processes acting on behalf of users. The left arrow represents the model business flow within a trusted environment, and the right arrow represents a more realistic view of the business flow, where perils exist in the operating environment.

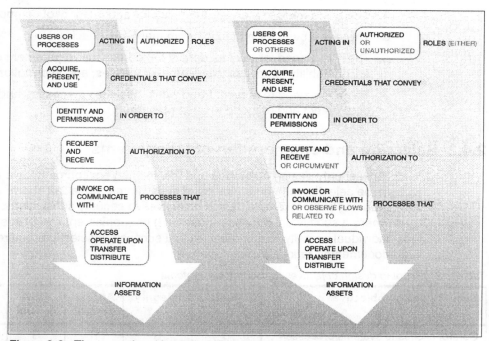

Figure 2-8   The normal and imperiled IT business process flow

2.4.2 Security design objectives

Traditionally, security requirements have been expressed by referencing the security services within the OSI model: authentication, access control, data confidentiality, data integrity, and non-repudiation. This practice introduces ambiguity when applied in the context of business processes. This ambiguity can contribute to a miscommunication of security requirements and a mismatch of functionality within the computing solution. As with other architecture disciplines, the technical objectives of the security design activity need to be articulated in quantifiable terms. Specific design objectives need to be developed and validated for each solution. For reference in this project, the following set of security design objectives were derived as a result of an analysis of the security-incident handling and reporting system for one corporation:

1. There is a need to control access to computer systems and their processes, consistent with defined roles and responsibilities.

2. There is a need to control access to information, consistent with information classification and privacy policies.

3. There is a need to control the flow of information, consistent with information classification and privacy policies.

4. There is a need to manage the reliability and integrity of components.

5. There is a need for protection from malicious attack.

6. There is a need for trusted identity to address the requirement of accountability of access to systems, processes, and information.

7. There is a need to prevent fraud within business processes and transactions, or to detect and respond to attempted fraud.

2.4.3 Selection and enumeration of subsystems

The security design objectives and the solution environment have a central role in the selection and enumeration of subsystems. Table 2-2 shows a possible mapping of the example design objectives to security subsystems. It indicates where a subsystem may be required (R) or supplementary (S) in satisfying an individual security requirement. Actual subsystem selection requires documented rationale.

Table 2-2 Mapping design objectives to security subsystems

Security design objectives	Audit	Integrity	Access control	Flow control	Credentials / Identity
Control access to systems/processes	S	S	R	S	S
Control access to information	S	S	S	R	R
Control the flow of information	S	S	S	R	S
Correct and reliable component operation	S	R	S	S	S
Prevent/mitigate attacks	R	R	R	R	S
Accountability through trusted identity	R	R	S	S	R

Security design objectives	Audit	Integrity	Access control	Flow control	Credentials / Identity
Prevent/mitigate fraud	R	R	R	R	R

There are many interrelated factors that determine how many instances of a given subsystem appear in the solution. Table 2-3 suggests motivations for instantiating security subsystems within a design. Actual subsystem enumeration requires documented rationale.

Table 2-3   Determining the security subsystems in a design

Subsystem	Number in a design	Characteristics of the computing environment
Security audit subsystem	Few	One subsystem for archive of related critical data One subsystem for analysis of related anomalies One subsystem for fraud detection in the solution
Solution integrity	Few	One subsystem per group of related critical components
Access control	1 to n	One subsystem per unique user-subject binding mechanism or policy rule set
Flow control	1 to m	One subsystem per unique flow control policy rule set One or more flow control functions per OSI layer service: physical, datalink, network, end-to-end transport, and application One or more flow control functions per domain boundary
Identity and credentials	1 to k	Some number of credential systems per domain Some number of credential systems per domain Some number of disparate credentials or uses for credentials per domain Some number of aliases/pseudonyms at domain boundaries

2.4.4 Documenting conceptual security architecture

Given the agreed-upon design objectives, a conceptual model for security within the IT solution can be created. Figure 2-9 on page 38 and Figure 2-10 on page 39 represent a conceptual security architecture. For clarity, security functions have been grouped by design objective.

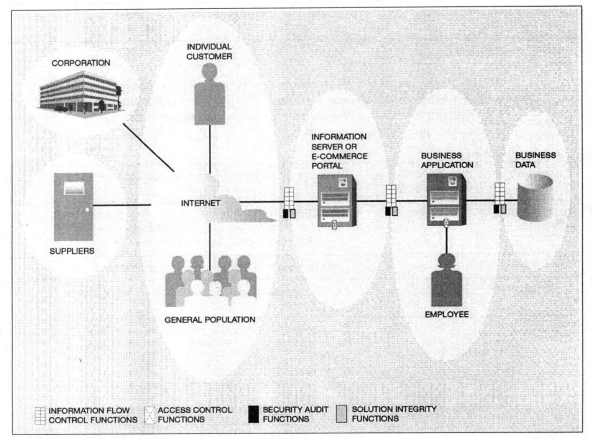

Figure 2-9   Defending against attacks

The diagrams represent the solution environment segmented by risk profile or operational affinity, along with icons for security functions. The legend for the diagrams maps the security subsystems to icons. The information flow control subsystem has a wide range of functions. For this reason, a rectangle is used to indicate a policy evaluation and enforcement function, whereas an oval indicates a data flow function, such as a communication protocol with security capabilities.

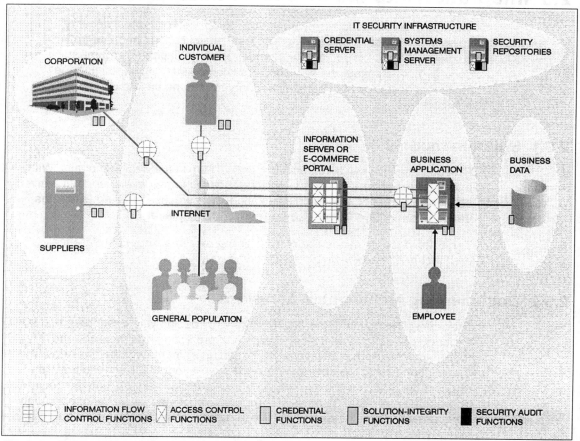

Figure 2-10   Ensuring correct and reliable operation

From the perspective of the enterprise deploying the solution, the security design objectives will dictate where security functionality is desired; however, the compliance to some or all of the security requirements may be limited by the enforceability of policies beyond the boundaries of the enterprise. Whether and how these credential subsystems and access control subsystems can be integrated into the security architecture can have a major impact on the trustworthiness of the solution as a whole. These issues and dependencies should be considered and documented within architectural decisions.

This type of conceptual model forms the baseline for developing and evaluating a "proof-of-concept" and further refinement of the functional aspects of security within the target environment.

2.5 Integration into the overall solution architecture

There are several steps involved in translating the conceptual security subsystem functions into component-level specifications and integration guidance. These include creating models of the solution environment, documenting architectural decisions, developing use cases, refining the functional design, and integrating security requirements into component architectures.

2.5.1 Solution models

Creating an initial solution model is a critical step in the design process. With skill and experience, one-of-a-kind solution models can be developed to fit a given set of requirements. For complex solutions, the practice of using templates derived from prior solutions is becoming commonplace.

The Enterprise Solutions Structure (ESS) provides a range of reference architectures[4] for e-business solutions.

2.5.2 Documenting architectural decisions

Previously, the notion of the duality of security design was described, that is, ensuring correct and reliable operation and protecting against error and maliciousness. Both motivations are based upon managing the business risks of the solution and of the environment. Risks represent the likelihood that an undesirable outcome will be realized from a malicious attack, unexpected event, operational error, and so on. Risks are either accepted as a cost of operation, transferred to some other party, covered by liability insurance, or mitigated by the security architecture.

Architectural decisions will dictate how robust the security system architecture should be, which security subsystems to incorporate into the system architecture, which functions and mechanisms within each subsystem should be deployed, where the mechanisms will be deployed, and how the deployment will be managed.

Examples of architectural decisions include:

► Viability of the countermeasures, including the threats addressed, the limitations and caveats of the solution, and the resulting window of risk

► Extensibility of the design, including whether or not the design will serve the total population and if there will be separate designs for defined population segments

---

[4] P. T. L. Lloyd and G. M. Galambos, "Technical Reference Architectures," IBM Systems Journal 38, No. 1, 51–75 (1999).

- ► Usability of the design, including whether or not the mechanisms integrate with the technology base and the extent of the burden of compliance for users

- ► Manageability of the design, including the extent of the burden of life-cycle management

2.5.3 Use cases

Architectural decisions will also drive the evaluation of prototypes and models of functions within the solution. One form of prototype is called a use case. Both security threats and normal interactions and flows can be validated with use cases.

Example 1: Interception of errant packet or message flow

Figure 2-11 represents several levels of detail for the operation of an information flow control subsystem that is designed to monitor, send, and receive operations that cross a boundary between two networks.

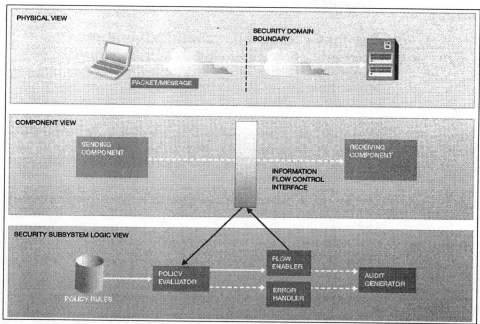

Figure 2-11   Boundary flow control with security subsystems

The computer systems are represented in the physical view. In the component view, an information flow control interface, positioned between source and destination, will examine one or more aspects of packets or messages sent across the boundary. Some components of this information flow control subsystem are shown in the logic view, where the monitored conditions and the programmed actions are carried out, based upon a set of rules.

Valid packets are allowed to flow across the boundary; however, packets or messages of a specified format, or from an invalid source, or to an invalid destination, are disabled by the security subsystem. A record of the event is generated by invoking an interface to a security audit subsystem.

This example is representative of the type of filtering, analysis, and response that is performed within packet filter firewalls or electronic mail gateways.

There are many architectural decisions to be evaluated within each iteration of the design. The effect on performance due to processing delays, plus the effect of data collection and analysis on the overall operation of the solution, are significant factors.

Example 2: Three-tier client/server input flow

Figure 2-12 on page 43 illustrates an input flow for a three-tier client/server process that is typical of the integration of enterprise computing with the Internet environment.

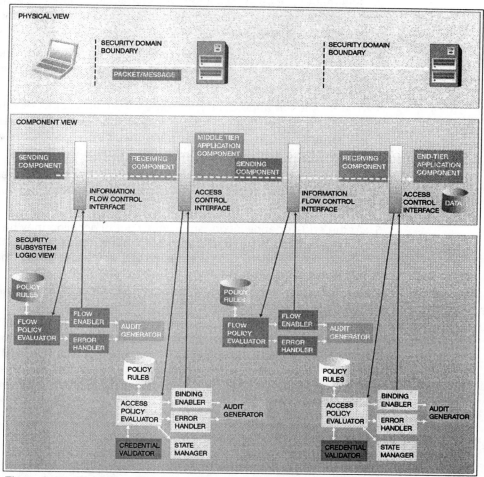

Figure 2-12   Three-tier client/server input flow with security subsystems

Several instances of security subsystems are depicted, spread among three network security domains. An information flow control subsystem is positioned at the boundary points between networks. An access control subsystem is positioned between a receiving component and its corresponding application component. Interfaces to related credential subsystems and security audit subsystems are shown in the security subsystem logic view. No integrity subsystem functions are referenced in this example. The scenario follows:

1. The business process interface is invoked by a user or a process and the request is transferred via a sending component.

2. The request flows across a security domain in a manner that is acceptable to the sending and receiving components, based upon the defined information flow control rules.

3. Identification, authentication, and access control decisions are made based upon the external identity associated with the request by an access control subsystem associated with the middle-tier application.

4. The middle-tier application is invoked via a user-subject binding. The actual processing is not covered here; it may include business presentation and data mapping logic, or it may be performed by an application-level information flow control subsystem, such as a proxy server.

5. The middle-tier application initiates, or relays, a request to the end-tier application. The request is scrutinized at another network boundary control point.

6. At the end-tier application, an access control decision may be performed on the request relative to the identity of the user represented by the middle-tier application, depending on the design of the application and the exchange protocols used.

7. The business process is invoked by a user-subject binding if the access control decision is positive.

This demonstrates how security functions from several subsystems are distributed throughout the solution. As with the first example, architectural decisions will guide the design of the security subsystem functions, which in turn may put constraints on the overall business flow in order to achieve the risk management objectives.

2.5.4 Refining the functional design

Walk-throughs of complete business processes, including exception conditions and handling processes, assist in creating a viable solution outline and refining requirements and interdependencies among the solution building blocks.

Example 3: PKI digital certificate enrollment

This example uses the credential subsystem model to describe the generalized flow for enrolling a user into an identity or credential system based upon PKI digital certificates as the first step in developing a security system architecture. The process involves combining the subsystem model with assumptions about the business environment, the business processes, the risk management requirements, the technical specifications, and possibly the legal and business compliance requirements associated with issuing PKI digital certificates.

In Figure 2-13, the yellow blocks represent manual processes, the blue blocks map to automated processes, and the peach blocks map to automated audit data capture points. The blue data storage icons represent sensitive repositories, the pink icons map to cryptographic secrets, the white icons represent unique contents of the certificate, and the lavender icon is associated with the certificate.

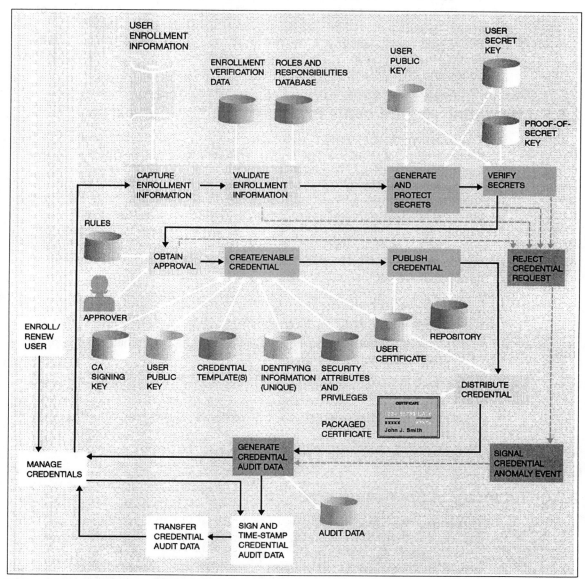

Figure 2-13   Sample PKI digital certificate enrollment process flow

The enrollment process flow depicted demonstrates the exchange of sensitive user information and secrets, plus the export of the credential outside the control of the issuer. The full enrollment scenario should include processes from a corresponding information flow control subsystem. For public key credentials, the format of certificates, along with details of how the credentials are formatted, transported, and stored, are important design considerations. All scenarios must be validated against existing and proposed business processes. Validation of the scenarios substantiates the architectural decisions discussed earlier. Subsequent design steps are needed to develop and map the functions of the security subsystems to Common Criteria specifications and ultimately onto the nodes and physical components.

2.5.5 Integrating requirements into component architectures

The security functions within the design need to be apportioned throughout the solution. However, many of the mechanisms and services within the IT solution that implement security functionality operate within other than security components, for example, database systems, application systems, clients, servers, and operating systems. The task of adopting security functions into the network, application, middleware, security, systems management, and infrastructure architectures is shared by the several architects and integration specialists involved in the design project. The process involves a structured approach, considering the purposeful allocation of functions and requirements throughout the component architectures by:

► Mandate, based upon a legal or contractual compliance requirement

► Best practice for security, or for balance of security and business process

► Component capability, knowing the existence of a mechanism that supports the required process or action

► Location in the configuration, based upon interaction with components or flows

► Impact, considering the risk, security objective, or the component capacity to perform

► Necessity, because there may be no better alternative

2.5.6 Summary of the design process

This section has described the process for translating the conceptualized security solution into a set of detailed specifications, for an integrated IT security control system, using the security subsystem construct. The design is documented, refined, and validated against the business processes through use cases and scenarios. The detailed security requirements, expressed in terms of Common Criteria component-level detail, are distributed throughout the operational model for the IT solution. At this point, integration-level detail can be finalized, and the implementation plan can proceed.

2.6 Conclusions

This chapter has examined the issues and circumstances that affect the design of comprehensive security functions for computing solutions. It has outlined a system model and a systematic process for security design with the Common Criteria international standard at its foundation.

Several summary observations can be made relative to this proposed model and process:

► Security is a shared responsibility among all IT design disciplines

► Security design is linked to business objectives beyond the need for protecting against attack, and conversely, protecting against attack does not in itself meet all the business requirements for security

► Many, if not most, security control points within IT solutions are found in portions of solutions that are not typically considered security components.

Reliable and correct operation of solutions using secure data exchange protocols, such as IPSec and secure sockets layer, is predicated on functions within all five of the security subsystems defined in the proposed model and design process. These protocols are based upon trusted identities that utilize cryptographic keys requiring storage integrity, reliable key exchange protocols, strong access control mechanisms, reliable data exchange protocols, and trusted audit trails for enrollment and key life-cycle management. Furthermore, the proposed model provides a new perspective for viewing Common Criteria protection profiles in the context of security subsystems. For example, the protection profile for an application gateway firewall suggests the functionality of all five security subsystems. The fact that a front-line security device, such as a firewall, might fit the definition of a credential subsystem highlights the critical nature of its design, integration, and operation.

2.6.1 Actions and further study

The concepts and the supporting detailed information presented in this chapter were incorporated into training for IBM Global Services architects this year. Additional work is underway to develop notations, models, and visualization techniques that enhance its adoption in related methods and architect disciplines. A patent application has been filed for the system and process, designated Method for Architecting Secure Solutions, or MASS.

Several of the notations, models and visualization techniques will be applied throughout this redbook.

3

IT infrastructure topologies and components

This chapter discusses the changing role of the network. While the focus of this redbook is not networking or the concepts and practices used in designing or implementing them, a discussion of "network basics" is crucial when designing or implementing a security architecture. In addition to the network basics, we also cover some of the major application framework components in an IBM based e-business approach, such as:

► Network frameworks

► Practical designs

► WebSphere Application Server

► WebSphere Edge Server

► Domino Application Server

► IBM Firewall

► Tivoli PKI

3.1 The network becomes mission critical

Network architectures are an integral part of e-business. Networks provide the framework for making IT investment and design decisions in support of business objectives. Because the design and construction of a reliable e-business infrastructure is no longer considered an IT only issue, reliability, scalability and flexibility are now on the minds of CEOs and CIOs alike.

The network and its components are the foundation on which an e-business is resting. It has become highly visible and if it and the IT structure fail, so fails the e-business. Total cost of ownership, lost revenue, lost customers, and eroded image are direct consequences. To be successful, the infrastructure should be optimized to support the business requirements.

3.1.1 Evolution

In the beginning, network security was focused on keeping intruders out using tools such as firewalls, routers, filters, and so on, independently installing and managing many different technologies from different vendors. The Web and its influence on today's business models has changed the assumptions and breadth of how we approach security. E-business means allowing access to someone who would have been considered a malicious intruder in the past into your network in a limited and careful fashion today. E-business means that clients, employees, customers, and business partners alike access applications not only from the company intranet, but from the unsecured Internet as well.

The Internet was not designed with security in mind. It was constructed to be an open environment with control and trust distributed among its users, not the providers. Rules, policies, and security functions can not be centrally administered, because physical rules are impossible to apply. The firewalls, routers, filters, and so on that once secured your network are now in the position to help prevent viruses from corrupting the network and thieves from stealing important company data, but they do little to keep the internal employees from accessing information they are not entitled to or securing the applications that your business partners and/or customers use.

3.2 Connectivity framework

Constructing a set of guiding principles to help develop the necessary infrastructure is the best starting point. In the past, networks evolved. Meaning specifically, as the need for a service, or access to an application became necessary, the network grew to accommodate the requests. There was no unique beginning or endpoint.

Network architectures now require the input of security specialists, application developers, network professionals. All of these individuals affect the process of the flow of data and clients on the network. Each individual brings the necessary information for assembling building blocks where the logical and physical design needs and expectations are, giving a clearer representation of the enterprise. Building an architectural model that represents key components and the connections or interfaces between components will allow for a visual picture of the business needs, as shown in Figure 3-1.

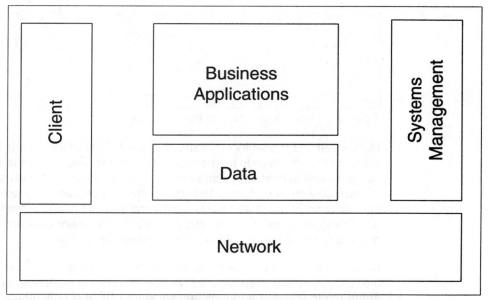

Figure 3-1   High level architectural model including all network components

Looking at the enterprise in this manner gives you the opportunity to visualize the relationship between your basic systems. It should also allow you to drill down into each component for the visualization of additional relationships.

Perhaps the most important relationship, in terms of this discussion, is that security no longer simply comprises the network, but surrounds the entire enterprise as depicted in Figure 3-2 on page 52.

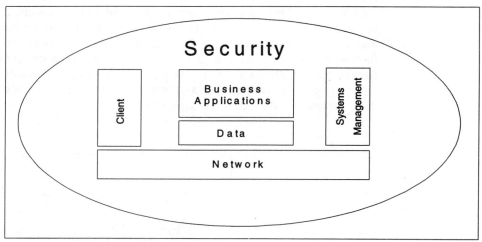

Figure 3-2   How security fits into the enterprise

Notice that this model incorporates the client. That action opens the door to realizing that the Web is the network of organizations, where the traditional client server model is now multi-dimensional and the security concerns are immediately more complex. The user population increases geometrically, identification of users and hosts accessing data is no longer "easy", and controlling the access and availability becomes a major concern. The security needed to protect your environment must evolve as well.

Does the evolution of your security requirements mean you abandon the methods you have used to date? Do you simplify the components by limiting your approach to firewalls and antivirus software? No, it simply means that you must globalize your security and localize your approach. Adopting, installing and independently managing different technologies from multiple vendors in many locations will not give you the reduced time to market required in the e-business environment or cost effective management of your enterprise.

3.2.1 A local global vision with MASS

A global vision suggests that the enterprise is more than its physical boundaries. But localizing that perspective will tame the complexity of trying to install, implement, and manage a security solution. How to achieve this? Base the solution on an integrated, standards based architecture. An open and adaptable architecture will help reduce the unseen flaws that could compromise the entire infrastructure and reduce the availability of applications and information.

Adding security design objectives into your architecture creates a framework to organize and validate the business environment and security risks. The immediate benefit is saved time and lower costs to reach the outcome. However, using a tried methodology gives you a better quality result with a quantitative tracking method. The security design objectives should outline how to achieve the following:

► Deploy and manage trusted credentials

► Control access to stored information consistent with roles, responsibilities and privacy policies

► Control access and use of systems and processes consistent with roles and responsibilities

► Protect stored or "in transit" information consistent with its classification, control, and flow policies

► Assure the correct and reliable operation of components and services

► Defend against attacks

► Defend against fraud

The IBM Method for Architecting Secure Solutions (MASS) provides you with design objectives or, more simply put, a starting point. Based on Common Criteria, MASS is compliant with international standards that are comprehensive and well accepted. MASS provides a set of security domains to help define the threats to an enterprise (this includes actors/users, flow control, authorization, physical security, and so on). It allows you to assign information assets to your security domains that become crucial in high-level designs of your architecture.

Using Figure 3-3 on page 54, think of these areas as uncontrolled, controlled, restricted, secured, and external controlled. The client utilizes the network to access applications and data. This client can be from either within your enterprise or outside of it. Using the concept of security domains you can translate Figure 3-3 into something more targeted, as shown in Figure 3-4 on page 56.

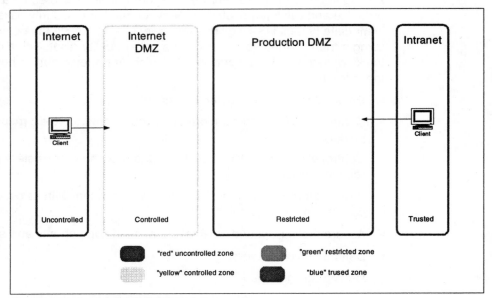

Figure 3-3   Applying MASS domain concepts

What these domain categories mean:

Uncontrolled   Refers to anything outside the control of an organization.

Controlled   Restricts access between Uncontrolled and Restricted.

Restricted   Access is restricted and controlled; only authorized individuals gain entrance and there is no direct communication with external sources (Internet).

Trusted   Access is only available to staff AND access to one area does not insure access into another trusted area.

External controlled   An external zone where data is stored by business partners external to the systems where there is limited trust in the protection of data (for example, credit reporting agencies, banks, and government agencies).

Constructing your environment in this way allows the internal users to "see" out, but the external users can not "see" in. The benefits of constructing security domains this way are:

► Clear and efficient

► Easy to explain

► Easy to work with

► Complete design and implementation view allowing you to avoid errors

► Fewer errors mean a lower risk of exposure and loss

You will see these domain designs again throughout the book. Figures 6-4 and 6-5 have firewalls clearly marked on them to help you become familiar and comfortable with the placement and domain concept.

3.2.2 E-business security requirement and MASS

IBM's e-business methodology fits nicely with MASS domain concepts. MASS is built on open and accepted standards. E-business patterns originate in IBM product divisions and are provided as operational models that are also based on open standards and technologies. Notice that the principles of the six "As" of e-business factor nicely into the overall plan as well:

Authorization	Allowing only users that are approved to access systems, data, application, and networks (public and private).
Asset protection	Keeping data confidential by making sure that privacy rules are enforced.
Accountability	Identifying who did what and when.
Assurance	The ability to confirm and validate the enforcement of security
Availability	Keep systems, data, networks, and applications reachable.
Administration	Define, maintain, monitor, and modify policy information consistently.

In order for your network security solution to work, it must be based on consistent, corporate wide policies. A successful deployment requires that an effective link be forged from the management definition of policy to the operational implementation of that policy.

> **Tip:** Plan your security polices around your business model, not the other way round. For more information on corporate policies, see Section 1.3, "Corporate policy" on page 8.

3.3 Practical designs

A demilitarized zone (DMZ) is an area of your network that separates it from other areas of the network, including the Internet. But it allows you to exchange information with limited, calculated risk. Creating a DMZ involves adding firewalls for added layers of security. Firewalls are often used in multi-machine systems to protect the resources that live on that private network, such as critical data, business applications, and sensitive information. There are a wide variety of topographies that can be appropriate for a DMZ; however, the basic units usually look something like the layout in Figure 3-4.

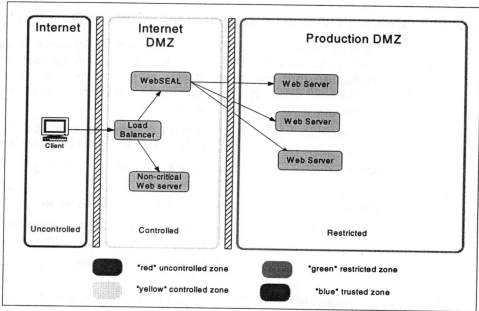

Figure 3-4   Basic DMZ design

This design allows for the separation of the presentation material on the non-critical Web server and the application logic on the Web servers in the private network. The infrastructure allows secure transactions and processing in stages, reducing the demands required.

Note: Obviously, there are many ways to implement a DMZ, and even more ways to build the foundation of a firewall. One of these is protocol switching (changing from one transport mechanism to another). While protocol switching will stop most IP based attacks on your network, it will not stop everything. It also adds to the complexity of your network and increases management requirements.

Most firewalls and security schemes are built to keep the Internet away from the internal network. However, in some situations, you may want to protect parts of the internal network from other areas of your internal network. It makes sense that not everyone needs access to the same services, information, or security protection. Figure 3-5 on page 57 shows the segregation of the intranet client from the production environment. Some parts of your enterprise need to be more secure than others, for example, demonstration networks (where there are often people from outside of the organization present), Human Resources data, development projects, financial data, and so on.

Adding the additional security of another junction point (WebSEAL, which is discussed in more detail in Section 4.2.1, "WebSEAL" on page 91) to the network would give you manageability of the internal user's access as well. In this example, the user has been allowed full access to one Web server (solid line), limited access to one other Web server (dotted line), and no access to the remaining server.

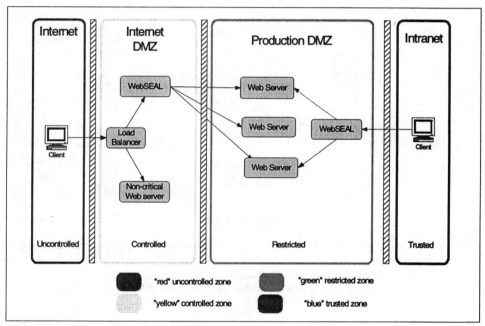

Figure 3-5   Segregating the intranet client

Let us take that concept one step further: in Figure 3-6 on page 58, we are adding an additional zone of protection and tying the idea of load balancing and high availability into the architecture. By moving the security management into its own area that is physically as well as virtually secure, you have created an area where the security administration will be performed and all the necessary data is contained only in that area.

You can undertake this type of segregation of the network for various reasons. You could create another protected area called Human Resources, where the applications and data would all be contained inside that specific network with access granted only as needed. Take care when applying this type of result. Separate the things that absolutely must be protected. Keep your solution straightforward and easily scalable for future growth.

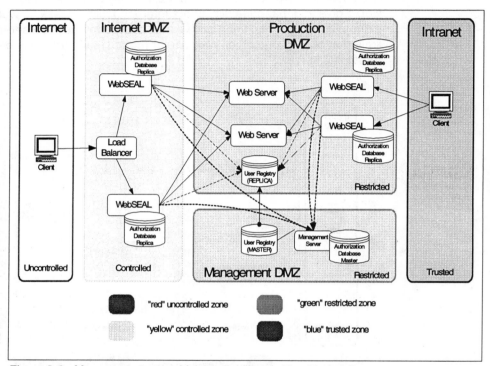

Figure 3-6   Management zone, high availability, and load balancing

3.4 Additional components

We have talked about network security structure, MASS, and zones. What we have not discussed is how to make these things happen. What constitutes a Web server? What do I need for a firewall? What are certificates?

The additional components that are discussed here were designed to work in conjunction with other Tivoli security products and are part of the overall IBM family of software products. However, these are not the only products available and not the only ones that Tivoli security products are capable of working with. Additional product information on Firewall, PKI, and Anti Virus software products can be found in Appendix A, "Additional product information" on page 407.

This section touches on:

► IBM WebSphere Application Server
► IBM WebSphere Edge Server
► Lotus Domino Application Server
► IBM Firewall
► Tivoli PKI

3.5 WebSphere Application Server

Application Servers are the heart of e-business. An application server runs the necessary programs for client usage and manages those user interactions. WebSphere Application Server provides an open distributed computing environment that allows for rapid deployment of applications and scalability.

Figure 3-7 on page 60 shows WebSphere Application Server being part of a large family of IBM products. All were designed to help you attain your e-business goals. The WebSphere software platform provides an e-business infrastructure that is flexible, extensible, and robust. As the foundation of the WebSphere software platform, WebSphere Application Server Version 4.0 provides the core software needed to deploy, integrate, and manage e-business applications. WebSphere Application Server supports the full range of applications from dynamic Web presentation to sophisticated transaction processing whether they are 100 percent custom-built, based on integrated WebSphere platform products, or provided by a partner, such as an ISV or systems integrator.

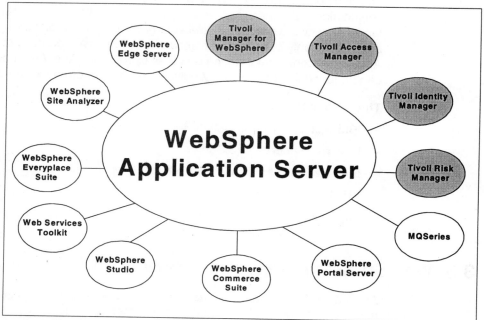

Figure 3-7   WebSphere family of products

WebSphere Application Server is a Java technology-based Web application server, integrating enterprise data and transactions with the e-business world. It provides an e-business application deployment environment with a complete set of application services, including capabilities for transaction management, security, clustering, performance, availability, connectivity, and scalability. It manages and integrates enterprise-wide applications and utilizes open technologies and application programming interfaces (APIs).

In addition to the Standard Edition, WebSphere Application Server is available in Advanced and Enterprise editions. The Advanced Edition provides an Enterprise Java Beans (EJB) run-time engine, high-performance database and transaction connections, and other similar application services. The Enterprise Edition contains all of the features of the Advanced and Standard editions, plus the transaction processing features of IBM TXSeries™ and the object management features of IBM Component Broker.

3.5.1 WebSphere Application Server overview

In this section, we will provide more information on the Standard and Advanced versions of WebSphere Application Server.

WebSphere Application Server Standard

The Standard Edition lets you use Java servlets, Java Server Pages, and XML to quickly change static Web sites into dynamic content sites. The server combines the control and portability of server-side applications with the performance of Java. WebSphere Application Server provides connectivity and integration with existing back-end systems, such as existing databases and transaction systems. It also lets you build and deploy personalized, dynamic Web content quickly.

The Standard Edition extends the value and versatility of your Web server with:

► Full Java servlet, JavaBeans™, Java Server™ Page (JSP) components, and Extensible Markup Language (XML) and eXtensible Style Language (XSL) support, including support for applications built with the Java servlet specification.

► The Java servlet 2.1 API, for easy, automatic creation of users sessions and state information.

► Database pooling for dynamic access to databases with Java Database Connectivity (JDBC) access, including DB2® Universal Database™ and Oracle.

► Improved integration with IBM VisualAge® for Java, allowing Java code and JSPs locally or remotely deployed to either the Standard or Advanced editions of the WebSphere Application Server to be debugged within WebSphere Studio (the integrated development suite for WebSphere based applications).

► Extended tagging support through JSP specification 1.0 for queries and connection management.

► An IBM HTTP Server powered by Apache, as well as support for other major Web servers (including Netscape and Microsoft), with enhancements for security, control, and a browser-based remote administration graphical user interface (GUI).

► Extensive monitoring tools that allow you to watch your site's servlets and sessions with nearly real-time capability.

XML management

The Standard Edition includes support for Extensible Markup Language (XML) and Extensible Style Language (XSL) technologies to improve data definition and sharing, allowing data presentation to be separated from your actual data. The Standard Edition includes tools that support:

► An XML and XSL parser utilizing the latest World Wide Web Consortium (W3C) XML 1.0 specifications

► Dynamic HTML generation based on XML document object model (DOM) Level 1 recommendations

- An XML Document Type Definition (DTD) library for local validation of a document's structure

- An XSL processor to transform your XML data into formatted HTML

- Additional tools enable you to tailor data to specific devices, including initial support for Wireless Markup Language (WML)

Security management

The Standard Edition contains a Lightweight Directory Access Protocol (LDAP) client for connection to an LDAP server. LDAP is an open, vendor-neutral standard that provides an extendable architecture for centralized storage and management of information. The secure access control lists can be established at a more granular level than in the past. In addition to setting up security at the user and group levels, control and policies can be established for specific calls or methods within the applications themselves, utilizing third-party authentication techniques. This provides much greater depth of control and protection within the server deployment environments.

Supported HTTP servers

The following HTTP servers are supported by IBM WebSphere Application Server Standard Edition:

- Apache Server Version 1.3.12 or higher for IBM AIX®, Sun™ Solaris™, Microsoft® Windows® NT, and HP-UX

- Netscape Enterprise Server Version 3.5.1 or higher for AIX, Solaris, and Windows NT

- iPlanet Enterprise Server 4.0 for AIX, Solaris, Windows NT, Windows 2000, and HP-UX

- Microsoft Information Server Version 4.0 for Windows NT

- Microsoft Information Server Version 5.0 for Windows 2000

- Lotus® Domino™ Application Server Release 5.0.2b for Windows NT, Sun Solaris, HP-UX, and AIX

WebSphere Application Server Advanced

The Advanced Edition has the same capabilities as the Standard version but also adds an Enterprise Java Beans (EJB) server for implementing EJB components that utilize business logic.

WebSphere Application Server Advanced Edition offers:

- Full Web services (SOAP, UDDI, WSDL, XML, and J2EE™ 1.2 (Java 2 Enterprise Edition platform) certification), including robust integration and transaction technology

- Unparalleled connectivity through Common Object Request Broker Architecture (CORBA) and ActiveX interoperability and expanded database support

- Message Beans and Java Message Service (JMS) Listener Support

- Enterprise Java Beans™ (EJB) extensions

- Internationalization allows for intelligent adjustments in business logic to accommodate client locales for time zones, currencies, and languages

- Business rules beans enable dynamic updates without coding when business practices change Business Process Beans Technology Preview

- Performance enhancements, including dynamic reload of EJBs, dynamic caching (muti-tier), and Java Naming and Directory Interface (JNDI) caching

- A single-server configuration featuring browser-based administration and new versions of Visual Age for Java and WebSphere Studio

- Integration with IBM e-business application development environments provided by WebSphere Studio packages and VisualAge for Java Enterprise Edition, while maintaining support of open Java technology standards and other third-party Integrated Development Environments (IDEs)

- Consistent, cross-platform support for Windows (NT and 2000), Sun Solaris, HP-UX, AIX/6000, OS/400, Linux (Red Hat, SuSE, and Turbo), and Linux/390

- Deepest and broadest, leading-edge implementations of the most up-to-date Java-based technologies and Application Programming Interfaces (APIs)

- Comprehensive connectivity support for interacting with relational databases, object databases, transaction processing systems, MQ-enabled applications, and hierarchical databases

- A migration path to a more scalable and transactional environment from WebSphere Application Server Standard Edition with a superset of capabilities for a complete production-level, J2EE-based Web application platform

- A focus on medium- to high-level transactional environments used in conjunction with dynamic Web content generation and Web-initiated transactions

- Inclusion of an Apache-based HTTP Server with enhancements for security and control as well as support for other major Web servers

- Performance and scaling attributes that support bean-managed and container-managed persistence for entity beans and session beans with transaction management and monitoring

- An easy-to-use XML-based administrator client and friendly server environment for easy setup right out of the box

- ► Container management and persistent storage within a transactional environment for Java servlets and Enterprise Java Beans™ components
- ► A rich eXtensible Markup Language (XML) parsing and configuration environment
- ► Extensive interoperability with other elements of WebSphere software platform, including:
  - – e-commerce: WebSphere Commerce Suite
  - – e-collaboration: Lotus Domino
  - – Business process management: MQSeries, MQSeries Integrator, and MQSeries Everyplace
  - – Business-to-business communications: WebSphere Business Integrator
  - – Pervasive computing: WebSphere Everyplace Access and WebSphere User Experience

For more information on WebSphere Application Server, please visit:

`http://www.ibm.com./software/webservers/appserv/`

3.6 WebSphere Edge Server

WebSphere Edge Server or, simply, Edge Server, is an application that specifically addresses scalability, reliability, and performance. It incorporates caching, filtering, and load balancing to deliver an enterprise's critical business applications across the Web. Edge Server is the latest IBM integrated solution for local and wide area load balancing, content based quality of service routing and Web content filters and caching for multi-vendor Web environments. Edge Server can be deployed in a variety of ways to improve scalability, reliability, and efficiency for Web content hosts and Internet access providers. It is an important component of the overall network topography.

3.6.1 What Edge means

Edge of the network, edge of the data center, edge of the enterprise, enabling you to distribute application processes to the edge of the platform as part of an end to end framework. Figure 3-8 on page 65 gives a basic idea of the placement.

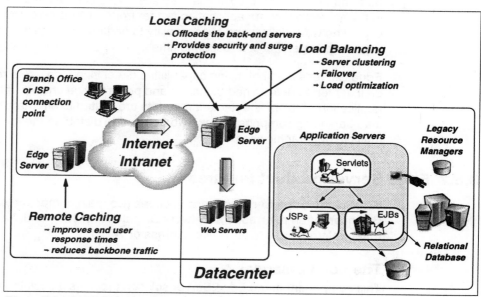

Figure 3-8   Basic Edge Server placement

Edge Server resides at local and remote network boundaries and provides services on behalf of back-end servers to improve Web application performance, availability, and scalability through distributed application processing under centralized administrative and application control. Edge Server provides an integrated solution for local and wide-area load balancing, content-based quality of service (QoS) routing, and Web content caching and filtering for multi-vendor Web server environments.

A comprehensive e-business solution also requires an uninterrupted infrastructure. Even a small amount of down time can make customers seek other sites that offer the same or like product or service but with a speedier and less trouble free experience. In today's market, the old notions of customer loyalty do not apply; the slightest perceived unpleasant experience can and often does send the client to the competition. Edge Server addresses the availability, reliability, manageability, security, and quality of service to provide a complete infrastructure for your enterprise that helps to ensure 24x7 operation.

Edge Server is positioned to play a strategic role in addressing an industry-wide issue involving the centralized Web application model. The current centralized Web application model has resulted in the concentration of applications and user traffic to one, or, at most, several central server sites, creating hot spots and overload at the centralized application. This impacts the scalability and performance of large e-business Web sites. This centralization has also resulted in the movement of the application farther from the end user, resulting in greater overall network delays and susceptibility to bottlenecks within the network, impacting the end user's response times.

Edge Server's load balancing capabilities direct incoming users requests to the best server as determined by health and performance checks. If a server or application problem is detected, requests are routed to alternate servers. The load balancing component may also be used to distribute the load across multiple geographic sites.

3.6.2 Edge Server product features

WebSphere Edge Server offering includes two main components: the Load Balancer (often referred to a Network Dispatcher or ND), and the Caching Proxy (often referred to as Web Traffic Express or WTE).

The Load Balancer

This component of the Edge Server solution provides a scalable answer for load balancing requests among your team of HTTP, FTP, or other TCP-based servers. This provides higher availability and scalability than with a single server. Incoming user requests are directed to the best server as determined by the health and performance of the servers and the applications running on them. If a server or application problem is detected, user requests are dispatched to alternate servers. The load-balancing component can also be used to distribute load across multiple geographic sites. The dynamic weighting factors used to make the load balancing decision can be augmented by customer-defined rules and requirements for client/server affinity.

Other load balancing features include:

► Mutual high-availability backup

Permits two WebSphere Edge Servers to load balance user requests, each acting as a standby for the other. Overall throughput and availability of the solution can be increased because both machines have identical roles.

► Interactive Session Support (ISS)

Integrates with domain name servers (DNS) to provide wide-area load balancing. ISS balances the load on servers by communicating with agents (ISS load-monitoring daemons) installed on each server machine, altering the IP address returned to the client via DNS.

- IP Address, cookie, and server-directed affinity

  Allows requests from a particular client session to be directed to the same server for a specified time period, based on the client's Internet Protocol (IP) address, client-supported cookie, or information provided by the application. The client can maintain the server connection until the transaction is complete.

- Cross-Port affinity

  Allows server affinity to be maintained across port transitions. SSL connections may be sent to the same server that receives HTTP transactions or vice versa. This maintains shopping cart integrity during a user-shopping session that alternates between secure and non-secure connections.

- Generic Routing Encapsulation (GRE) Support

  Ability to load balance packets to multiple server addresses associated with one MAC address by encapsulating client IP packets inside IP/GRE packets and forwarding them to GRE-enabled servers, such as @server zSeries and S/390.

- Custom Advisors

  Enables load balancing based upon unique application and platform criteria. A sample custom advisor for use with WebSphere Application Server is provided with Edge Server as sample code together with a Java servlet that would be the server-side counterpart of the custom advisor.

Web Traffic Express - the Caching Proxy

The Edge Server's Caching Proxy component serves as both a caching proxy server and as a content filter. In addition to serving the traditional proxy server tasks of acting as a gateway for multiple clients, and forwarding client requests to destination content servers, the Edge Server Caching Proxy can cache the Web documents it receives and serve subsequent requests from its local cache. Caching reduces bandwidth usage and improves response time for users when the same content is requested multiple times or by multiple users.

Specific Proxy features are as follows:

- Support for multiple SSL connections terminated at the proxy server (for reverse proxy configurations), in addition to SSL tunneling capabilities (for forward proxies)

- Transparent proxy capabilities (with some platform-specific restrictions) that ensure the client software is unaware of the existence of the intermediate proxy server

- Support for LDAP-based authentication

- Support for both memory only mode and disk/memory mode caching. The disk mode caching allows very large cache sizes (on the order of 100 GB)

- The ability to cache dynamic content in the form of Java Server Pages™ (JSPs) and servlet results generated by WebSphere Application Server, as well as basic support for redirecting streaming media presentation requests to a RealProxy server

- Support for virtual hosting, which allows the pointing of multiple domain names to a single server.

The Caching Proxy also provides customizable content filtering to censor Web page content at the proxy server level. Proxy-level filtering gives the administrator closer control over content than browser-based filtering. Filtering can be based on URL, independently available content labels, or a custom application.

WebSphere Edge Server Version 2 enhancements

Version 2 introduces significant new capabilities to the Edge Server platform. Although the Edge Server can function like a simple caching proxy or load balancer, its new functions for Version 2, defined by the Edge Services Architecture, offer additional capabilities far beyond basic availability, scalability, and price-performance.

The Edge Services Architecture has been defined to enable the delayering of application programs to more fully exploit the distributed execution environment created when one places Edge Servers at the edge of the network. "Delayering" means decomposing an application into smaller modules for placement on appropriate platforms throughout a distributed network topology. It is advantageous in fitting a variety of business models, which may be evolving over time. Delayering applications into "edgable" components will open new opportunities for e-businesses, service providers, and independent software vendors, allowing application scalability and improved user response times.

Edge locations for in-house enterprise solutions include the edge of the data center and the edge of the enterprise or branch office, as shown in Figure 3-8 on page 65. Edge locations for outsourced enterprise solutions and new service-provider offerings include geographically distributed content points of presence within a content distribution network, as well as Internet access points, such as ISP gateways and proxies, where end-user traffic is aggregated.

The following is an overview of the new Edge Server Version 2 features:

- Enhanced Caching capability that, in addition to the robust Version 1.0.3 features, such as dynamically caching JSP results from the Application

Server, also provides the ability to handle dynamic invalidations of both static and dynamic cached content, integrated with the Content Distribution Framework for higher scalability.

► Enhanced Load Balancing that will provide an even greater improvement to a Web site's availability, scalability, and performance by transparently clustering edge, Web, and application servers. It also provides site selection, workload management, session affinity, and transparent fail-over.

► Content Distribution deploys published Web content (Web pages, fragments, application components, and streaming assets) to caches and re-hosting servers throughout the network.

► Policy-Based Quality of Service allocates computing and network resources according to a transaction's business value and interoperates with networking hardware (for example, Cisco, Nortel, Alcatel, Lucent, and so on). This allows customers the ability to prioritize and secure traffic based on user classes and groups, optimizing resource utilization, and improving network scalability using Tivoli Access Manager.

► Manageability addresses functions such as installing and upgrading software, managing and storing standardized configurations, aggregating software components, and viewing and reporting events.

► Centralized security policy administration using Tivoli Access Manager secures access to protected Web resources using the SSL protocol with optional hardware-assisted cryptography as required. In addition, Edge Server V2 can maintain SSL endpoint affinity using either the SSL ID or SSL Connection Pooling.

► The Offloadable Application Component capability (referred to as Application Offload) enables the delaying of an application so that application modules can execute on an edge node and offload the presentation module workload from the costly origin application servers, allowing them to concentrate on core business logic. Edgable components can contain servlets and Java Server Pages, and are distributed using the Content Distribution Framework. This capability allows page composition at the Edge Server from cached fragments and Web objects. Both the composition servlets (JSPs) and fragments may be distributed using the Content Distribution Framework. WebSphere Application Server is the run-time environment for executing distributed application components under the coordination of the central site.

► WebSphere Transcoding Publisher automatically adapts (transcodes) content for mobile devices. The adaptation includes sophisticated XSL-based lexical parsing and workflow processing. WebSphere Transcoding Publisher and the Edge Server have been integrated using a WebSphere Transcoding Publisher plug-in into the caching proxy that allows the Edge Server to cache multiple transcoded versions of content (for example, one for a PDA, one for a mobile phone, and so on).

3.6.3 Benefits of integrating Edge Server and Access Manager

By coupling Access Manager with the Edge Server, customers will be able to implement an integrated Edge-of-the-Network solution. This solution would consist of robust Load Balancing capabilities, a sophisticated Caching Proxy, Content Distribution Framework, Quality of Service features, Application Offload, and the authorization engine of Access Manager to ensure only authorized users can access cached and non-cached Web resources. This integrated solution not only ensures control at the edge of your network, preventing unwanted users from entering your network, but it also enhances user experiences by improving Web application performance, availability, and scalability.

The Access Manager Plug-in for WebSphere Edge Server integrates the caching Web proxy of the Edge Server with the authentication, authorization, and single sign-on capabilities of Access Manager. Some of the specific security attributes of the Edge Server Caching Proxy, once its been customized to use the Access Manager plug-in, are:

► Elimination of the "Islands of Security" problem, allowing Web security to be enforced at the Edge Server, and integrated under a common authorization platform and unified namespace that also encompasses security for Java/Java 2 Platform Enterprise Edition (J2EE), MQSeries, UNIX, @server zSeries and S/390 platforms.

► Secure Dynamic Caching, to allow users to store the Web documents the proxy receives and serves subsequent requests from its local cache. This caching reduces bandwidth usage and improves response time for users when the same content is requested multiple times or by multiple users.

► LDAP-based user authentication via basic authentication, forms-based login, or client-side certificates.

► Flexibility to use the full extent of Access Manager-supported LDAP user registries.

► Web Single Sign-on (SSO) across WebSphere and non-WebSphere resources. Although SSO mapping is not supported, the Edge Server Caching Proxy Plug-in allows the user to create custom SSO tokens for accepting and submitting user information (that is, the name and format of the token can be specified). Using the plug-in's flexible mechanism, it can emulate most of WebSEAL's SSO support (that is, iv_header). It allows pre-authentication servers to authenticate to it using an IP address, basic authentication header, or a client certificate. It authenticates to the back-end server using a basic authentication header. In addition, it supports the LTPA token.

► Virtual hosting capabilities for support of multiple, isolated domain names on the same server.

- The ability to authorize forward proxy requests to enable an enterprise that uses the Edge Server caching proxy as their HTTP forward proxy to restrict who has access to the Internet and when.

For more information on WebSphere Edge Server, visit:

`http://www.ibm.com/software/webservers/edgeserver/`

3.7 Domino Application Server

The Domino Application Server platform focuses on collaborative Web applications. Domino's integrated application services, such as security, workflow, and content management, optimize the platform for rapid delivery of the collaborative Web applications you need to initiate and strengthen key business relationships. Built-in connection services provide live access to leading relational databases, transaction systems, and ERP applications. You can use leading third party Web development tools along with Domino's integrated development environment. You may start anywhere with Domino; it is flexible and extendable, meaning that you may implement any or all infrastructure components.

Domino is standards-based and offers one of the industry's most comprehensive support mechanisms for Internet messaging standards, with Internet addressing, SMTP routing, and MIME content support all native, plus full support for E/SMTP, S/MIME, SSL, POP3, IMAP4, LDAP, HTTP, HTML, SNMP, and so on. Domino delivers interoperability with your current tools and systems and the ultimate in extensibility, so you can more easily reach out to your customers and partners.

Product features

The Domino Application servers offers a comprehensive array of services:

- Flexible security model. Integrated X.509 support. S/MIME support ensures message integrity for all client types. Authentication via trusted third-party directories.

- LDAP Directory V3 that integrates with other directories and utilizes an extensible schema, allowing you to store any information you choose. Also synchronizes user accounts with Windows NT directory.

- Workflow tracking: Easily define processes to route and track documents to coordinate activities both inside your enterprise and out.

- Search services: Domain wide searching across all Domino applications and file systems. Includes built-in search security and filters.

- Integrated development environment: Domino Designer is optimized to work with Domino and includes a complete set of visual tools for rapid development and deployment of secure e-business solutions. Also support various HTML authoring tools as well as Java development and scripting.

► Includes Domino Enterprise Connection Services (DECS) for live access to enterprise systems. DECS supports such products as DB2, Oracle, Sybase, A/SQL, SAP, PeopleSoft, JD Edwards, Oracle Applications, MQSeries, Customer Information Control System (CICS), and so on.

3.7.1 Using two IBM application server products

For high volume, transactional applications, there is no better choice than a Web application server, such as WebSphere Application Server. For collaborative, document-based applications, there is no better tool than a collaborative application server (CAS), such as Lotus Domino. All of IBM Software Group, including WebSphere and Lotus, have committed to Web services as the next focus for integration. Doing so will enhance the integration of Domino, WebSphere, Tivoli, and DB2, of course, but will also open up the market to any other Web services-compliant system from any vendor.

IBM has extended a philosophy throughout its software group: all of the brands (WebSphere, Lotus, DB2, and Tivoli) have the freedom to innovate and lead in a particular market, but a mandate to integrate and interoperate in ways that offer distinct customer benefits.

For more information, visit:

http://www.lotus.com/home.nsf/welcome/dominoapplicationserver

3.8 IBM SecureWay Firewall

Firewalls are part of the security architecture of a network. They protect resources from other networks and individuals by controlling access to the network and enforcing a security policy that can be tailored to suit the needs of the enterprise. IBM SecureWay Firewall allows for a safe, secure e-business environment by controlling all communications to and from the Internet. This firewall technology was developed by IBM research in 1985 and has been protecting IBM and global corporations' assets for more than 10 years. Unlike most other firewalls, the IBM firewall contains all three critical firewall architectures (filtering, proxy, and circuit level gateway) to provide customers both a high level of security and flexibility.

IBM SecureWay Firewall for Windows NT and AIX offers a combination of advanced e-mail protection features that help block unwanted e-mail, such as unsolicited promotional messages, and help thwart "mail spoofing" (trickery that makes a message appear as if it came from an authorized address).

IBM SecureWay Firewall also supports the SOCKS V5 standard, securing applications such as Real Audio and Real Video by authenticating a user with a user ID and password or by other user authentication methods. SOCKS V5 is a generalized, cost-effective method for securing high throughput Internet multimedia applications and "home-grown" UDP applications.

IBM SecureWay Firewall is part of IBM's Security Software family of products, which provide the foundation for you to extend e-business applications to employees, customers and business partners.

Other features include:

► Symmetric Multi-Processor (SMP) Support

SMP describes a computer system that can use more than one computer processor, and do so in such a way that the jobs carried out by pieces of operating systems and applications can be divided up and run across multiple processors using a common memory space.

► HTTP Proxy

An enhanced version, derived from IBM's WebSphere Web Traffic Express software technology, provides efficient handling of browser requests through the IBM firewall. This includes added support for standard report utilities (that is, IBM SecureWay Firewall will comply with commonly used industry logging schemes), support for persistent Web sessions with HTTP 1.1 (that is, users only need to enter their ID and password once to secure Web access), and URL blocking.

► Network Address Translation

This feature provides support for many-to-one (versus one-to-one) address mappings from the secure-to-unsecure network. Customers can use a single external address to represent many internal machines, reducing the requirement for registered IP addresses, and simplifying the planning process for the secure IP structure of an internal network. Support for the ICMP protocol also helps with firewall setup and testing.

► IPSec VPN Enhancements

Implementation of Triple DES encryption (the strongest level of encryption currently available) and support for the current version of the IPSec standards for Virtual Private Networks allow customers to use the Internet for secure, private communications instead of expensive leased lines.

► Enhanced filter rule processing and interface

Features the ability a customer has to manage the filter rules which process traffic. A graphical user interface allows you to track rule activity. You can prioritize filter rules which minimize processing and improve performance, especially if they have many filter rules.

► Usability

An installation wizard is provided for the IBM SecureWay Firewall. This allows customers to install and configure the firewall from a simple set of configuration questions once they have determined their security policy.

In short, IBM Firewall provides:

► Three firewalls in one, allowing you to optimize security and performance through the choice of filtering, circuit gateway, or application gateway.

► Network Security Auditor proactively scans the firewall and other hosts to find potential security exposures.

► Includes VPN support based on the IPSec standard.

► Reduces cost through predefined services for fast setup.

► Disables unsafe applications to ensure a secure platform for the firewall.

► Provides seamless Internet access using standard client software.

► Supports TCP and UDP applications through SOCKS Version 5.

► Provides real-time performance statistics and log monitoring.

► Provides easy and secure administration and centrally manages and configures multiple firewalls.

► Eliminates the need for expensive leased lines by using the Internet as a virtual private network.

More information is available at `http://www.ibm.com/software/security`.

3.9 Public Key Infrastructure

X.509 Public Key Infrastructure (PKI) is an Internet official protocol standard that is, in the simplest terms, a digital method of identification. It is used to verify that a message or document was authored by a certain person, and that it was not altered or modified by anyone else. (The process of verifying the integrity of a document is authentication.) Digital IDs are a standard way to establish proof of identity using a variety of protocols. They certify that a document was signed by a person with a certain public key when opened by the recipient that holds the private key. It does not matter if someone else holds the original public key, because it is of no value in decrypting the document.

The discussion regarding how this is achieved is lengthy and beyond the scope of this redbook. More detailed information may be found in the IBM Redbook *Deploying a Public Key Infrastructure,* SG24-5512 or in the *RFC2459 Internet X.509 Public Key Infrastructure* at `http://www.ietf.org/rfc.html`.

3.9.1 Tivoli Public Key Infrastructure (TPKI)

Tivoli PKI is a cross platform, integrated PKI solution that contains all the components needed to enable an X.509 based public key infrastructure in your enterprise. More than a certificate server, it supports the life cycle of a certificate, including requesting, validation, issuing, publishing, and administration of certificates. It provides applications with ease to authenticate users, ensure trusted communications, and establish the level of trust needed to conduct your e-business.

Tivoli PKI allows transactions to travel across organizational boundaries without compromising privacy, security, or confidence. It provides secure authentication for parties involved in e-business transactions via digital signing and an audit trail for all transactions.

Tivoli PKI features:

► Organizations can issue, publish, and administer digital certificates in accordance with their registration and certification policies.

► Support for Public Key Infrastructure X.509 version 3 (PKIX) and Common Data Security.

► The Common Data Security Architecture (CDSA) for cryptographic standards allows for vendor interoperability.

► Digital signing and secure protocols provide the means to authenticate all parties in a transaction.

► Browser- and client-based registration capabilities provide maximum flexibility.

► Encrypted communications and secure storage of registration information ensure confidentiality.

► A trusted Certificate Authority (CA) manages the complete life cycle of digital certification.

► Cryptographic hardware, such as the IBM 4758 PCI Cryptographic Coprocessor, can be used to protect the CA's signing key.

► A Registration Authority (RA) handles the administrative tasks behind user registration. The RA ensures that only certificates that support permitted business activities are issued, and that they are issued only to authorized users.

► The administrative tasks can be handled through automated processes or human decision-making.

► A Web-based enrollment interface makes it easy to obtain certificates for browsers, servers, and other purposes, such as virtual private network (VPN) devices, smart cards, and secure (S/MIME) e-mail.

- ► A Windows application, the Tivoli Public Key Infrastructure Client, enables end users to obtain and manage certificates without using a Web browser.

- ► A Web-based administration interface, the RA Desktop, enables authorized registrars to approve or reject enrollment requests and administer certificates after they have been issued.

- ► An Audit subsystem computes a message authentication code (MAC) for each audit record. If audit data is altered or deleted after it has been written to the database, the MAC enables the intrusion to be detected.

- ► Flexible policy exits enable application developers to customize the registration processes.

- ► Core product components are signed with a factory-generated private key. Security objects, such as keys and MACs, are encrypted and stored in password-protected areas.

For additional information, please visit:

`http://www.tivoli.com/products/index/secureway_public_key/index.html`

3.10 Conclusions

There are many ways to diagram an environment or implement it, as shown in the first part of this chapter. There are also many ways to keep your security and network environment safe, as we have shown with the different products available.

Networks have been around for some time, and security for applications and data have as well. Now, they are interconnected more than before. Technologies will change, business will evolve, but the need to keep information out of the hands of those that have no authorization to use or see it will only increase.

Building a secure system is not enough. Keeping it functional, testing it, and improving and reviewing it with management, your security, network and development professionals is mandatory. When you deal with the Web and network security, reviewing your procedures and policies regularly will help keep the enterprise protected from new threats as well as old.

A question to keep in mind as you review your environment: "Will the cost of this improvement/refinement be more or less than repairing or replacing the assets compromised or lost?"

It is generally more cost effective to be proactive rather than reactive.

Part 2

Managing
access control

In this part, we discuss the solutions Tivoli has to offer in the access control subsystem of the overall security architecture. Access control information, which generally evolves around authentication and authorization mechanisms, is mainly handled by Tivoli Access Manager for e-business (TAME) and its different blades. Access Manager handles a multitude of integration aspects with all sorts of IT infrastructures and application environments, which are detailed throughout this part of the book.

Introduction to Access Manager components

In this chapter, we introduce the components of Access Manager. We will discuss three types of components:

► Base components, which are generally common to all Access Manager installations

► Blades, which support authorization for specific application classes

► Interface components, which permit application programs to directly interact with Access Manager functions

Discussion of these components will provide the foundation for introducing the elements of the Access Manager architecture.

> **Note:** Due to the latest IBM Tivoli changes in naming and branding you will be confronted with the new name for Tivoli Policy Director: IBM Tivoli Access Manager for e-business. On some occasions, when we are referring to older versions of the product, we still use Policy Director V3.8 or V3.7. All references to Tivoli Access Manager are based on the current Version 3.9, which becomes available in April 2002.

4.1 Base components

Access Manager provides several components that support basic product functionality. The Access Manager "base" consists of a small set of architecturally "core" components and management facilities that are generally required to support and administer the environment.

4.1.1 Overview

Access Manager's base functions are provided through a set of core components and various management components.

Core components

Access Manager is fundamentally based upon two components:

► A user registry
► An authorization service, consisting of an authorization database and an authorization engine

These components support the core functionality that must exist for Access Manager to perform its fundamental operations, which are:

► Knowing the identity of who is performing a particular operation (users)
► Knowing the roles associated with a particular identity (groups)
► Knowing what application entities a particular identity may access (objects)
► Knowing the authorization rules associated with application objects (policies)
► Using the above to make access decisions on behalf of applications (authorization)
► Auditing and logging of all activity related to authentication and authorization

Versions of Policy Director prior to 3.8 also required Distributed Computing Environment (DCE) services as a core operational component. This is no longer the case, and those Access Manager components which previously relied on DCE services have been modified to use alternative functionality. In particular, inter-component communication now uses an Access Manager specific protocol based on SSL rather than DCE mechanisms. This has significant positive impact on production Access Manager architectures, which rely on firewalls to control access to network zones/demilitarized zones (DMZs).

In summary, a user registry and an authorization service are the fundamental building blocks upon which Access Manager builds to provide its security capabilities. All other Access Manager services and components are built upon this base.

Management components

The Access Manager environment requires certain basic capabilities for administrative control of its functions. Management facilities are provided through the following base components:

► The Policy Server, which supports the management of the authorization database and its distribution to authorization services

► The `pdadmin` utility, which provides a command line capability for performing administrative functions, such as adding users or groups

► The Web Portal Manager, which provides an Web browser based capability for performing most of the same functions provided by the pdadmin utility

4.1.2 User registry

Access Manager requires a user registry to support the operation of its authorization functions. Specifically, it provides:

► A database of the user identities that are known to Access Manager

► A representation of groups in Access Manager (roles) that may be associated with users

► A data store of other meta data required to support authorization functions

Identity mapping

While it can be used in authenticating users, this is not the primary purpose of the user registry. An application can authenticate a user via any mechanism it chooses (ID/password, certificate, and so on), and then map the authenticated identity to one defined in the user registry. For example, consider a user John who authenticates himself to an application using a certificate. The application then maps the DN in John's certificate to the Access Manager user named john123. When making subsequent authorization decisions, the internal Access Manager user is john123, and this identity is passed between the application and other components using various mechanisms, including a special credential known as an EPAC (Extended Privilege Attribute Certificate).

Note: One of the primary goals of the authentication process is to acquire credential information describing the client user. The user credential is one of the key requirements for participating in the secure domain.

Access Manager distinguishes the authentication of the user from the acquisition of credentials. A user's identity is always constant. However, credentials, which define the groups or roles in which a user participates, are variable. Context-specific credentials can change over time. For example, when a person is promoted, credentials must reflect the new responsibility level.

The authentication process results in method-specific user identity information. This information is checked against user account information that resides in the Access Manager user registry. WebSEAL maps the user name and group information to a common domain-wide representation and format known as the Extended Privilege Attribute Certificate (EPAC).

Method-specific identity information, such as passwords, tokens, and certificates, represent physical identity properties of the user. This information can be used to establish a secure session with the server.

The resulting credential, which represents a user's privileges in the secure domain, describes the user in a specific context and is only valid for the lifetime of that session.

Access Manager credentials contain the user identity and groups where this user has membership.

User registry structure

The user registry contains three types of objects:

► User objects, which contain basic user attributes.

► Group objects, representing roles which may be associated with user objects.

► Access Manager meta-data objects, containing special Access Manager attributes that are associated with user and group objects. The meta-data includes information that allows a Access Manager user ID to be linked to its corresponding user object.

The default user registry is LDAP-based and Access Manager 3.9 consolidates its registry support around a number of LDAP directory products. Previous releases of Access Manager supported a DCE user registry; however, with the elimination of DCE from the product, this registry type is no longer supported.

Access Manager is capable of using the following directory products for its user registry:

- ► IBM SecureWay Directory server
- ► Critical Path LiveContent Directory
- ► Netscape iPlanet Directory
- ► Microsoft Active Directory (Windows 2000 advanced Server only)
- ► Lotus Domino Name Address Book (Access Manager (AM) on Windows only)
- ► OS/390 Security Server
- ► z/OS Security Server

The IBM SecureWay Directory is included with Access Manager and is the default LDAP directory for implementing the user registry.

Access Manager components support the use of directory replicas, and in production installations, it is generally advantageous to use replicas for scalability and availability purposes.

Directory schema

To support its critical and private registry data, Access Manager requires certain support in the directory schema. There are certain object classes and attributes that are specific to Access Manager and are configured as needed during product installation. Access Manager, however, only adds new subclasses to existing Directory entries, for example, *inetOrgPerson*.

Attention: While it might seem relevant to inquire about the details of the directory schema that Access Manager uses, such information is not necessarily useful (and may in fact be somewhat "dangerous" to have). It is important to keep in mind that Access Manager components are the exclusive users of these special object classes and attributes. The schema definitions and their usage can change from release to release. As such, application components should not assume any knowledge of Access Manager-specific schema definitions or how they are used. Instead, application interaction with registry information or functions should only be performed using published Access Manager interfaces.

4.1.3 Authorization database

Separately from the User Registry, for its authorization functions, Access Manager uses a special database containing a virtual representation of resources it protects. Called the "protected object space", it uses a proprietary format and contains object definitions that may represent logical or actual physical resources. Objects for different application types may be contained in different sections of the object space, and the object space may be extended to support new application types as required.

Security policy for these resources is implemented by applying appropriate security mechanisms to the objects requiring protection. Security mechanisms are also defined in the Authorization Database and include:

► Access control list (ACL) policy templates

ACLs are special Access Manager objects that define policies identifying user types who can be considered for access and specify permitted operations. In the Access Manager model, ACLs are defined separately from and then attached to one or more protected objects. So an ACL has no effect on authorization until it becomes associated with a protected object.

Access Manager uses an inheritance model in which an ACL attached to a protected object applies to all other objects below it in the tree until another ACL is encountered.

► Protected object policy (POP) templates

A POP specifies additional conditions governing the access to the protected object, such as privacy, integrity, auditing, and time-of-day access.

POPs are attached to protected objects in the same manner as ACLs.

► Extended attributes

Extended attributes are additional values placed on an object, ACL, or POP that can be read and interpreted by third-party applications (such as an external authorization service).

Figure 4-1 depicts the relationships between the protected object space, ACLs, and POPs.

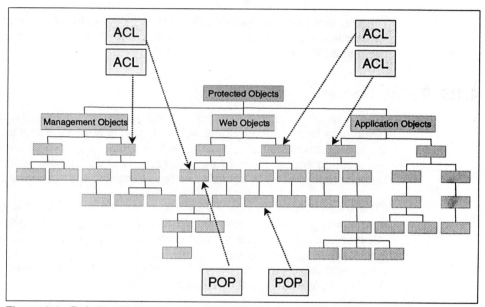

Figure 4-1   Relationship between the protected object space, ACLs, and POPs

Successful implementation of security policy requires that the different content types are logically organized (and the appropriate ACL and POP policies applied). Access control management can be complex and is made much easier by careful categorization of the content types. It should implement the general corporate security policy (refer to Section 1.3, "Corporate policy" on page 8).

4.1.4 Authorization Service

The foundation of Access Manager is its Authorization Service, which permits or denies access to protected objects (resources) based on the user's credentials and the access controls placed on the objects.

The Policy Server (described in the next section) provides a basic authorization service that may be leveraged by applications and other Access Manager components that use the Authorization Application Programming Interface (aznAPI) (described in Section 4.3.1, "aznAPI" on page 106). Optionally, additional Authorization Servers may be installed to offload these authorization decisions from the Policy Server and provide for higher availability of authorization functions. The Policy Server provides updates for Authorization Database replicas maintained on each Authorization Server.

The Access Manager Authorization Service can also be directly embedded within an application. In this case, the functions of an Authorization Server are contained in the application itself.

4.1.5 Policy Server

The Access Manager Policy Server maintains the master Authorization Database for the secure domain. This server is key to the processing of access control, authentication, and authorization requests. It also is responsible for distributing and updating all authorization database replicas and maintains location information about other Access Manager servers in the secure domain.

There can only be a single Policy Server in an Access Manager domain. For availability purposes, a standby server can be configured to take over Policy Server functions in the event of a system failure. This can be supported via manually executed recovery actions, or automatically, using an appropriate high-availability product (for example, HACMP on AIX platforms). This is further discussed in Section 7.2, "Availability" on page 159.

4.1.6 The pdadmin utility

pdadmin is a command-line utility which supports Access Manager administrative functions. In Policy Director versions prior to 3.8, multiple, specialized command line utilities supported various administrative needs. These functions (including management of WebSEAL junctions) have now been combined within **pdadmin**.

4.1.7 Web Portal Manager

The Access Manager Web Portal Manager (WPM) provides a Web browser-based graphical user interface (GUI) for Access Manager administration. It replaces the Management Console used in earlier releases of Access Manager.

A key advantage of the Web Portal Manager over the **pdadmin** command and the earlier Management Console is the fact that it is a browser-based application that can be accessed without installing any Access Manager-specific client components, or requiring special network configuration to permit remote administrator access. In fact, the authorization capabilities of WebSEAL (described in Section 4.2.1, "WebSEAL" on page 91) can be used to control access to the Web Portal Manager. This allows greater flexibility in where administrators are located with respect to the physical systems they are managing.

The Web Portal Manager was designed to be an alternative to the **pdadmin** command line interface (CLI) for many administrative functions. However, not all **pdadmin** functions are supported (for example, managing WebSEAL junctions must be done using **pdadmin**), and the command line interface will still be required in certain cases.

The Web Portal Manager also provides a delegated user administration capability. This allows a Access Manager administrator to create delegated user domains and assign delegate administrators to these domains, as shown in Figure 4-2 on page 88.

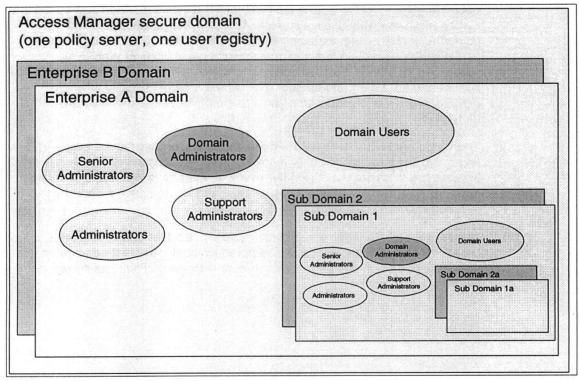

Figure 4-2 Access Manager delegation model example

The initial aim of the Web Portal Manager is to allow multiple independent enterprises to manage their own user population in a single **Access Manager Secure Domain**. This functionality could be used where a **Service Provider** that is using Access Manager to provide access control to Web resources wants to allow their customers to define and manage their own user population.

> **Note:** The Web Portal Manager Version 3.9 has been aligned with Tivoli's Identity Manager user interface for better administrative usability.

The WPM provides a simple Web-based interface to the existing Delegated Administration function of Access Manager. It allows a super user (fore exampl, sec_master) to define a number of Enterprise Domains, each with one or more Domain Administrators that are the super users in that domain. WPM is supported on WindowsNT SP6a, Windows 2000 advanced Server SP2, AIX Version 4.3.3. and 5.1.0, and Solaris 7 and 8 platforms.

A Domain Administrator can create, modify, and delete domain users within the domain and can delegate administration within the domain. Domain administrators can also create sub-domains inside the domain they control.

All Administrative users in a domain (including the Domain Administrators) can be limited so they can only view and/or modify the users within their domain.

Depending on their assigned roles, the delegate administrators can perform a subset of the administration functions aligning the security administration with different organization and business relationships, such as:

► Departments

► Dealerships

► Branch offices

► Partnerships

► Suppliers

► Distributors

There are four different levels of administration in Access Manager with the following basic fields of action, as shown in Table 4-1.

Table 4-1   Delegated administration roles in Access Manager

Action/Role	Domain Admin	Senior Admin	Admin	Support	Any other
View user	X	X	X	X	X
Reset password	X	X	X	X	
Add existing Policy Director user as an administrator	X	X	X		
Create domain user	X	X			
Remove user	X	X			
Domain control	X				

Architecture

The Web Portal Manager is built using Java Server Pages (JSP), which support the various administrative functions. It uses a Web application server servlet engine; WebSphere Application Server 3.5 is provided with Access Manager to support this capability. Figure 4-3 on page 90 provides an architectural view of how the Web Portal Manager works.

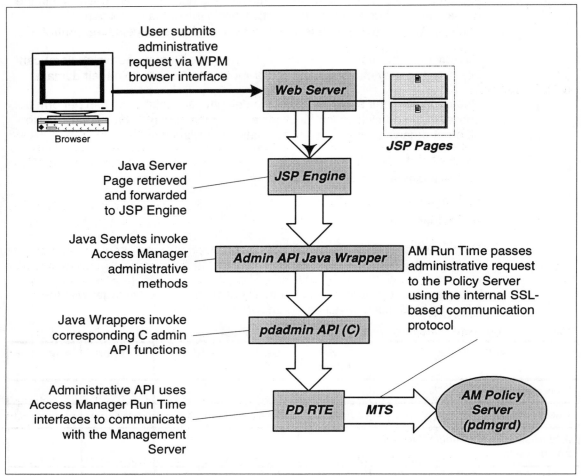

Figure 4-3   Web Portal Manager architecture

Other issues

There are a number of other issues that should be kept in mind when deploying the Web Portal Manager:

► There is no limit to the number of Web Portal Manager instances that may be deployed.

► It is possible to provide access to the Web Portal Manager via a WebSEAL junction (discussed below); however, transparent sign-on is not supported in the current (3.8) release. In other words, a user logged on to WebSEAL must also log on to the Web Portal Manager.

4.2 Blades

Blades are components that provide Access Manager authorization support for specific application types.

4.2.1 WebSEAL

WebSEAL is a high performance, multi-threaded Web server that applies a security policy to a protected object space (which is defined in the authorization database, described in Section 4.1.3, "Authorization database" on page 84). WebSEAL can provide single sign-on solutions and incorporate back-end Web application server resources into its security policy.

In addition to its ability to support local HTML and basic CGI content, WebSEAL is capable of operating as a reverse proxy, front-ending back-end Web services.

More details on an architectural discussion on positioning Access Manager components, especially WebSEAL, within an Internet centric environment can be found in Chapter 5, "Access Manager Web-based architecture" on page 111.

Platforms

WebSEAL is supported on all Access Manager platforms, except Intel-based Linuxes.

Junctions

The back-end services to which WebSEAL can proxy are defined via "junctions", which define a set of one or more back-end Web servers that are associated with a particular URL.

For example, suppose a junction on WebSEAL host "www.abc.com" is defined such that a request for any URL specifying the path "/content/xyz" (relative to the Web space root, of course) is to be proxied to the back-end Web server "def.internal.abc.com". "/content/xyz" is the "junction point", which can be thought of in a loose sense as being similar in concept to a file system mount point.

A user at a browser then makes a request for "http://www.abc.com/content/xyz/myhtmlfiles/test.html"; WebSEAL will examine the URL and determine that the request falls within the Web space for the "/content/xyz" junction point. It will then proxy the request to "def.internal.abc.com" and forward the resulting response back to the browser.

From the perspective of the browser, the request is processed by "www.abc.com". The fact that it is actually handled by the target server "def.internal.abc.com" is not known to the user. To support this, WebSEAL performs various transformations on the response sent to the browser to assure that the back-end server names are not exposed. This exemplifies one of the powerful capabilities provided by WebSEAL junctions, that is, the "virtualization of the Web space". Junctions may be defined to the individual Web spaces on various back-end servers, yet from the browser's point of view, there is only one single Web space.

It was hinted above that more than one target server may be defined for a particular junction point. For example, the server "ghi.internal.abc.com" could be defined as an additional target for the "/content/xyz" junction point. In this case, WebSEAL can "load-balance" among the servers, and should a back-end server be unavailable, WebSEAL can continue forwarding requests to the remaining servers for the junction. For situations where it is important that subsequent requests for a particular user continue going to the same back-end server, WebSEAL is capable of supporting this via what are called "stateful junctions".

The above assumes that processing a request does not involve any security considerations. While WebSEAL is capable of doing a fine job of simply managing access to Web-based content and applications via simple junctions, this, of course, leaves out a primary purpose of utilizing WebSEAL. Its integration with the base Access Manager services to provide access control for Web resources is its main reason for existence.

WebSEAL security functions

One of WebSEAL's key functions is to protect access to Web content and applications. To do this, it uses Access Manager's authorization services. The authorization service must know which Web objects (that is, URLs) require protection, and what level(s) of access to these objects are permitted for the Access Manager users and groups defined in the User Registry.

The protected object space is defined in the Access Manager authorization database. It is populated using a special CGI program that runs on each back-end junctioned Web server. This program, named "query_contents", is run by the Web Portal Manager and scans the Web directory hierarchy on the server. It populates the authorization database with representations of the various objects it finds. ACLs and POPs can be "attached" to these objects, and WebSEAL can then use Access Manager's authorization engine to make access decisions on requests for various URLs.

Of course, the authorization engine cannot make access decisions without being told something about the identity of the user. WebSEAL supports the ability to authenticate a user and assign a Access Manager identity for use when making authorization decisions. Whenever a URL is requested that is not accessible by an unauthenticated user, WebSEAL will attempt to authenticate the user by issuing an HTTP authentication challenge to the browser (it supports multiple authentication mechanisms, which are discussed in Section 8.4, "Supported WebSEAL authentication mechanisms" on page 184). Upon establishment of an authenticated "session", the authorization engine is then consulted to determine whether the user may access the content specified by the requested URL. This WebSEAL session is maintained until the user exits the browser or explicitly logs off, or until the session times out from inactivity. Subsequent URL requests for this session continue to be checked to see if access is permitted. In this manner, WebSEAL provides single sign-on capabilities for Web-based content and applications.

The access control granularity provided can be anywhere from a coarse-grained protection of particular directories (containers) in the Web space to specific, fine-grained protection of individual Web objects, for example, an individual HTML file. Additionally, URL "patterns" may be defined that represents "dynamic" URLs. For example, application parameters are often defined in URLs, and may differ across invocations. By defining a pattern to Access Manager's Web object space that matches such a URL, it is possible to accommodate these situations.

Authentication to back-end servers

Often, it is necessary to provide special authentication information to junctioned Web servers, for the purpose of verifying the identity of the WebSEAL server, providing the identity of the logged-in user, or both. WebSEAL provides a number of mechanisms to support such authentication requirements.

WebSEAL authentication

If necessary, WebSEAL can authenticate itself to a junctioned server using either server certificates, forms based authentication, or HTTP basic authentication. When using an SSL communication channel for this junction, WebSEAL and the junctioned server can also mutually authenticate each other. This is very important in order to establish the trust relationships between WebSEAL and back-end Web application servers.

As an added functionality, WebSEAL supports *Forced Login* and *Switch User* functions. Reauthentication is used to force a user to log in again, based on a policy setting or a session timeout. Switch User allows administrators to log on to Access Manager as a user without having to supply their password. This will aid help desk administrators with customer support issues. It can also be used by administrators to easily troubleshoot and vefify the correct functionality of Access Control Lists without the need to create test users.

Delegated user authentication

WebSEAL supports a number of mechanisms to supply a junctioned server with the identity of the logged-in user, including:

► Providing the user's identity via HTTP header values, which can be read and interpreted by the junctioned server.
► Insertion of an HTTP basic authentication header to provide the junctioned server with login information for the user, including a password. This basic authentication header can optionally permit login to the junctioned server with a different identity than the one for the user who is logged-in to WebSEAL.
► For junctions that support it (for example, WebSphere Application Server and Domino), insert an LTPA (Lightweight Third-Party Authentication) cookie identifying the user into the HTTP stream that is passed to the junctioned server.

WebSEAL delegated authentication capabilities are discussed more fully in Section 8.5, "WebSEAL delegation mechanisms" on page 190.

Replicated WebSEALs

It is possible to replicate WebSEAL servers for availability and scalability purposes. There are specific configuration requirements to create WebSEAL replicas, and a front-end load balancing capability must be used to distribute incoming requests among the replicas. Also, because each WebSEAL replica maintains active session states for its own authenticated users, the load balancing mechanism used must support a "sticky" capability to route subsequent requests to the same replica (in other words, users "log on" to a specific WebSEAL server). The use of WebSEAL replicas will be discussed and illustrated in Chapter 7, "Increasing availability and scalability" on page 157.

Virtual hosting

Multiple instances of WebSEAL can be created on a single machine using the WebSEAL configuration/unconfiguration utility. Each WebSEAL will require its own unique IP/Port combination. This approach enables a virtual hosting solution by running multiple WebSEALs with unique URL identifiers.

Communication protocols

WebSEAL can communicate with the clients and back-end servers with both encrypted (SSL) and unencrypted (TCP) protocols. The supported encryption types are SSLv1, SSLv2, SSLv3, and TLSv1.

SSL hardware acceleration support

For performance improvement, WebSEAL supports SSL hardware acceleration. Utilizing the functionality of GSKit5, hardware acceleration can minimize the CPU impact of SSL communications, improving the overall performance of the system.

The nCipher nForce 300 card will be supported for the AIX, Solaris, and Windows platforms. Please refer to the product documentation for the complete description of all the cards we will support when the product is generally available.

This support applies to any SSL session that WebSEAL is involved in, but the performance impact that the users see is exclusive to the browser/WebSEAL session. The performance advantage the SSL hardware acceleration card can give us is the initial SSL handshaking between two communicating parties. Once an SSL tunnel is set up, the card does not help any more. In other words, the card provides benefits only for the RSA public key authentication part (happening in the initial SSL handshaking), but not for the DES encryption part used in normal data transmission afterwards. Most SSL sessions are built during the configuration time or the junction setup time and will be reused. So, we will not get performance improvement from SSL hardware acceleration. The browser-to-WebSEAL SSL session is built whenever a user with a browser tries to communicate with WebSEAL. The customer value is the improved performance in browser-WebSEAL SSL session setups and the higher numbers of users that can be supported, due to the offloading of work from the WebSEAL host's processor to the card.

There is no Access Manager-specific documentation to cover this enhancement; the support of the card is simply a function of GSKit, and so the card's documentation is all that is needed.

Other WebSEAL functionality

WebSEAL supports an e-Community Single Sign-on functionality that allows Web users to perform a single sign-on and move seamlessly between WebSEAL servers in two separate secure domains. We take a closer look at e-Community Single Sign-on in Chapter 10, "Access control in a distributed environment" on page 227.

WebSEAL also supports a capability which permits "failover" of logged on users to another replica in the same domain in the event their assigned WebSEAL server becomes unavailable. This failover cookie feature is also supported by the Plug-in for Edge Server, which is discussed in Section 4.2.2, "Plug-In for Edge Server" on page 97.

Architecture

The WebSEAL architecture is summarized in Figure 4-4. The WebSEAL server directly interacts with the browser and proxies requests to junctioned Web servers, determining which junction to pass the request to by examining the URL.

Before passing the request, WebSEAL also uses the authorization engine to check the URL against the Web objects. If the URL is not protected, the request is simply proxied to the appropriate junction. If the URL is protected, an access control check must first be made. If the user is not yet authenticated, an authentication challenge is sent to the browser and WebSEAL uses its authentication services to validate the user's claimed identity and map it to an appropriate Access Manager identity in the user registry. Access to the object is then checked against this identity, and if allowed, the request is proxied.

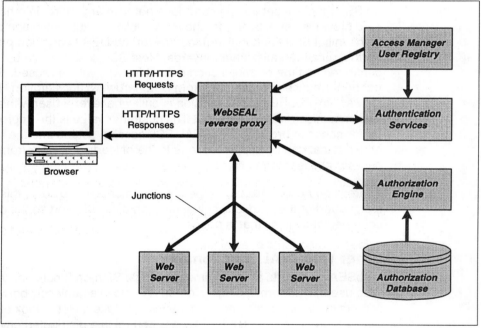

Figure 4-4   WebSEAL architecture

4.2.2 Plug-In for Edge Server

The Access Manager Plug-in for Edge Server is a plug-in for the Edge Server Caching Proxy component of the IBM WebSphere Edge Server. It adds Access Manager authentication and authorization capabilities to the proxy, and in certain scenarios, it provides an alternative to WebSEAL for managing access to Web content and applications. More information on WebSphere Edge Server can be found in Section 3.6, "WebSphere Edge Server" on page 64.

While the Plug-in for Edge Server shares many of the same capabilities as WebSEAL, its configuration is different. However, architecturally, it fits into most Access Manager scenarios in the same manner as WebSEAL.

While there are other differences, two key differentiators between the plug-in and WebSEAL are:

► Use of the plug-in with the Edge Server Caching Proxy provides direct support for virtual hosting.

► The plug-in can be used in both forward and reverse proxy configurations (WebSEAL only supports a reverse proxy).

The plug-in also integrates with the WebSphere Everyplace Suite, and supports forms-based login, IBM WebSphere LTPA cookies, and Access Manager WebSEAL failover cookies.

Architecture

Figure 4-5 on page 98 provides a simplified view of the Plug-in for Edge Server architecture used as a reverse proxy (a forward proxy scenario is virtually identical, except that the proxy operations are to the outside rather than back-end servers). It should be noted that while this architecture is similar to that for WebSEAL (Figure 4-4 on page 96), the specific functionality and configuration of various components does differ.

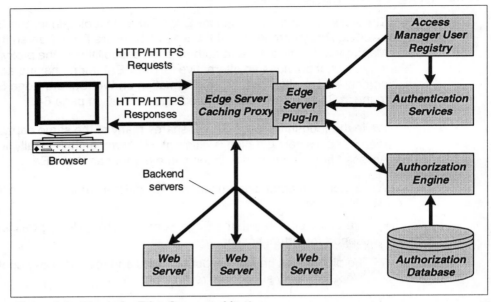

Figure 4-5   Plug-in for Edge Server architecture

4.2.3 Plug-in for Web Servers

In Access Manager 3.9, we have full capability for Web Server plug-ins. This Web Server plug-in architecture provides a solution where the customer has decided on deploying a Web plug-in architecture for their solution architecture rather than a reverse proxy approach.

Table 4-2 summarizes the capabilities that are provided by this implementation based on a WebSEAL comparison.

Table 4-2   Plug-in for Web servers functionalities

Authentication support	
Authentication based on client IP address	Supported.
User name/password (basic authentication and forms-based), certificate and SecureID authentication	Supported.
Step-up authentication	Supported.
Cross Domain Authentication Service (CDAS)	Supported.
Interoperability with WebSEAL fail-over cookies	Supported.

Authentication support	
Web SSO (Basic Authentication and Forms-Based Authentication)	Supported.
SSO from plug-in Web server to back-end BEA WebLogic Server (BEA WLS) or WebSphere Application Server	Supported.
e-Community SSO (requires a WebSEAL Master Authentication Server (MAS)	Supported.
SSO from WebSEAL to plug-in	Supported.
Forms-based SSO	Supported.
Password policy support, including password strength, password expiration, extensible password policy native implementation of "N strikes out password policy"	Supported.
Junction from WebSEAL to plug-in	Supported. Will accept WebSEAL to WebSEAL junctions.
Authorization support	
ACL and POP policies	Supported.
Tag/value support	Supported.
PD_PORTAL support	Supported.
Pass user/groups/creds in HTTP header	Supported.
Fail over (Same as Authentication fail over)	Supported.
Platform support	
Note: One Web server per host is assumed.	
IIS on Windows 2000	▸ IIS 5.0 (Need to clarify service packs and security fixes). ▸ Windows 2000 Server and Windows 2000 Advanced Server.
IPlanet on Solaris	▸ IPlanet 6.0. ▸ Solaris 7 (Sparc). ▸ Solaris 8 (Sparc) - "run at".

Authentication support	
Apache	► Apache 1.3.20. ► Red Hat Linux 7.1 (x86). ► Mod_ssl 2.8.4.
Other	
Directory support: IBM SecureWay Directory, Netscape iPlanet Directory, MS Active Directory, and Domino NAB Registry	Supported.
Virtual hosting	Provided by the host Web server.
Install/configure/uninstall	Simple and intuitive.
URL and HTTP protocol transparency	Supported.
Globalization-languages supported	Same as PD Base, except bi-directional languages will not be supported.

For an architectural overview of the Web server plug-in implementation, look at Figure 4-6.

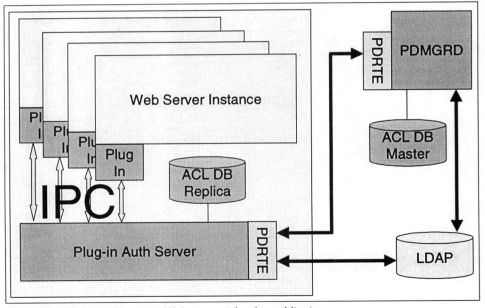

Figure 4-6   Access Manager Web server plug-in architecture

In most Web server environments, there are multiple server threads in operation on the machine. These might be different threads of the same Web server instance or threads of different Web server instances. Having a distinct authorization engine for each thread would be inefficient, but would also mean that session information would have to be shared between them somehow.

The architecture used contains two parts:

1. Interceptor

   This is the real *plug-in* part of the solution. Each Web server thread has a plug-in running in it that gets to see and handle each request/response that the thread deals with. The interceptor does not authorize the decisions itself; it sends details of each request (via an Inter-Process Communication interface) to the Plug-in Authorization Server.

2. Plug-in Authorization Server

   This is where authorization decisions are made and the action to be taken is decided. There is a single Plug-in Authorization Server on each machine and it can handle requests from all plug-in types. The Plug-in Authorization Server is a local aznAPI application that handles authentication and authorization for the plug-ins. The Authorization Server receives intercepted requests from the Plug-ins and responds with a set of commands that tell the plug-in how to handle the request.

4.2.4 Access Manager for Business Integration

Tivoli Access Manager for Business Integration provides comprehensive security services for IBM MQSeries. It extends the MQSeries environment to support end-to-end security across queues, and includes the following capabilities:

► User identity based upon Access Manager (Standard MQ Series uses the local process user identity on and is platform/OS specific).

► Centralized management of access control to application messages on queues (using the Access Manager authorization engine).

► End-to-end message encryption for confidentiality and data integrity (messages are encrypted when placed on a queue and then decrypted when received from a queue).

These services are provided transparently to MQ Series, meaning that existing applications are supported without requiring any changes to them. Access Manager actually exchanges the original MQ.DLL with one that provides an interceptor to Access Manager.

Architecture

Access Manager for Business Integration provides an "interceptor" process that sits between an MQSeries application and MQSeries itself. Calls made by the application to MQSeries for services are captured by this interceptor, which determines:

► Whether the request for MQSeries services is authorized, based upon an authorization check against a Access Manager object representing the resource.

► Whether the data in the transaction should be encrypted and/or digitally signed, before being placed in the queue requested.

Access Manager for Business Integration can also provide access control services for local applications attempting to access remote queues on servers running on platforms that its interceptor does not run on today. For example, Access Manager for Business Integration can prevent an application running on Solaris or NT from getting or putting messages to a local queue that maps to a remote queue actually on a mainframe or AS/400.

Encryption and digital signing of messages requires that the Access Manager for Business Integration interceptor be running on both sides of the transaction. If services are needed to a mainframe or other platform the interceptor does run on today, a customer can set up a proxy system running the interceptor. A typical environment is a remote network of distributed servers running MQSeries transactions across public networks to a central IS center. With Access Manager for Business Integration, transaction flows across the public network can be protected.

User/application authentication for Access Manager for Business Integration employs PKI credentials. PKI Client services are required to provide the S/MIME encryption services used to protect MQSeries message data integrity.

Figure 4-7 on page 103 illustrates the flow of messages within the Access Manager for Business Integration (AM/BI) Architecture.

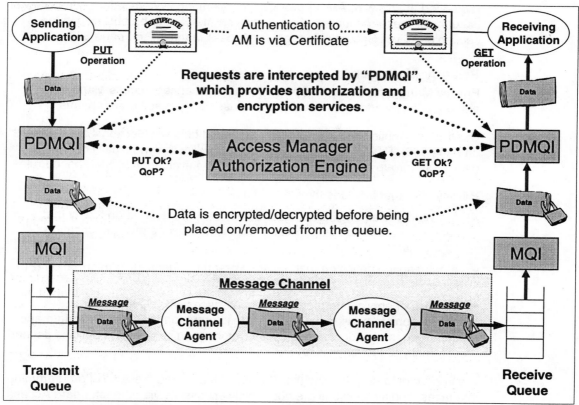

Figure 4-7   Access Manager for Business Integration architecture

4.2.5 Other blades

There are several other blades available for Access Manager, some of which are targeted at a more system level integration and others at an application level integration.

Access Manager for Operating Systems

Access Manager for Operating Systems (AMOS) provides the security engine for Tivoli Security Manager (TSM) and Tivoli Identity Manager (TIM) on UNIX platforms. It is composed of a security engine that intercepts certain operating system calls requiring authorization checks, such as for file access. The native operating system authorization checks are supplanted by checks against Access

Manager objects that represent the system resources for which access is requested. In this way, AMOS provides an operating system independent view of security for these resources. More details on AMOS can be obtained in the section on "Tivoli Security Manager for Access Manager" on page 327.

Privacy Manager

Privacy Manager is an add-on product which enhances Access Manager authorization by adding the ability to address data privacy requirements.

Used in conjunction with the aznAPI (described below in Section 4.3.1, "aznAPI" on page 106), Privacy Manager provides the ability to dynamically change a user's role (group membership), based upon the evaluation of XML-based rules.

Privacy Manager includes the following functions:

► A dynamic roles engine that allows policies to be defined on the fly that cannot be encoded using existing Access Manager static authorization mechanisms.

► A namespace definition that defines Personally Identifiable Information (PII) fields.

► The use of application programming interfaces (APIs), which allow applications to provide the appropriate information to Privacy Manager and then request authorization to access information based upon policies defined externally to the application.

It is important to keep in mind that Privacy Manager requires use of programming interfaces, and its functions are not directly accessible via other standard Access Manager blades, such as WebSEAL.

Access Manager for WebSphere Application Server

AM 3.9 provides the industry's first Java 2 Platform Enterprise Edition (J2EE) container-level integration with WebSphere Application Server 4.0.2.

Access Manager for WebSphere Application Server consists of the WebSphere 4.0.2 Authorization plug-in and an associated Migration Utility. This J2EE integration provides an Access Manager compatible implementation of the WebSphere version 4.0.2 Authorization Table interface for most *workstation* platforms supported by WebSphere Advanced Edition. In addition, a J2EE to Access Manager user/role migration utility will be provided to assist customers in populating the Access Manager Policy Database with users and roles.

This enables enterprises to leverage a common security model across WebSphere and non-WebSphere resources leveraging common user identity and profiles, AM-based authorization, and using Access Manager's Web Portal Manager to leverage a single point of security management across J2EE and non-J2EE resources.

The integration is transparent to the J2EE applications, because no coding or deployment changes are needed at the application level. More details can be obtained in Chapter 9, "WebSphere application integration" on page 201.

Access Manager for BEA WebLogic Server

Access Manager for WebLogic Server is an Access Manager 3.9 based implementation of a BEA WebLogic Server 6.1 *Custom Realm*, which supports Single Sign-on via WebSEAL as well as a common, AM administered user registry. SSO is achieved when WebSEAL acts as a front-end authentication server that establishes a trust relationship with the AM Custom Realm. WebSEAL authenticates the external user and vouches for the user to the AM realm. Internal users can still authenticate themselves to the WebLogic Server in the usual way. The AM Custom Realm distinguishes between those users that are vouched for by WebSEAL and those that need to be authenticated in Access Manager.

The advantages of the AM custom realm support include:

► Providing a common user registry administration across many different protected resources.

► Supporting Web single sign-on when used in conjunction with WebSEAL. This allows many authentication mechanisms to be used, including certificates, without any impact to the target application.

► Providing centralized access control of WebLogic resources in two ways:

   a. Changing a user's group memberships alters their access privileges to WebLogic's J2EE resources in accordance with the group to role mappings contained in each application's deployment descriptors.

   b. WebSEAL controls access to URLs that correspond to objects in the Access Manager policy database. These can be static URL strings or be represented by pattern matching.

Note that WebLogic Server does not expose authorization interfaces. So, centralized control of user access to WebLogic's J2EE resources is limited to moving users between groups that have been assigned to roles in application deployment descriptors.

4.3 Interfaces

Access Manager supports a number of programming interfaces which permit direct application interaction with its components. While these interfaces support a rich set of functionality and are useful in many situations, it is important to point out that there is substantial product function that does not require their use. Initially, many organizations do not need to utilize these interfaces, allowing rapid deployment of security components such as WebSEAL. However, as the needs of the organization evolve, these interfaces allow for a high level of security integration and customization.

4.3.1 aznAPI

The Access Manager aznAPI provides a standard programming and management model for integrating authorization requests and decisions with applications. Use of the aznAPI allows applications to utilize fined-grained access control for application controlled resources.

Both C and Java aznAPI function bindings are provided. Application-specific resources may be individually defined and added to the protected object space and maintained in the authorization database in the same manner that WebSEAL and other standard Access Manager blades define their respective resources. ACLs and POPs may be attached to these application objects, and aznAPI calls may then be used to access the Access Manager authorization service to obtain authorization decisions.

4.3.2 Java API for AM-based authorization

A powerful feature is to use Access Manager as an authentication and authorization backend inside the Java 2 security model.

The Access Manager Authorization Java Classes provide an implementation of Java security code that is fully compliant with the Java 2 security model and the Java Authentication and Authorization Services (JAAS) extensions. More detailed information on this topic can be found in Section 9.4, "Access Manager and WebSphere integration" on page 210.

4.3.3 Management API

Also known as the "pdadmin API", the Management API provides C language bindings to the same functions supported by the `pdadmin` command line utility. It may be used by custom applications to perform various Access Manager administrative functions.

It is Tivoli's stated direction to provide Java wrapper interfaces to Access Manager administrative functions in the future. These will be available through http://www.alphaworks.ibm.com.

4.3.4 External Authorization Service

The External Authorization Service (EAS) interface provides support for application-specific extensions to the authorization engine. This allows system designers to supplement Access Manager authorization with their own authorization models.

An EAS is accessed via an authorization "callout", which is triggered by the presence of a particular bit in the ACL that is attached to a protected object. The callout is made directly by the authorization service.

Policy Director versions prior to 3.8 implemented the EAS interface using DCE Remote Procedure Call (RPC) interfaces. In the current release of Access Manager, the EAS interface is supported via a simple authorization service "plug-in" capability. This allows an EAS to be constructed as a loadable shared library and is a much more efficient model than the previous RPC-based mechanism.

Access Manager 3.9 does support legacy DCE RPC-based EAS modules via a special DCE RPC EAS plugin. This plugin provides the DCE RPC client-side interface required for the EAS and, of course, DCE client services are required on the client machine when using this legacy EAS interface.

The EAS architecture is summarized in Figure 4-8 on page 108.

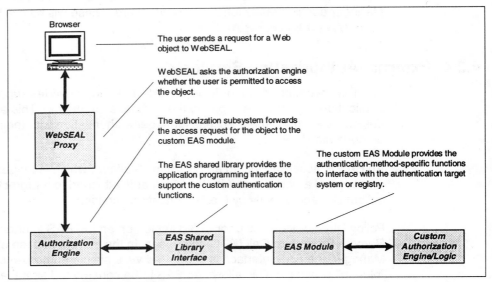

Figure 4-8   WebSEAL EAS architecture

4.3.5 Cross Domain Authentication Service

The Cross Domain Authentication Service (CDAS) is specific to WebSEAL. It provides a shared library mechanism that allows you to substitute the default WebSEAL authentication mechanisms with a custom process that ultimately returns a Access Manager identity to WebSEAL.

When WebSEAL determines that it must authenticate a user, an installation-specific CDAS can be invoked that performs the authentication using whatever mechanism is desired (for example, the user could be authenticated against a "foreign" user registry). Upon authenticating the user, the CDAS then "maps" the user to an identity defined in the Access Manager User Registry (for example, one could "log on" via a foreign registry as "joe" and then be mapped by a CDAS to the Access Manager user "fred").

Versions of Policy Director prior to 3.8 provided a DCE RPC based CDAS interface. This interface is no longer supported and all WebSEAL CDAS functions must use the shared library interfaces.

An overview of the CDAS architecture is show in Figure 4-9 on page 109.

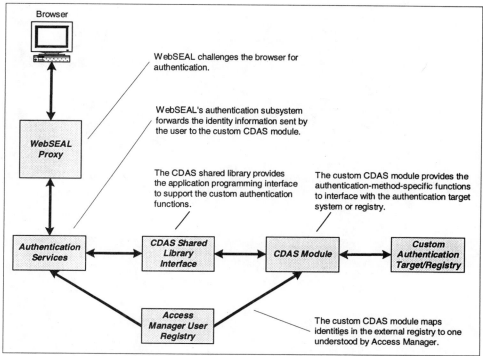

Figure 4-9   CDAS architecture

4.3.6 Cross Domain Mapping Framework

The Cross Domain Mapping Framework (CDMF) is a programming interface that may be used in conjunction with WebSEAL e-Community SSO and Cross Domain Single Sign-On (CDSSO). It allows a developer to customize the mapping of user identities and the handling of user attributes when e-Community SSO functions are used.

Conceptually, the mapping in a CDMF function works in a similar manner to a CDAS, except that it is used to map a Access Manager user in one secure domain to a Access Manager user defined in a different secure domain.

5

Access Manager Web-based architecture

Today, a Web presence has become a key consideration for the majority of businesses and other organizations. Almost all organizations see the Web as an essential information delivery tool. Increasingly, however, the Web is being seen as an extension of the organization itself, directly integrated with its operating processes. As this transformation takes place, security grows in importance.

This chapter introduces the elements of the Access Manager architecture in a Web-centric environment. While it focuses on the use of WebSEAL, it covers key architectural issues associated with any Access Manager deployment, and provides a foundation for the architectural discussions in later chapters.

5.1 Typical Internet Web server security characteristics

Perhaps the best place to begin the discussion of Access Manager architecture is with the issues typically encountered by organizations as they begin to address Web security requirements.

It is generally accepted practice for organizations to place Internet-facing Web servers in a protected zone (also known as a demilitarized zone (DMZ)), which is generally firewalled and separated from the Internet. There are many ways of doing this, depending on the needs of the business. For example, many organizations do not even maintain their Web servers in-house; instead they rely on hosting services to provide the appropriate network infrastructure to support their Web content. Other organizations, especially large ones with significant Web content and application infrastructure, maintain protected zones within the context of their own network infrastructure. In any case, it is generally recognized that it is not a good idea to place Web servers in an organization's internal network directly on the Internet. A typical Internet Web server architecture is shown below in Figure 5-1.

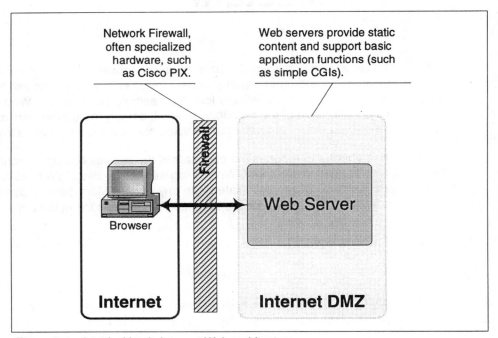

Figure 5-1   A typical basic Internet Web architecture

In the above example, note that the Web server(s) directly serve content and may perform substantial application processing. Obviously, there is some level of security risk, depending on the sensitivity of the content and applications provided by the Web server.

In more advanced scenarios, where content is increasingly driven by complex applications, there are usually back-end components in the environment. For example, an application may rely on a large mainframe database, or substantial portions of the application may execute on back-end systems.

Direct Internet access to such components may present a significant security risk. Even assuming the Internet-facing firewall uses appropriate filtering to prevent access, compromise of the firewall could prove disastrous. For this reason, back-end components may be placed in an internal network, firewalled from the Internet DMZ, leaving only the Web server component exposed to direct browser access, as illustrated in Figure 5-2. This "double firewall" architecture has become common, not only for Internet application access, but increasingly for internal organization access to critical computing resources as well.

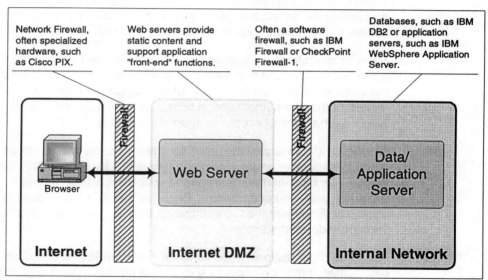

Figure 5-2 Typical advanced Web application architecture

While such architectures successfully address security from a network perspective, they do not address a larger set of concerns, including:

► Security sensitive information may reside in the static content of Web servers (for example, human resources, sales, and personal information)

► Authentication/authorization may be driven by platform-specific mechanisms.

- ► Authentication, authorization, and audit functions may not be centralized.
- ► Managed security policies may be inconsistent and vary from server to server (access policies controlled by many different individuals or groups).

In such environments, there may be sensitive functions and content which, if compromised, could represent a significant business risk.

Access Manager is capable of addressing the above issues. Combined with an appropriate network architecture, an organization can deploy Web content and applications with a high degree of assurance that the environment is secure, and that the security functions and policies may be consistently applied.

In the following sections, we will introduce the elements of Access Manager architecture, using the deployment of WebSEAL as a focal point.

5.2 Access control of Web content and applications

While most Web servers contain basic mechanisms to provide authentication and authorization, such capabilities prove woefully insufficient to deal with the access management requirements being encountered today.

Many organizations want to enable a single sign-on capability to Web applications. This can prove difficult, as most organizations have a diverse set of components, each with their own authentication requirement. It is also often important that the authentication capability is directly tied into the authorization functions that control access to specific resources.

WebSEAL allows organizations to tie authentication and authorization for Web resources together under a common umbrella. Users need only log on once, and WebSEAL's back-end authentication capabilities "mask" authentication to individual back-end components. Because WebSEAL also directly controls access to Web resources, authorization may be controlled using a common, platform-independent model.

For some organizations, in conjunction with WebSEAL's URL-level authorization capabilities, it may be necessary to control access to Web-based content and applications at an even more granular level - for applications, even down to specific functions or data values. With appropriate integration, Access Manager is capable of supporting such fine-grained access control in the context of a common security model. This is a significant advantage over other security products. Let us take a closer look at the architectural component layer using MASS.

5.3 Access control subsystem

An access control subsystem is reponsible for data and component protection by providing mechanisms for identification and authentication as well as authorizing component access. In addition to these major functions, it also provides security management and cryptographic support.

Figure 5-3 on page 116 shows a use case model of an access control subsystem. The physical view shows the systems involved in the transaction. The component view depicts the information flow control function that will examine messages being sent and, based upon a set of rules, will allow valid messages to to flow. Invalid messages are rejected and recorded. The logical view breaks down the access control process into distinct functions.

The Access Policy Evaluator is the major component that gets involved when it comes to an access control decision. Since it is positioned between two security domain boundaries, every transaction or information request has to be routed through this component.

If the sending component has not yet been authenticated, the Access Policy Evaluator involves the Credential Validator service in order to verify the requester and issue a credential package that will be returned to the Access Policy Evaluator. If the requester could not be successfully authenticated, the Error Handler will be involved, and the Audit Generator writes an entry into the Error Log.

If the sending component has already been authenticated, the Access Policy Evaluator involves the State Manager to verify the current status of the session.

If the session is still active and everything proves valid, the Access Policy Evaluator proceeds with the evaluation of the request by applying access control rules from the Policy Rules database.

If access is granted, the Access Policy Evaluator updates the information in the State Manager and hands the task over to the Binding Enabler. If configured, the Binding Enabler might ask the Audit Generator to write a positive log entry. It also configures the requester's HTTP header according to the active configuration and allows the Reverse Proxy to handle the requested information flow.

If access is not granted, the Access Policy Evaluator updates the information in the State Manager and hands the task over to the Error Handler, which will write a log entry. It then informs the Binding Enabler of the negative decision, which in return will inform the requester of the denied access.

This example use case flow demonstrates that we can easily depict the functions necessary for an access control subsystem. There are several other possible use cases for the access control subsystem, but for our purpose, this will remain the only example.

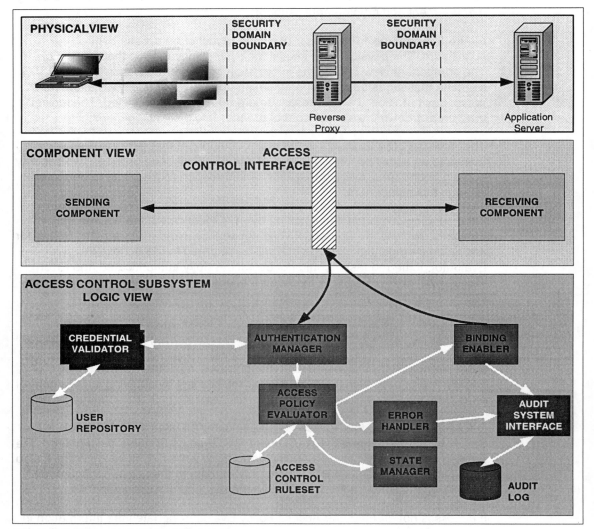

Figure 5-3   Access control subsystem

The remaining sections of this chapter discuss the fundamental architecture issues associated with deploying Web single sign-on and URL-based authorization with WebSEAL.

5.4 WebSEAL requirement issues

As discussed in Section 4.2.1, "WebSEAL" on page 91, WebSEAL junctions provide powerful capabilities for managing access to multiple Web servers through a common access portal. The use of WebSEAL often is driven by key business requirements, which are reflected in specific design objectives, or technical requirements as particularly lined out in the IBM MASS approach.

5.4.1 Typical business requirements

There are a number of commonly encountered business requirements which tend to drive Web security solutions such as those using WebSEAL:

► Different back-end and Web content hosting systems require users to authenticate multiple times and is generating a negative user experience.

In order to improve customer satisfaction, a method for single user authentication has to be implemented.

► The Web-based functions of the business are extending into content and applications, which increasingly require sophisticated security management.

Almost all businesses that are on the Web are encountering this. The moment one goes beyond basic, static informative content, the inadequacies in the simple security mechanisms typically present in many Web servers become clear. The enforcement of Web security across the enterprise cannot be successful without something more sophisticated and manageable at the enterprise level.

► Web security policies must be consistently applied across the business.

Without a common security infrastructure, Web content and application security policies tend to be applied differently by various parts of the business. This results in a hodge-podge of differing security mechanisms that enforce policy in different ways, often to the point where one cannot easily understand what the organization's overall security policies are.

► The costs of Web security management must be predictable.

Security requirements will evolve with the business. Ultimately, the costs of a commonly leveraged solution that is reliable and scalable to the needs of the business will be far more predictable than other approaches.

► Threats of inadvertent security compromises or hacker attacks represent significant risks to business operations and company goodwill.

The direct costs of investigation and recovery after a security incident may be significant, but the indirect costs may be even greater. Especially when doing business on the Web, a perception that security is inconsistent and may be compromised can cause substantial revenue loss.

> ► Competitors are leveraging security solutions to explicitly generate user trust.
>
> This is related to the above. Even if threats are minimal, it still may be essential to maximize the trust that users have in the business' ability to protect itself from compromise. Competitors which can successfully present a "rock-solid" image may often have an advantage over a business which does not.

5.4.2 Typical design objectives (technical requirements)

In conjunction with the business requirements that drive the need for a Web security solution, the following design objectives (technical requirements) are often encountered:

► There is a need to apply security policy independent of application logic.

► A common security control point for Web infrastructure is needed.

► Security policy management must be operating system platform independent.

► Single-sign-on for access to Web content and applications is needed.

► Authorization policy management and enforcement mechanisms must be consistent across applications.

► Exposure of Web content and applications to potential attack must be minimized.

► There must be a common audit trail of accesses to all Web applications.

These are only examples of some of the possible design objectives that might drive Web security solutions, such as those utilizing WebSEAL. Applying MASS to individual scenarios will generate fine grained design objectives that can be applied within the solution.

5.5 WebSEAL architectural principles

The most common Access Manager scenarios involve management of access to Web content using WebSEAL. Our approach to WebSEAL architecture is based on three principles, consistently applied.

5.5.1 Principle 1

Web security must begin at the front gate.

First, this means that first, there should in fact be a logical Web "front gate" to your content and applications. Side and back gates create vulnerabilities. Second, you must control access at this point, because once someone gets inside, there are many more available channels through which vulnerabilities may be exploited. Your Web front gate is also the initial "choke point" for auditing access attempts.

WebSEAL is the Access Manager component that provides this logical Web front gate. Its authentication capabilities and integration with the Access Manager authorization services allow us to know who a user is and make appropriate access decisions before exposing any additional Web infrastructure.

5.5.2 Principle 2

Minimize the number of direct paths to each component.

Ideally, we should have only one HTTP/HTTPS path to our Web server(s) from a browser. To enforce this, we can utilize the stateful packet filtering capabilities of firewalls to allow/disallow certain traffic.

This is fine to protect us from certain types of attack - unless the firewall itself is compromised. The attacker then may be able to launch a multitude of direct attacks on the Web server in an attempt to gain direct access to sensitive content and control of applications. By interposing a reverse proxy such as WebSEAL, the range of possible attack scenarios in the event of a firewall compromise is lessened.

5.5.3 Principle 3

Keep critical content and application functions away from hosts that directly interface to Web clients (that is, browsers).

The further away components are from a potential attacker, the easier it is to minimize the number of available direct paths to exploit them.

5.6 Basic WebSEAL component interactions

As discussed in Chapter 4, "Introduction to Access Manager components" on page 79, all Access Manager architectures share a common set of base components. Specifically, all Access Manager deployments have a User Registry and a Policy Server. WebSEAL interacts with these components to provide its security functions, as shown in Figure 5-4.

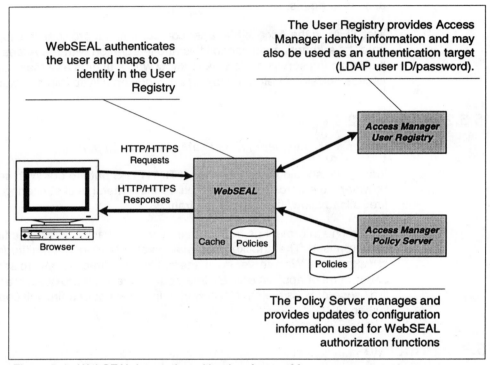

Figure 5-4 WebSEAL interaction with other Access Manager components

In the most basic of WebSEAL architectures, as shown in Figure 5-5 on page 121, a user at a Web browser contacts WebSEAL with a URL request, and then WebSEAL directly serves the content itself (recall that while it functions as a reverse proxy, WebSEAL is also a Web server with the ability to use locally stored content).

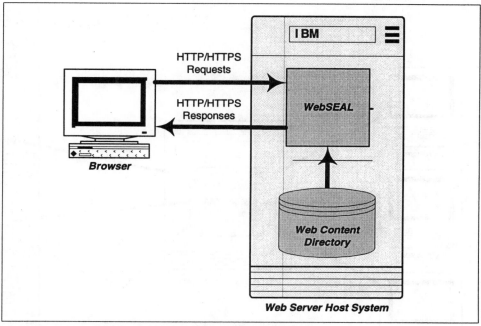

Figure 5-5   Direct serving of Web content from WebSEAL

While illustrative of WebSEAL capabilities, such a scenario may not be terribly interesting, given the evolution of Web-based application architectures that employ significant back-end infrastructure. Also, while directly serving non-sensitive content may be acceptable, when sensitive content is involved, it is generally better to serve it via proxy. Such environments are, in fact, ones where WebSEAL proves to be an ideal solution.

Web applications may involve significant back-end infrastructure, and there are advanced Access Manager scenarios in which direct security integration with such components is important. However, even in complex scenarios, the basic elements of Access Manager architecture still apply. In the current discussion, we will only address applications in the context of back-end Web servers that are junctioned to WebSEAL.

With WebSEAL junctions, a browser user does not directly interact with the target Web server. Instead, WebSEAL takes care of initial user authentication as required and performs appropriate authorization checks on URL requests. Authorized requests are then proxied via the appropriate junction. Figure 5-6 on page 122 shows the basic flow involved in processing such a request.

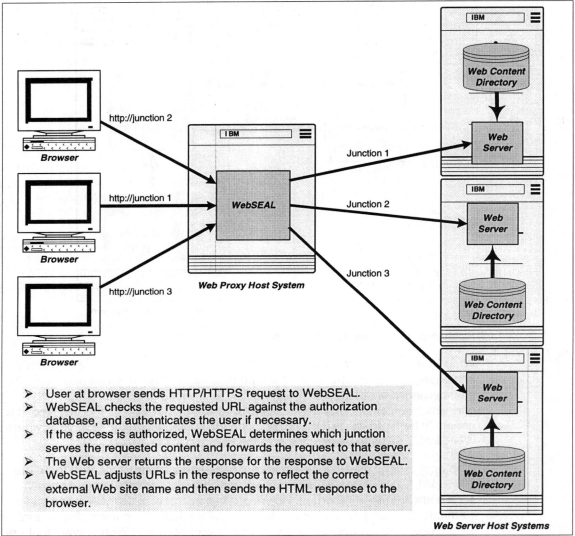

> - User at browser sends HTTP/HTTPS request to WebSEAL.
> - WebSEAL checks the requested URL against the authorization database, and authenticates the user if necessary.
> - If the access is authorized, WebSEAL determines which junction serves the requested content and forwards the request to that server.
> - The Web server returns the response for the response to WebSEAL.
> - WebSEAL adjusts URLs in the response to reflect the correct external Web site name and then sends the HTML response to the browser.

Web Server Host Systems

Figure 5-6 Basic WebSEAL proxy functionality

The flow in Figure 5-6 represents the common architecture for all WebSEAL deployments. The differences that come into play include such things as how components may be combined or distributed among host systems, junction configuration, and back-end authentication issues. However, WebSEAL deployments are built from the same basic architectural elements.

At this point, we have not yet introduced the role of the network into an Access Manager WebSEAL architecture. Obviously, as we discussed earlier in Section 5.1, "Typical Internet Web server security characteristics" on page 112, network configuration does play a role, and it is important to understand how WebSEAL and other Access Manager components fit into typical secure network infrastructures.

5.7 Component configuration and placement

Obviously, it is possible to deploy Access Manager components within a single network. While this kind of architecture may be reasonable for a lab or development environment, it is generally not for a production setting. Most Access Manager deployments must fit within the context of network security requirements.

We discuss how various Access Manager components relate to the network configuration, and provide recommendations for how they should be distributed in a typical architecture. While much of what is in this section may be applied to Access Manager generally, the focus is on deployment of a WebSEAL architecture.

5.7.1 Network zones

In Chapter 3, "IT infrastructure topologies and components" on page 49, we have discussed network zones and their relationship to security. At this point, we shall discuss these zones in the specific context of Access Manager architecture.

We have to consider four types of network zones in our discussion of Access Manager component placement:

► Uncontrolled (the Internet)

► Controlled (an Internet-facing DMZ)

► Restricted (a production or management network)

► Trusted (an intranet)

Since we will not place any components in an uncontrolled zone, we take a closer look at the remaining three zones.

Internet DMZ (controlled zone)

The Internet DMZ is generally a controlled zone that contains components with which clients may directly communicate. It provides a "buffer" between the uncontrolled Internet and internal networks. Because this DMZ is typically bounded by two firewalls, there is an opportunity to control traffic at multiple levels:

► Incoming traffic from the Internet to hosts in the DMZ.

► Outgoing traffic from hosts in the DMZ to the Internet.

► Incoming traffic from internal networks to hosts in the DMZ.

► Outgoing traffic from hosts in the DMZ to internal networks.

WebSEAL fits nicely into such a zone, and in conjunction with the available network traffic controls provided by the bounding firewalls, it provides the ability to deploy a highly secure Web presence without directly exposing components that may be subject to attack by network clients.

Production or management DMZ(s) (restricted zone)

One or more network zones may be designated as *restricted*, that is, they support functions to which access must be strictly controlled, and of course, direct access from an uncontrolled network should not be permitted. As with an Internet DMZ, a restricted network is typically bounded by one or more firewalls and incoming/outgoing traffic may be filtered as appropriate.

These zones typically would contain *back-end* Access Manager components that do not directly interact with users.

Intranet (trusted zone)

A trusted zone is one which is generally not heavily restricted in use, but appropriate span of control exists to assure that network traffic does not compromise operation of critical business functions. Corporate intranets may be examples of such zones.

Depending on the specific level of trust existing in a trusted zone, it may be appropriate to place certain Access Manager components within it.

Other networks

Keep in mind that the network examples we are using do not necessarily include all possible situations. There are organizations that extensively segment functions into various networks. Some do not consider the intranet a trusted zone and treat it much like the Internet, placing a DMZ buffer between it and critical systems infrastructure contained in other zones. However, in general, the principles discussed here may be easily translated into appropriate architectures for such environments.

Placement of various Access Manager components within network zones is, on the one hand, a reflection of the security requirements in play, and on the other a choice based upon existing/planned network infrastructure and levels of trust among the computing components within the organization. While requirement issues may often be complex, especially with regard to the specific behavior of certain applications, determination of a Access Manager architecture that appropriately places key components is generally not difficult. With a bit of knowledge about the organization's network environment, and its security policies, reasonable component placements are usually easily identifiable.

Figure 5-7 summarizes the general Access Manager component type relationships to the network zones discussed above.

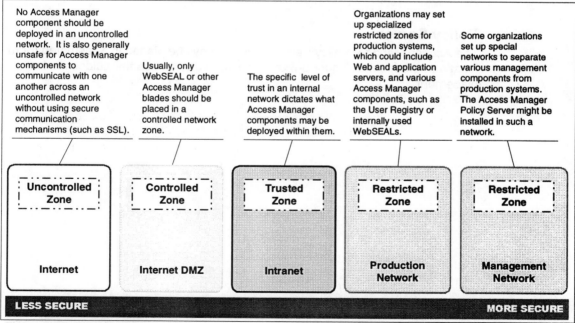

Figure 5-7   Network zones

5.7.2 Secure communication issues

All communication among Access Manager components is, or is configurable to be as needed, secure, using SSL. Given this, one might assume that it is fine to simply place all components within an Internet DMZ and rely on SSL to deal with protecting the communication among them. However, if it were that simple, there would only be a single Access Manager architecture pattern, and this part of the book would be quite short.

SSL only addresses the issues of privacy and integrity of communication among components. It does not deal with other types of security exposures that are inherent in the physical placement of those components within the network infrastructure. The choice to use SSL among certain components should be primarily based upon the trust relationships which exist *within* the network zones in which they operate. While trust may influence the placement of various Access Manager components within different network zones, the use of SSL itself does not necessarily govern such placements.

5.7.3 Specific Access Manager component placement guidelines

Now that we have discussed the basic issues involved in component placement, we can go into greater detail regarding specific components typically found in a Access Manager WebSEAL architecture.

Policy Server

The Access Manager Policy Server should always be placed in a restricted (or at least a trusted) zone. Figure 5-8 on page 127 summarizes the guidelines for placement.

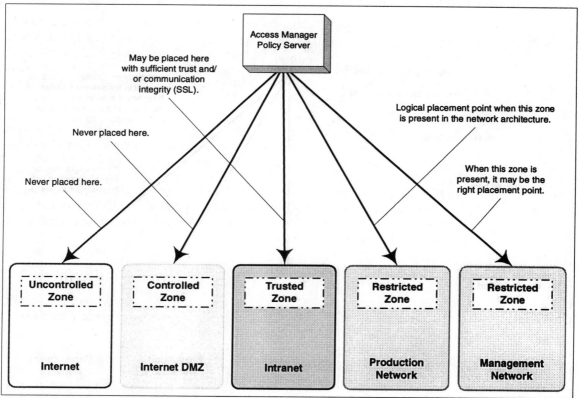

Figure 5-8   Policy Server placement guidelines

User Registry

As we have discussed previously, WebSEAL interacts with the Access Manager User Registry to perform some of its functions. This means that the registry must be accessible to WebSEAL. However, it probably should not be accessible to general users, especially from the Internet.

The registry should be in a restricted zone to which access may be strictly controlled, or at least a trusted network. Firewall configurations should disallow any possibility of access to the User Registry from the uncontrolled zones such as the Internet (for example, port 389 access might be disallowed by an Internet-facing firewall, and outgoing port 389 accesses only allowed to pass from the Internet DMZ to another zone if initiated by a WebSEAL server).

Figure 5-9 on page 128 summarizes network zone placement guidelines for the User Registry.

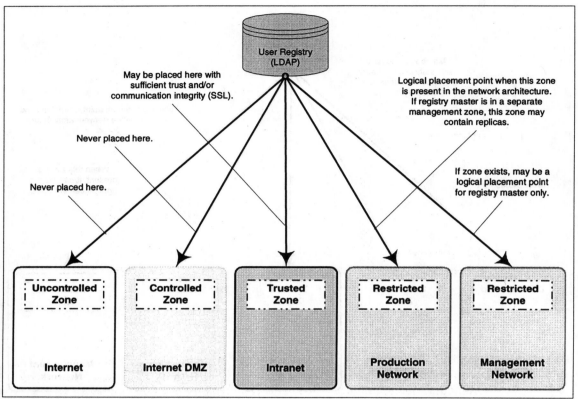

Figure 5-9   User Registry placement guidelines

An example User Registry placement using network filtering rules to limit access is shown in Figure 5-10 on page 129.

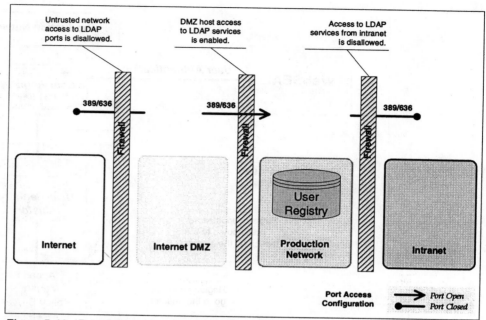

Figure 5-10   Restricting network access to User Registry

Additionally, it may make sense to separate the *read* functions of the registry that are needed by WebSEAL from the *write* functions that are required by Access Manager management components. This can be done by creating a registry replica used for *read only* access (such as authentication) and leaving the registry master only for making updates. If there is a special *management DMZ* into which all management components must be placed, such a configuration may be appropriate. An example of doing this is shown in Figure 5-11 on page 130.

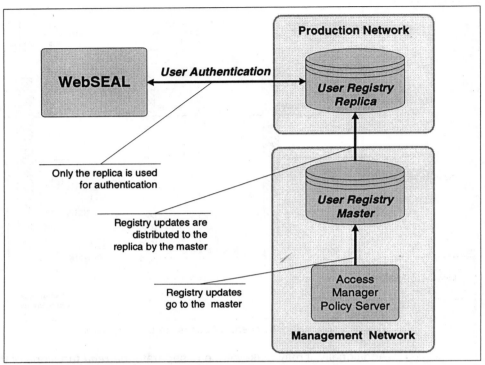

Figure 5-11   Separating User Registry read and write functions

Web Portal Manager

The Web Portal Manager should always be placed in a restricted (or at least a trusted) zone. If a separate Management DMZ is used, there may be issues in how best to structure the configuration of the Web Portal Manager in such an environment.

Because the Web Portal Manager's functions are accessed via HTTP/HTTPS, access to it can be configured via a WebSEAL junction. If this is done, special consideration should be given to its placement and how access should be controlled.

Figure 5-12 on page 131 summarizes placement guidelines for the Web Portal Manager.

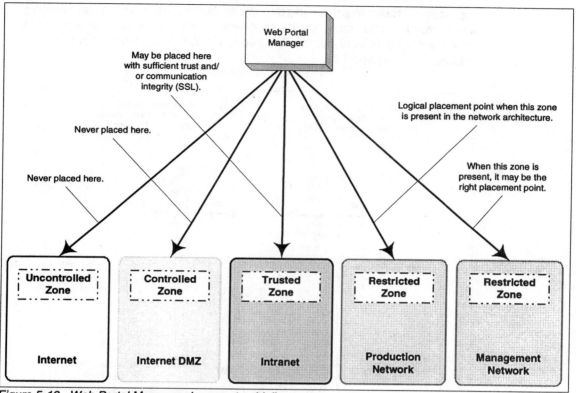

Figure 5-12 Web Portal Manager placement guidelines

WebSEAL

WebSEAL should always be the sole HTTP/HTTPS contact point for a Web server from an Internet client. When using WebSEAL in an intranet setting, this is usually desirable as well.

Internet

Based upon our discussion so far, it should be clear that WebSEAL servers accessible via the Internet should be placed in a DMZ. WebSEAL in such a setting should generally be in a network zone separate from those that contain other Access Manager components upon which it relies, and from the Web servers to which it is junctioned.

The DMZ network boundaries are generally best secured through firewalls, and appropriate traffic filters are used to strictly control the flows into and among components. In this case, the Internet-facing firewall should be configured to make ports 80/443 only accessible through WebSEAL. This is shown in Figure 5-13 on page 132.

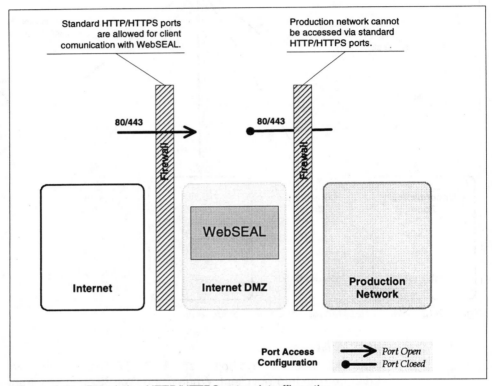

Figure 5-13   Restricting HTTP/HTTPS network traffic paths

This approach has several advantages:

► It focuses all Web traffic through a single path.

► Secured Web content is not directly accessible.

► Compromise of the Internet-facing firewall results in a limited security exposure.

This points out one of WebSEAL's key strengths. As a reverse proxy, it provides security capabilities that cannot be supported by any other approaches, such as plug-ins.

WebSEAL minimizes the numbers of hosts that must be placed in an Internet DMZ. In addition to the security benefits, for businesses that utilize hosting services to support their DMZs, this may allow them to reduce costs by moving substantial amounts of Web infrastructure back into their internal networks, leaving WebSEAL hosts as the key component in their hosted environments.

Intranet user access via WebSEAL

WebSEAL may also be used to serve Web content to internal clients. There are some specific issues that must be addressed when using it in this manner.

It may seem reasonable to simply force internal clients to use the same WebSEAL hosts that are serving Internet clients. However, such an approach may not be the best, because a security compromise of the Internet DMZ could create direct attack paths to internal clients.

An alternative approach is to dedicate a separate WebSEAL server for internal uses, and place it in an appropriate internal network zone. Depending on the level of trust and other configuration factors, the following choices exist for placement of an internal WebSEAL server:

1. Place the WebSEAL server in the same network zone as other Access Manager components.

2. Place the WebSEAL server in an internal DMZ that is separated from other Access Manager components - essentially, mirror the Internet DMZ scenario internally.

Given a sufficient level of trust internally, it may be reasonable to choose the first approach and put the internal WebSEAL in the same zone as other components. This is quite often the approach chosen when architecting WebSEAL solutions for internal user access.

For environments in which the internal trust is insufficient to justify placing WebSEAL into a common zone with other components, the second approach may be more appropriate.

WebSEAL placement summary

Figure 5-14 on page 134 summarizes the guidelines for WebSEAL placement.

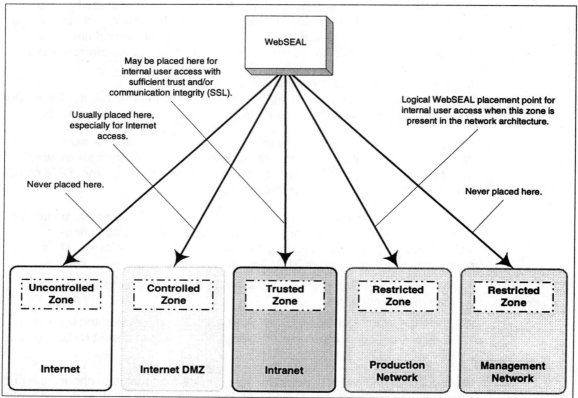

Figure 5-14   WebSEAL placement guidelines

Junctioned Web servers

In a WebSEAL configuration, it is recommended that junctioned Web servers not reside in an Internet DMZ. While WebSEAL does not restrict Web server placement in any way, the further away one can move critical resources from uncontrolled zones, the better.

Ideally, Web servers should be in a special, restricted zone, but could also be placed in a more open, yet trusted network zone if appropriate configuration steps are taken (such as utilizing SSL for communication with WebSEAL and configuring the Web server so that it will only accept connections from a WebSEAL host). Figure 5-15 on page 135 summarizes the zone placement guidelines for Web servers that are junctioned via WebSEAL.

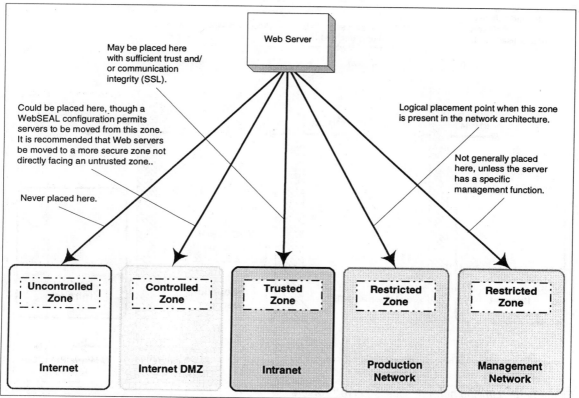

Figure 5-15   Web server placement guidelines

It may be a good idea to configure junctioned Web servers to use ports other than 80/443 (for example, 81/1443). This permits the Internet DMZ firewall configuration to be structured such that port 80/443 accesses can only be made to the Internet DMZ, and the internal-facing firewall to be configured to disallow ports 80/443 and only allow these alternate ports into the restricted/trusted zone. Such a configuration is exemplified in Figure 5-16 on page 136.

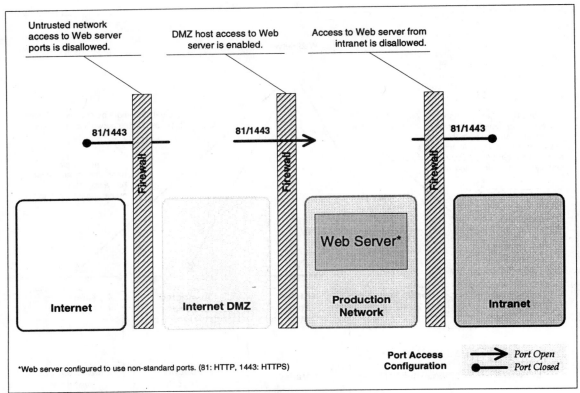

Figure 5-16   Limiting network access to Web servers

Putting it all together

Now that we have discussed the placement of the various components in a WebSEAL configuration, let us put it all together in a typical architecture. Assume that the following network zones exist:

► An uncontrolled Internet zone

► A controlled Internet DMZ zone

► A restricted Production Network zone

Without discussing the specific requirements of the organization, let us assume a basic WebSEAL configuration for both Internet and internal user access. One possible architecture could be as depicted in Figure 5-17 on page 137.

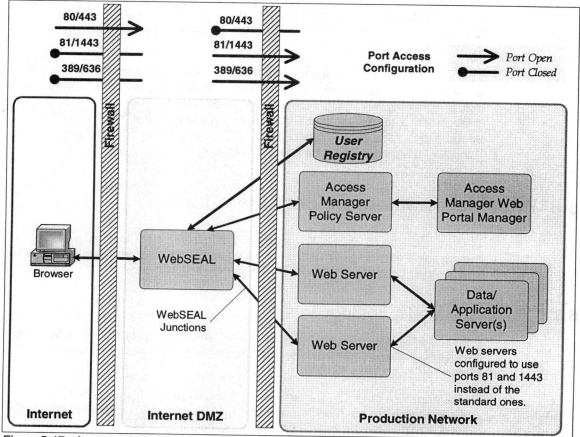

Figure 5-17   An example Access Manager WebSEAL architecture

It should be clear that by simply following the guidelines, many Access Manager WebSEAL architectures are relatively straightforward. The real complexities often come into play when addressing things other than the overall architecture itself, which are normal issues involved in enterprise systems deployment. This includes such things as configuration, deployment plans, capacity requirements, operational policies and procedures, and specific application integration issues.

5.7.4 Summarizing Access Manager component placement issues

In the above discussion, it must be emphasized that, to a large extent, the placement of Access Manager components represent a set of choices. Nothing in Access Manager itself dictates what kind of network configuration is required. The above component placement guidelines are actually related more to overall security principles than any particular need Access Manager has. In fact, in a WebSEAL deployment such as we have discussed in this chapter, Access Manager actually offers greater component placement flexibility than many other approaches to Web security.

This said, keep in mind that you cannot simply separate network configuration issues from Access Manager. While Access Manager components perform their duties extremely well, good sense dictates that they must operate in an environment that prevents them from being bypassed and protects them from undue exposure to other forms of attack. With *any* security solution, not just Access Manager, this must be kept in mind.

5.8 Physical architecture considerations

In our discussion of WebSEAL architecture above, we have focused primarily on the logical relationships among software components, and not necessarily on specific system configurations upon which they are installed.

5.8.1 Access Manager components

It should be clear from our earlier discussion that, at least for Internet scenarios, WebSEAL should reside on a separate host from other Access Manager components.

However, where other (back-end) components should go is not as clear. Honestly, there are no "rules" regarding this. Where these components should be placed is dependent on a number of factors, including:

► The specific network configuration within which Access Manager is installed.

► The capacity/capability (that is, "horsepower") of the host systems upon which these components are installed.

► The amount of flexibility required for future expansion of the security infrastructure.

► Specific security or operational policies that may dictate certain Access Manager configurations.

It is certainly possible to place all required back-end Access Manager components on a single host system. However, other than in a very simple WebSEAL deployment or a lab setting, this may not be the best approach. For example, a common way of breaking things out would be to place the management functions on one host and the User Registry on another.

Figure 5-18 below shows a physical system layout mapping of the example architecture shown previously in Figure 5-17. Keep in mind that this is simply an example and it does not represent the only way in which components may be combined on host systems.

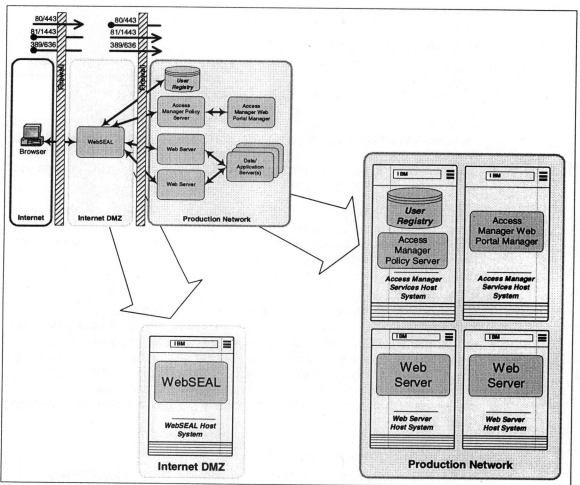

Figure 5-18   An example physical component layout

5.8.2 Other infrastructural components

In addition to Access Manager components themselves, there are other components that are a natural part of the infrastructure in most typical environments, including:

► Domain Name Service (DNS) or other, similar naming services

- ► Time services, such as Network Time Protocol (NTP)
- ► Host configuration services, such as Dynamic Host Configuration Protocol (DHCP)
- ► Mail transport agents (MTAs), such as sendmail
- ► File transfer services, such as FTP

Domain Name Service

In general, Access Manager components themselves should avoid the use of naming services for address resolution. It is usually best to directly configure host addresses locally, both for availability and security reasons.

In cases where access to a name service is needed by a Access Manager host, consideration should be given to installing a DNS secondary on the host itself or in close proximity to the host in an appropriately protected network zone. In no case should the security infrastructure share DNS services with the general user community, either internal or external.

Another note regarding the use of DNS in an Internet WebSEAL setting. It is recommended that a "split-level" DNS configuration or other approach be employed to assure that external clients have no IP address resolution visibility beyond the WebSEAL hosts themselves.

Time services

Releases of Policy Director prior to version 3.8 depended upon time synchronization among the components (this was due to Distributed Computing Environment (DCE)). Though Access Manager no longer requires that time be synchronized, it is still a good idea, if for no other reason than to assure that audit logs contain consistent time stamps. Network Time Protocol (NTP) is the recommended choice for time synchronization and an appropriate implementation should be available on all platforms upon which Access Manager runs.

Host configuration services

Host configuration services, such as DHCP, should never be used by any host running Access Manager components. IP addresses should be statically configured. It is also recommended that DHCP services not be provided by hosts that are running Access Manager components.

Mail transport agents

Mail transport agents, such as sendmail, are often present within the network infrastructure to route mail both internally and externally. Such mail gateways should not be configured on Access Manager hosts, as their use may substantially affect the performance characteristics of the system and diminish performance predictability.

Additionally, a WebSEAL host, especially one that is accessible via the Internet, should not respond to SMTP (port 25) connection requests.

File transfer services

File transfer services, such as anonymous FTP, are often present within the network infrastructure to support access to program archives or other information. It is recommended that such services should not be configured on Access Manager hosts, as their use may substantially affect the performance characteristics of the system and diminish performance predictability.

Additionally, a WebSEAL host, especially one that is accessible via the Internet, should not respond to FTP (port 20) connection requests.

5.8.3 General host "hardening" considerations

In addition to the recommendations above, it may make sense to "harden" certain hosts which participate in a Access Manager configuration. This may be especially true for Internet-facing WebSEAL hosts.

While the specifics of hardening an operating system are beyond the scope of this book, the following items are representative of the types of issues addressed:

► The number of incoming paths through which it may be accessed is minimized (for example, turning off certain network services that are not necessary for system operation).

► The number of outgoing paths from the system to other hosts is minimized (for example, limiting the system's knowledge of other hosts to those absolutely necessary for proper operation).

► Appropriate system auditing functions are enabled to assure traceability of accesses.

► The set of users that may access the system is minimized to a level that is necessary for system operation, and clear roles and responsibilities are defined for those users (and where possible, enforced).

Additionally, certain network firewall configurations may be employed to enforce the restrictions of a hardened environment.

5.9 WebSEAL in an overall security solution

It would be a mistake to assume that deployment of WebSEAL alone is sufficient to fully address all security requirements. WebSEAL provides key functionality, which is essential for Web security, but it is not a "silver bullet". As should be evident from the discussion of other topics within this book, there are other security considerations which should be addressed in conjunction with WebSEAL.

Some things we have not touched on include other security components that may work in conjunction with WebSEAL and other Access Manager components to address broader security concerns. In particular, Identity Director and Risk Manager, which are discussed in Part 3, "Managing identities and credentials" on page 257 and Part 4, "Managing a security audit" on page 329, provide functionality complementary to Access Manager and can be of substantial value as components of an overall security solution.

A basic WebSEAL scenario

Our earlier discussion of Access Manager has been helpful in describing the basic elements of architecture for deployment. At this point, we will apply those guidelines to a simple Web scenario for an example organization with a typical set of requirements.

In our discussion, we will deliberately avoid certain issues, including availability considerations and specific issues relating to application integration. These areas are discussed in later chapters.

Also, while host machine configuration and capacity is touched on in this chapter, we will deliberately avoid providing much in the way of specifics. This is because without appropriate capacity planning activities, which consider simulated/real loads of the actual application, it can be difficult to make accurate determinations.

6.1 Company profile

Stocks-4u.com is a wholly owned subsidiary of a major brokerage company, Medvin, Lasser & Jenkins (ML&J). ML&J's online presence has, to this point, been limited, consisting mainly of informational Web content. Online trading has not been a priority. The clientele has traditionally been major accounts with assets greater than $5 million, and transactions are almost exclusively done via direct contact with a broker. While the company, a privately held corporation, has maintained solid profitability over the past several years, largely due to a stable client base, the company's growth has stagnated, remaining at approximately the same revenue levels since 1995.

Market trends have forced a rethinking of ML&J's approach to business. The individual investor community has increased substantially in recent years, and the company has not shared in that growth. Consequently, the company's market share has eroded. Also, the rise of online trading has begun to affect a portion of ML&J's client base. In the last year, there has been a net outflow of investment funds cutting across approximately ten percent of all client accounts. Research has shown that 95 percent of these outflows are being redirected to online brokerages. This trend, if it continues, threatens to affect the long-term viability of the business.

An online component to complement ML&J operations has been judged a necessity. Stocks-4u.com was started with assets recently acquired from a failed Internet startup, and additional capital has been provided to fund completion of the company, which recently began full production operation ramp-up, services the online trading requirements of ML&J's current clients, while focusing on developing additional clients who are primarily online traders with trading capital in excess of $250,000.

> **Attention:** As of April 2002, our fictitious domain name Stocks-4u.com was not reserved by anyone.

6.1.1 Technology background

Stocks-4u.com has been deployed as a Web-based online trading system with capabilities similar to those found at other online trading sites. This software is composed of a number of underlying applications, all of which perform functions based upon the each user's privileges. For example, only users who have paid for Level II quotes may access that application.

In concert with the ongoing application development activities, the company has been examining alternatives for providing secure access to their Web site. Originally, a "master" application was developed, which provided a single access point for providing user authentication and authorization utilizing the underlying capabilities of the operating system.

Following initial deployment, additional requirements became apparent. It became clear that the level of effort required to fully address all functional requirements was cost-prohibitive. The tie-in to the operating system security mechanisms began to limit certain deployment options. The CIO felt that this approach was locking them in architecturally to an in-house solution that would require long-term sustaining and support services. After examining marketplace alternatives in a proof-of-concept (POC) setting, a decision was made to deploy a Access Manager security capability, leading with Web security.

The company wants to transition its user base from the in-house Web security system to a WebSEAL-based one over the next several months. They initially wish to deploy adequate capacity to address their anticipated loading over the six months, and then incrementally add more as needed.

6.1.2 IT infrastructure

The Stocks-4u.com concerns on becoming an integral part of the ML & J IT infrastructure are partitioned into three major categories:

- Data centers
- Network
- Operational plans

A closer look at these individual aspects is provided in the following sections.

Data centers

Stocks-4u.com has two major data centers. One is located in San Diego, California, and the other is in Savannah, Georgia. At this time, all Internet application access and key internal application access is provided through the San Diego center, in which the company's IT Operations (OPS) group is based. The Savannah center is currently supporting a few other internally used applications and houses the company's IT Architecture, Development, and Deployment Support (ADDS) business unit.

While Stocks-4u.com did consider hosting its Web servers through a third-party provider, it was decided that all subsidiaries deploy its servers in-house. However, they have not ruled out migrating certain Web operations to a hosting provider in the future. This could bring additional data centers into play.

Network

The data centers are connected by redundant T3 (45mbps) access. At this time, Internet connectivity is provided through the San Diego center, with multiple T3 lines from three different providers. The diagram depicted in Figure 6-1 shows the national Stocks-4u.com network.

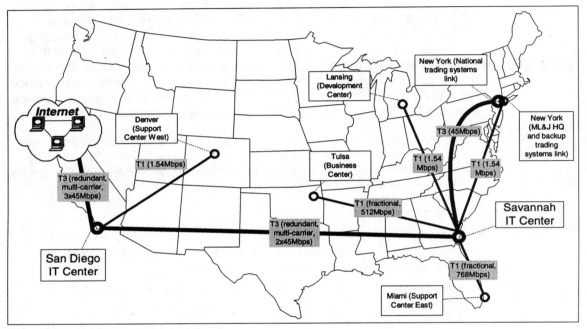

Figure 6-1   Stocks-4u.com data network

Within the San Diego center, all Internet access is channeled through Web servers residing in a demilitarized zone (DMZ). These Web servers provide front-end application logic, including presentation services. Back-end application logic is hosted on systems residing behind the DMZ in an internal production network.

The Savannah center has no direct Internet access. It has a production network for internal application systems.

In addition to the specific network capabilities at each of the sites, there is also a general company intranet shared across all corporate locations. This network is not considered secure, and is not authorized for hosting production systems.

Operational plans

Early plans are in the development stage for future expansion of Internet operations into the Savannah center to provide for a redundant access capability with load-balancing for customers on the US East and West coasts. At this time, there is no requirement to actually support this. However, the Stocks-4u.com chief architect wants to be certain that the security solution they deploy is capable of meeting such a requirement. During the Access Manager proof-of-concept, it was determined that this should not be a problem.

6.1.3 Business requirements

The CIO has provided input on the business drivers for the targeted solution:

► Provide an enabler for consistent application of security policy across the business. The business cannot afford to create multiple, competing security infrastructures.

► Assure client confidence by offering a flexible, yet perceptively secure solution. It is essential that the security system not get in the way, while at the same time protecting client information and assuring that financial transactions are conducted securely.

► Competitively position the business to react quickly in deploying secure premium services and content. Quickly deploying value-add capabilities is important to gaining and maintaining market share.

Allow for the integration of special premium applications capabilities to Medvin Lasser's "Select" clients. Medvin Lasser is very focused on maintaining their existing high-income client base by providing them with special capabilities that are not available through any other online service. For example, additional bond management capabilities within the portfolio management application are being developed specifically for these clients.

► Provide for expansion of services with minimal incremental investment. It is essential that, once in place, the security solution grow with the company. It is unacceptable to require extensive and continuing re-engineering efforts for the security infrastructure as the company expands its operations.

► Meet applicable US Securities and Exchange Commission (SEC) requirements. There are certain legal requirements for assurance that client assets and transactions are handled properly. The security infrastructure should be supportive of these requirements.

6.1.4 Security design objectives

Based upon initial discussions and a security workshop, it has been determined that the following key technical requirements exist:

▶ Provide a single sign-on capability for all Web-based applications. A user should only need to log in one time, to one entity to obtain access to all authorized applications and content which may reside on various servers.

▶ Remove the need for application developers to authenticate users. The company does not wish to invest in developing any authentication capabilities within its new applications.

▶ Provide a cross-platform security solution. Previous experience with the in-house security application clarified the need to maintain operating system independence for Web-based application security.

▶ Provide the ability to control access to Web applications and content, which may be hosted through multiple Web servers, at the URL-level.

▶ Provide the ability to make fine-grained authorization decisions within applications. While this is not an immediate deployment requirement, the solution must allow for this capability to be added.

▶ Support browser based access to applications from both employees and customers. From their desks, internal users may access both Internet-hosted applications and internal applications. At this time, there is no requirement for employees to have access to internal applications from the Internet.

▶ For the first six months following deployment, load requirements are for up to 40,000 Internet users, with an annual growth rate of 50 percent over the next five years. In five years, the online client base is expected to exceed 300,000 users. Approximately 25 percent of all clients are expected to conduct at least one transaction on any given day.

▶ The internal employee user base is currently around 250, and is expected to approximately 1000 in the next five years. Approximately 80 percent of employees are expected to conduct at least ten transactions on any given day.

6.1.5 Requirements analysis

The requirements for this access control subsystem are typical of those found in many Web application environments. Also, Stocks-4u.com's experience with home-grown security is not unique. With today's Web-centric application focus, many organizations approach the security issue from that perspective, yet they often utilize existing host-based security systems that prove inadequate in addressing key requirements. The fact is that, while some host-based security capabilities are extensive, they are tied to a specific platform. This is inconsistent with the reality of today's Web-based applications. These applications often run on several different machines on several different platforms, and on various Web server implementations.

An Access Manager WebSEAL capability is an obvious fit for Stocks-4u.com's current needs. In fact, most Access Manager deployments start with a Web focus. However, there are clear requirement statements that discuss future infrastructure expansion, and the same Access Manager environment that supports WebSEAL will also be capable of addressing those needs.

For example, it is clear that the company has a future need to support a tighter application level integration with security, using Authorization Application Programming Interface (aznAPI) or JAVA2 security-based functionality to allow very detailed authorization for application components. The inherent architecture of Access Manager allows these requirements to easily be met.

In this example, we will address the immediate requirements of Stock4.com with a WebSEAL solution. However, in a later chapter of this book, we may introduce additional requirements or revisit some of the remaining issues to illustrate how they may be addressed as the company expands its use of Access Manager.

To summarize from the requirements discussion above, we know the following:

► We need to have a WebSEAL capability covering both internal and external users.

► There is a relatively small number of users initially, but this will dramatically grow.

We also know that:

► All Internet access will go through a single site (San Diego).

► All Web servers we need to access are housed at a single site (San Diego).

► Web servers reside in an Internet DMZ network.

► Production systems reside in a special production network.

► All internal users share a common intranet across company site locations.

From this, we can easily address an initial WebSEAL-based Access Manager architecture for Stocks-4u.com.

6.1.6 Access control architecture

As we know it today, the diagram in Figure 6-2 on page 150 summarizes the existing security architecture deployed by Stocks-4u.com with multiple Web server host systems deployed in the Internet DMZ.

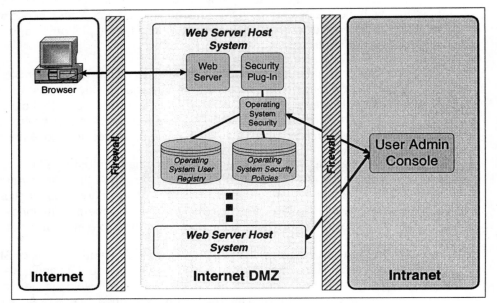

Figure 6-2   Current Stocks-4u.com architecture

The following are the most pressing issues:

► The operating system security model is too centric.

► Key components are exposed within the DMZ.

► It is difficult to apply a uniform security model.

► Long-term maintenance staffing is required.

► It is difficult keeping up with evolving standards.

► Authentication is not flexible for requirements.

This is our starting point for developing an Access Manager architecture to meet current requirements, which, as we shall see, is actually simple and straightforward.

Initial architecture approach

Recalling the discussions in Chapter 4, "Introduction to Access Manager components" on page 79 and Chapter 5, "Access Manager Web-based architecture" on page 111, we obviously know that we will place a WebSEAL server in the DMZ, which will provide for Internet user access. We also know that the user registry, policy server, and Web Portal Manager (WPM) should not reside in the DMZ, and we will place those components in the San Diego center internal production network.

As you will recall, the company currently has its Web servers in the DMZ. With WebSEAL, there is obviously no longer a need to do that, and these Web servers may be migrated to the production network. This is a good thing, as it enhances the security of the overall solution by moving the front-end application logic out of the DMZ.

Our initial architectural diagram is displayed in Figure 6-3.

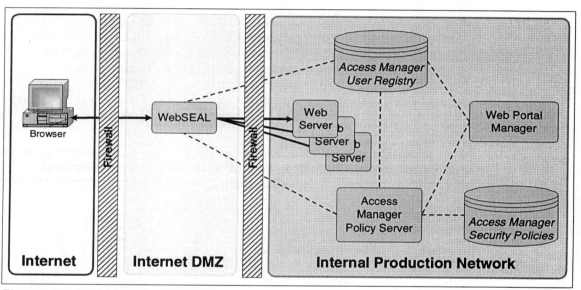

Figure 6-3   Initial WebSEAL architecture

This initial architecture provides us with the following benefits:

► The security model is independent of the operating system.

► We have a limited component exposure within DMZ.

► It is architecturally consistent and we have a uniform security model.

► It is not dependent on internal resources to support core security component code.

► As standards evolve, the security infrastructure may be readily upgraded.

Internal user access
Now let us discuss the internal user access. There are potentially many issues here, but to keep things simple for the moment, we know that we only need to support employee access to internal applications from inside the company. In other words, Internet application access is currently only being provided for client applications and content.

We could route browser traffic to internal applications through the same WebSEAL that resides in the Internet DMZ. However, this is not a recommended approach, partly for security reasons, and partly for manageability and performance reasons. So in this case, we will go with another WebSEAL server that is dedicated solely to internal access. This allows us to create a different set of junctions for the internal and external WebSEAL servers, which permits better segregation of content between the two access classes.

> **Tip:** There is an interesting issue here that we will touch on briefly, but not dwell on. That is, there may be scenarios where it makes sense to have different user namespaces for employees and clients. This can easily be accomplished by creating a second Access Manager secure domain. However, in this scenario, such requirements do not exist. In this architecture, we will keep it simple and use a single Access Manager user registry covering both employee and client users in a common user ID namespace.

Where should this internal WebSEAL server reside? In our case, based upon the Stocks-4u.com network structure, the logical place for this is in the production network. The updated architecture diagram is depicted in Figure 6-4.

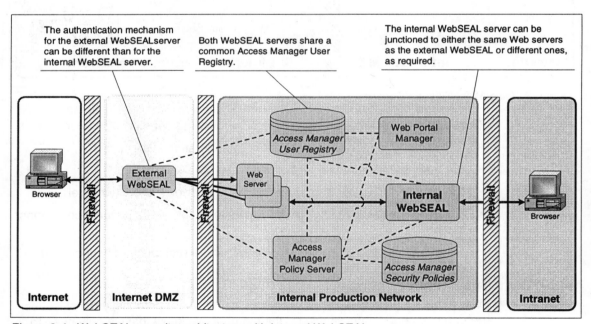

Figure 6-4   WebSEAL security architecture with internal WebSEAL

Connecting the pieces

Now that we have placed the key components in this scenario, let us discuss how they will all interact with one another.

The Internet-facing WebSEAL will be listening on ports 80 and 443 (SSL). We will also modify the configuration of the Web servers slightly to have them listen on alternate ports - in our case, we use ports 81 and 1443. This will permit us to close ports 80 and 443 on the firewall between the DMZ and production networks in the manner described previously in Chapter 5, "Access Manager Web-based architecture" on page 111. We will also disallow LDAP port (389/636) access from the Internet, because WebSEAL is the only entity that needs to communicate from the DMZ to the user registry.

There is also the question of whether the junctions between the Internet-facing WebSEAL and the Web servers require the use of SSL. Because, in this case, the Web servers are in a controlled zone, it is not strictly necessary to do so. If the Web servers were in the open corporate intranet, SSL should probably be used. The choice to use SSL may be made based upon the specific risk associated with the content involved. The answer is similar with respect to communication with the user registry.

The internal WebSEAL in the production network, unlike the Internet-facing WebSEAL, will be co-located with the Web servers it is junctioned to. It will listen on ports 80 and 443 and the firewall between the intranet and production network will be configured to disallow access via these ports. If, for some reason, it is not possible to disable these ports, for example, there could be Web servers that are separate from the Access Manager infrastructure, the junctioned Web servers may be configured to only accept connections from the WebSEAL server. This would allow both WebSEAL and non-WebSEAL controlled resources to coexist in the same network while maintaining the integrity of the back-end Web servers.

Important: If you place a production Web server under WebSEAL access control, it is recommended that you do not allow access to it via non-WebSEAL channels without careful consideration. Prior experience has shown that this can lead to confusion, manageability issues, and most important, security breaches.

Generally, co-locating internal WebSEALs with Web servers is acceptable to many organizations; however, groups that may wish to impose an internal DMZ in front of a production network may do so in the same manner as is done for the Internet-facing WebSEAL. This is a legitimate architecture and may make sense in some cases. However, in the current scenario, the requirements may be satisfied as we have described.

Now that we have addressed the communication among the components, our new architecture is shown in Figure 6-5.

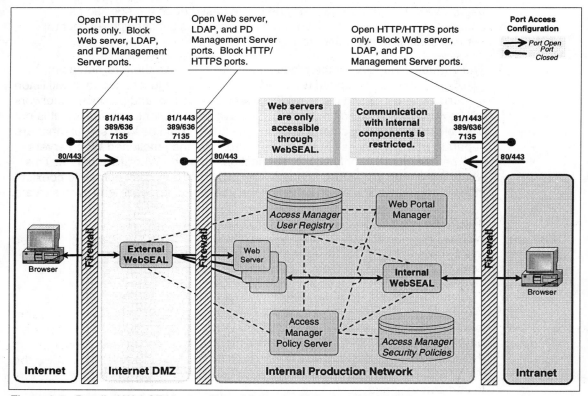

Figure 6-5 Detailed WebSEAL security architecture with internal WebSEAL

6.1.7 Building the physical architecture

With the locations of the pieces decided, now we need to know how many machines we need and what parts have to be configured on what systems.

Internet DMZ

Obviously, because the Internet-facing WebSEAL is in the DMZ by itself, it will need to be on a separate machine. This is typical for most WebSEAL scenarios. While technically this machine could support other applications or services along with WebSEAL, such configurations are not generally recommended, especially in an Internet-facing scenario.

A single WebSEAL host, appropriately configured, should be able to handle the expected client load over the next six months.

Production network

In the production network, things get a little more complicated, although not by much.

An obvious place to consolidate components would be to put the Access Manager Policy Server and the User Registry on the same machine, provided it has sufficient capacity. The policy server uses little overhead in a basic deployment such as this one, which has a relatively small number of components and users. The major user of memory and processor capacity will be the user registry. We will place these components on a single machine.

> **Tip:** However, it is important to point out that, as the company expands its operations, it may make sense to eventually split these functions out onto separate machines. This should be easy to do when the time comes.

The WPM component can run on a Windows NT or Windows 2000 platform as well as on AIX and Solaris. One thing to keep in mind is that a midrange desktop system which meets minimum WebSphere memory requirements will generally work well to host WPM.

The internal WebSEAL is the remaining issue. Unlike the Internet-facing WebSEAL, we have got more flexibility here. First, we know the number of users is relatively small. However, they each are performing several transactions per day. It may be possible to consolidate this WebSEAL onto the same host running the user registry and policy server. However, in this case, we will opt to place the WebSEAL on a separate machine to avoid any potential performance effects due to component interactions.

The final physical architecture for this initial deployment is depicted below in Figure 6-6.

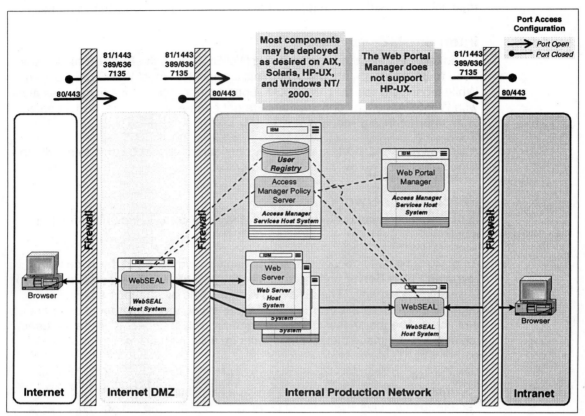

Figure 6-6   WebSEAL physical architecture

6.1.8 Architectural summary

In this chapter, we have used the guidelines discussed previously in this book to illustrate the thought process involved in developing a typical WebSEAL solution architecture. You can easily understand that a Web security solution with Access Manager is often straightforward.

With this as a base, we can easily extend any Access Manager architecture to add additional capability and capacity, as we will see in later chapters.

7

Increasing availability and scalability

In this chapter, we continue the discussion from the previous section with our customer Stocks-4U.com. Previously, the concern was access control and user and account integration, as well as systems and network integration. Now, the focus has shifted slightly and the need to address additional requirements of a growing business have come to the fore front. This growth and the increased expectations pose new challenges to the architecture.

Availability is the major concern that a failing part within the infrastructure will cause the overall solution to languish. This will eventually lead to unsatisfied customers and decreasing business success.

Scalability describes the capacity to be able to instantaneously change and adapt the I/T infrastructure in order to handle an increased number of information and transaction requests without reducing the quality of online experience for customers.

7.1 Further evolution

Stocks-4U.com has seen steady growth of their business. This growth, and the continued sucess of the business, has introduced new business requirements that mirror the evolving business. Based on these new requirements, we have to alter the security design objectives.

You, as the architect, now face the added design objectives of availability and scalability. Content, access control, and centralized audit and policy enforcement, as well as a single entry point into the site, are still very much a part of the scenario and must be included with the new requirements.

7.1.1 Business requirements

After the initial Web presence approach, the Web based functions have functionally extended into content and applications and the security management becomes more viable. With the sucessful reception by the public, and an increasing client base, the availability of the Stocks-4U.com Web site is crucial. E-businesses have no set hours of operation and must be reachable and operational twenty four hours a day, seven days a week (24x7).

At this stage, the CEO is looking for a way to guarantee the availability of the business application around the clock. Customers are entrusting their financial investments more and more to Stocks-4U.com, and they have to be rewarded with a reliable e-business application infrastructure that is always there for them.

After some serious downtime of the WebSEAL portal (due to some operating system problems and some issues with the backend Web server availability, due to security vulnerabilities), the CEO demands some measures in the availability and portability of the corresponding systems.

A second concern of his is the constantly increasing number of customers visiting the Web site. The CEO asks for future flexibility and ways to dynamically add functional empowerment of the single systems to better cope with new e-business opportunities.

7.1.2 Security design objectives

The major design objectives of these business requirements target two areas of the e-business implementation:

► The access control infrastructure

   Embracing the internal and external WebSEAL portals as well as the underlying security base with the Access Manager Policy Server and the LDAP User Registry

- The e-business application

  Consisting of the HTTP Web servers and the applications running on those servers

Basically we have to consider two different approaches as lined out by the CEO:

- Availability

  Allowing systems to be available on a 24x7 schedule by providing enough resources in additional, duplicated systems or other failover mechanisms.

- Scalability

  Allowing the e-business solution to scale to any number of future capacities by adding additional components of the same sort and providing smart load balancing mechanisms to perfectly utilize these new components. In a second viewpoint, this can also imply to move a current functional implementation to a new, more powerful operating platform.

Let us take a closer look at how to approach these design objectives.

7.2 Availability

The Internet has changed forever the idea of fixed hours of operation. Suddenly, there is the need to have your customers access your site at any time, day or night, increasing your visibility and profitability. The IT systems must be reliable and offer consistent content in a timely fashion to the client at any time. In our initial architecture, there are different points of failure in the infrastructure.

Each element in a configuration must be analyzed for failure points, including the hardware. Most hardware appliances, such as routers or switches, can be configured for failover or alternate paths, and cold standbys can be kept available, should a hardware failure occur.

The discussion in this section will focus on the availability of all components that are part of the Web application, we will not consider infrastructure elements, such as firewalls and routers.

7.2.1 Failure situations

Web servers and applications can and do fail. The reasons for failure vary: program code, "bleeding" edge technologies, disk failures, and even human error. In Figure 7-1 on page 160, the instance of only one WebSEAL, User Registry, Access Manager Policy Server with its authorization master database, Web Portal Manager, and each individual Web server are in themselves single points of failure.

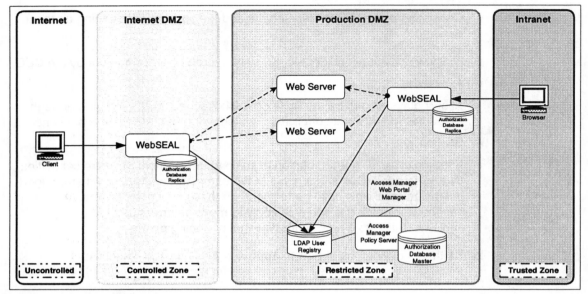

Figure 7-1   Initial Web architecture

What happens if the WebSEAL server fails? What happens if a Web server fails? What happens if the User Registry server stops working? Let us take a closer look at the individual components.

WebSEAL failure

If the WebSEAL portal to either the Internet or the intranet fails, and there is no operational replacement, the client attempting access will be denied access to the site. While the content and the application might be fully functional behind WebSEAL, the failure of the WebSEAL server leads the user to perceive that the site is "down".

Web server failure

If a Web server stops operating, the applications and/or services that reside on it are no longer available. While other applications are still working, the client that tries to access offerings on this particular machine perceives the site or the application as "down".

User Registry failure

If the User Registry is down, WebSEAL will no longer be able to authenticate incoming users in order to access Web content and applications that are protected and require user authentication. While WebSEAL and the Web servers may still be operational, the client is unable to gain access and thus perceives the site is "down".

Access Manager Policy Server failure

Although it is definitely not funny if your Policy Server fails, at least it will not affect the availability of your Web site. WebSEAL can still perform all necessary authorization operations because it uses the local cache mode, which means that the authorization service running on the WebSEAL machine uses a local authorization database replica. You only lose the ability to administer your Access Manager secure domain while your Policy Server is down.

The same is valid for the Web Portal Manager, which provides the administration graphical user interface (GUI) Web application for the Access Manager administrators. The Web application will not be affected if WPM is not available. The only impact is that the administration of the Access Manager secure domain has to be postponed until the service is available again.

In addition to problems or failures of these components, sheer volumes can affect availability as well. With the growth of the Internet and your business, the ability to handle the traffic to your site has changed the scope and appearance of the architecture. Internet sites can become unstable or even fail under severe load conditions.

> **Tip:** Besides adding multiple replicas for increasing availability and performance, you should also consider that your Web environment can scale on different operating system platforms with different availabilty characteristics. If you are stuck with only one supported platform, you might lose the ability to grow your business later.
>
> The best example is the Web server itself. The IBM HTTP Server or the Apache Web Server can scale from entry platforms like Windows NT or Windows 2000 to other powerful platforms like Solaris, HP-UX, AIX, or even OS/390 or z/OS. As a side effect, you also have to consider developing your Web applications supporting only open standards like basic HTML, JAVA, Java Server Pages (JSP), or Enterprise Java Beans (EJB). Otherwise, you might get stucked with one particular platform.

7.2.2 Providing high availability

Adding replicas of crucial servers increases your site's availability. After depicting an overview of this configuration in Figure 7-2, we describe the different areas with their solution.

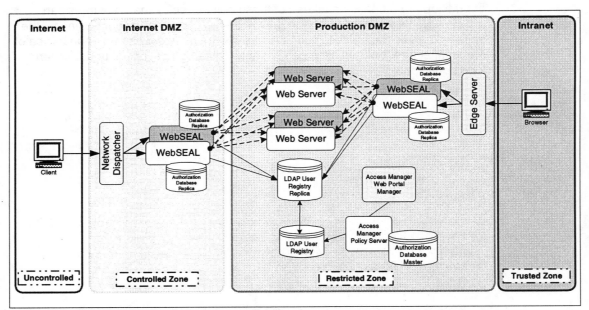

Figure 7-2   Server replication to increase availability

WebSEAL availability

Increasing the availability of your WebSEAL controlled Web site starts with at least two front-end WebSEAL servers. Replicated front-end WebSEAL servers provide the site with load balancing during periods of heavy demand as well as fail-over capability - if a server fails for some reason, the remaining replica server(s) will continue to provide access to the site. Successful load balancing and fail-over capability results in high availability for users of the site. The load balancing mechanism is handled by a mechanism such as the Network Dispatcher component of the IBM WebSphere Edge Server or Cisco Local Director.

In a redundant WebSEAL configuration environment, as depicted in Figure 7-3, there are several places where the configuration must be duplicated.

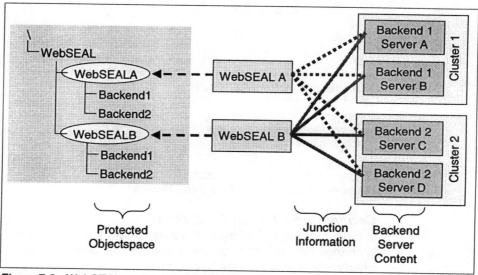

Figure 7-3   WebSEAL availability overview

► Back-end server content:

This must be the same on every server in the same cluster. Maintaining this is the responsibility of the individual systems administrator for the corresponding servers. More information can be found in "Web server availability" on page 165.

► Junction information

Each duplicated WebSEAL server must have the same junction information. This is made easy in Access Manager because all that is required is to copy the junction database from one WebSEAL to another. All the junction information is kept in XML formatted files.

► Protected objectspace

Both WebSEALs must have the same access control lists (ACLs) attached to the same places in their objectspace. In a normal configuration, both WebSEALs have their own object space, so work must be duplicated. However, it is possible to make WebSEAL servers share a single objectspace, as shown in Figure 7-4.

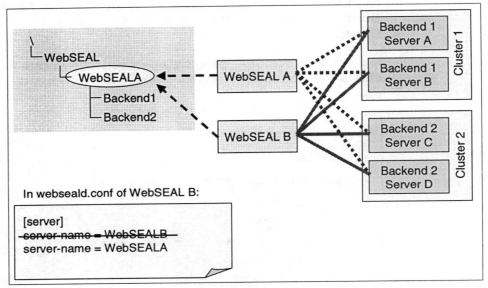

Figure 7-4   WebSEAL availability configuration

Configuring a WebSEAL cluster

In order to make two WebSEAL servers share the same object space, we need to change the part of the object space that one of the WebSEAL servers uses when making authorization decisions.

Normally, when WebSEALB checks permissions on /index.html, the object checked is /WebSEAL/WEBSEALB/index.html. However, if the server-name parameter in webseald.conf is changed to WEBSEALA, WEBSEALB will now check the object /WebSEAL/WEBSEALA/index.html.

The portion of the objectspace under /WebSEAL/WebSEALB is now redundant; all checks are done against the objects under /WebSEAL/WEBSEALA. As long as the file space of both servers is identical (which means they have the same junctions and the same back-end servers), then this will be fine, and will remove the need to duplicate work. You have to ensure that a copy of the XML junction information gets distributed to all clustered WebSEAL servers if new Web server junctions are being configured.

WebSEAL failover cookies

Failover cookies are used in Access Manager to allow a user to access a redundant WebSEAL server (in case of failure) without having to re-authenticate. Access Manager supports the use of failover cookies over HTTP or HTTPS.

The failover-cookies-keyfile entry in the webseald.conf file points to a file containing a triple DES key created using the cdsso_key_gen utility. This keyfile must be shared by all WebSEAL servers in the Access Manager secure domain that the user might be redirected to in the event of a failure.

> **Note:** The processing of failover cookies is processor intensive and they should only be used for failure recovery. They should not be used for load balancing.

More information on this configuration can be obtained in the section "Replicating Front-end WebSEAL Servers" in the *Tivoli SecureWay Policy Director WebSEAL Administration Guide Version 3.8.0*, GC32-0684.

Web server availability

In order to increase the availability of your Web server space you have to exactly duplicate your servers. The Web administrator has to ensure that the content of the Web root directories on the duplicated servers are kept in sync. After you have created an initial WebSEAL junction for your first Web server, you can add your replicated Web servers to the same junction.

By default, Access Manager WebSEAL balances back-end server load by distributing requests across all available replicated servers when the replicated servers use the same junction point, as depicted in Figure 7-3 on page 163. Access Manager uses a "least-busy" algorithm for this task. This algorithm directs each new request to the server with the fewest connections already in progress.

For static Web content this approach is very easy to implement. However, there are some other considerations you have to regard.

Maintaining a stateful junction

Most Web-enabled applications maintain a "state" for a sequence of HTTP requests from a client. This state is used, for example, to:

► Track a user's progress through the fields in a data entry form generated by a CGI program

► Maintain a user's context when performing a series of database inquiries

► Maintain a list of items in an online shopping cart application where a user randomly browses and selects items to purchase

Servers that run Web-enabled applications can be replicated in order to improve availability through load sharing. When the WebSEAL server provides a junction to these replicated back-end servers, it must ensure that all the requests contained within a client session are forwarded to the correct server, and not distributed among the replicated back-end servers according to the load balancing rules.

This approach is a good solution for high availability, but it cannot provide true load balancing, as the current user session will be forced to utilize one specific server.

Authorization Server availability

Although not initially depicted in the basic scenario in Figure 7-2 on page 162, let us assume we have extended our Web application using some fine grained Authorization Application Programming Interface (azn_API) authorization calls. This authorization information is provided by Access Manager and the application servers can be configured to request this information from a specific Access Manager Authorization Server. This scenario is shown in Figure 7-5.

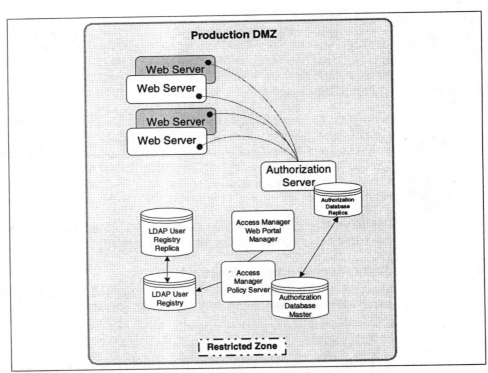

Figure 7-5   Authorization Server scenario for Stocks-4U.com

However, when this Authorization Server fails, the application cannot perform its fine grained authorization calls and will therefore fail. In order to provide high availability of the application authorization services, the scenario configuration would result as shown in Figure 7-6.

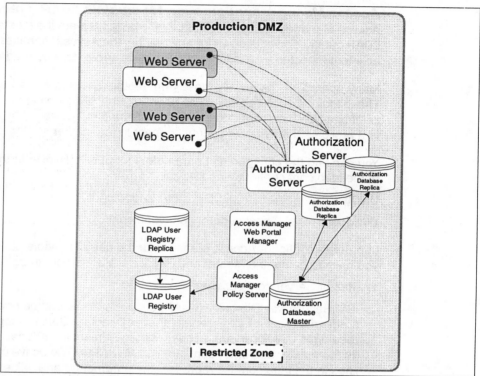

Figure 7-6   Authorization Server scenario with high availability

After implementing a second Authorization Server, you would only need to configure your azn_API applications to be aware of the new replica. This is done by executing the `bassslcfg - add_replicas` command.

User Registry availability

The IBM SecureWay Directory Server supports the concept of Master and Replica LDAP servers.

A Master server contains the master directory from which updates are propagated to replicas. All changes are made and occur on the Master server, and the Master is responsible for propagating these changes to the replicas.

A Replica is an additional server that contains a database replica. The Replicas must be exact copies of the Master. The Replicas do not allow updates to them (except from replication from the Master). The Replica provides a backup to the Master server. If the Master server crashes, or is unreadable, the Replica is still able to fulfill search requests, and provide access to the data.

Access Manager configuration for multiple LDAP directories

Access Manager connects to the LDAP master server when it starts up. If the LDAP master server is down for any reason, the Access Manager server must be able to connect to an available LDAP replica server for any read operations.

Many operations, especially those from regular users, are read operations. These include such operations as user authentication and sign-on to back-end junctioned Web servers. After proper configuration, Access Manager will fail-over to a replica server when it cannot connect to the master server.

You can find the configuration parameters for LDAP fail-over in the [ldap] stanza of the ldap.conf configuration file:

UNIX   /opt/PolicyDirector/etc/ldap.conf

Windows   <install-path >\etc \ldap.conf

In order to configure Access Manager for the use of multiple LDAP directories, you have to define the Master and Replica LDAP servers to be used:

1. Master Server configuration

    IBM SecureWay Directory (LDAP) supports the existence of a single read-write master LDAP server. iPlanet Directory Server supports multiple read-write LDAP servers. Access Manager treats the iPlanet "supplier" server as the master server for configuration purposes. The active configuration lines in the ldap.conf file represent the parameters and values for this master LDAP server. You determine these values during Access Manager configuration. For example:

    ```
    [ldap ]
    enabled =yes
    host =outback
    port =389
    ssl-port =636
    max-search-size =2048
    ```

    If you make a change to the LDAP database, such as adding a new user account through the WPM, Access Manager always uses the read-write (master) LDAP server.

2. Replica Server Configuration

IBM SecureWay Directory (LDAP) supports the existence of one or more read-only replica LDAP servers. iPlanet Directory Server (LDAP) supports the existence of one or more read-only replica LDAP servers referred to as "consumers".

You must add lines to the [ldap] stanza that identify any replica servers available to Access Manager. Use the following syntax for each replica:

```
replica =<ldap-server>,<port>,<type>,<preference>
```

Changes to the ldap.conf file do not take effect until you restart Access Manager. Further details on configuration can be found in the *Access Manager Version 3.9 Base Administration Guide*.

Access Manager Policy Server availability

The only portion of Access Manager that cannot be replicated within the same secure domain is the Policy Server. You can, however, have a second server in standby to provide manual failover capabilities as a first aid response. If you want to assure a 24x7 availability of your Access Manager Policy Server you would need to implement a high availability cluster solution like HACMP for AIX. For further details check the *HACMP Enhanced Scalability Handbook*, SG24-5328.

> **Note:** The purpose of the Policy Server is to maintain the master authorization database that contains the protected object space with the access control information (ACLs and POPs). The Policy Server replicates the authorization database to all other Access Manager Authorization Servers in the secure domain. Every application, configured in local cache mode, that uses this authorization service (like WebSEAL and third party utilization of the aznAPI) has its own local copy (replication) of the master authorization database and can therefore provide authentication and authorization services, even if the Policy Server is not available for a brief period of time.

Web Portal Manager availability

Again, the same is valid for the Web Portal Manager, which provides the administration GUI Web application for the Access Manager administrators. If the implementation requires a 24x7 availability of the Web administration interface, more than one Web Portal Manager should be deployed. This can very well be the case if you have delegated administration for your business partners to external domain administrators or if you are in the ASP business.

Since WPM runs on a WebSphere Application Server base, you would need to deploy the application using another WebSphere Edge Server dispatcher unit in front of your multiple WPM or set up a WebSEAL junction for the WPM application in order to use the Edge Server/WebSEAL deployment as a frontage for high available access.

Conclusion

Again, this point is clear: the Internet has changed the rules on how business is conducted. It has also changed the rules or concepts concerning customer loyalty. When users are experiencing slow response times or refused connections, they are having what is considered an unsatisfactory experience, which may cause them to never visit your site again and instead prefer one of your competitors. This line of thought leads us to the next discussion about scalability and performance.

7.3 Adding scalability

Scalability means that your systems have the capability to adapt readily to the intensity of use, volume, or demand. Designing scalability into your architecture also allows for failover of critical systems and continuous operation at the same time. A lot of the availability discussion can be applied to the scalability issue as well; the topics are all very similar. Let us take a closer look at some specific viewpoints concerning scalability.

Access Manager component scalability

Access Manager automatically replicates the primary authorization policy database that contains the policy rules and credentials when a new application component, configured in local cache mode, or an Access Manager Blade (like WebSEAL or an Authorization Server) is configured. This capability provides the foundation of Access Manager's scalable architecture. After you have designed and installed your Access Manager secure domain and your Policy Server, you can easily extend and configure this IT security landscape.

WebSEAL scalability

In order to add another WebSEAL machine to your existing cluster you would need to execute the following tasks:

► Install and configure a new WebSEAL server; an initial copy of the authorization database gets copied from the Policy Server.

► Edit the [server] stanza in the webseald.conf file as shown in Figure 7-4 on page 164.

► Copy the existing junction definitions (XML files) to the new server.

- Add the new WebSEAL IP address to the load balancing table of your IBM Network Dispatcher or Cisco Local Director.

- Install and configure the neccessary certificate information if you are using SSL communication, mutual authentication with your back-end Web servers, or failover-cookies.

- Start the new WebSEAL.

The new WebSEAL will immediately receive browser requests that are routed from the load balancer product. This way, you can easily extend or change your WebSEAL infrastructure.

Authorization Server scalability

In order to add another Authorization Server component to your infrastructure, you would need to execute the following tasks:

- Install a new Authorization Server; an initial copy of the authorization database gets copied from the Policy Server.

- You need to define this server as a new Authorization Server replica to your applications by using the `bassslcfg - add_replicas` command.

- Install and configure the neccessary certificate information if you are using SSL communication.

The new Authorization Server will immediately be available to receive authorization requests from your applications. This way, you can easily extend or your application infrastructure.

Infrastructure component scalability

In order to achieve overall scalability, we need to take a closer look at the other infrastructure components.

Web server scalability

When your current Web server installed base is not capable anymore of handling incoming requests, it is time to add a new server, maybe on a different, more powerful hardware and operating system platform. In order to get the new system incorporated into your existing Web server infrastructure, you need to apply the following tasks:

- Install a new HTTP server on a new machine and create an exact mirror of your published root directory structure from your existing Web server.

- Add a WebSEAL junction to the same junctionpoint as your existing Web server.

- If you were previously using only one Web server at this particular junction, you have to consider defining a stateful junction at this time, if your Web application is relying on session states.

- If you require SSL connections between WebSEAL and your Web server, you have to configure the junction apropriately.

Using WebSEAL as a mechanism for Web server loadbalancing and high availability makes it a simple task to scale your Web server environment to your individual demands. You could even replace a grown Web server cluster of multiple Intel machines with a new high power server platform by reconfiguring your WebSEAL junction information without losing one second worth of business or redefining any of your security access control information.

User Registry scalability

In order to enhance the overall scalability of the implementation, LDAP replica servers can be added at will to improve the response time for user applications relying on LDAP access. In conjunction with using preference values, you can place LDAP replica servers close to the application functionalities - logically or location dependant.

Preference values for replica LDAP servers

Each replica LDAP server must have a preference value (1-10) that determines its priority for selection as:

- The primary read-only access server

- A backup read-only server during a failover

The higher the number, the higher the priority. If the primary read-only server fails for any reason, the server with the next highest preference value is used. If two or more servers have the same preference value, a least-busy load balancing algorithm determines which one is selected.

Remember that the master LDAP server can function as both a read-only and a read-write server. For read-only access, the master server has a hard-coded default preference setting of 5. This allows you to set replica servers at values higher or lower than the master to obtain the required performance. For example, with appropriate preference settings, you could prevent the master server from handling everyday read operations.

You can set hierarchical preference values to allow access to a single LDAP server (with failover to the other servers), or set equal preferences for all servers and allow load balancing to dictate server selection. Further details on configuration can be found in the *Access Manager Version 3.9 Base Administration Guide*.

Authentication and delegation with Access Manager

This chapter describes the flexibility of user authentication mechanisms with Access Manager. It presents several mechanisms for the identification of users and shows how they can be used in various Web-based scenarios. It also introduces the basic concepts of achieving single sign-on solutions in Web-based environments.

This chapter does not look into any particular customer scenario, but rather presents the technological groundwork for the scenario in Chapter 9, "WebSphere application integration" on page 201.

Different approaches are needed to provide different types of user access, for example, unrestricted access or restricted access with passwords, SecurID tokens, or PKI certificates, to a variety of back-end applications. This flexibility should be provided within one security solution and the maintenance of this security solution has to be done by a centralized security staff, while maintenance of the Web applications can be done by other individual groups.

The goal of this security solution is to enforce user authentication and to perform target-based, coarse or fine grained authorization before forwarding a user's request alongside with his credentials to any of the Web application servers. This way, the Web application developers can stay free of maintaining any security infrastructures.

The security solution is implemented as a reverse proxy, Access Manager WebSEAL, which is located in the Internet demilitarized zone (DMZ). In order to serve as the single point of access control, it has to be used as the only access point for all incoming HTTP and HTTPS connections. Its major task will be to initially authenticate the user and to forward the user's request together with sufficient information about the user's identity to a Web server in a more secured network.

There are several issues we have to look out for:

► We have to make sure that WebSEAL does not allow any bypassing of the access control system. All internal and external access to Web based resources should be channeled through WebSEAL.

► When using SSL connectivity to and from WebSEAL, you have to administer a private key for each WebSEAL and Web server participating in the SSL traffic flow. You should carefully control and document the usage of the private keys.

► You have to protect WebSEAL against unauthorized physical access. Because the reverse proxy has to terminate incoming SSL connections, all connection data will be unencrypted on WebSEAL. Although the data will be encrypted again when using an SSL connection to a back-end application server, physical access to WebSEAL or its memory might allow you to listen to communications even if the data is not being held in a cache.

► It is recommended to use a hardened operating system for WebSEAL. Do not use the machine for any other purposes. Restrict physical and logical access and use Intrusion Detection Tools to monitor any type of unauthorized connection attempts.

We have already focused on general WebSEAL architecture issues in Section 4.2.1, "WebSEAL" on page 91 as well as throughout Chapter 5, "Access Manager Web-based architecture" on page 111 and Chapter 6, "A basic WebSEAL scenario" on page 143. In this specific chapter, we will concentrate on the different authentication and delegation mechanisms that can be utilized with WebSEAL.

8.1 Typical business requirements

In addition to the typical business requirements described in Section 5.4.1, "Typical business requirements" on page 117, which were driven by an overall Web security approach, we want to add the following concerns from the authentication aspect:

▶ The business application developers should only focus on business functions and not on security in order to eliminate hidden security management costs.

Today, a lot of applications use their own authentication and authorization mechanisms as well as security information repositories. There are also a lot of fields where basic operating system security is being used to achieve authentication. These approaches are forcing applications to be constantly maintained when changes to either security policy or operating system have to be implemented.

▶ Increase authentication flexibility without the need of changing any application logic.

Separate user registries for internal and external applications are used, as well as separate security administration for inside and outside applications.

Another flexibility requirement is to allow different authentication methods for certain applications. A basic Web order system might be sufficiently protected with user ID and password authentication, while access to the same ordering system by business partners with high volume orders has to be controlled by providing a certificate or token based authentication.

▶ Increase authentication strength within one session without the need of changing any application logic.

Sometimes it is necessary to process a step-up authentication when an already authenticated user tries to access data that is identified as critical. This would result in the user being prompted for an additional authentication after he already signed in.

8.2 Typical security design objectives

In addition to the typical security design requirements described in Section 5.4.2, "Typical design objectives (technical requirements)" on page 118, which were driven by an overall Web security approach, we want to add the following concerns from the authentication aspect.

Here are some of the technical requirements for authentication that WebSEAL has to address:

► Authentication

   Enforce authentication of users, where the type of authentication depends on the resources they want to access. Sometimes all users need to be authenticated, sometimes only users that want to access some protected URLs or applications need to identity themselves.

► User-based authorization

   Perform an initial user-based authorization check, for example, decide if a user should be allowed to initially contact any of the Web applications. This step prevents certain users from accessing the system at all.

► Target-based authorization

   Perform a resource-based authorization by deciding if a user should be allowed to contact a certain Web application.

► Delegation

   If user authentication and authorization was successful, forward the user's request and user's credentials to a certain Web application server for further processing.

► Allow usage of a separate component for authentication

   It might be necessary to allow a separate and already existing authentication application and repository to perform the initial user authentication. These additional authentication methods should be usable without having to rewrite any of the applications.

8.3 Solution architecture with WebSEAL

The best way to achieve the design objectives is by using a reverse Web proxy with sufficient security functions in front of the existing Web application servers. Figure 8-1 on page 177 shows a basic architecture for protecting Web applications.

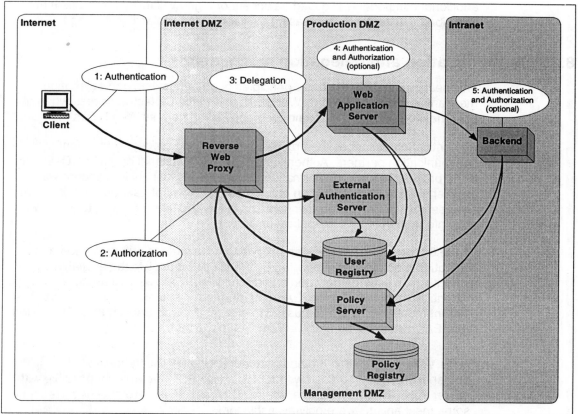

Figure 8-1 Reverse proxy flow for authentication, delegation, and authorization

The reverse proxy is used as a mediator between the end user and the Web application servers. The functions of the reverse proxy have to be provide the following details:

► Accept either HTTP or HTTPS connections

► If needed, gather user credentials

► If needed, perform user authentication (locally or by using an external authentication service)

► Gather authorization information and make an authorization decision

► Delegate user's connection together with user credentials to the applicable Web application server

Because this is a pure architectural discussion on functionality, the placement of additional components like load balancers or high availability mechanism are described in Chapter 7, "Increasing availability and scalability" on page 157.

8.3.1 Authentication and delegation mechanisms

This section presents the basic principles of authentication and delegation mechanisms that are used by WebSEAL to enforce protected access when a user tries to connect to a certain Web application from its Web browser.

Authentication describes the process of exchanging credentials to identify the communication partners. Authentication can be directional or mutual. Delegation is the process to forward information about a user's identity in a secure way to another system. WebSEAL can enforce certain types of user authentication and can use several delegation mechanisms to forward user requests together with user information to a Web application server.

Figure 8-2 on page 179 gives an overview of the various authentication and delegation mechanisms supported by WebSEAL. It depicts the available authentication schema between a user and WebSEAL, as well as the authentication between WebSEAL and other back-end application servers. The different mechanisms are discussed in greater detail in Section 8.4, "Supported WebSEAL authentication mechanisms" on page 184.

> **Note:** All authentication methods, except for the certificate based authentication, can be used with HTTP or HTTPS. This was not possible with earlier Policy Director versions, where HTTP sessions were not supported and some mechanisms were only available for HTTPS.

Let us take another look at Figure 8-1 on page 177 in order to describe the single steps during the authentication process:

1. The user contacts the Web site by entering the HTTP address of a Web page or Web application. His first point of contact is the WebSEAL portal. Because WebSEAL works as a reverse proxy, the user does not realize that there is another system involved in the communication between him and the Web server he tries to contact.

   If access to the requested information is restricted, WebSEAL requests authentication information and authenticates the user. After successful authentication, WebSEAL generates user credential information.

2. Once authenticated, WebSEAL achieves an authorization decision based on the user credentials and the policy information that protects the information. WebSEAL decides if the user is allowed to contact the system at all.

3. WebSEAL selects the junction for the user's requests and forwards the user credentials and user request to the Web application server.

4. Based on the forwarded user credentials, the Web application server can proceed with further, more fine-grained authorization decisions.

5. Based on the forwarded user credentials, the back-end application server can proceed with further, more fine-grained authorization decisions.

WebSEAL provides enough flexibility to support multiple authentication and delegation mechanisms to act as a reverse Web proxy between different user groups and different types of Web application servers in a secure way.

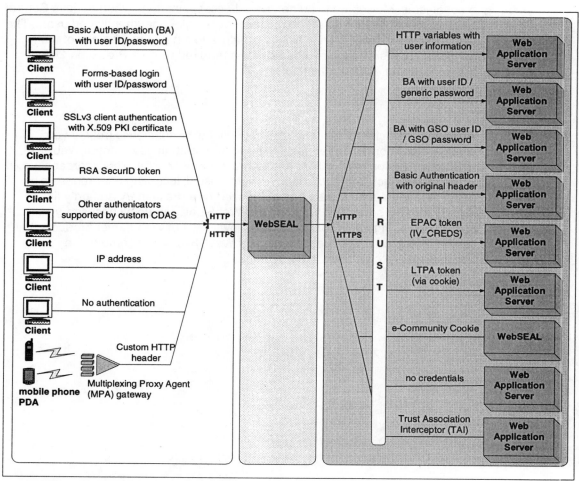

Figure 8-2   Access Manager authentication methods with WebSEAL

The left portion in Figure 8-2 lists all authentication mechanisms available between a user and WebSEAL. The right side lists all delegation mechanisms between WebSEAL and another Web application server.

Some of those mechanisms can be combined, for example, access to a certain URL can be restricted to require a certain IP source address and the correct user ID/password combination. It is also possible to combine any authentication mechanism with any delegation mechanisms.

A single WebSEAL server may be configured for three different levels of authentication, of which unauthenticated is the first. Usually the next one is the user ID and password, but it can be any of the supported authentication mechanisms. Moving up to authenticated access happens when Access Control Lists on the requested object do not allow access for unauthenticated users. The next level of authentication, which is usually a token (but can be any of the supported authentication mechanisms), is required when a Protected Object Policy requiring it is set on an object.

8.3.2 Trust

An important factor for a centralized security portal solution is trust. If you configure all information requests to be routed through your central WebSEAL reverse proxy, you only want to authenticate the user once. This approach would imply that all back-end application servers trust all incoming user requests as being properly authenticated and authorized by a preliminary authority like WebSEAL.This solution is very useful if WebSEAL can do all necessary authorization. Figure 8-3 on page 181 shows a list of Web server products that can be protected with Access Manager's WebSEAL using some of the mechanisms listed above.

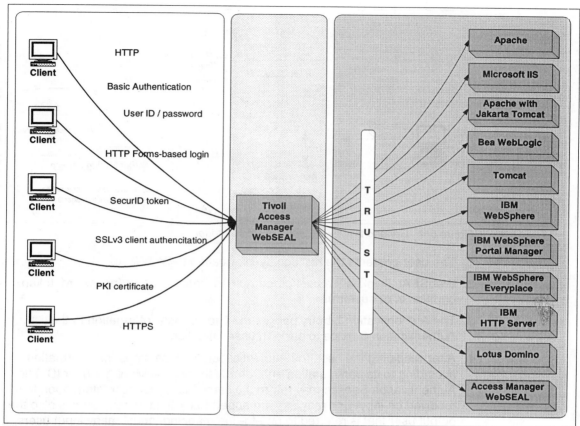

Figure 8-3   Overview of Web server products protected with WebSEAL

In order to fully implement a secure trust relationship, you would also have to configure each and every back-end application server to only accept incoming requests from WebSEAL on the specified port. No other direct connections, internal or external, are to be allowed to any of the servers. In cases where this is not yet practical or possible to achieve, you would have to specify the junctions to forward the user credentials in a way for the back-end servers to re-authenticate the user principal. This discussion has also been addressed in Chapter 5, "Access Manager Web-based architecture" on page 111.

8.3.3 Generic authentication mechanism with WebSEAL

Before going into the specific authentication model details, let us use Figure 8-4 on page 182 to take a look at a generic picture of the WebSEAL authentication model.

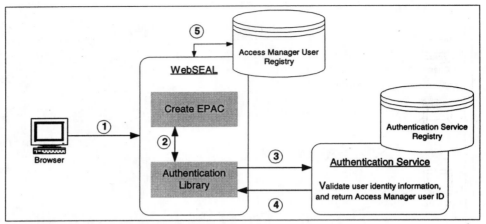

Figure 8-4   Generic WebSEAL authentication model

1. The user presents the his identity information to WebSEAL.

2. WebSEAL invokes the configured Authentication Library (password, token, certificate, or custom).

3. The Authentication Library passes the user identity information to the Authentication Service to perform user validation.

4. After validating the user, the Authentication Service maps the information according to its configuration and returns an Access Manager user ID. The Authentication Service may return the same individual user information that it received on input or it may use a mapped-to ID, if each input user is also the output user that is referred to one-to-one mapping, and if many input users are mapped to the same output user that is referred to as many-to-one. In both cases, the returned user must be defined to the Access Manager's user registry.

5. WebSEAL now uses the Access Manager User Registry to create the Access Manager credential - Extended Privilege Attribute Certificate (EPAC) - that is cached for the duration of the session and used for any authorization decisions.

> **Note:** The EPAC is a token that details the user's identity and the roles that he can use. It can also contain additional attributes if required. EPACs are often misunderstood, they are not encrypted or signed, and they do not time out. They should only be trusted from within the Access Manager secure domain.

8.3.4 Generic delegation mechanism with WebSEAL

As discussed in Section 4.2.1, "WebSEAL" on page 91, WebSEAL junctions provide powerful capabilities for managing access to multiple Web application servers through a common access portal. Figure 8-3 on page 181 shows the different junctions WebSEAL can establish.

If you want to delegate further authentication and/or authorization tasks to the back-end application, you have to provide information about the user and the session. In order to pass on that kind of information, you have to define your junctions accordingly. You can actually provide the following information for your junctioned servers.

Supplying client identity in HTTP headers

You can insert Access Manager-specific client identity and group membership information into the HTTP headers of requests destined for junctioned third-party servers. The Access Manager HTTP header information enables applications on junctioned third-party servers to perform user-specific actions based on the client's Access Manager identity.

Supplying client IP addresses in HTTP headers

You can insert the client IP address information into the HTTP headers of requests destined for junctioned application servers. The Access Manager HTTP header information enables applications on junctioned third-party servers to perform actions based on this IP address information.

Passing session cookies to junctioned portal servers

A Web portal is a server that offers a broad array of personalized resources and services. You can send the Access Manager session cookie (originally established between the client and WebSEAL) to a back-end portal server. This option currently exists to directly support the integration of WebSEAL with the Plumtree Corporate Portal solution.

Global Sign-On solution

Access Manager supports a flexible single sign-on solution that features the ability to provide alternative user names and passwords to the back-end Web application server.

Dynamic business entitlements

Access Manager offers a dynamic business entitlement functionality for passing information to back-end Web applications. This is implemented with two steps:

1. It is now possible to insert any field from an Access Manager users LDAP record into their credential at login time. These values can be extracted by an application using the Authorization Application Programming Interface (aznAPI) accessing the delegated client identity information.

2. Being able to insert arbitrary values from LDAP into the credential (without writing new authentication code) is a useful addition to Access Manager; however, the next step goes one step further, allowing back-end Web applications to access the information without the needing to use aznAPI.

   WebSEAL can extract the values from the credential and pass them to the back-end Web server as fields in the HTTP request header. This allows most Web applications to access them without using any special code.

8.4 Supported WebSEAL authentication mechanisms

This sections shows the authentication mechanisms that are supported by WebSEAL to protect access to a Web environment. All mechanisms in this section can be combined with any of the delegation mechanisms in the next chapter to make the connection between a user and a Web application.

WebSEAL uses the concept of Plug-on Authentication Modules (PAMs) to use different authentication methods. The programming interface is now available so users could write their own modules.

The following Plug-on Authentication Modules exist in Access Manager:

► passwd-ldap: Password Authentication (Forms/BasicAuth)

► token-cdas: Token Authentication (SecureID)

► cert-ldap: SSL Client Certificate Authentication

► http-request: HTTP Header Authentication

► cdsso: e-Community Single Sign-On

8.4.1 Basic authentication with user ID/password

Basic authentication (BA) is part of the HTTP standard and defines a standardized way in which user ID/password information is passed to a Web server. When WebSEAL sends a BA challenge to the browser, the browser pops up a dialog panel requesting user name and password from the user. Once this information is entered, the browser sends its original request again, but this time with the user name and password included in the BA header of the HTTP request. WebSEAL extracts this information from the header and uses it to verify the user's identity. In this case, a specific library shipped with Access Manager implements a built-in authentication service and performs a check against the Access Manager user registry. If successful, an EPAC is created and cached.

Once a user has authenticated, through the browser, an ID and password, the browser caches this information in memory and sends it with each subsequent request to the same server. Even by configuring a session log out parameter, which is possible for HTTPS sessions, the user will automatically log on to WebSEAL with each new request he sends. The only way to clear this cache (and log the current user out) is to close all browser panels.

8.4.2 Forms-based login with user ID/password

The alternative to using basic authentication is to use forms-based login. Rather than sending a basic authentication challenge in response to a client request, WebSEAL responds with a sign-in form in HTML format. The client browser displays this and the user fills in his user ID and password. When the user clicks on the send or logon button, the form is returned to WebSEAL using an HTTP POST request. WebSEAL extracts the information and uses it to verify the user's identity by using the Access Manager authentication service, where it performs a check against the Access Manager user registry.

As the user ID and password information is not cached on the browser, it becomes possible to perform a programmatic log out for the user. On a client request, WebSEAL presents a customizable log-out form to a user. After the user confirms the log-out, the session is considered closed and the EPAC is deleted from the WebSEAL cache.

8.4.3 Authentication with X.509 client certificates

In response to a certificate request from WebSEAL, as part of the SSL v3 tunnel negotiation, the browser prompts the user to select a certificate from the local certificate store or smartcard. The user is asked for a password before he can access the private key. Once the user has chosen a certificate, it is passed to WebSEAL, which passes it on to the certificate authentication library, where the signature of the client certificate using the Certificate Authority (CA) certificates that it trusts is checked. It also checks the validity period to ensure the certificate has not expired. Assuming the certificate is OK, the identity in the certificate is mapped (one-to-one) to an Access Manager identity. Once the Access Manager identity is passed back to WebSEAL, WebSEAL pulls the user information from the Access Manager user registry and builds the EPAC.

If you configure Access Manager to use X.509 client certificates for authentication, but the user does not have a certificate available, WebSEAL can fall back to Basic Authentication, if required.

8.4.4 Authentication with RSA SecurID token

Access Manager includes a Cross Domain Authentication Service (CDAS) that supports authentication of clients using user name/token pass code information from an RSA SecurID token authenticator (TAR), a physical device that stores and dynamically generates a piece of authentication data (token).

The TAR is used in tandem with an authentication server (the Ace/Server), which actually performs the authentication. During authentication to WebSEAL, the client enters a user name and pass code. The pass code consists of:

► The unique PIN number associated with the client's SecurID TAR

► The current number sequence generated by the SecurID TAR

The Ace/Server uses its own registry database to determine the PIN that the user should be using, checks it, and strips it off of the pass code. It then checks the remaining number sequence against its own internally generated number sequence. A matching number sequence completes the authentication.

At this point, the role of the token CDAS is complete. The CDAS does not perform identity mapping, but simply returns to WebSEAL an Access Manager identity containing the user name of the client. This user name must match a user ID stored in the Access Manager user registry.

8.4.5 Custom authentication using CDAS

All the authentication mechanisms described above assume that the user identity validation information is held in the Access Manager user registry or can be verified locally on WebSEAL. Of course, there are situations where this is not the case, and user authentication has to be performed outside the Access Manager trusted Domain: One-Time Password Servers (for example, RSA SecureID), RADIUS, Resource Access Control Facility (RACF), and so on. On the other side, depending on the requirements, it may become necessary to extend or enrich the capabilities provided by built-in authentication libraries.

WebSEAL provides a capability referred to as *Cross Domain Authentication Service* (CDAS) in order to meet these requirements.

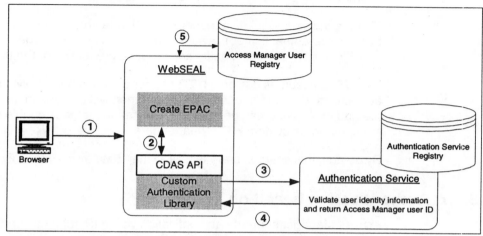

Figure 8-5 WebSEAL authentication model with CDAS

As shown in Figure 8-5, the CDAS allows you to substitute the default built-in WebSEAL authentication mechanism with a highly flexible shared library mechanism that allows custom handling and processing of client authentication information. The CDAS application programming interface (API) is available for download by registered customers.

You can customize the CDAS shared library to handle authentication data according to your security requirements given the following options.

The custom CDAS can process authentication data internally and return an Access Manager identity. This is especially useful if it is desired to have enriched authentication mechanisms in comparison to built-in ones, for example, checking client certificate validity via Online Certificate Status Protocol (OCSP). The user identity validation information may reside in the user registry and not be used for authentication by default, for example, providing a customer number along with user ID and password in B2B scenarios.

Extending the built-in capabilities of authentication mechanisms provided by Access Manager is another reason to built a custom CDAS. This method allows you to authenticate clients who are not direct members of the Access Manager security domain. In that case, the custom CDAS can direct authentication data to be processed by an external authentication mechanism and third-party registry (for example, RACF, One-Time Password Server, or authentication via personal question). Ultimately, the CDAS returns an Access Manager identity to WebSEAL for querying the Access Manager user registry and creating an EPAC.

8.4.6 Authentication using customized HTTP headers

Access Manager supports authentication via customized HTTP header information supplied by the client or a proxy agent.

This mechanism requires a mapping function (a shared library) that maps the trusted (pre-authenticated) header data to an Access Manager identity. WebSEAL can take this identity and create a credential for the user.

WebSEAL assumes custom HTTP header data has been previously authenticated. For this reason, it is recommended that you implement this method exclusively with no other authentication methods enabled. It is possible to impersonate custom HTTP header data.

By default, this shared library is built to map data from Entrust Proxy headers.

8.4.7 Authentication based on IP address

Access Manager supports authentication via an IP address supplied by the client.

This mechanism is best used in combination with other mechanisms. For example, you can use IP network addresses to identity a certain group of users, give them access to a certain application, and then use additional authentication mechanisms to give access to more protected applications.

Such a configuration can be used to implement a two-factor authentication as well. It will possibly be more secure than plain password authentication.

8.4.8 No authentication

Any user that can reach WebSEAL belongs to the group of unauthenticated users. This group can also get certain permissions.

This group of unauthenticated users generally is used to define public Web access. WebSEAL can force unauthenticated users to use another authentication method when selecting certain protected URLs.

All users that can reach WebSEAL might already have enough permissions to contact certain junctioned Web servers. For example, if WebSEAL is connected to a VPN gateway, only authorized VPN users will be able to reach that server and additional authentication might not be needed. In this situation, it might be OK to treat unauthenticated users similar to a group of password-authenticated Internet users.

8.4.9 MPA authentication

Access Manager provides an authentication mechanism for clients using a Multiplexing Proxy Agent (MPA). This is a special variation of the authentication with customized HTTP headers, often used for mobile phones and PDAs today, but not limited to these.

Multiplexing Proxy Agents are gateways that accommodate multiple client access. IBM Everyplace Wireless Gateway (EWG) is an integrated part of the IBM WebSphere Everyplace Suite that provides security-rich wired and wireless connectivity between the IT network and the Communications Network for example

- ► Cellular networks, including GSM, CDMA, TDMA, PDC, PHS, iDEN, and AMPS
- ► Packet Radio networks, including GPRS, CDPD, DatatTAC, and Mobitex
- ► Satellite and Wireline environments, including DSL, cable modems, Internet Service Providers, ISDN, Dial, and LAN

In addition, the Everyplace Wireless Gateway provides protocol translation as a Wireless Application Protocol (WAP) gateway, information push as a WAP push proxy gateway, and support for short messaging services (SMS). EWG establishes a single SSL channel to the origin server and "tunnels" all client requests and responses through this channel.

To WebSEAL, the information across this channel initially appears as multiple requests from one client. WebSEAL must distinguish between the authentication of the MPA server over SSL and the additional authentication requests for each individual client.

Because WebSEAL maintains an SSL session state for the MPA, it cannot use SSL session IDs for each client simultaneously. WebSEAL instead authenticates the clients using HTTP authentication techniques over SSL.

If the user is authenticated at the EWG, for example, to a RADIUS Server, then WebSEAL can be configured to receive an "authenticated ID" from the gateway and not re-authenticate the user.

Today, WebSEAL support for the Entrust Proxy and the Nokia WAP Gateway exists.

8.5 WebSEAL delegation mechanisms

After a user has been authenticated by WebSEAL and an authorization decision has been made, WebSEAL has to forward the user's request to a back-end Web application server. If needed, WebSEAL can include information about the user, for example, X.509 Distinguished Name, Group memberships, or any other value.

The mechanisms to forward that information can vary. It is possible to use standard protocols, for example, the HTTP Basic Authentication header, or to use proprietary mechanisms when talking to specific server products. WebSEAL supports several mechanisms to forward requests to Web application servers.

This section presents alternatives on how to pass information about the user and the user's request to the back-end application.

When a protected resource is located on a junctioned Web application server, a client requesting that resource can be required to perform multiple logins - one for the WebSEAL server and one for the back-end server. Each login may require different login identities. The problem of administering and maintaining multiple login identities can often be solved with a single sign-on (SSO) mechanism.

The Open Group defines single sign-on as a "mechanism whereby a single action of user authentication and authorization can permit a user to access all computers and systems where that user has access permission, without the need to enter multiple passwords"[1] (compare with the discussion in Appendix B, "Single Sign-On - a contrarian view" on page 417). While Tivoli Global Sign-On addresses the authentication issues on various applications running on different operation systems, WebSEAL's realm is to provide the single sign-on functionalities for Web infrastructures. Acting as a Web reverse proxy to the company's Web environment, WebSEAL communicates with the junctioned servers on behalf of the users. It allows the user to access a resource, regardless of the resource's location, using only one initial login. Any further login requirements from back-end application servers are handled transparent to the user.

Depending on integration requirements, different data should be sent to the WebSEAL secured Web application using different formats. However, most of the Web applications support standard HTTP-based mechanisms for the user identification, which are exploited by WebSEAL.

---

[1] Taken from the security section of the Open Group Web site (http://www.opengroup.org/security/topics.htm)

8.5.1 Tivoli Global Sign-On (TGSO)-lockbox

Most Web applications support Basic Authentication for checking authenticity and obtaining a user's identity information. When using this support, an application or a server the application is running on maintains a database with user IDs and passwords (in the most simple case). In our initial example in Chapter 6, "A basic WebSEAL scenario" on page 143, it was operating system based user management on multiple Web servers, containing lists of user IDs and passwords. After challenging a user and obtaining user ID and password, an application made a look up for the matching entry, and if one was found, the user was considered authenticated and his or her identity has been associated with the provided user ID. In more sophisticated environments relational databases, legacy applications or LDAP-based repositories are targeting that scope.

Access Manager supports a flexible single sign-on solution that features the ability to provide alternative user IDs and passwords to the Web application servers.

The integration is achieved by creating "SSO-aware" junctions between WebSEAL and Web servers hosting the applications. TGSO resources[2] and, eventually, TGSO resource groups must first be created in Access Manager for every application. When WebSEAL receives a request for a resource located on the "SSO-junctioned" server, WebSEAL queries the Access Manager user registry for the appropriate authentication information. The user registry contains a database of mappings for each user registered for using that application, which provides alternative user IDs and passwords for specific resources. Evidently, that information has to be in the repository prior to initial using. The values (user IDs and passwords) should match those stored in the application "home" registry.

> **Note:** Although junctions are set up on a Web server basis, it is possible to provide different SSO-data to different applications hosted on the same server. In order to achieve it, multiple TGSO junctions to the same Web server are created. However, using access control lists (ACLs), the access to the resources is defined that way, so that only appropriate URLs can be requested through a specified junction.

---

[2] The SSO functionality in early Policy Director releases relied on Tivoli SecureWay Global Sign-On technology, where user IDs and passwords for resources were stored based on a Distributed Computing Environment (DCE) infrastructure. Although LDAP is the repository for that kind of information today and the implementation has no connection to the Tivoli SecureWay Global Sign-On technology anymore, the name has been preserved. Further, the technology is referred to as SSO and junctions as TGSO-junctions.

The visible advantage of the solution is, that no changes are supposed to be made on the application side. However, the following issues should be considered:

► Synchronization of the user IDs and passwords in the application's "home" user registry and Access Manager user registry

► Storage of SSO passwords in the Access Manager user registry in the clear, as they should be passed through to the application in the clear (they could be protected from the disallowed access, for example, LDAP ACLs).

A special situation emerges if Access Manager and the secured application are sharing the same repository for storing user data, as shown in Figure 8-6 on page 193. An LDAP directory is the most suitable platform for maintaining application specific information about users and groups. Given compatible LDAP schemas[3], many applications may share the same LDAP directory. LDAP provides a standardized way of authenticating users based on user ID and password stored as user attributes. However, it provides no flexibility in defining object classes to be used for authenticating a user, rather than performing a call based on primary identification attributes of a user (user ID and password). While using an Access Manager TGSO-junction, Access Manager uses specific LDAP attributes for storing TGSO-information for every TGSO user. As a result, the TGSO user ID and password provided for a specific junction are not necessary the same as primary ones. However, a "junctioned" application sharing the same LDAP repository would then try to authenticate a user using these values against primary ones (by doing LDAP bind or compare). The need to keep the values of primary user IDs and passwords and TGSO ones arises.

---

[3] LDAP schema describes the way of storing the information in a LDAP directory in terms of object classes and attributes.

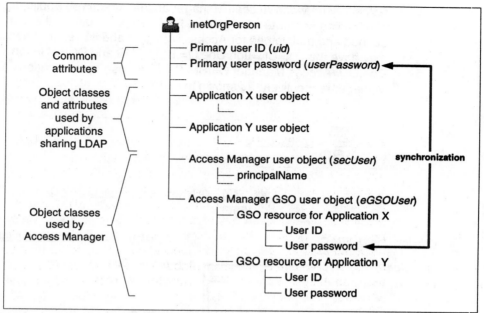

Figure 8-6   LDAP shared by Access Manager and other applications

The following issues should be considered while looking for solutions for integrating Access Manager and Web applications using the same LDAP repository:

▶ Main user passwords are allowed to be in the clear (keep in mind, Access Manager TGSO passwords are always in clear). The possibility of protecting LDAP data based on ACLs always exists.

▶ Changing the main password should be reflected in the change of the TGSO password for a particular user. This can happen immediately, for example after a user changes his password[4], or in a batch run on a regular basis. The last situation presumes that main passwords are in clear.

---

[4] Note that a custom Web application should be developed in order to achieve the "on-the-fly" synchronization of main and TGSO passwords. All password changes should be handled by users through that application that will subsequently carry out the changes for main and TGSO passwords. This would allow main user passwords to be encrypted. However, the Access Manager mechanisms for setting up and maintaining password policies may not be in place any longer. Otherwise, the Access Manager native interface for changing passwords, and not the custom application, would be invoked, for example, in the case of password expiration.

Another way to resolve the LDAP "bind-issue" while sharing the same LDAP repository between Access Manager and secured Web applications is maintaining separate user entries. For example, a different subset of users is defined and maintained for Access Manager and its secured application. A user may have the DN=CN=Jon Doe,O=IBM,C=US and DN=CN=Jon Doe,OU=Access Manager,O=IBM,C=US for use by applications and Access Manager respectively, as shown in Figure 8-7.

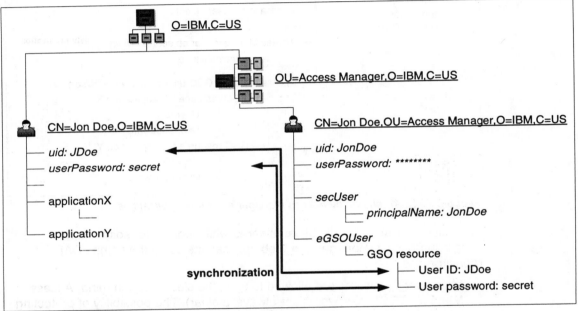

Figure 8-7   Shared LDAP with separate user entries

As a result, while performing authentication, the application will try to bind using its own user IDs and passwords. The TGSO user IDs and passwords could be more easily kept in sync with those maintained by an application. The trade-offs of this solution are:

► The need to maintain the user information sets per application sharing is the same LDAP

► As the same user identity would exist multiple times, it would raise the direct cost, if the licensing of the LDAP software is on a per-user base

8.5.2 Integrating applications requiring forms-based login

A special situation arises if an application performs authentication requesting user ID and password by using forms-based login. A customizable Web page (login form) is presented to a user. The page contains HTML fields for entering a user ID and password. As these fields and values are passed back to the application server transparent to WebSEAL, no interception occurs. In order to achieve SSO, a custom Web application (for example, an SSO servlet) can be developed, as depicted in Figure 8-8.

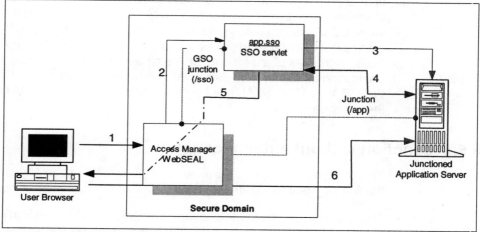

Figure 8-8   SSO servlet

1. The user logs on to the Access Manager WebSEAL. He clicks on a link (https://www.webseal.com/sso/app.sso) from the system's main page, such as index.html, to access the junctioned application server.

2. The request is passed through the TGSO junction "/sso" where the user's authentication data, particularly for the junctioned application stored in Access Manager, will be passed to the SSO servlet.

3. The SSO servlet uses a GET request to obtain the login page and any possible session information (such as cookies) from the junctioned application server. The SSO servlet filters the login form, fills in the Access Manager TGSO user name/password, together with any possible hidden data fields and session cookies, generates a POST request, and sends it back to the junctioned application server.

4. The application performs the authentication and returns the result and session information, if any, back to the SSO servlet.

5. The response is filtered by the SSO servlet and sent as an HTTP redirect containing the URL with the WebSEAL's host name and the junction "/app" and any session information back to the browser through WebSEAL.

6. The browser processes the redirected request and generates a new one to the junctioned application server through the WebSEAL junction (/app).

8.5.3 Passing an unchanged Basic Authentication header

WebSEAL can be configured to pass the received Basic Authentication data unchanged to the junctioned application. If Access Manager and the application share the same LDAP registry, Access Manager authenticates a user against the same LDAP attributes as an application performing a regular LDAP bind, that is, using a main user ID and password. In this case, there is no need to maintain the TGSO attributes of a user and the main password may be encrypted. However, Basic Authentication is the only available authentication method used by WebSEAL, as WebSEAL has to obtain the BA header values in order to pass them through.

8.5.4 Junction without authentication

This may be useful if WebSEAL does all the authentication and authorization and there is no need to forward any information to the back-end servers.

This scenario seems applicable for either servers without any reliable security functions or where there is no need of extra back-end authentication and authorization, for example, providing only static Web pages. Nevertheless, this approach requires full trust towards WebSEAL, and the back-end servers should be configured to only accept incoming requests from WebSEAL proxies.

8.5.5 Providing a generic password

At this point, the following subchapters are based on the assumption that trust between WebSEAL and the back-end application server is established.

Given a Web application that may be contacted through WebSEAL only, an integration solution based on providing a user ID along with a uniform generic password, shared by WebSEAL and the application, can be considered. As the process of authenticating a user is performed by WebSEAL, and given WebSEAL is the only gateway into the application, there is no need to carry out the authenticity check again. Although no changes have to be made in the application, it still could perform authentication in its obvious manner. However, its scope should only be the gaining of user identity. There should be no other possibilities available to contact the application avoiding WebSEAL.

The application can maintain its own user repository or share that of Access Manager (LDAP-based). In the second case, however, the LDAP-bind issue, discussed before (see Section 8.5.1, "Tivoli Global Sign-On (TGSO)-lockbox" on page 191), has to be considered. That leads to the necessity of maintaining separate entries for a single user for Access Manager and the secured application.

8.5.6 Supplying user and group information

WebSEAL can be configured to provide information about user ID, groups, and resources the user has access to, to a junctioned application. That is accomplished by supplying the values of defined HTTP variables:

iv_user	For user ID
iv_user_l	For user's LDAP distinguished name
iv_groups	For groups a particular user belongs to
iv_creds	For the user's credentials

The variables supplied in the HTTP stream can be easily mapped to the CGI environment variables that can be interpreted by a Web application. As no password information can be supplied this way, no authentication can be · performed by the junctioned Web application. However, it is possible to combine this option with any previously described.

Secure credential exchange

We would like to briefly introduce the notion of secure credentials and how they could be exchanged between Web applications.

Credentials are basically created as a result of a successful authentication. Credentials created by a WebSEAL reverse proxy can be understood by other WebSEALs in the same Access Manager security domain and even beyond (see Chapter 10, "Access control in a distributed environment" on page 227). However, the credential exchange with the junctioned Web server is not necessarily trivial mainly due to the lack of standardization. Kerberos, PKI, DCE, and Active Directory (with related products) are the most well-known security technologies, providing security interoperability for different platforms and applications, including Web based environments; however, the applications have to be enabled for that. Not less important is the fact that these technologies do not interoperate seamlessly with each other, neither do the applications.

In order to support the interoperability of Web applications, WebSEAL today uses a generic HTTP-based interface as described in the previous sections.

8.5.7 Using LTPA authentication with WebSEAL

WebSEAL can provide authentication and authorization services and protection to an IBM WebSphere environment. When WebSEAL is positioned as a protective front end to WebSphere, accessing clients are faced with two potential login points. Therefore, WebSEAL supports a single sign-on solution to one or more IBM WebSphere servers across WebSEAL junctions.

WebSphere provides the cookie-based lightweight third party authentication mechanism (LTPA). You can configure WebSEAL junctions to support LTPA and provide a single sign-on solution for clients.

When a user makes a request for a WebSphere resource, the user must first authenticate to WebSEAL. Upon successful authentication, WebSEAL generates an LTPA cookie on behalf of the user. The LTPA cookie, which serves as an authentication token for WebSphere, contains user identity and password information. This information is encrypted using a password-protected secret key shared between WebSEAL and the WebSphere server.

WebSEAL inserts the cookie in the HTTP header of the request that is sent across the junction to WebSphere. The back-end WebSphere server receives the request, decrypts the cookie, and authenticates the user based on the identity information supplied in the cookie.

To improve performance, WebSEAL can store the LTPA cookie in a cache and use the cached LTPA cookie for subsequent requests during the same user session. You can configure lifetime timeout and idle (inactivity) timeout values for the cached cookie.

The creation, encryption, and decryption of LTPA cookies basically introduces processing overhead. The LTPA cache functionality allows you to improve the performance of LTPA junctions in a high load environment. By default, the LTPA cache is enabled. Without the enhancement of the cache, a new LTPA cookie is created and encrypted for each subsequent user request.

Note: With previous versions of WebSphere you needed to enable SSO for the Access Manager LTPA authentication to work correctly. This meant that WebSphere sent a cookie containing an LTPA token back to the browser with the HTTP response. This cookie was not used or required for Access Manager LTPA to work. However, because this cookie contained the LTPA token is sent back to the browser, there was an exposure. The LTPA keys could be cracked in an off-line attack. This meant it was important to periodically regenerate the LTPA keys within WebSphere and redistribute them to Access Manager.

With WebSphere V4 SSO and WebSEAL, it is no longer required for Access Manager LTPA authentication to work. Even if it is enabled, the LTPA token is no longer sent to the browser, eliminating this exposure.

Having the LTPA cookie enabled is independent of the Basic Authentication (BA) header. This means that with the LTPA cookie inserted into the request header, it is still possible to have the BA header to carry any authentication information to the back-end server depending on the -b option specified during the junction creation. The usage of the BA header depends on the configuration of the back-end WebSphere server.

Access Manager LTPA authentication can also be used to provide a single sign-on solution with Lotus Domino servers. Figure 8-9 on page 200 shows the available usage scenarios with the LTPA authentication.

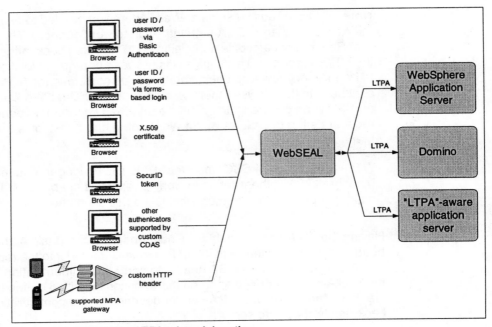

Figure 8-9   WebSEAL LTPA token delegation

WebSphere application integration

One of the nightmares in IT security management is application managed security. When different applications on different platforms driven by different project groups are implementing their own view of security functionalities, the result is an expensive, unmanageable turmoil that opens security holes instead of providing a strong access control solution. In developing new Java-based e-business Web applications, we can start to build a solution that lets us distinguish and differentiate between security and application functions.

Looking at application development platforms within today's e-business environments, we have to take a closer look at Java 2 Platform Enterprise Edition (J2EE) based Web application servers. Two major products have already been integrated with Access Manager to some extent: BEA's WebLogic Application Server and IBM's WebSphere Application Server. This chapter examines the details of integration between Access Manager and WebSphere application Server.

9.1 Business requirements

Security is such a fundamental enabler of e-business that in the emerging B2C and B2B markets, effective security can make the difference between owning the market and becoming an "also ran". The promise of e-business and its ability to create new revenue streams is predicated upon the ability of these new business processes to reach these new markets and customers. But that promise evaporates if security issues are not addressed properly.

In this world of e-business, WebSphere has become a Web application server market leader. A growing number of customers are deploying WebSphere and WebSphere-based solutions as their core e-business software platform. Few, if any, customers will put their WebSphere-based applications and solutions into production without the assurance that their business processes and data will be protected from malicious and inadvertent loss. More importantly, as enterprises extend their business applications to reach new markets and customers, security and trust issues become of paramount importance. This has always been true in core, mission-critical intranet-based applications. This is even more true as these applications are leveraging the Internet's Web-based computing model for B2C and B2B.

As customers have moved to a Web-based computing model, some have found it very difficult to implement security on an application-by-application basis. And with disparate applications that require disparate security approaches, it becomes clear very quickly that there is no security policy when there are numerous *islands of security* that cloud the picture. There is nothing nefarious about the islands of security approach; in fact, it can be a natural evolution for customers, because many products, including IBM's WebSphere, come with some form of security built in. But when the islands begin to diminish, the ability to clearly manage security according to policy for your organization decreases, so there is tremendous value in securing applications in a way that is consistent and compatible with securing applications and application-components running on other middleware and platforms in the enterprise.

For this scenario, we define the following business requirements for existing as well as new e-business applications based on WebSphere family products:

► Reducing the costs of implementing and maintaining proprietary Web security solutions (islands of security)

► Fast time-to-production

► Reduce cost and complexity of application development

► Consistently managed end-to-end security (from browser to Web application) in order to mitigate risks of fraud

- ▶ Develop applications according to standards and standard architectures in order to achieve independence of specific vendor solutions

9.2 Security design objectives

Based on business requirements, we define the following security design objectives to be achieved by integrated solutions:

- ▶ Simplification of application development and off-loading the security policy of the application
- ▶ Simplification of system administration by maintaining a consistent security model across Web applications and related systems

Regarding the implementation of an access control subsystem, the systems fall into one of the following three categories.

Category 1 systems implement their own authorization decision processes based on security policies, defined in proprietary formats, as well as enforcement of those policies, as shown in Figure 9-1.

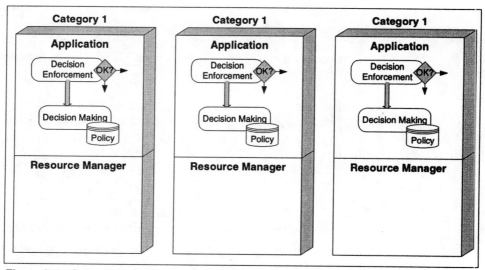

Figure 9-1   Category 1 systems

Obviously, these are home-grown applications that may even precisely reflect the existing security policies. However, the risk is rather high that such implementations go outside the designed limits in rapidly extending and changing IT environments. As security decision making, as well as their enforcement, is implemented inside the application, any change in the policies requires reflection in the application code. Moreover, it becomes difficult to ensure that all category 1 systems enforce the same policy. As an outcome in category 1 systems, maintenance cost for updating security in the applications are rising, and the valuable development time is spent on writing security, not business functions.

Systems of category 2 address this issue by off-loading the authorization decision making process out of the application to a resource manager, as shown in Figure 9-2. The resource manager takes over the role of providing the requested resources to the application and decision making process. If a resource is requested by the application, it calls the authorization decision making process residing in the resource manager. The resource manager consults its policy database and provides the application with a simple yes or no decision. It is then up to the application to enforce the received decision and provide information on the user's request or decline it. A series of subsequent authorization decision calls may be necessary to come to the final go or no go decision.

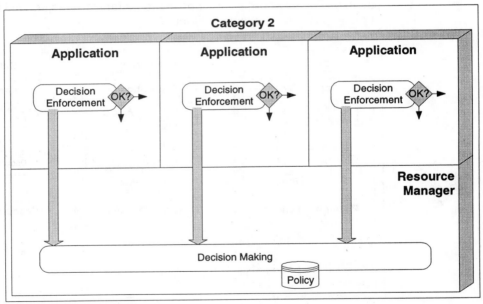

Figure 9-2   Category 2 systems

By separating the two functions (decision making and decision enforcement), it is much easier to achieve reusability of the decision making processes and consistency of the policies. The Tivoli Access Manager software architecture supports this category, providing a uniform framework for authorization decisions and Open Group's Authorization application programming interface (API) for its querying. Decision enforcement takes place on the blades in order to meet the needs of distributed applications acting in disparate environments with different security requirements.

However, an application based on a system of category 2 has to implement its own decision enforcement and, if not standardized (for example, based on Authorization API provided by Open Group), the decision requester as well, which may be considered to be more error-prone.

To avoid this problem, systems of category 3 rely on mechanisms provided by a resource manager and have no need to even maintain decision enforcement, as shown in Figure 9-3.

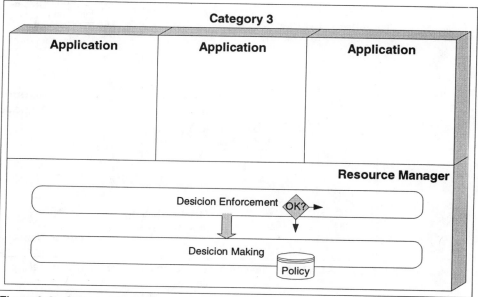

Figure 9-3   Category 3 systems

A Web server providing access to files in a defined directory is an application that falls in this category. In a simple case, it uses security mechanisms of the operating system that act as a resource manager. If a user is requesting an HTML document, the operating system's file permissions are decisive for granting access. The application (Web server) requests a resource (file), managed by the operating system. While serving the request, the operating system makes a decision, based on the permission attributes (policy) of the requested file, and, if allowed, provides access to the file (decision enforcement) by the Web server. WebSphere Enterprise Java Bean (EJB) based applications work in a similar fashion.

This approach works just fine as long as applications reside together with the resource manager on the same system. But it becomes much more difficult to manage if multiple applications of the same kind are distributed through the IT-environment and communicate with the same resource manager. Moreover, as soon as a need arises to establish security policies throughout applications based on different resource managers of different kinds, a new consolidation layer is required. As shown in Figure 9-4, Access Manager provides that uniform authorization framework, which allows you to consolidate the decision making process based on a consistent policy database.

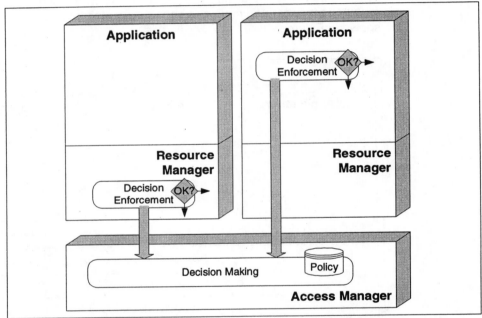

Figure 9-4   Policy Enforcement based on consistent decision making

9.3 WebSphere Application Server Version 4.0 security

WebSphere Application Server Version 4 is a Java 2 Enterprise Edition, or J2EE 1.2 compliant Java application server. It implements the required services as they are specified. There have been a number of changes in the architecture and functionality of WebSphere Application Server Version 4.0 in order to become compliant with J2EE 1.2. Probably the most noticeable change is the structure of the artifacts that make up an application and are installed into WebSphere. All components intended to run in WebSphere are now packaged as Enterprise Archive files (EAR). Another change is the addition of a major new tool, the

Application Assembly Tool (AAT). The AAT is used to build an EAR from component modules, and configure all the deployment descriptors. In this chapter, we concentrate on the J2EE security features implemented in WebSphere Version 4.0:

- ► Role-based security
- ► Declarative security
- ► Programmatic security

Role-based security

One of the goals of the EJB 1.1 specification was to lessen the burden of application security on application developers. Previously, if a portion of code could only be executed by particular types of users, the code itself had to handle the authorization, often right within the business logic. For example, if only managers were allowed to execute a function, then each user attempting to call that function would have to be identifiable as a manager. This might require a lookup in an employee database to determine the user's employee type or group type. This lead to the development of category 1 systems, as described in Figure 9-1 on page 203.

EJB 1.1 and J2EE 1.2 attempt to move this security burden to the application *assemblers* and *deployers*. It allows them to define security roles, sets of permissions for access to Web resources, and specific EJB methods. The use of roles provide a level of indirection that allows the subsequent assignment of those roles to users and groups to be done at application installation time, rather than during development. It also allows security constraints within modules developed by different teams to be resolved at assembly, deployment, or installation time.

The J2EE specification defines a security role as a logical grouping of users that is defined by an Application Component Provider or assembler. It is then mapped by a deployer to security identities, for example, principals or groups, in the operational environment. A security role can be used either with declarative security or with programmatic security. Thus, WebSphere's security model has changed from permission-based to role-based.

Declarative security

The declarative security mechanisms, as part of J2EE, are stored in a document called deployment descriptor using a declarative syntax. Global security roles for a WebSphere application are stored in the XML deployment descriptor. Security roles for WebSphere components are stored in their corresponding deployment descriptors inside the EAR, Java archives (JARs), and Windows archives (WARs).

WebSphere uses method permissions, introduced in the EJB 1.1 specification, to describe security roles for EJBs. For a particular EJB resource, method permissions are the association of role names with the sets of methods, based on what types of permissions should be required to invoke the methods. Example 9-1 demonstrates a slightly abbreviated sample role description for EJB methods within an ejb-jar.xml deployment descriptor. Only a user that can be mapped to the security role Teller is allowed access to the methods getBalance and getLastTransaction of the bean AccountBean.

Example 9-1   Method permissions in the ejb-jar.xml deployment descriptor

```
<method-permission>
        <role-name>Teller</role-name>
        <method>
           <ejb-name>AccountBean</ejb-name>
           <method-name>getBalance</method-name>
        </method>
        <method>
           <ejb-name>AccountBean</ejb-name>
        <method-name>getLastTransactions</method-name>
        </method>
</method-permission>
```

If WebSphere security is enabled and EJBs have no method at all configured with security, then the default is to grant access to the EJB methods. If WebSphere security is enabled and at least one method has a security constraint, then the request to the EJBs is denied. This kind of behavior is different compared to the Web modules' components. By default, access is allowed to all Web resources. Parts of the Web resources can be protected using security constraints.

For a particular Web resource (servlet, JSP, and URL), security constraints are the association of role names with the sets of HTTP methods, based on what types of permissions should be required to access the resource. These are defined in the WAR's deployment descriptor. Example 9-2 shows a WAR deployment descriptor that restricts access to any URL containing the URL-pattern /sales/ to the methods HTTP-POST and HTTP-GET and to users, that can be mapped during runtime to a security role called SalesPerson.

Example 9-2   Security constraints and permissions in a WAR deployment descriptor

```
<web-app>
        <display-name>Retail Application</display-name>
        <security-constraint>
           <web-resource-collection>
              <web-resource-name>SalesInfo</web-resource-name>
              <url-pattern>/sales/*</url-pattern>
              <http-method>POST</http-method>
```

```
              <http-method>GET</http-method>
<             /web-resource-collection>
              <auth-constraint>
                <role-name>SalesPerson</role-name>
              </auth-constraint>
          </security-constraint>
     </web-app>
```

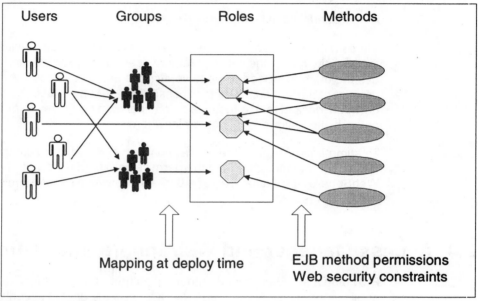

Figure 9-5   Role based security

Figure 9-5 depicts declarative security based on security roles. The objects (EJB methods, static Web pages, servlets, and JSPs) are protected by method permissions or security constraints. Permissions and constraints are mapped to security roles. The deployer grants access to roles for users and groups. So far, there is no need for a developer to implement a single line of code to achieve security.

Programmatic security
Declarative security is not always sufficient to express the security model of the application. Let us look at the example of a payment transaction. A customer has to have access to a bean method in order to transfer money. If he is granted access, he can perform any transaction he wants. In order to limit the amount of money that can be transferred by this user, the application needs to have knowledge about the role of the customer.

Developers can check security constraints programmatically using the name of the role. The API for programmatic security in J2EE 1.2 consists of two methods of the EJB EJBContext interface and two methods of the servlet HttpServletRequest interface:

► isCallerInRole (EJBContext)

► getCallerPrincipal (EJBContext)

► isUserInRole (HttpServletRequest)

► getUserPrincipal (HttpServletRequest)

These methods allow components to make business logic decisions based on the security role of the caller or remote user. In our example, the application may use the method isUserInRole to verify if the user is allowed to transfer the amount of a given sum. Another possibility would be to use the method getUserPrincipal to use the user's principal name as a key to get more authorization information stored elsewhere.

To summarize, WebSphere Application Server 4.0 authorization uses a role-based model rather than the permission-based model of previous versions. WebSphere Application Server 4.0 treats a role as a set of permissions to access particular resources.

9.4 Access Manager and WebSphere integration

Providing a standard-based authorization framework for WebSphere applications, Tivoli Access Manager supports the Java 2 security model as well as the Java Authentication and Authorization Services (JAAS) and Java 2 Enterprise Extensions (J2EE).

Integrating WebSphere and Access Manager adds WebSphere resources to the significant list of elements that can be managed via Tivoli Access Manager's consistent authorization policy, and it also adds to WebSphere applications the benefits that accrue in an Access Manager protected environment. The examples of this discussed in the previous chapters include URI-based access control, availability and scalability characteristics inherent in Access Manager implementations and the ability to support many authentication mechanisms without any impact to the target application and Web single sign-on, which are fully applicable for WebSphere Application Server.

The integration of WebSphere Application Server and Access Manager offers the following additional options/possibilities:

► Shared user registry

- Web single sign-on using:
  - Tivoli Global Sign-On (TGSO) junctions
  - Web Trust Association Interceptor (TAI)
  - WebSEAL LTPA cookie support
- Application integration utilizing:
  - Authorization Application Programming Interface (aznAPI)
  - JAAS
  - PDPermission
  - J2EE security

9.4.1 Shared user registry

Both WebSphere and Access Manager need a user registry to store user information, such as IDs and passwords. The first area of integration is for both products to use the same user registry, and so have a single, common set of users defined to both WebSphere and Access Manager. They each support a number of Lightweight Directory Access Protocol (LDAP) servers for this purpose. Obviously, to share the same user registry you must choose a server that both products support. Table 9-1 provides on overview of supported user registries for WebSphere 4.0.2 and Access Manager 3.9.

Table 9-1 LDAP directories supported by WebSphere and Access Manager

LDAP Directory	WebSphere 4.0.2 support	Access Manager 3.9 support
Netscape iPlanet Directory Server 5.0	X (not on AIX 5.x)	X
Lotus Domino Enterprise Server 5.0.5	X	Access Manager (AM) for Windows
IBM SecureWay Directory 3.2.1	X	X
Windows 2000 Active Directory 2000	X	X
Critical Path InJoin Directory		X

For the newest information about LDAP support in WebSphere 4.0.2 refer to:

`http://www-3.ibm.com/software/webservers/appserv/doc/v40/prereqs/ae_v402.htm`

Information for WebSphere 3.5.3 can be found at:

`http://www-3.ibm.com/software/webservers/appserv/doc/v35/idx_aas.htm`

Administration considerations

WebSphere has no interface for administering users in an LDAP server, so you have to use the tools that are provided with the LDAP Server product. Access Manager, on the other hand, does have tools: the `pdadmin` command and the WPM Administrator Console.

WebSphere never changes the default installation of the LDAP server, but Access Manager does. WebSphere and the LDAP server need additional configuration after Access Manager has been installed to allow them all to work together. The changes to be aware of are:

► Anonymous access to LDAP is no longer permitted. WebSphere must be configured with a Bind Distinguished Name.

► Schema is modified. The default WebSphere group filter defined for the particular LDAP server must be updated.

► LDAP access control lists (ACLs) are modified. You require a special privilege to be able to perform a directory-search. WebSphere needs to be able to perform directory-searchs to retrieve users and groups and populate user and group-selection lists, so the WebSphere administration ID must be added to the LDAP's Security group.

9.4.2 Single sign-on

Single sign-on between Access Manager and WebSphere can be achieved using three different mechanisms:

► TGSO junctions
► Trust Association Interceptor
► LTPA cookies

TGSO junctions

Access Manager's Global-Sign-On provides a mapping between the primary user identity (used for login to WebSEAL) and another user ID/password that exists in another user registry.

In a pure WebSphere environment, accessing a protected URL will cause an HTTP 401 challenge to the browser. The end user enters their authentication details (user ID and password) and this information is passed in a basic authentication (BA) header back to WebSphere. WebSphere Application Server then uses the authentication information to perform an LDAP-bind to authenticate the user.

The different TGSO options and capabilities are described in detail in Section 8.5.1, "Tivoli Global Sign-On (TGSO)-lockbox" on page 191.

Web Trust Association Interceptor (TAI)

In a customer's corporate distributed environment, the Access Manager security architecture utilizes a reverse proxy security server, WebSEAL, as an entry point to all service requests. The intent of this implementation is to have WebSEAL as the only exposed entry point. As such, it authenticates all requests that come in and provides course-granularity junction point authorization.

When WebSphere is used as a back-end server it further exploits its fine-grained access control. WebSEAL can pass to WebSphere an HTTP request that includes credentials of the authenticated user. WebSphere can then use these credentials to authorize the request.

Former versions of WebSphere did not understand the format of the credential information passed by WebSEAL. WebSphere 3.5.3 and its later versions, include a new execution mode in its security framework, the Trust Association Interceptor Mode, in which it can interface with third-party objects that intercept requests issued by trusted proxy servers, such as WebSEAL. These objects are collectively known as *Trust Association Interceptors* or simply *interceptors*.

TAI implies that WebSphere's security application recognizes and processes HTTP requests received from WebSEAL. WebSphere and WebSEAL engage in a contract in which the former will give its full trust to the latter, which means that WebSEAL will apply its authentication policies on every Web request that is dispatched to WebSphere.

This trust is validated by the interceptors that reside in the WebSphere environment for every request received. The method of validation is agreed upon by WebSEAL and the interceptor. Setting values for parameters defined in the webseal.properties file that resides on the WebSphere Application Server server will determine the method of validation for the interceptors.

The TAI version that ships with Access Manager 3.9 can be configured in three different ways:

► Trust Association with -b supply option

- ► Trust Association without -b supply option (improved version)
- ► Trust Association using mutually authenticated SSL

In the following sections, we describe the different options and requirements.

Using TAI with a -b supply junction

In order to get TAI to work, there must be a WebSEAL junction to the WebSphere Application Server. In the earlier version of TAI, the only available authentication of WebSEAL was to secure the junction with the -b supply option, which has an associated risk for security attacks. The WebSEAL user ID/password used in TAI is not authenticated by WebSEAL, but is used by WebSphere to authenticate the traffic coming from WebSEAL. The following steps, as depicted in Figure 9-6, explain this in more detail:

- ► When a user requests access to a WebSphere protected resource through his browser, WebSEAL authenticates the user, generates the Extended Privilege Attribute Certificate (EPAC) (based on userid=John) and obtains his own WebSEAL user ID/password (ws_itso/chuy5) from the pd.conf file located on the WebSEAL server.

- ► WebSEAL sends this WebSEAL user ID/password in the BA header along with the authenticated user credentials in the iv-user, iv-groups and iv-creds fields.

- ► WebSphere extracts the WebSEAL user ID/password in the BA header to bind to LDAP in order to authenticate the traffic from WebSEAL.

- ► The user ID in the iv-user header is extracted by WebSphere and used to authorize the request to access the protected resource.

- ► Because WebSphere trusts the TAI authentication over the junction (-b supply), the password for the user requesting access is not required or used by WebSphere.

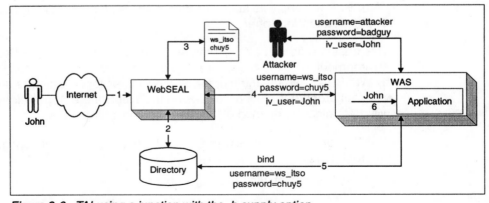

Figure 9-6   TAI using a junction with the -b supply option

Suppose now that we have an attacker who is a legitimate user of some other part of the system. This attacker can impersonate any other user by creating a packet with his own user ID and password in the BA header and any other user's ID in the iv-user header. WebSphere will bind to LDAP and use the attacker's ID to authenticate the traffic. The user ID in the iv-user header is used to authorize access to a protected WebSphere resource. This is not a good situation if the protected resource is, for example, a payroll system.

Using TAI without a -b supply junction

The new and current version of TAI provides better security. Only WebSEAL's password is sent in the BA header, which is being defined as the basic-dummy-passwd value in the pd.conf file located on the WebSEAL server. WebSphere uses the password sent in the BA header and then extracts WebSEAL's UserID value from the webseal.properties file located on the WebSphere Server to authenticate the traffic from WebSEAL.

> **Note:** The com.ibm.websphere.security.WebSEAL.username value in the webseal.prpoperties file contains the WebSEAL UserID.

Attackers who are legitimate users of some other part of the system would no longer be able to use their own user ID and password to impersonate a valid user. They would need access to the WebSEAL password. This version of TAI is shown in Figure 9-7.

Where an internal network is defined as secure, TAI without the -b supply option can be used without SSL.

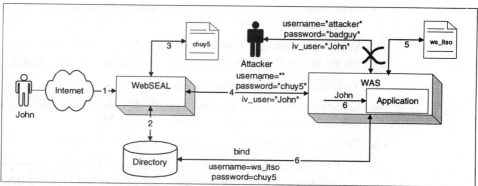

Figure 9-7 TAI using a junction without the -b supply option

Using TAI with mutually authenticated SSL junction

This approach improves the performance by eliminating the necessity of WebSphere calling LDAP for authentication of each WebSEAL connection. The webseal.propeties file is located on the WebSphere Application Server and by setting the value of the `com.ibm.websphere.security.WebSEAL.mutualSSL` to yes, we can eliminate a BIND to LDAP to validate WebSEAL's identity. It can only be used when the junction between WebSEAL and WebSphere is a *mutually authenticated* SSL junction, as described in the section "Mutually Authenticated SSL Junctions" in the *Access Manager WebSEAL Administration Guide*. WebSphere will *trust* this junction and no additional mechanism is used to authenticate WebSEAL. This situation is depicted in Figure 9-8.

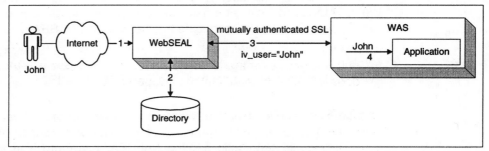

Figure 9-8   TAI using a mutually authenticated SSL junction

Summary of how TAI works

Let us see how Trust Association works using the WebSphere Administration Applications:

1. The browser requests a URI that WebSEAL recognizes to be a protected resource.

2. WebSEAL prompts the user to provide a user ID and password (this can either be via Basic Authentication challenge or via a Custom Form).

3. WebSEAL authenticates the user.

4. Once properly authenticated, WebSEAL forwards a modified HTTP request to the back-end WebSphere server.

5. Depending on the configuration:

   – If the junction has been defined without -b supply, the modified HTTP request contains the `basic-dummy-passwd` value in the BA header field that is only used between WebSEAL and WebSphere. This password and the value of the `com.ibm.websphere.security.WebSEAL.username` property is used to bind to LDAP. If this bind is successful, WebSphere will trust this session and the values sent with the http headers (this is done in method: validateEstablishedTrust()).

- If the junction has been defined with -b supply, the modified HTTP request contains the user ID and password value of WebSEAL in the BA header field and the requestor's user ID in the iv-user field. WebSphere binds to LDAP using the user ID and password specified in the BA header.

- Alternatively, if the junction between WebSEAL and WebSphere is a mutually authenticated SSL junction and the property value of com.ibm.websphere.security.WebSEAL.mutualSSL is yes, WebSphere trusts the session and does not need to bind to LDAP.

6. TAI then extracts the value of the iv-user http header and returns this as the authenticated user that should be used by WebSphere authorization (this is done in method: getAuthenticatedUsername()).

WebSEAL LTPA cookie support

WebSphere Application Server uses an LTPA Token (a cookie by another name) to provide single Sign-On across multiple WebSphere servers. After the user has been authenticated by WebSphere, an LTPA cookie is created and sent to the browser. The browser will return this cookie on subsequent requests, allowing the origin WebSphere Application Server (or other WebSphere Application Server within the same TCP domain) to recognize the user. The LTPA cookie is protected by a 3DES key, which also proves that it was created by a trusted source.

Access Manager WebSEAL can generate an LTPA cookie that will be accepted by the WebSphere Server. The WebSphere server will trust this LTPA cookie because it is encrypted with the correct shared key.

Figure 9-9 on page 218 shows a WebSEAL junction that is configured for LTPA. An LTPA key is generated on the WebSphere machine and then exported to a keyfile (protected by a password). This keyfile must then be manually copied to the WebSEAL machine. When the junction to the WebSphere server is configured, it is specified as an LTPA junction, and the keyfile and password are given as parameters.

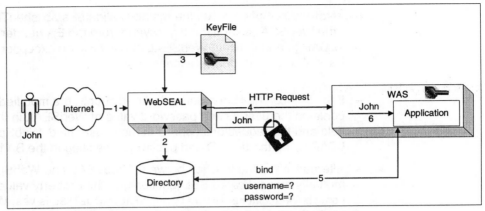

Figure 9-9 WebSEAL creates LTPA cookies for authenticated users

When a user authenticates to WebSEAL and requests a resource on this junction, WebSEAL creates an LTPA cookie using the key from the keyfile. This encrypted cookie contains the Access Manager UserID of the user and is included in the HTTP request sent to the WebSphere server. When WebSphere receives the HTTP request, it extracts the UserID from the LTPA cookie and uses it to build WebSphere's credential for the user. It would be usual for WebSEAL and WebSphere to share a registry to avoid synchronization problems. WebSphere then applies its own authorization decision to the request. A general description of LTPA is provided in Section 8.5.7, "Using LTPA authentication with WebSEAL" on page 198.

How to select the SSO option

In fact, if you assume that Access Manager and WebSphere share a user registry, then TGSO would be the last choice for SSO. Instead, using either the Trust Association Interceptor (TAI) or the LTPA support would be the preferred solution. TGSO is only an option for the following scenarios:

► WebSEAL and WebSphere rely on different user registries. Under this circumstance, you may need to supply a different user ID and password combination for the user to WebSphere that is meaningful to WebSphere's user registry.

► There might be situations, even in the case of a shared user registry, where -b gso might be useful. For example, if internal users should be able to connect to WebSphere directly using basic authentication, and then they should have indirect access through WebSEAL with WebSEAL being configured to provide forms based login.

Otherwise, we recommend the TAI option, because it is easy to configure and maintain. There is no key distribution or periodic update required. TAI is also the method used when WebSphere supports integration with third party reverse proxy security servers in general.

9.4.3 Application integration

If we want to integrate WebSphere applications with Tivoli Access Manager we have to distinguish between:

► Integration of new applications that are to be developed or existing applications that will be changed

► Integration of existing applications without any changes

Access Manager provides a C version of the Authorization API (aznAPI) and pure Java classes: *PDPermission*, *PDPrincipal* and *PDLoginModule*. Java wrapper classes for the aznAPI are also available from Open Source. PDPermission is usable in both a Java Authentication and Authorization Services (JAAS) and non-JAAS environment. These methods can be used for securing new applications or to adjust existing applications. We provide an overview of these methods in "aznAPI" on page 219 and "PDPermission and JAAS" on page 219.

Often, there are already existing J2EE applications secured by WebSphere declarative security and/or using J2EE security methods. Tivoli Access Manager for WebSphere Application Server offers the possibility to import WebSphere security definitions into Access Manager's object space. The function that determines if a user is granted any permitted roles is now handled by Access Manager. We describe Tivoli Access Manager for WebSphere Application Server in "Access Manager for WebSphere Application Server" on page 221.

aznAPI

aznAPI is an API specifically designed for Access Manager. It has been approved by the OpenGroup as the standard implementation of the Authorization Model. Access Manager provides a C version of the API, and Java Wrappers are available as Open Source. WebSphere applications may use the aznAPI to retrieve fine-grained authorization information about a user.

PDPermission and JAAS

The original Java security model dealt almost exclusively with the needs of the Java environment's first major user, the Web browser. It focused on the complexities of secure usage of mobile code, so it worried about the origins of code and its authors, as indicated by digital signatures. The Java 2 environment generalizes that model to concern itself with all code, not just that loaded from remote locations. The Java 2 architecture also restructures the internals of the Java run-time environment to accommodate a very fine-grained usage of security. JAAS, a standard extension of the Java 2 environment, adds in the concept of who the user is that is running the code and factors this information into its security decisions.

All levels of Java security have been policy based. This means that authorization to perform an action is not hard coded into the Java run time or executables. Instead, the Java environment consults policy external to the code to make security decisions, and therefore maps to systems of category 2 or 3, as described previously in Section 9.2, "Security design objectives" on page 203. In the simplest case, this policy is implemented in a flat file, which somewhat limits its scalability and also adds administrative overhead.

To overcome the flat file implementation of Java 2 policy, and to converge to a single security model, the authorization framework provided by Access Manager can be leveraged from inside a normal Java security check. As mentioned earlier, the most natural and architecturally pleasing implementation of this support is inside a JAAS framework. Support for this standard provides the flexibility for Java developers to leverage fine-grained usage of security and authorization services as an integral component of their application and platform software.

With the Java 2 and JAAS support delivered in Tivoli Access Manager, Java applications can:

► Invoke the Tivoli Access Manager supplied JAAS LoginModule to acquire authentication/ authorization credentials from Access Manager

► Use the PDPermission class to request authorization decisions

This offers Java application developers the advantages that:

► The security of Java applications that use PDPermission is managed using the same, consistent model as the rest of the enterprise.

► Java developers do not need to learn anything additional beyond Java 2 and JAAS.

► Updates to security policy involve Tivoli Access Manager-based administrator actions, rather than any code updates.

Today, JSPs, servlets, and EJBs can take direct advantages of these services. When WebSphere containers support Java 2 security, EJB developers can avoid the need to make security calls by having the containers handle security while they focus on business logic.

There are two options for implementing fine-grained authorization (at the level of actions on objects) within servlets and EJBs today:

- Given the Access Manager credential information (EPAC) passed in the HTTP header, the servlet or the EJB would have to use the PDPermission class extensions directly to query Access Manager for access decisions. The access enforcement is still the responsibility of the application (servlet or EJB).

- Develop a proxy bean (a session bean) within an EJB. This proxy bean will intercept all method invocations and communicate with Access Manager (using the PDPermission class) to obtain the access decision and enforce it.

Access Manager for WebSphere Application Server

If the application is designed as a J2EE application, it would rely on the J2EE security methods to get a user ID and role. Tivoli Access Manager for WebSphere Application Server provides container-based authorization and centralized policy management for WebSphere Application Server Version 4.0.2. Tivoli Access Manager for WebSphere Application Server is implemented as an Access Manager aznAPI application running on the WebSphere Application Server instance.

A graphical user interface utility, the Access Manager Web Portal Manager, and the `pdadmin` command provide a single point for security management of common identities, user profiles, and authorization mechanisms.

Access Manager for WebSphere Application Server supports applications that use the J2EE Security Classes without requiring any coding or deployment changes to the applications.

Tivoli Access Manager for WebSphere Application Server is used to evaluate access requests from a user to protected resources based on the following tasks:

- Authentication of the user

- Determination if the user has been granted the required role by examining the WebSphere deployment descriptor

- The WebSphere container will use Access Manager to perform role membership checks for security code added directly into an application (programmatic security)

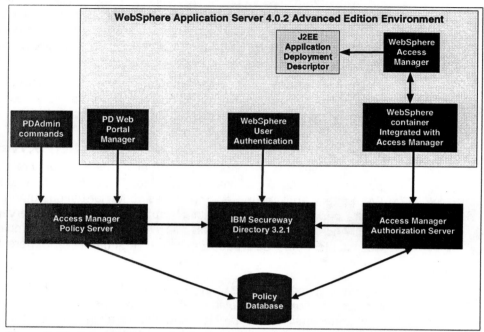

Figure 9-10   Access Manager integration with WebSphere Application Server

Figure 9-10 shows the integration of Access Manager with WebSphere Application Server Advanced Edition Version 4.0.2. When a user tries to access a protected resource by running an application with J2EE security, the following sequence of events occur:

1. WebSphere Application Server authenticates the user. For WebSphere Advanced Edition, the authentication is against SecureWay Directory Version 3.2.1 LDAP user registry. This LDAP user registry is shared with Access Manager.

2. WebSphere container collects information from the application deployment descriptor to determine the required role membership for the protected resource.

3. The WebSphere container uses the integrated Access Manager module to request an authorization decision from the Access Manager authorization server.

4. The Authorization Server obtains the user credentials from the SecureWay 3.2.1 LDAP users registry and checks the users permissions for a specified role. The Access Manager security model uses the definitions stored in the protected object namespace to build a hierarchy of resources to which ACLs can be attached. These ACLs define the mapping of roles in the J2EE

application deployment descriptor to users and/or groups defined in SecureWay LDAP 3.2.1 user registry.

5. The Authorization Server returns the access decision to the WebSphere container, which either grants or denies access to the protected resource.

Migration of roles to principals and groups

Tivoli Access Manager for WebSphere Application Server has a migration utility that maps the roles in WebSphere Application Server to Access Manager principals and groups.

The *Tivoli Access Manager for WebSphere Application Server User Guide Version 3.9* provides a fully detailed chapter on this migration utility and is recommend for further study. In this chapter, we will give a brief description of the migration utility.

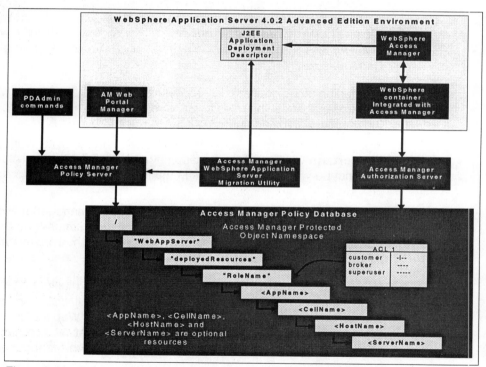

Figure 9-11   Access Manager utility to map roles to principals and groups

Figure 9-11 depicts the single steps executed by the migration utility. This utility extracts information on roles from the J2EE deployment descriptor and maps them to group/principal information in Access Manager.

This information is converted into Access Manager format and it is passed to the Access Manager Policy Server using the PDAdmin API, which is used to add entries to the protected object namespace to represent roles defined for the application. The appropriate principals and groups are added to the ACLs that are attached to the new objects. This migration utility is executed on the machine that has access to the J2EE application deployment descriptors (EAR files).

After migration, the system administrator can use the `pdadmin` commands or the Access Manager Web Portal Manager to modify the ACLs and add new roles and users.

> **Attention:** The migration utility is executed only once, prior to application run time. It must not be used as a maintenance tool for roles. Use either the `pdadmin` command or the Access Manager Web Portal Manager to manage roles.

Central policy management for multiple WebSphere servers

Tivoli Access Manager can manage security policy across multiple WebSphere Servers.

After using the migration utility as described earlier, the Access Manager Web Portal Manager can be used to manage changes in security definitions related to the mapping of roles to principals and groups.

> **Important:** Changes to role mapping made through the WebSphere console will not be visible in the Access Manager security model.

The Access Manager security model may also be managed using the `pdadmin` commands. Access Manager also provides a programmatic interface to administration tasks accomplished by `pdadmin` and the Web Portal Manager. The APIs can be used by programmers to develop tasks specific to an application.

In our security architecture, we have chosen to use multiple WebSphere servers to host a new Internet application. This is a high availability consideration; Server 2 is a mirror copy of Server 1. Each server accepts Web traffic simultaneously routed to it through the load balancing capabilities of WebSeal. Central administration of the security policy is required to achieve this.

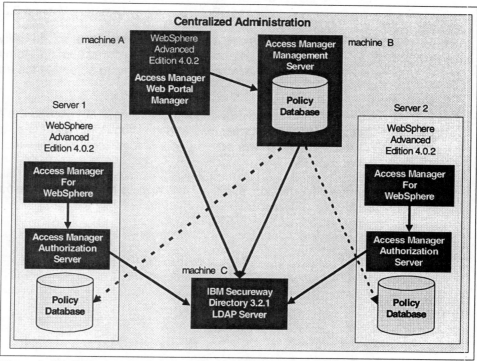

Figure 9-12   Central administration for multiple WebSphere servers

Figure 9-12 illustrates central administration of two WebSphere servers. The Access Manager Web Portal Manager has been installed on *machine A*. Access Manager Policy Server with the master policy database is installed on *machine B*. The Web Portal Manager uses the Access Manager Policy Server to administer the security policy.

Two WebSphere Advanced Edition Version 4.0.2 machines are shown, *server 1* and *server 2*. Access Manager Authorization Server is also installed on these machines. Co-location of Access Manager Authorization Server with WebSphere Application Server optimizes performance when making authorization decisions. This is because Tivoli Access Manager for WebSphere Application Server is an aznAPI application, and it communicates with the Authorization Server. Therefore, placing the Authorization Server on the same machine as the WebSphere Application Server application eliminates network connection overhead. This configuration is recommended.

The Access Manager policy databases on *server 1* and *server 2* are replicated from machine B, which improves performance and fail-over capability.

Access Manager servers and the WebSphere servers share the same LDAP user registry, in this case, IBM SecureWay Directory Version 3.2.1.

Access Manager provides a powerful command-line based utility (**pdadmin**) for the management of the Access Manager security domain. Administrators can also use this utility within scripts or programs to automate the administrations tasks.

Access Manager also provides a programmatic interface to the administration tasks accomplished by **pdadmin** and the Web Portal Manager. Application developers can use this API to perform administration tasks that are specific to the application.

For more information, see the *Tivoli Access Manager Administration API Developer Reference.*

Access control in a distributed environment

To this point, our discussions of Access Manager have focused primarily on WebSEAL scenarios in which all components are typically deployed in a relatively contained single security domain deployment environment at a single site. This chapter addresses key issues relating to situations where components of both single and multiple Access Manager secure domains may be distributed among multiple sites. We also touch on the use of Access Manager for Business Integration as a component of a distributed application.

Note: Due to the latest IBM Tivoli changes in naming and branding, you will be confronted with the new name for Tivoli Policy Director for MQ Series: IBM Tivoli Access Manager for Business Integration. On some occasions, when we are referring to older versions of the product, we still use Policy Director Version 3.8 or Version 3.7. All references to Tivoli Access Manager are based on the current Version 3.9, which becomes available in April 2002.

10.1 Cross-site distribution of a single security domain

In order to introduce the aspects of multiple security domains, let us take a closer look at the distributed Web security requirements at Stocks-4u.com.

Earlier, in Chapter 6, "A basic WebSEAL scenario" on page 143, we introduced Stocks-4u.com's key Web security requirements. Our scenario discussion focused on supporting a Web security infrastructure at a single site - the San Diego IT Center. We mentioned the need for future expansion of Internet operations into the Savannah center to provide for a redundant access capability with load-balancing for customers on the US East and West coasts. After the initial Access Manager deployment in San Diego, Stocks-4u.com management has initiated planning for an extension of the security infrastructure to the Savannah IT Center, starting with a review of key business and technical requirements.

10.1.1 Business requirements

The need to distribute Web security is related to some key business issues:

► The growth rate of the customer base will require Internet application capacity to double over the coming year, and double again the following year. The San Diego site will require expansion to support this growth. However, Savannah has substantial additional space which, if utilized, could reduce the San Diego expansion need by 70 percent.

► Stocks-4u.com competitors have been promoting higher service availability levels. Competitive pressures require the company support equivalent capability. A recent partial site power failure at the San Diego IT center demonstrated that expected availability levels cannot be achieved by simply replicating Access Manager servers at a single site.

► Related to the above, as part of its premium service offering, Stocks-4u.com has recently established service level agreements in place with a number of its key customers. Should it fail to achieve service level targets, these customers are entitled to substantial levels of compensation.

► The majority of internal applications are deployed in Savannah. To utilize Access Manager security capabilities, internal user browser access must be routed through a WebSEAL server in San Diego. However, 68 percent of company employees are connected to the company intranet through the Savannah IT Center. A consultant has found that 15 percent of the company's total long-haul telecom cost is associated with routing internal HTTP/HTTPS traffic through San Diego.

From the above, the following business requirements have been proposed by management:

- Savannah facilities be fully utilized to minimize the San Diego expansion requirement.

- Internet customer application access must be immune to a San Diego site failure.

- Management has directed that cross-site telecom costs for internal applications be reduced by 25 percent and the savings be used to expand network support for customer applications.

10.1.2 Technical requirements

An analysis of Stocks-4u.com business requirements has established the following key technical requirements:

- Internet users must be able to securely access applications via a Web browser through either San Diego or Savannah.

- In the event of a site failure or shutdown, all security functions must be provided through the surviving site.

- Internal HTTP/HTTPS application traffic must be routed through the closest IT center (San Diego or Savannah).

- The Stocks-4u.com network must provide direct network linkages from San Diego to New York trading systems.

If these technical requirements are met, the business requirements will be easily satisfied, and Stocks-4u.com will also be well positioned for future expansion.

Security architecture changes

Currently, Access Manager components are deployed only in San Diego. The updated architecture will add new Access Manager components in the Savannah IT Center. There will be a single security domain sharing a common user registry, as shown below in Figure 10-1 on page 230.

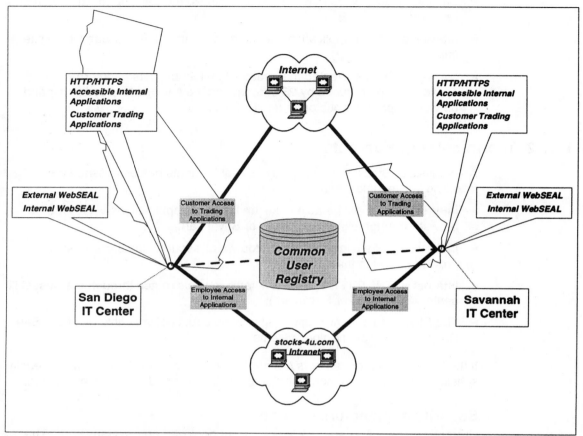

Figure 10-1   Stocks-4u.com security domain

Network changes

To support a distributed environment, the company has planned some changes to their network. Previously, customer trade transactions required routing through Savannah and ML&J in New York. A new T3 link is planned which will directly connect San Diego to New York trading systems. Another link from the Internet to Savannah is planned to support direct access as customer application web servers are deployed there. Figure 10-2 on page 231 shows the new Stocks-4u.com corporate network connectivity.

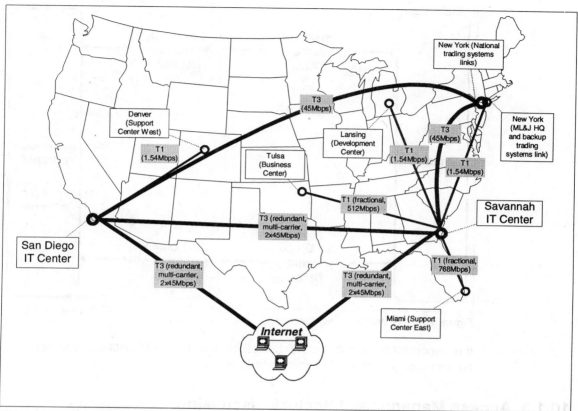

Figure 10-2   Stocks-4u.com updated data network

Within the Savannah IT Center, the internal network configuration will also change to support the new requirements. The new configuration will add an Internet demilitarized zone (DMZ), providing both IT centers with similar zone structure, as shown below in Figure 10-3 on page 232.

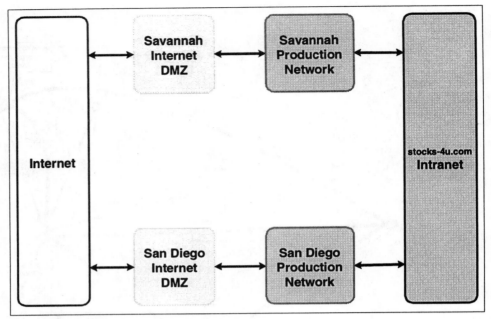

Figure 10-3   IT center network zones

It is important to note that communication between the IT center production zones must go through the corporate intranet.

10.1.3 Access Manager architecture discussion

In the initial WebSEAL deployment, all Access Manager components were installed in San Diego. In the distributed architecture, new Access Manager components must be deployed in Savannah. The question is, which components? In this scenario, we must be concerned about:

► WebSEAL servers
► The Access Manager Policy Server
► The User Registry
► The Web Portal Manager

WebSEAL servers

Certainly, we know that we will need to put WebSEAL servers in Savannah to avoid rerouting requests unnecessarily through San Diego. There will be both internal and external WebSEAL servers at each IT center. As in the existing Access Manager deployment, shown in Figure 6-5 on page 154, the external WebSEAL servers will go into the Internet DMZs, and the internal WebSEAL servers will go in the production networks.

WebSEAL junctions

WebSEAL junctions may be cross-site, that is, WebSEAL servers in San Diego may be junctioned to back-end Web servers in Savannah and vice versa. This is not a problem as long as the cross-site communication between WebSEAL and the junctions is appropriately secured.

For external (Internet-facing) WebSEAL servers, there is another issue that must be addressed when junctioning cross-site. That is, an appropriate network configuration must be created to permit them to pass traffic from their respective DMZs into the production network at the remote site. This obviously is a more complex network scenario than the local site case. We will discuss some of these networking issues below.

As an alternative, Stocks-4u.com may choose to replicate all Web servers between sites so that all WebSEAL junctions are local. Figure 10-4 on page 234 below illustrates both approaches.

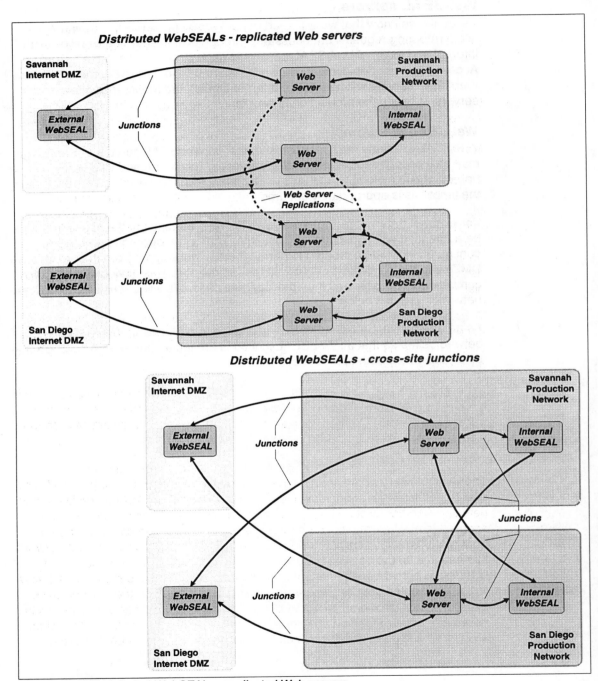

Figure 10-4   Distributed WebSEALs - replicated Web servers

Access Manager Policy Server

Because there currently can be only one Access Manager Policy Server for a security domain, the current server in San Diego will remain in place and will support both sites.

In the event of a San Diego site outage, Savannah WebSEAL servers will continue to operate. However, configuration changes cannot be made. To address an extended site outage situation, a backup system will be available to take over the Policy Server function. Configuration of a replacement Management Server involves special considerations.

Cross-site backup takeover considerations

Availability issues are often more involved when dealing with migration of functions across site locations. In a local fail-over situation, it is much easier to utilize specialized high-availability software (such as HACMP or Microsoft Cluster Server) to provide an automated recovery capability. Such products generally utilize special network/device connectivity and *heartbeating* to determine failure conditions and initiate a service takeover. Generally, a shared disk is used to assure data consistency

Consider that in a cross-site fail-over scenario, the network subnet addressing, depending on the particular network architecture, may be different between the sites. This means that a simple IP address takeover may not be sufficient to bring a backup system online.

In the case where the backup has a different IP address, services which access it will need to be told of the new address, either by reconfiguration or via domain name server (DNS) changes (and to successfully accomplish an address change via DNS, services must not be caching the old address).

In the alternative, a *shadow* standby network may be created at each site. These shadow networks are configured to the same subnet as the peer site, and are kept offline unless a takeover is required. The backup systems reside in this network. Another twist to this, which would permit the shadow network to be accessible at all times, would be to use NAT (Network Address Translation) in front of the shadow network during normal operation. This would permit network traffic to flow to the backup systems (for example, capturing of configuration updates, and so on). Then, should a takeover be required, the router would have to be removed in order for the backup systems to appear on the local network under the peer site subnet. This approach, of course, assumes a total peer site network failure or loss of communication, because the peer network cannot be accessible simultaneously with the shadow using the same subnet address.

Another problem is that of replicating the existing configuration. Generally, for Access Manager, this can be sufficiently handled by doing a periodic backup of critical files and replicating them to the backup site (There are also more sophisticated mechanisms, which can capture updates at the device level and replicate changes across sites).

Perhaps the most difficult issue of all, however, is that of how to deal with the following:

► How can a failure of the primary server be reliably determined across site locations?

► If a backup server takes over, what happens when the primary comes back up?

The reason these issues are so important is because there are unpleasant scenarios that can occur should a backup takeover occur by mistake or without appropriate advance process planning - especially if it occurs when the primary is still actually active (which creates what is known as a *split-brain* scenario).

A communication failure across sites is not sufficient to determine with certainty that the primary has failed. And once a backup takes over Policy Server functionality, the primary cannot be permitted to return to full operation without assurances that updates that may have occurred in the interim have been reconciled.

In addition to a manual processes that may be executed to bring a backup server online in a cross-site situation, there are products that provide sophisticated cross-site fail-over capabilities. They are beyond the scope of this book.

The User Registry

In the existing San Diego configuration, there is a master LDAP server for the User Registry, and an LDAP replica of the registry that is used by WebSEAL for authentication. In our distributed configuration, we will place an additional replica in the Savannah production network. This replica will be used by the Savannah WebSEAL servers for user authentication, with the San Diego replica as a backup. The master will remain in San Diego.

In this configuration, if the San Diego site goes down, the Savannah WebSEAL servers will still have registry services available for authentication. However, updates go through the San Diego master. In the event of an extended San Diego outage, a backup replica server will be *promoted* to a new master.

Web Portal Manager

An additional instance of the Web Portal Manager will be installed in Savannah.

Distributed server configuration

Figure 10-5 shows the distributed Access Manager server configuration.

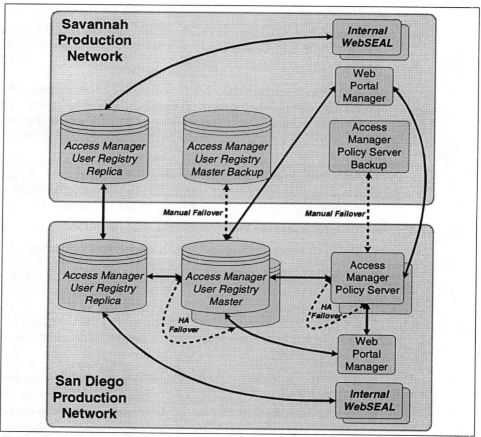

Figure 10-5   Stocks-4u.com production network distributed server configuration

10.1.4 Communication between distributed components

While we have established where Access Manager components will be placed, we have not yet addressed cross-site network communication issues.

Cross-site component interactions

WebSEAL servers will generally communicate with a local User Registry instance for authentication. Cross-site communication issues occur with managing and updating configuration data. The master LDAP server and the Policy Server in San Diego must communicate with WebSEAL servers in the Savannah Internet DMZ and Production networks.

The LDAP master in San Diego must communicate with its Savannah replica(s), and must also be accessible from the Savannah Web Portal Manager.

The Policy Server in San Diego must communicate with the WebSEAL servers in Savannah, and must also be accessible from the Savannah Web Portal Manager.

In the network configuration described earlier, communication between production network hosts must go through the Stocks-4u.com intranet. Clearly, it may not be acceptable for security server communications to cross through the Stocks-4u.com intranet unprotected. This requires special considerations.

Cross-site communication alternatives

To assure the integrity and privacy of cross-site traffic between security components, there are three approaches we will consider:

► Using SSL across the open Stocks-4u.com intranet
► Using VPN capabilities to tunnel between network zones
► Bridging of network zones

SSL

All Access Manager components support the ability to interact via SSL:

► The Access Manager Policy Server communicates with WebSEAL and other blades via SSL.

► The Web Portal Manager communicates with the Access Manager Policy Server via SSL.

► The SecureWay LDAP User Registry can be configured to communicate via SSL. (Other supported LDAP servers may support SSL as well.)

► WebSEAL may be configured to communicate with junctioned servers via SSL, provided the servers support it.

If all components can be configured to use SSL, then Stocks-4u.com cross-site communication may be securely implemented using the company intranet. This may be a viable approach, especially in situations where the amount of cross-site communication is relatively small, and the SSL overhead remains low.

Figure 10-6 below shows the use of SSL between Stocks-4u.com IT centers.

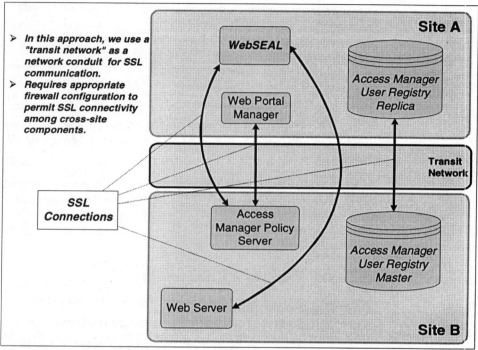

Figure 10-6   Cross-site SSL communication

A VPN approach

An alternative approach to cross-site communication involves the use of VPN technology to *tunnel* between the production networks. For example, a VPN tunnel can be created through the company intranet, which effectively permits unrestricted communication among the cross-site components without additional measures. The VPN traffic may be encrypted, providing for the integrity and privacy of communication between San Diego and Savannah without using SSL.

This approach has the advantage that local communication among Access Manager components does not have to incur encryption overhead as it may if SSL were used. Also, because the hardware/software cost of VPN technology has lowered, it is no longer cost-prohibitive in many cases. Figure 10-7 illustrates the use of a VPN for Stocks-4u.com cross-site Access Manager traffic.

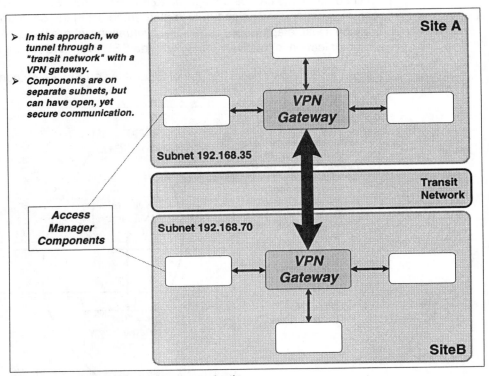

Figure 10-7   Cross-site VPN communication

Bridging production networks

A third approach may be to effectively *merge* the San Diego and Savannah production networks by *bridging* them. The two production networks may then co-exist within a single IP subnet. Current network hardware capabilities and costs may make this an attractive approach, especially because it may provide for cross-site IP address takeover when bringing up a backup Policy Server or LDAP master.

Note: The ability to migrate IP addresses across sites does not eliminate the *split-brain* issue mentioned earlier. What it does do, however, is eliminate the need to reconfigure other systems to use alternate IP addresses for backup servers, or to create a *shadow* backup network at the site. In any case, caution and proper planning is still necessary in implementing any availability solution.

Figure 10-8 on page 241 illustrates the use of a bridged approach to distributing Access Manager components between San Diego and Savannah.

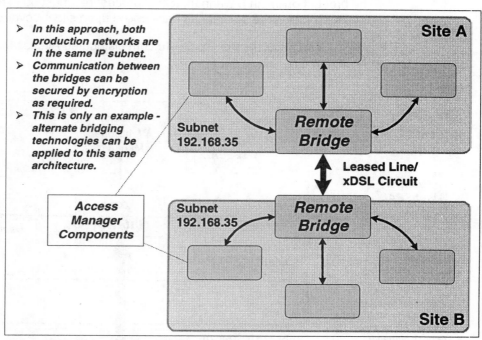

In this approach, both production networks are in the same IP subnet.

Communication between the bridges can be secured by encryption as required.

This is only an example - alternate bridging technologies can be applied to this same architecture.

Site A

Subnet 192.168.35

Remote Bridge

Leased Line/ xDSL Circuit

Access Manager Components

Subnet 192.168.35

Remote Bridge

Site B

Figure 10-8   Bridged cross-site communication

10.1.5 Stocks-4u.com distributed architecture

Summarizing the above architecture discussion, the Stocks-4u.com distributed Access Manager architecture will include the following:

► An architectural choice has been made to utilize a VPN tunnel to connect the Stocks-4u.com production networks together.

► WebSEAL hosts will junction across sites for internal applications. For external (customer) applications, Web servers will be replicated across sites and WebSEAL junctions will be local.

► Within the San Diego site, a standard high-availability configuration using HACMP will be used with the Access Manager Policy Server and the LDAP master. This will assure availability of services as long as the San Diego site remains operational.

► In the event of a communication disruption between San Diego and Savannah, operation will continue without configuration update capability at the Savannah IT Center.

► In the event of a confirmed San Diego site outage lasting more than eight hours, a backup Access Manager Policy server and a new LDAP master will be brought online in Savannah. (Strict procedures must be in place for this and for bringing the old servers back online upon site recovery.)

Figure 10-9 summarizes the Stocks-4u.com distributed Access Manager architecture.

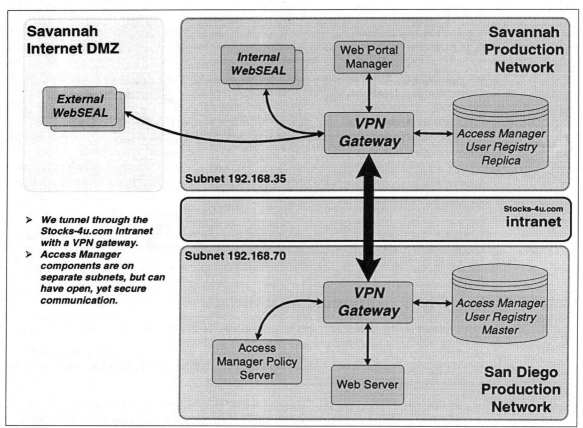

Figure 10-9   Stocks-4u.com distributed WebSEAL architecture summary

10.2 Distributed security domains

Another type of distributed scenario involves single sign-on for access to resources in multiple security domains (that is, each domain has its own user registry and security policy definitions). Consider two divisions of a company, each offering Web-based services to Internet customers. Each division has deployed WebSEAL in separate security domains. However, there is a requirement for certain users in one domain to access resources in the other domain without needing to authenticate twice. WebSEAL supports two different types of cross-domain authentication to address such scenarios: Cross Domain Single Sign-On (CDSSO) and e-Community single sign-on.

10.2.1 CDSSO

WebSEAL supports the ability to forward an authenticated identity from a user in one security domain to a WebSEAL server in another security domain. The *receiving* WebSEAL then maps the identity provided by the *sending* WebSEAL to an identity which is valid in its security domain. CDSSO can also be viewed as a *push* model with respect to authentication.

This functionality is known as Cross Domain Single Sign-On (CDSSO). In CDSSO, the user makes a request to a special link on a WebSEAL server, which then initiates the process to forward the request, along with credential information to a WebSEAL server in a different Access Manager domain. If the user were to instead directly access the link in the target domain, he would have to authenticate to that domain.

The CDSSO process contains the following steps:

1. A user initially logs on to a WebSEAL server in one security domain.

2. At some point, the user accesses a link controlled by the user's WebSEAL which contains a special directive (pkmscdsso). This directive results in redirecting the user to a URL controlled by a WebSEAL server in another security domain and passing encrypted credential information to the new WebSEAL.

3. The user is redirected to the other WebSEAL and this server decrypts the credential information passed to it, maps the identity to one defined in its own user registry, and then creates a secure session with the browser.

4. At this point, the user has established secure sessions with two WebSEAL servers in different domains, but has only had to log in once.

Another way of looking at CDSSO is that it provides a mechanism by which a WebSEAL server in one security domain can send something analogous to a *letter of introduction* to a WebSEAL server in another security domain.

Figure 10-10 on page 244 summarizes a typical CDSSO flow.

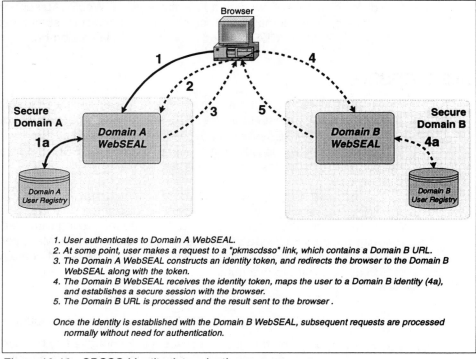

1. User authenticates to Domain A WebSEAL.
2. At some point, user makes a request to a "pkmscdsso" link, which contains a Domain B URL.
3. The Domain A WebSEAL constructs an identity token, and redirects the browser to the Domain B WebSEAL along with the token.
4. The Domain B WebSEAL receives the identity token, maps the user to a Domain B identity (4a), and establishes a secure session with the browser.
5. The Domain B URL is processed and the result sent to the browser.

Once the identity is established with the Domain B WebSEAL, subsequent requests are processed normally without need for authentication.

Figure 10-10   CDSSO identity determination process

The only significant CDSSO implication for a given security domain involves the mapping of user identities. How this mapping is done is not really an architectural issue *per se* - it is more a detailed-design/implementation concern. The important thing to remember is that the mapping must make sense for the specific situation.

It is possible (using the Cross Domain Mapping Framework (CDMF) interfaces discussed in Section 4.3.6, "Cross Domain Mapping Framework" on page 109) to map from an ID in one domain to a different ID in another. However, if the IDs in both domains are the same, a direct mapping may be done - this is the default and does not require the use of any special programming interfaces.

Using CDSSO at Stocks-4u.com

Let us briefly examine a possible CDSSO scenario at Stocks-4u.com.

Assume that ML&J has installed Access Manager in its New York offices to manage security for a new set of Web-based tools. This Access Manager domain is separate from the Stocks-4u.com domain, and has its own user registry. Stocks-4u.com wants to make these tools available to certain ML&J customers without requiring them to log in twice (once to a Stocks-4u.com WebSEAL and then to an ML&J WebSEAL).

By setting up CDSSO between the Stocks-4u.com and ML&J Access Manager domains, these users are required to authenticate only once. Also, with CDSSO, things can be set up to allow initial authentication in either domain - users initially authenticating to an ML&J WebSEAL server can access their Stocks-4u.com account and vice versa.

Another thing to point out is that with CDSSO, an authorization decision can be made at the Stocks-4u.com WebSEAL to control participation in cross-domain single-sign-on. The ability to do this may be important for business reasons.

Figure 10-11 on page 246 illustrates the above CDSSO scenario.

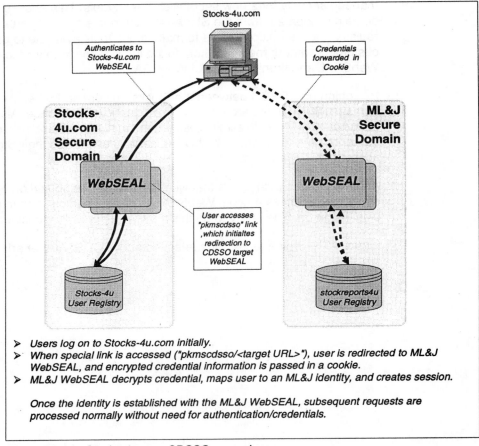

Figure 10-11   Stocks-4u.com CDSSO scenario

10.2.2 e-Community single sign-on

e-Community single sign-on supports a cross-domain authentication capability. However, it differs from CDSSO in a few key respects. Recall that in CDSSO, authenticated identities are *forwarded*. In an e-Community scenario, identities are instead retrieved - it is a *pull* model. The use of e-communities has certain advantages over CDSSO, yet have architectural impacts that are not encountered in a CDSSO environment.

In this model, multiple Access Manager domains are defined to be part of a single e-Community. While each participating domain has its own user registry, one of the domains is designated to be the *home domain*. Users requesting protected resources in any of the participating domains initially authenticate to a

Master Authentication Server (MAS) in the home domain. Once the initial authentication has taken place, the user has an e-Community identity based upon the home domain's user registry. A user's e-Community identity may subsequently be mapped, as required, to local identities by WebSEAL servers in other domains within the e-Community.

The e-Community model is shown in Figure 10-12.

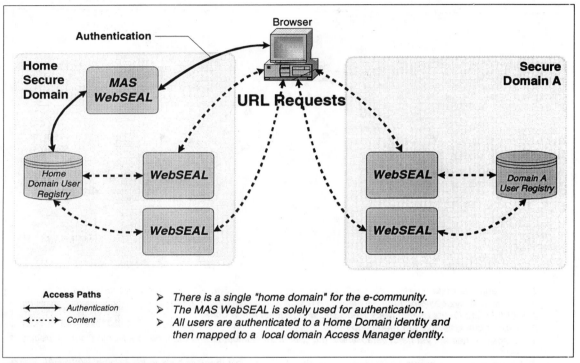

Figure 10-12   The e-Community model

The e-Community mechanism involves the following steps, generally:

1. A user makes a request for a protected resource controlled by a WebSEAL server in one of the e-Community domains. This WebSEAL does not yet have an established secure session with this user.

2. The WebSEAL server redirects the user to the MAS and sends with the request a special directive (pkmsvouchfor) which requests that the MAS provide identity information for the user.

3. The MAS checks to see if the user has already been authenticated to the e-Community, and if not, the MAS then authenticates the user.

4. The MAS then sends a token back to the original WebSEAL server that contains credential information that vouches for the user's identity.

5. The WebSEAL server then maps the identity provided to it by the MAS to an appropriate Access Manager within its local domain and establishes a secure session with the browser.

Figure 10-13 summarizes the flow of an initial e-Community user authentication.

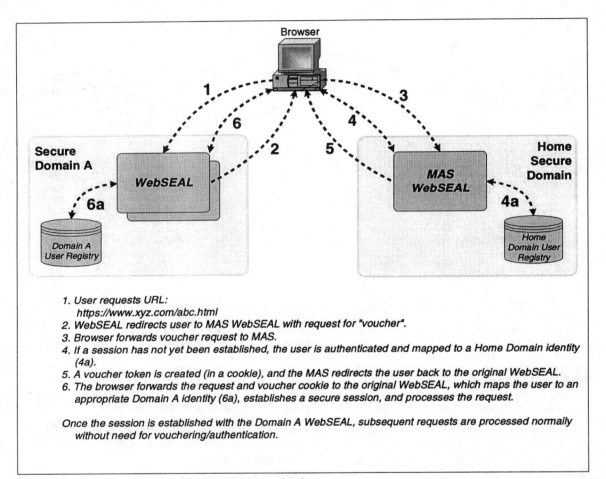

1. *User requests URL:*
   https://www.xyz.com/abc.html
2. *WebSEAL redirects user to MAS WebSEAL with request for "voucher".*
3. *Browser forwards voucher request to MAS.*
4. *If a session has not yet been established, the user is authenticated and mapped to a Home Domain identity (4a).*
5. *A voucher token is created (in a cookie), and the MAS redirects the user back to the original WebSEAL.*
6. *The browser forwards the request and voucher cookie to the original WebSEAL, which maps the user to an appropriate Domain A identity (6a), establishes a secure session, and processes the request.*

Once the session is established with the Domain A WebSEAL, subsequent requests are processed normally without need for vouchering/authentication.

Figure 10-13   e-Community initial identity determination process

Within the *home domain*, unauthenticated requests are always vouched for via the MAS. In other participating domains, once the user has initially logged in to the MAS, subsequent authentication activities to other WebSEAL servers in those domains are handled locally - the first WebSEAL in the domain that validates the user's identity against the MAS then vouches for that user's identity within the local domain. This is depicted in Figure 10-14.

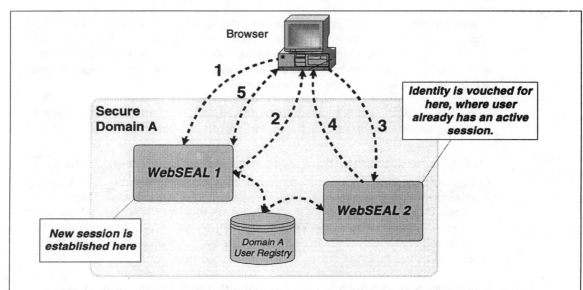

(User has authenticated to an e-community MAS in a previous request to WebSEAL 2. WebSEAL 2 now will vouch for subsequent identity "voucher" requests by other WebSEALs for this user in this domain.)

1. *User requests URL from WebSEAL 1:*
   https://www.xyz.com/abc.html
2. *WebSEAL 1 redirects user to WebSEAL 2 with request for "voucher".*
3. *Browser forwards voucher request to WebSEAL 2.*
4. *WebSEAL 2 provides a voucher cookie token, and redirects the user back to WebSEAL 1.*
5. *The browser forwards the request and voucher cookie to WebSEAL 1, which maps the user to the correct Domain A identity, establishes a secure session, and processes the request.*

Once the session is established with the WebSEAL 1, subsequent requests are processed normally without need for voucher/authentication.

Figure 10 4   e-Community subsequent identity determination process

The key advantage of e-Community single sign-on over CDSSO is that the initial URL request can be made directly to the target WebSEAL server. Recall that with CDSSO, the URL request must go through the WebSEAL to which the user is currently authenticated. In an e-Community configuration, the target WebSEAL is specifically configured to *retrieve* credential information through the vouching mechanism, and the URL request itself need not be accompanied by special processing or contain special characteristics, as in the CDSSO case.

There are many detailed issues regarding the operation of e-Community single sign-on, but they are not architecturally important. The main architectural impact of e-Community single sign-on involves the role of the MAS. The key issue is, with all user authentication for the e-Community going through a single domain, where should the MAS server(s) be located?

In a geographically distributed situation, this question is especially important. For example, let us look at the Stocks-4u.com distributed scenario.

Applying e-Community single sign-on at Stocks-4u.com

Let us assume that Stocks-4u.com has just signed an agreement with a company that provides stock analysis reports via the Web. This company, stockreports4u.com, has an existing client base to which they charge individual usage fees. The Stocks-4u.com agreement allows all Stocks-4u.com users to have access to stockreports4u.com through a special Web site for a flat fee (no individual usage charges).

Stockreports4u.com does not want to manage a user registry of valid Stocks-4u.com users. Instead, they wish to allow users to login to their site against the Stocks-4u.com user registry, and then map those IDs to a small set of special IDs at their Web site.

Further, they wish to permit direct access to this site without a requirement to link to it through Stocks-4u.com first (that is, it may be directly *bookmarked*). This is a scenario, depicted in Figure 10-15 on page 251, where an e-Community approach may be useful.

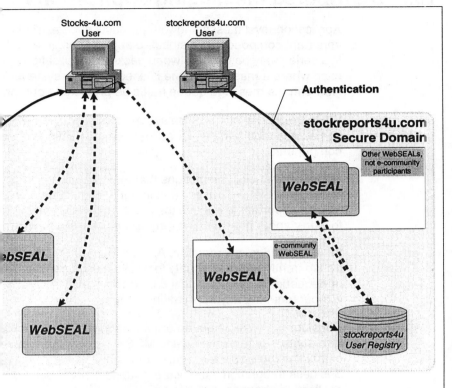

Stocks-4u.com User

stockreports4u.com User

Authentication

stockreports4u.com Secure Domain

Other WebSEALs, not e-community participants

WebSEAL

e-community WebSEAL

WebSEAL

WebSEAL

bSEAL

WebSEAL

stockreports4u User Registry

> ➤ Stocks-4u.com is the "home domain" for the e-community.
> ➤ stockreports4u.com has a WebSEAL server dedicated to serving Stocks-4u.com users.
> ➤ stockreports4u.com has its own user base that directly connects through WebSEALs that do not participate in the e-community.

.com e-Community scenario

ng CDSSO and e-Community single sign-on

ifficult to state hard-and-fast rules regarding when it is best to use an nmunity versus a CDSSO approach. Certainly, one factor is the desired ie of control over the users.

e-Community scenario, one site gets to control the users - business models ire focused on profiling, branding, or other factors as mechanisms for ue generation may be well-served by this approach.

with e-Communities, if authentication at the MAS fails, users may have the n of authenticating directly to the local domain.

10.3 Distributed messaging applications

Application-level messaging with products such as IBM MQSeries is often an important component of distributed applications. In a Web application scenario, MQSeries may be used between back-end application components. Consider a case where a message queue is used between systems located at two sites. How can the message queue traffic be protected appropriately?

While WebSEAL can provide secure communication with a browser, there are sometimes requirements for secure communication between back-end components.

Consider financial transactions that must traverse across unsecured networks. It is essential that the privacy and integrity of such data be maintained - yet it may also be important to remove the need for the application components themselves to worry about providing the appropriate security functions.

In an MQSeries environment, Access Manager for Business Integration can transparently provide security for messages. It can control the ability to enqueue or dequeue messages, and it can transparently encrypt in-transit messages without requiring any application changes.

Consider the case where an organization wishes to exchange application data with another organization using MQSeries over the Internet to eliminate the cost of maintaining a special secure communication link. Access Manager for Business Integration can securely support this capability without requiring any application changes.

10.3.1 An MQSeries distributed application at Stocks-4u.com

Let's briefly take a look at the use of Access Manager in a distributed situation, with IBM MQSeries as a solution component.

Expanding on our current scenario, Stocks-4u.com intends to deploy a new stock transaction record application that uses MQSeries for data exchange between front-end and a back-end application components. In this case, the front-end application component is deployed in the San Diego IT Center and the back-end component is deployed in Savannah on a corporate mainframe host. The front-end application component is embedded within a servlet running on an IBM WebSphere Application Server platform. Clients may access the application via WebSEAL. Figure 10-16 on page 253 illustrates these components.

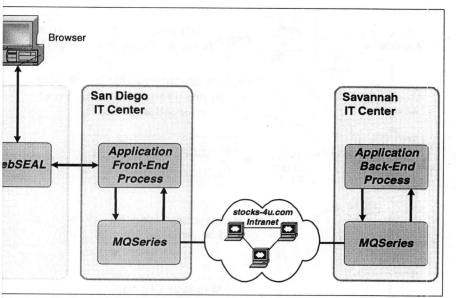

10-16   A Stocks-4u.com MQSeries application

case, the MQSeries channels represent a cross-site communication
onent that, depending on the specific network configuration, might not be
e. In this case, let us assume that the MQSeries communication occurs
s the Stocks-4u.com intranet, leaving the traffic largely unsecured. The
ion is, how can we use Access Manager to secure this communication and
e data privacy and integrity?

s Manager for Business Integration (AM/BI) is specifically designed to
ss such situations. As mentioned earlier, it provides queue security and
arently applies encryption to message channel traffic, permitting highly
e use of MQSeries over otherwise insecure channels.

provides two key functions:

rovides access control for enqueue and dequeue (put/get) operations
ng Access Manager's authorization engine.

an encrypt individual messages to protect their integrity and privacy. It
es this transparently to the application.

to Figure 10-17 on page 254, which depicts AM/BI components and
ctions.

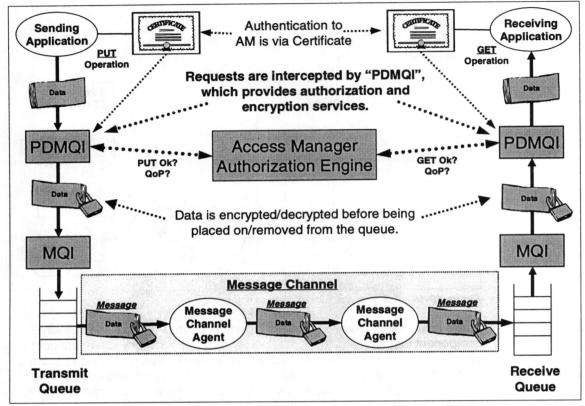

Figure 10-17   AM/BI architecture

AM/BI places a run-time library *shim* in the path between the application and MQSeries. The application continues to call the standard MQSeries run-time functions. These calls are intercepted transparently, where authorization checks and message encryption/decryption is done. Neither MQSeries itself or the application are aware of AM/BI functions. Architecturally, this permits AM/BI to be deployed in existing MQSeries environments with minimal changes.

In the stock4.com environment, AM/BI can be *overlaid* on top of the MQSeries components used by the stock transaction application. Transaction records queued as MQ messages in San Diego are encrypted while in transit.

Finally, because queue access can now be managed, it is easier to leverage a single queue for multiple applications securely. Stocks-4u.com can deploy a common set of messaging channels used by all of its MQSeries applications, as shown in Figure 10-18 on page 255.

u.com AM/BI scenario

ning this with a WebSEAL front end, which is interfaced to the application
nd process, one can see how Access Manager components may be
at multiple levels within the application framework to meet various
y requirements.

ion

chapter, we have focused on more advanced Access Manager
ctural issues that relate to its use in distributed environments. As you can
ere are a number of choices that may be required to complete an
onal architecture in a distributed scenario.

id, however, this chapter has hopefully shown that distributed
ctures with Access Manager are actually not terribly complex. By following
imple guidelines, and asking the correct questions up-front to determine
uirements, even advanced architectures may be straight-forward.

Part 3

Managing Identities and Credentials

part, we discuss the solutions Tivoli has to offer in the identity and
tial management space of the overall security architecture. Identity and
tial information, which generally revolves around managing individuals, is
handled by Tivoli User Administration, Security Manager, and Identity
er. These products handle a multitude of integration aspects with all sorts
frastructures and application environments, which will be detailed
hout this part.

ısic management for
ᴏntities

ᴵapter deals with potential security management problems related to
ᴵ management in large heterogeneous networks and user groups. Let us
ᴵe the individual problems encountered when a company experiences
by using some challenging remarks.

11.1 The weak link

The weakest link in security puts the whole team effort in danger. Companies are mainly using two types of security strongpoints:

- ► The ones that will improve your resistance, such as firewalls, proxies, and antivirus software
- ► The ones that will improve your reaction speed by monitoring your network and systems and warn of any unauthorized usage and risks

These packages are utilized to mitigate the risk of external attacks on our Internet connection first, with the Internet being the most visible and advertised type of attack. However, the majority of the attacks on an enterprise are being conducted from the inside. The number of industrial espionage cases are growing all the time, and many security related problems are perceived as errors. But these errors, if exploited, can have a huge impact, making the protection of your intranet a key element in your enterprise security.

That is why dealing with intranet security is extremely difficult. You have two contradictory positions: the protection of the environment and the flexibility required to work efficiently. If you enforce a too heavy security, users will be tempted to circumvent it. So the goal is to get it light and transparent while still effective.

11.2 Efficient managing of an IT environment

When a business is at start up stage, a limited IT environment is easy to manage, update, and control. However, the bigger the environment and the number of users are, the more dynamic the process of user management will be. The number of user creations, modifications and deletions start to be problematic. To preserve efficiency in managing your user and access environment, procedures will need to be put in place.

Another problem is also inherent: the human error factor. With a large number of accounts and a complex network of computers, the chance that mistakes will occur becomes higher and the chance to notice them lower.

Despite the procedures put in place, manual handling is still a cause of errors. A common example is temporary accounts that are never deleted. Why? The operating systems employed do not support account aging and these temporary accounts must be deleted manually.

situations like this occur, *how to* is important. Tools that provide the ed security features can enable the management team to integrate tasks a single process and maintain security by enforcing enterprise security irds for accounts and access rights.

ıy profile

iterprise we are using as an example is running a retail business and does :us on any information technology in particular. It started out in a single ın but has grown significantly and established multiple regional offices. The unction of these offices is to support the local sales force.

he last few years, the company acquired property in several locations its home country. The decision was made to connect them to two computer s using a fast networking backbone. The I/T systems are balanced ın the two separate computer centers, allowing for resilience and :ity. These centers provide and maintain the Internet, intranet and extranet ctivity, as well as the partner's and employees home office VPN ctions.

11-1 on page 262 shows an overview of the enterprise layout.

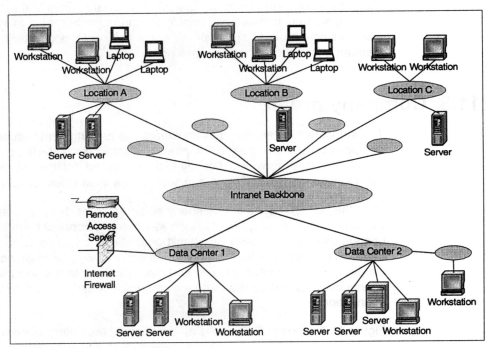

Figure 11-1   Enterprise layout

While the company was growing, several projects where launched with different teams. This resulted in successful implementations but with environments based on the preferred infrastructure of the individual project managers. It lead to a heterogeneous environment with a large team managing each specialized project environment. The typical systems used today are based on Microsoft Windows NT, Windows 2000, AIX, HP/UX, Solaris and a few LINUX servers in test, with accounting operations being implemented on an IBM AS/400. The regional offices, however, have limited staff available to handle day-to-day operations on the Windows NT/2K and UNIX systems.

Today's administration is done by requesting access via e-mail to each project team. There are no policies or practices to support these procedures. All the project teams have their own rules and the response to user requests is done on a best effort.

11.3.1 Security related problems

There are major problems the way user management is implemented that may impact the overall I/T security:

► Lack of policies and consistent user management

le users are facing different approaches in the way their requests are
indled; they will get different IDs with different passwords. This is a common
oblem and most users have the tendency to record their ID and password
imbinations by using very insecure methods.

fferent security levels across the network

I the computers will likely be on the same network; however, some
iplications (HR, accounting, and so on) require a higher level of security.
ving access based on the computer or an operating system level instead of
application easily results in potential access to sensitive information.

irge number of users and high percent of changes

ie amount of time spent (when using different management teams) to
indle a large user population becomes impressive. The management teams
ll spend a lot of time to just get up-to-date with the change requests. They
ve no time to control or verify what enforcement is in place, and end-of-life
accounts are not often enforced.

; requirements

an audit, the CEO learned about the high costs of administering the IT
rces. An impressive number of days are lost each time an employee joins
impany before he can really start being productive. There is a lag time
en assigning and access to the required resources. In the past, the cost for
anagement staff kept increasing over the years, despite a deterioration of
sults and quality. Another highlight of this audit was that several accounts
isted for people who have left the company. Additionally, there were some
ccounts that could not be matched to *real* physical people at all, and since
issword *trust levels* are not consistently implemented, some passwords
iven set to blank.

isult of this audit, the following plan must be achieved:

blish policies and practices

iolicy on how the accounts and accesses are to be handled as well as how
item oriented practices will be produced and published. The company
irmation must be protected in a more effective way.

ntralize the management functions

The I/T management teams will be reorganized into an administration team with two levels of expertise. The first level will handle the day-to-day operations, such as creating/modifying/blocking/deleting accounts, while the second level will consist of specialists with high skills per platform and/or application. Another mission of the first level management staff is to ensure that the policies and practices regarding user account management are enforced.

► Increase productivity by reducing latency time for changes

There will be a new Service Level Agreement (SLA) for IT requests in order to improve the response times. This is possible because the more time consuming problems are directly handed to the second level staff while the first level can focus on user management related issues.

► Decrease training cost of management staff

The first level of the management team will receive training on the management tools they use, as well as basics on the managed platforms. Only the second level team will need to be trained more extensively. This helps to reduce overall I/T costs and maintain a higher level of function oriented help desk people.

11.3.3 Security design objectives

In the first place, a project like this is initiated to reduce the I/T management cost; however, by implementing a well organized user management, it delivers some new key elements to the overall security infrastructure, such as:

► A central repository of user identities among all the systems

As all the I/T systems have different ways of handling IDs; tracking a user among heterogeneous computers is a hard task. A central repository that is able to maintain the user and ID relationship quickly allows control and investigations in an efficient way. When combining this repository with a central auditing and reporting system, it can easily help consolidate information per employee.

► Provide system independent capabilities

Operating systems and applications are designed and built with different capabilities in term of security. Some offer password aging, other password patterns or account aging. These capabilities are all interesting, but not commonly standardized. To implement a central repository that can handle these matters while designed to enforce security, all the systems will receive a common set of capabilities, enforced locally or from the central system.

► Use standard access templates

reating templates, the required access can be determined by the user's
le, which can also help reduce the implementation time and the risk of
an errors, as the number of manual manipulations is reduced. Any
sequent change to this template, such as the addition of a system, a
em name change, and so on, will be propagated to all the existing users
matically.

ide quick deletion and/or locking

heterogeneous environment, deleting and/or blocking a user's account is
ficult and time consuming task. When an account must be immediately
inated or blocked for security reasons, manual intervention on all the
ved systems will take a lot of time and can easily be incomplete due to
an errors. If this task cannot be performed automatically, immediate
rity risks are introduced.

owing summarizes the key elements of this section based on standard
areas:

ss control

estrict access to information to authorized users only

nforce the same authentication scheme to all the systems

rovide a single password to as many systems as possible

low accountability

entials

ovide central repository of user IDs for all I/T systems

ovide consolidated reporting per user

ovide system access reports

architecture overview

the previously described elements, we can start building the solution.
elements are described in an abstracted mode that is not related to any
product.

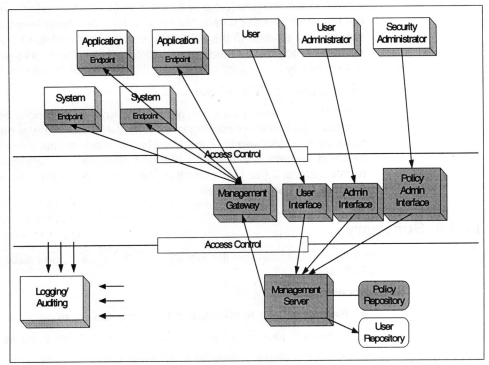

Figure 11-2 Planned architecture

Figure 11-2 represents the information flow between the following key components:

▶ System or Application

These systems or applications are to be managed.

▶ *User*

The normal users should be allowed to view and modify their personal data and to initiate certain requests like password changes or access to new applications. Users will not be authorized to perform administrator tasks. Users may be located anywhere in the internal network and should be able to use the online user interface at anytime.

▶ User/Group Administrator

This role has the permission to perform administrative tasks like adding, modifying, or deleting data in the user/group repository. The user/group administrator is not authorized to perform any changes to policy settings.

▶ System Administrator

role describes a senior administrator who is authorized to modify rules in corporate policy repository, for example, security profiles. Within highly ure environments, it may be required that knowledge of the administrator's ID and password alone are not sufficient to perform changes to policy ngs. The new solution should be able to request proper authentication entials and to enforce proper authorization decisions before allowing any ges to the policy repository.

agement Gateway

management gateway is a component that helps to manage target ms and applications. The management gateway communicates with the ral management server and remote systems.

Interface

user interface allows users to initiate requests for tasks like password ges, new registrations, or new access rights. It should be an easy-to-use based interface. All user activity has to be logged and it should be idered that not all users are well-behaved. Authentication should be rced using an user ID and password stored in the user/group repository.

► User/Group Administration Interface

This interface allows authorized users, like first level support administrators, to perform certain administrative tasks, such as accepting or rejecting user requests, resetting passwords, or viewing user information. The interface should be an easy-to-use Web interface and might behave differently than the user interface. The administration interface is considered separate from the general user interface but, in most situations, it might later be combined on the same system with the general user interface.

► Policy Administration Interface

This interface has to be available to authorized enterprise administrators only. It can be used to administer changes to the global security settings and to view activities of administrators and users. Separating the three interfaces for users, user/group administrators, and policy administrators allows you to build separate interfaces with separate security options for those user types. Later on, it might be decided to implement all three interfaces on a single server. This interface might be implemented as a Web interface as well, but it should also have command line capabilities to allow the automation of certain tasks. All permanent administrative information should either be stored in the user/group repository or in the policy repository.

► Policy Repository

This component is used to store policy-related information.

► User Repository

The user repository is used to store all user and group related information.

► Management Server

The management server controls the new central management solution. It contains all the logic to implement the required business processes. The management server has direct access to the policy and user repository and it interacts with several of the other components. It receives requests from any of the user or administrator interfaces and communicates with managed systems or managed applications using the management gateway. It contains subcomponents to implement and enforce the required workflow.

► Logging/Auditing Services

These can be existing components that are used to collect, store and analyze logging and auditing information. It is assumed that log servers and auditing mechanisms exist and that they can be reused by the new components.

ess Control Services

se components are used to control and monitor access to new service
support components. Depending on the strength of the security
uirements, access control can be implemented in different ways using
valls, filtering routers, certain networking technologies (IPsec and VLANs)
ecured application gateways.

architecture (solution design)

st step of the project will use Tivoli User Administration (TUA) as the core
ory and user management system. TUA handles both the policies and the
oup administration details.

epository is implemented on Tivoli's ODB, which is an *object database*
n store various types of objects. This database will hold any new objects
be added to the user/group/system profiles. The repository will be fully
rent for the product user.

ial implementation requires three ways to interact with TUA, as depicted
e 11-3 on page 270.

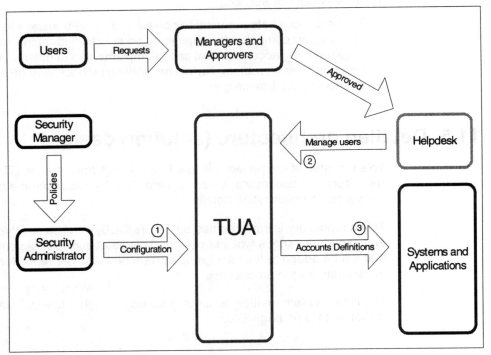

Figure 11-3   TUA interactions

1. The security administration provides the policies it must apply.

   Initially defined by the senior enterprise management, the security administrator maps the enterprise policies into configuration rules that can be maintained within the TUA environment. These rules can specify:

   a. Password policies

   b. User and group mappings for well defined roles, such as sales, HR, research and development (R&D), and marketing

   c. Access definitions to specific resources based on role membership

2. The help desk is maintaining the user accounts.

   This project phase still requires end users to apply for a new ID or access to an additional resource using their e-mail systems. Requests have to be sent to their line managers, who will manually check the justification for the request. The managers will forward the approved request to the help desk administrators, who will perform the administrative changes in TUA.

endpoints are receiving information.

After changes have been made to the TUA user and policy repositories, the new information gets distributed to the endpoints.

olicies

s are an important guideline for the operation of the enterprise. Providing ⟩ automate the implementation of policies using management products is ctive way to enforce them at all times.

Jser Administration will provide a graphical user interface (GUI) to define elated policies. A very common and useful definition is the password action. Any new password will be checked using the TUA rules before it stributed to the managed systems and application. Enforcing the 'ises password policy here will automatically enforce it on all the managed s and applications. An example of the policy GUI is shown in Figure 11-4.

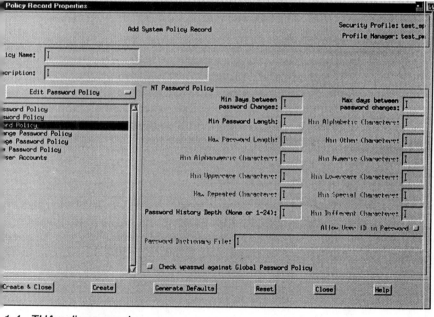

1-4   *TUA policy example*

11.5.2 Account management

The user management takes advantage of the central administration capability of Tivoli User Administration. Consistent approaches are applied to all the platforms and applications based on the globally defined enterprise policies. In addition, not only the user details are managed but also the user access rights. The administrative roles define what a particular administrator may perform in the environment.

The privileges are not only the standard TUA attributes, but also all the customized ones created to cope with the enterprise environments or the new platforms/applications supported by the toolkit.

11.5.3 Endpoint

The endpoint is a component of the underlying Tivoli Management Framework. TUA can either push information to the endpoint or it can retrieve it. When the Tivoli Framework is installed, the endpoint can provide a collection point for products such as Risk Manager, as described in Part 4, "Managing a security audit" on page 329.

Lotus Notes provides another good example, where there can be a bi-directional link between TUA and Notes. TUA can be used to initially create Lotus Notes accounts and populate the Notes address book using the endpoint connection, while Notes is being used for self-care afterwards. The user uses the Notes client to update his phone number, office location, and so on. This information can now be sent back to the TUA repository, where it gets redistributed to other systems or applications via the endpoints.

11.5.4 Logical network view

TUA manages access to various distributed UNIX servers without the need of changing the network topology. Its ability to manage groups of machines while applying roles to the users and groups allow you to efficiently manage communities within your network. Figure 11-5 on page 273 shows an overview of such an UNIX environment.

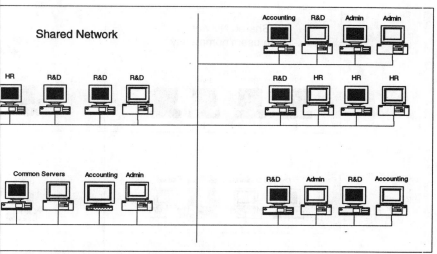

1-5   Mixed UNIX environment

twork is connecting several groups of users with some groups like HR
.D definitely not sharing any day-to-day information. These two areas can
considered as sensitive, the first one for privacy towards your
ees, the second one for confidentiality, as it holds your company assets.
iitial network, all the users defined using basic UNIX NIS (Network
tion System) capabilities only, sharing the user accounts through the
etwork.

g TUA, the servers and workstations will be split into different groups with
nplates (roles) not allowing the other group to connect to the secured
e, as shown in Figure 11-6 on page 274.

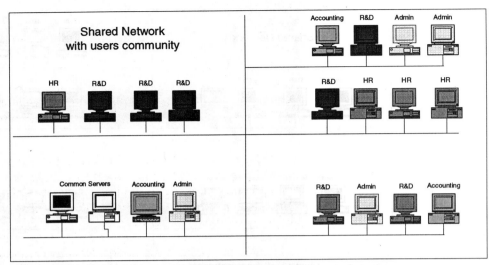

Figure 11-6   User and server groups installed

In this environment, we are managing the various groups from a single point. This will be particularly useful when adding a new server where, once installed, the Tivoli endpoint will distribute the profiles and integrate the new computer easily.

The difference in this approach compared to the NIS, for example, is that the user accounts are distributed securely to all the servers. This allows an uninterrupted availability to the existing users even when the TUA server is down (only modifications will be delayed).

11.6 Tivoli User Administration

Tivoli User Administration is enabling and controlling end user access to information and systems by creating, modifying, and deleting user accounts, groups, and roles. As the number of heterogeneous systems proliferate, administrators are faced with increased complexity. Tivoli's approach is one that focuses on shielding the administrator from having to understand all the details about their complex environment. Instead, it focuses the administrator on the value-add tasks that they need to perform.

Tivoli User Administration is designed to provide the system administrator with centralized control over widely distributed host systems, and incorporates a number of key concepts:

► Consistent Tivoli methodology

licy-based management

ınagement-by-subscription

cure delegation

ıtform-independent interface

roduct supports a wide variety of platforms, and with a *Default* and
ıtion policy, allows you to be sure that even your remote sites are being
istered correctly.

User Administration is a profile-based application that runs on the Tivoli
ɟed Region (TMR) server according to the management by subscription
. In this model, profiles contained in a profile manager define specific
ts of system configuration, such as user account information or group
ation. A profile record represents the actual configuration information
one user or group. In order to receive this configuration information, TMA
ints, managed nodes, PC managed nodes, NetWare Managed Sites, NIS
ins, or LDAP directories are subscribed to the profiles. The data stored in
ɔfile can be distributed to subscribers and is ultimately used to update
ation in the appropriate system files.

entries can either be manually added one at a time, or they can be initially
ed (populated) from one or more subscribed TMA endpoints, managed
, or an LDAP directory. The profiles are stored in the object database on
ıR server.

ɘr to make the information contained in the User Administration profiles
in the target systems, the profiles must be distributed to them. To be able
ʻibute profiles, an association has to be made between profiles and targets
ɟes, known as subscribers. This is done by using the profile manager's
ʻiption list.

ɪd validation policies

time you modify or create a profile entry, it is checked against a set of
ion policies that ensure that the data you are providing complies with the
t policy. Validation is performed in the same way when populating a profile.
ʻevents you from creating or getting an entry that does not meet your
cations. You can also request a validation for a specific profile at any time.

The default policies determine the default values used when creating a new entry for a profile. These default values can help you minimize the amount of data that you have to enter when creating a new record. The default policy can specify a default value for one or more of the attributes associated with a profile; therefore, any default policy values that you define will work as a template for each new record you add to the profile.

11.6.2 OnePassword

Password management is a relatively common function that must be performed by both users and administrators. Users require a simple interface to change their password, and administrators often perform password resets for users who have forgotten or misplaced their passwords. The OnePassword utility provides users and administrators with a Web interface to administer user passwords in the Tivoli Managed Environment (TME) database and distribute the updated passwords to subscribed endpoints. Users can access the common OnePassword Web site, enabling them to change their own passwords, and administrators can access a restricted Web site to assign new passwords for users.

To use OnePassword, the user or administrator connects to the HTTP server where the application has been installed and supplies a login name and requested passwords. For security purposes, users must supply both old and new passwords. The OnePassword utility then looks up the user in a user profile. If the old password matches the common password in the profile, the OnePassword utility replaces the old password with the new password for all supported and administered platforms. This process actually updates the user's password attributes in the user profile, which will then be distributed to all subscribed endpoints.

11.6.3 Integration with the existing infrastructure

This project is running on an existing infrastructure. As all the different user databases are already filled, it is cost effective to take advantage of these databases by importing user information. In addition, when a user must be created or deleted, TUA is either mastering this new information or relying on an external source. As the option for our implementation, we have selected to interface our system with SAP/HR, one of the available software tools in this industry space.

In the first phase, TUA will import its user information from the SAP/HR module to set up the database. A trigger based data exchange will also be configured so that when any TUA relevant information is changed (Name, Group, Date Out, locked account, and so on), this information will be passed to TUA in real time. In

se of a temporary contractor being employed for our company, this
tion also means that if the contract is properly typed in SAP, the
ision date of this account will be set too. This can prevent accounts from
operational after the contract end date.

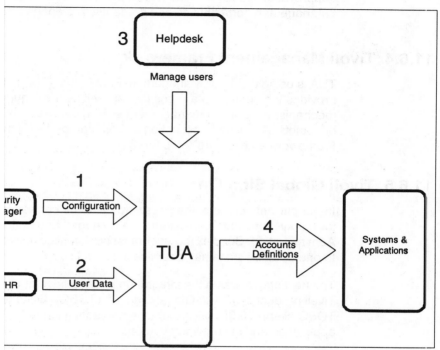

1-7 Functional TUA solution diagram

I 1-7 summarizes the various sources of information:

enterprise policies enforced by the user management

SAP/HR module used to feed TUA with the basic user Information

daily user management

propagation of the accounts to the necessary targets

> **Note:** Tivoli released a new product, called Tivoli Identity Manager Version 1.1, that will implement a large part of the user management through a self care workflow mode. This mode helps in enforcing security policies for the approval of access. It is discussed in more detail in Chapter 12, "Advanced management for identities and credentials" on page 283.

11.6.4 Tivoli Management Framework

TUA is using the Tivoli Management Framework (TMF) as a 'middleware' layer. It provides the central data repository as well as the required communication mechanisms between management server, gateways, managed nodes, and endpoints. A detailed description of TMF can be found in Section 13.3, "Tivoli Framework architecture" on page 337.

11.6.5 Tivoli Global Sign-On

In our current scenario, the passwords and the corresponding rules and policies for our systems and applications are managed and maintained by Tivoli User Administration. But still, the user must type in his password anytime he connects to one of these systems or applications.

The next step towards the integration and the ease of use is to introduce another Tivoli product call Tivoli Global Sign-On (TGSO). Once the user logged on to the TGSO client, TGSO will handle the authentication to the other system or application and securely log you on.

In addition to passwords, TGSO can handle fingerprint or smartcard authentication. You could use a combination of fingerprint and smartcard authentication in the TGSO client in order to completely omit any necessity for a user password.

As part of a complete Tivoli security management solution, Tivoli Global Sign-On integrates fully with Tivoli User Administration, Tivoli Security Manager, and the Tivoli Management Framework. In this environment, a designated Tivoli administrator can manage Tivoli Global Sign-On users and targets from a centralized console. Role-based administration is also available with this support.

Infrastructure and platforms

The overall infrastructure, as shown in Figure 11-8 on page 279, relies on the Tivoli Management Framework and the implementation of a DCE cell.

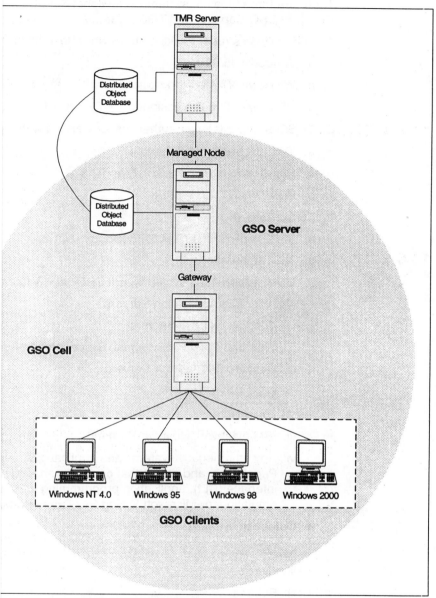

1-8   Tivoli Global Sign-On (TGSO) infrastructure

There are three types of systems in a Global Sign-On environment: TGSO Clients, TGSO Servers, and TGSO Targets.

1. TGSO Clients (user desktops from which to access other systems)
   a. Windows 95/98
   b. Windows NT 4.0 Workstation
   c. Windows 2000 Professional
2. TGSO Servers (secure authentication servers with logon information)
   a. IBM AIX Version 4.3.2 and 4.3.3
   b. Sun Solaris Version 2.6, 2.7, and 2.8
   c. Windows NT 4.0 + SP6a
3. TGSO Targets
   a. 3270 applications (RACF, TopSecret, ACF2)
   b. 5250 applications
   c. UNIX applications/systems via TCP/IP and VTXXX emulation
   d. Network File/Application Servers
      i. Windows NT 4.0 Servers
      ii. Windows 2000 Professional, Server and Advanced Server
      iii. Netware 3.X and 4.X Servers
      iv. OS/2 Warp Server
      v. Lotus Notes
      vi. IBM eNetwork Host On-Demand
      vii. Any other legacy systems and applications (such as cc:Mail, SAP R/3, PeopleSoft, and so on) that can be interfaced via command line interface (CLI), application programming interface (API), Terminal emulation, or Microsoft Dialog Box (*screen watching*)
   e. Database systems
      i. DB2
      ii. Oracle
      iii. Sybase
      iv. Informix
      v. MS SQL Server

uct prerequisites

Global Sign-On requires Tivoli Management Framework, Tivoli User
istration, and Tivoli Software Distribution. Other software distribution
cts, such as Microsoft SMS, can be supported as well.

ore product information, go to the following Tivoli product Web site:

`/www.tivoli.com/products/index/user_admin/`

dvanced management for
entities and credentials

chapter, we describe an advanced solution for a company that is already
basic mechanisms to manage user accounts and security settings on their
tems. They want to handle their security management processes in a more
l and efficient way, while being able to reduce existing security risks. We
ue with the scenario from Chapter 11, "Basic management for identities"
ge 259 and describe additional business reasons that lead to the
mentation of new security solutions.

scribe how Tivoli Identity Manager, which includes Tivoli User
istration and Tivoli Security Manager technology, can be integrated into
enario in order to respond to the new business needs. We show how to
ge user accounts and how to manage security settings consistently on
le systems and applications within their corporate network.

chapter, we mention some of the potential security risks that exist in an
et environment. Unfortunately, intranet environments are too often
dered as safe and trusted environments, so that the level of security
tion for its systems and applications is very low. Even without considering
aused by hostile intranet users, there is a growing requirement to protect
n sensitive systems within an intranet in a better way.

Due to the increasing number of interconnections between internal and external networks, it becomes more and more difficult to distinguish between the "secure" intranet, the "semi-secure" extranet, or the "insecure" Internet. New e-Business or e-Commerce solutions require that systems on one side can somehow communicate with systems on the other side. This introduces additional security risks for Intranet systems and demands that sensitive parts of the internal network receive better protection against attackers from any of those connected networks.

Sometimes, security weaknesses on the internal network (caused by operation failures, by misuse or by manipulation) may result in weaknesses that get exploited by attackers from the Internet. External attackers may then use these weaknesses as an entry point into a company's intranet and may start discovering or misusing intranet systems from the Internet. With some insider information, with some clever combination of security exploits, or with some intelligent trojan horses, external attackers might gain unauthorized access to systems, cause damage to systems, or read or manipulate important data.

Therefore, protection of the intranet environment not only helps against misbehaving internal network users, but may also help to prevent against more complex attacks originating from the Internet or other external networks. Systems that are important to a company's business need proper protection, even if they are *only connected to the secure intranet*. This chapter contains some recommendations on how to protect critical systems and to protect critical sub-networks within a corporate intranet using additional security products and concepts like network segmentation.

ıy profile

ˈtual company is the same as in the previous chapter. It can be described
ɔn-IT company with a large internal network spanning multiple locations,
e computing centers, and using multiple server platforms. An overview of
ˉ infrastructure is shown in Figure 12-1.

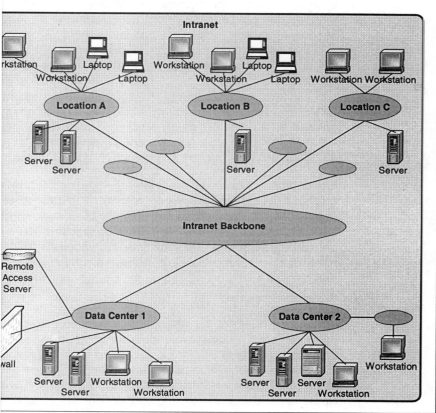

ironment of our virtual company

l corporate network users are placed in various locations. Each location
e or more local servers running Windows NT or Windows 2000 and may
few AIX, Solaris, or Linux servers. those servers are used as file servers,
ˌrvers, database servers, domain servers, Internet proxy servers and they
n some other local applications. Users have to identify themselves with an
ᵒ and password before accessing most of those services. Because our

company already has build a solution for improved user administration, as described in the previous chapter, users can contact the central corporate help desk in order to request new user IDs, change their passwords, change their user information, or to request access to new services.

We assume that our company uses the Tivoli Management Framework for software distribution and distributed monitoring for most of their servers and that they use the Tivoli User Administration product to manage user accounts on their systems. For various reasons, there might even be some systems that are still managed by local administrators. The overall status concerning usability and security of all their servers still has some room for improvements, and some of those servers are not configured in accordance to the existing corporate security policy. Most of the existing security problems have not been fixed over a long period of time, because our company does not have enough resources to set up processes for proper security management, and they are sometimes not able to fix some of their known security exposures. Our company does not have a solution for automatic security auditing, and the technical staff does not want to list all known problems in their manually generated status reports, so management might not be fully aware of most of their security exposures.

Our company has two or more large computing centers, where most of the business critical applications are located. The data centers also contain Internet connections, extranet-like connections to business partners, connections to other service providers, and remote-access connections used by mobile workers. The networking support group administers the firewalls, and they try to keep their network as secure as possible, but sometimes quick-and-easy solutions are needed and errors occur, so that the overall network security is not as secure as assumed.

For historic reasons, the infrastructure in those data-centers is very heterogeneous. Although intended, our company has not been able to migrate all their applications to a common server platform. Most applications have been migrated to UNIX, where two different support groups provide AIX and Solaris platforms. The new e-Business Web applications are already utilizing Linux. Some applications are running on Windows NT. Financial applications are using an AS/400 in one of the computing centers. Databases are managed using Oracle and IBM DB/2.

Today, our company has multiple independent groups of system administrators and application developers. The UNIX support groups are separate from other platform support groups and this has caused some problems in the past. Because good system administrators are getting harder to find, some of those servers are not as well maintained and as secure as they are supposed to be.

ately, our company has not yet experienced a major security incident in
st, although a recently security assessment performed by external security
tants in one of their data centers has shown that attackers, maybe some
itled employees from the intranet, might be able to manipulate or cause
e to some of the business-critical systems.

s requirements

gh-level business requirements (why the CEO of our company decides to
r a more advanced IT management solution) are cost reduction and
ed efficiency for management of the internal IT infrastructure. Additionally,
O wants to be prepared to merge support departments for the intranet and
g Internet infrastructure. Building a good solution should help them to
new ways of doing business and to gain competitive advantages.

g at the current IT processes shows that our company needs to implement
force processes for improved user and security management. Various
s may have caused them to come up with those new requirements at that
time. Maybe the implementation of formal and documented processes is
ary to prepare for an ISO9001 certification. Maybe administration of user
ts on many platforms could not handle the growing dynamics of end users
the company, moving to new responsibilities, or leaving the company.
our company has been threatened by a serious security incident that
d to one of their competitors. Maybe the company decided to follow some
ecurity recommendations they received out of a previous security
ment performed by security consultants. Maybe our company is growing
d wants to prepare for some new e-business projects, where improved
/ is considered a key requirement.

of business requirements to build an advanced IT security management
are:

t reduction: Manage the growing or more dynamic IT environment without
tional resources. Use reduced and less experienced staff to manage
mon tasks within the existing IT environment. Use experienced people to
orm new projects and high-level IT administration tasks.

iency: Perform IT administration tasks in a more efficient way and allow
s-platform support. Improve response time on user requests.

ageability: Use proven technology and common interoperability
dards. Integrate solutions with current system management tools.

urity: Enforce corporate policies and standards. Manage systems and
ss in a more formal way. If a corporate security policy does not yet exist,

then start a security policy development project and apply the best security practices for protection of critical components.

► Usability: Provide a single online interface for IT administration requests from users. It should be user-friendly and easy-to-use so that it can heavily reduce the number of help desk calls for everyday tasks, such as password changes. Allow automatic processing of subscription requests for certain services.

► Provide delegated management capabilities via an online interface.

► Prepare for future integration with new e-Business applications. Avoid a stand-alone intranet solution.

► Use common repositories to manage user and policy information. Allow separate databases for authentication data (in user registry) from authorization data (in policy registry). Allow partitioning of repositories for delegated administration. Avoid creating incompatible solutions. Allow central logging and auditing of security-related IT activities.

12.3 Security design objectives

Using the business reasons from above allows you to describe the security-related objectives that need to be considered, when architecting a good and secure solution for our company:

► Access Control:

- Protect access to systems, applications, and data. Enforce and control their usage.

- Provide access control to a new online administration interface.

- Enforce strict access control to new management systems and prevent unauthorized access attempts. If required, restrict access to users from authorized networks.

► Authentication:

- Allow different authentication mechanisms and allow selection for individual systems or applications.

- Allow simple user authentication with passwords.

- Provide stronger authentication mechanisms on request. Support RSA SecurID tokens and basic usage of PKI certificates.

► Integrity:

- Allow consistent administration of users and systems. Avoid undocumented servers. Make sure that the documented system settings are consistent with the documentation.

Enforce compliance with business policies.

Enforce security settings for systems and applications.

iting:

Allow monitoring of user activity and resource usage (systems, applications, and data).

Allow generation of status and history reports.

architecture overview

on the given business reasons and security requirements, we can now architect a suitable solution for our company. The first step is to plan ey components that should be part of our solution. At this point, those ents are only described on a conceptual or logical level. In the next hey will be described more specific and the components will be mapped products, such as systems, networks, software, databases, or ions, and to concrete solutions.

2-2 on page 290 shows the key components that should be part of the for our company. The lines indicate some of the communication ships between them.

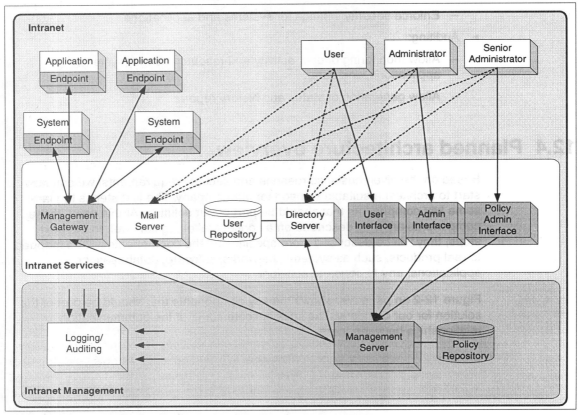

Figure 12-2   Components for advanced security management solution

The dark shaded components need to be implemented to build the new solution. The other components already exist in our company and they are included in the architecture overview, since they have to interact with the new components.

The following components are either users of the new solution or will be managed by the new solution:

► System: These are the target systems to be managed.

► Application: These are target applications to be managed.

► User: The normal user should be allowed to view and modify their personal data and to initiate certain requests like password changes or access to new applications. Users will not be authorized to perform administrator tasks. Users may be located anywhere in the internal network and should be able to use the online interface anytime. All changes and requests performed by users need to be logged in a reliable way.

ninistrator (Account Administrator): This role has the permission to
orm administrative tasks and to add, modify or delete data concerning a
ip of assigned systems, users, or resources in the User/Group registry.
administrator is not authorized to perform any changes to policy settings.
dministrator activity needs to be logged in a reliable way.

urity Administrator (Senior Administrator or Policy Administrator): This
defines a qualified administrator that is authorized to modify rules in the
orate policy registry, that is, security profiles and security settings. The
rity administrator's responsibility is to implement a technical solution for a
n corporate security policy. Within highly secure environments, it may be
ired that these kind of activities require strong authentication and that the
vledge of the security administrator's user ID and password are not
cient to allow making changes to policy settings. The new solution should
ble to request stronger authentication credentials and to enforce proper
orization decisions before allowing any changes to the policy registry.

owing components are directly used to provide the new services:

Server: This component already exists and can be used by the new
agement server to send notifications to users or administrators.

ctory Server (LDAP) with User/Group registry (Identity and Credential
base): The Directory Server provides access to user and group
mation via the LDAP protocol. The registry stores user-specific
mation like passwords or personal information. The user/group registry
t also be used to store additional information, such as policy-related user
utes. It is assumed that an LDAP server already exists and can be used
ore additional information for the new solution. Proper access control for
itive information is required. The actual Directory contents might be
d in a native LDAP Directory, in registries like Microsoft Active Directory
5), Novell NDS eDirectory Services, iPlanet LDAP Directory, or even in a
ional database management system (RDBMS, that is, DB/2 or Oracle).

agement gateway: Components that help to manage servers and
cations. The management gateway communicates with the central
agement server and remote servers. Using intermediate components
s managing systems more efficiently.

interface: This interface allows users to initiate requests for tasks like
word changes, new registrations, or new access rights. It should be an
-to-use Web interface. All user activity should be logged and it should be
idered that not all users are well-behaved. Authentication should be
ced using an user ID and password, as stored in the user/group registry.
ger authentication mechanisms should only be used if reliable
entication mechanisms like PKI certificates on smart cards or SecurID
is are already deployed for all users in the company.

- Administrator interface: This interface allows authorized users to perform certain administrative tasks like accepting or rejecting user requests and to view user information. The interface should be an easy-to-use Web interface and might behave differently than the user interface. In some network environments, it might be desired to combine both interfaces and to run the administrator interface and user interface on the same system. In other environments, it might be appropriate to keep both interfaces separate from each other in order to allow advanced control and auditing for all user activities and for all administrator activities.

- Senior Administrator interface: This interface should be available to authorized enterprise administrators. It can be used to make changes to global security settings and to view activities of administrators and users. Separating the three interfaces for users, user/group administrators, and policy administrators allows you to build separate interfaces with separate security options for those user types. Later, it might be decided to implement all three interfaces on a single server. This interface might be implemented as a Web interface, but it should also have command line capabilities to allow automation of certain tasks. The three types of interfaces should not store any user information; all permanent information should either be stored in the user/group registry or in the policy registry.

The following group of components that are needed to support and to implement the new services. These components do not need to be directly accessible for general users and they might need special security protection.

- Policy registry: This component is used to store policy-related information.

- Management Server: This system controls the new management solution. It contains all the logic to implement the required business processes. The management server has direct access to the policy registry and the LDAP directory and interacts with several of the other components. It receives requests from any of the user or administrator interfaces and communicates with managed systems or managed applications using the management gateway. It contains sub-components to implement and enforce the correct workflow.

- Logging/Auditing: Existing components that are used to collect, store, and analyze logging and auditing information. It is assumed that log servers and auditing mechanisms exist and can be reused by the new components. For the best protection, the log server should not run any other applications.

- Access Control: These components are used to control and monitor access to new service and support components. Depending on the strength of the security requirements, access control can be implemented in different ways using firewalls, filtering routers, certain networking technologies (IPsec and VLANs), or secured application gateways.

urity risk assessment

ing the security aspects of those components allows you to perform an
ecurity risk assessment. The following possible weaknesses, threats, and
juences should be considered to estimate the resulting security risks.
ding on the corporate security policy, you need to decide if some of those
e acceptable or if additional security measures should be implemented for
igation.

e security threats are:

uthorized access by an external attacker (minimal)

use by users from an internal network

use by administrators from an internal network

use by senior administrators from an internal network

e weaknesses are:

cure systems or applications

or stolen passwords

ication failures

e consequences are:

age, disclosure, or manipulation of data in an user registry

age, disclosure, or manipulation of data in a policy registry

ipulation of configuration information in critical systems or applications

age or misuse of systems or applications

recommendations:

ove network security to control access to servers.

se security zones to control access to sensitive servers and applications.

se firewalls or other gateways to control communication between
fferent security zones. Block unwanted traffic and monitor authorized
affic.

se reverse proxy with authentication/authorization capabilities for access
administration interfaces.

lace critical service and support servers in separate networks and block
cess using routers or firewalls.

ove system security to control activity on systems.

emove unneeded components.

- Add security components.
- Check and update all default settings.
- Enable system and application logging and send event information to a remote log server.

► Use and enforce authentication mechanisms to access interfaces in order to prevent misuse.

► Monitor usage of all interfaces for users, administrators, and security administrators in order to detect misuse

Other security risks that may have to be accepted:

► Senior administrator needs to be trusted (medium risk)

► Administrators need to be trusted (low risk)

► Software needs to be trusted (low risk)

12.5 Detailed architecture (solution design)

This section describes the solution design for our company using Tivoli Identity Manager Version 1.1, which contains Tivoli User Administration, Tivoli Security Manager, and additional new technology.

Tivoli Identity Manager is a management solution that provides the following key functions:

► Self Registration Interface: Enables new users to register themselves

► Self Care Interface: Allows users to manage their own data and to request additional permissions and services

► Integrated Workflow: Automates processes for identity management and implements business policies

► Delegated Web Administration: Allows dynamic delegation of administrative responsibilities via Web-based interface

► User Administration Agent: Manages account information on various systems and applications

► Security Manager Agent: Manages security settings and provides role-based authorization on various systems and applications

ivoli Identity Manager Version1.1 requires you to have the following other
e components installed:

li Management Framework Version 3.7.1 with Patch 2 is used as the
erlying infrastructure to handle management information and to
municate with remote managed systems and managed applications.

li User Administration Version 3.8 with Patch 1 and 3 is part of Tivoli
itity Manager, but is still available as a separate product.

li Security Manager Version 3.8 is part of Tivoli Identity Manager, but is
lable as a separate product.

Directory 3.2.1 (LDAP Server with DB2 UDB Version 7.1 and IBM HTTP
'er Version 1.3.19) is required to manage the user registry. Information
the directory is used to authenticate users and administrators. User
mation from the internal Tivoli Management database is synchronized
information in the user registry via LDAP.

WebSphere Standard Edition 4.0.1 (IBM HTTP Server 1.3.19 + JDK 1.3)
ed to provide the Servlet environment for the User Administration Web
face.

li Access Manager (Version 3.7) is required when using Tivoli Security
ager for UNIX systems. This allows to enforce centrally managed policy
sions on all UNIX systems.

The current version of Tivoli Identity Manager requires IBM LDAP
ory Server to store user and policy information. It is Tivoli's stated
on that future versions of Tivoli Identity Manager will also support other
of registries, including Microsoft Active Directory, Novell Directory
es, iPlanet Directory, and relational database management systems.

now use Tivoli Identity Manager to implement the components described
evious architecture overview. Most of the conceptual components can
mapped to Tivoli Identity Manager components. Figure 12-3 on
6 shows the logical flow of information in the proposed solution and
2-4 on page 297 shows a more detailed view with individual components
r communications. The server components of Tivoli Identity Manager will
lled on an existing Tivoli Management Server (TMR Server), existing
gateways will be reused to manage the endpoints, additional software
stalled on all endpoints, and the Identity Manager Web interface will be
on a separate system running IBM WebSphere.

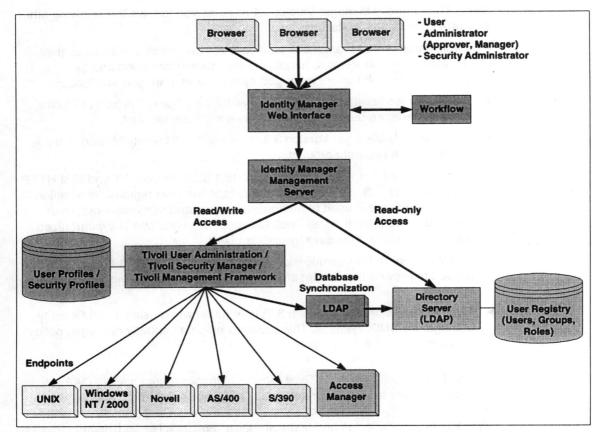

Figure 12-3   Tivoli Identity Manager overview

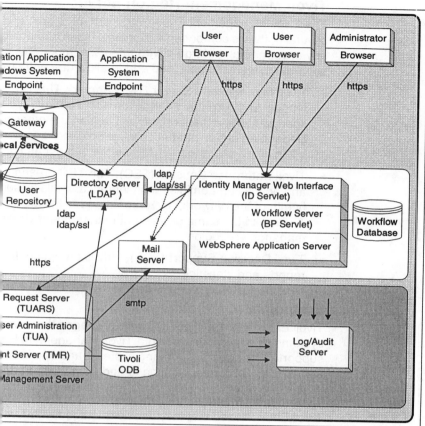

*...*n with Tivoli Identity Manager

*...*gement Framework

*...*bed in Chapter 11, "Basic management for identities" on page 259, we
*...*hat our company already uses the Tivoli Management Framework to
*...*host systems within their intranet environment and they already use
*...*r Administration for a more consistent and efficient management of
*...*unts on their systems. We will now introduce additional components
*...*i Identity Manager V1.1 and show how they can be used to build a
*...*anced security management solution.

*...*detailed information about the Tivoli Management Framework, refer to
*...*edbooks *All About Tivoli Management Agents*, SG24-5134, *Tivoli*
... *Management Across Firewalls*, SG24-5510 and *Extending Network*
*...*ent Through Firewalls*, SG24-6229.

Tivoli Management Region Server

The Tivoli Management Framework separates management functions into several software components. Not all of these components have to be installed in any environment. In large environments, components can be installed on separate systems to split load and to allow de-centralized management.

► Tivoli Management Server (TMR Server): This is the central component to receive and correlate information about various types of events within a specific management region and to manage other components in that region. Depending of the intranet size, multiple management regions can be established and another TMR server can act as the overall manager.

► Tivoli Enterprise Console (TEC): The TEC presents operational information and acts as an administration interface. It allows support staff to monitor the health of the network environment and to initiate corrective actions. Multiple TECs with the same or different management views can be installed in any management region.

► Tivoli Decision Support (TDS): This is an optional component to generate reports and statistics.

Endpoints

Tivoli Endpoints are client software packages that are required to manage systems or applications within a Tivoli Management Region. Endpoints are supported for specific operating systems and applications. Proprietary protocols are used for all communication to and from Tivoli Endpoints.

Tivoli Identity Manager contains additional software to extend functionality of Tivoli Endpoints so that they can be managed with Tivoli User Administration and Tivoli Security Manager. The following client platforms are fully supported:

► Windows 2000 and Windows NT

► UNIX Versions: Solaris, AIX, HP-UX, and Linux

► OS/390

► AS/400

► OS/2

► NetWare

Supported platforms for Tivoli Identity Manager's server components are:

► Solaris, AIX, and Windows NT

support, for example, only Tivoli Security Manager or Tivoli User
ration, is available for a list of additional platforms. In addition, a toolkit
User Administration and Tivoli Security Manager is available to allow
on of other systems or applications.

int Gateways

nication between server and endpoints within the Tivoli Management
ork is realized via Endpoint Gateways. They are used to manage a group
ered endpoints within their neighborhood. Endpoint Gateways can either
led on a management server or can be distributed throughout the
to improve performance or availability. They are always included on
d Nodes and on TMR Servers. For our virtual company, at least one
Gateway will be installed in each location so that all endpoints can
eir management gateway locally and do not have to rely on highly
WAN connections to complete certain management operations.

Gateways provide the following communication functions:

for initial endpoint logins, which are needed to register in a Tivoli
gement Region

for upcall requests from endpoints to management server

for downcall requests from management server to specific endpoints

oute certain requests to all registered endpoints (server broadcast)

gateways do not need to be installed on separate physical systems, but
be installed on a non-busy system in combination with endpoints,
l nodes or management servers.

or busy environment, Endpoint Gateways can be used to take load
n the management server. As an estimate, each TMR server supports
Endpoint Gateways and each Endpoint Gateway supports up to 2000
s.

-5 on page 300 shows a list of supported endpoints that can be used
i User Administration and Tivoli Security Manager.

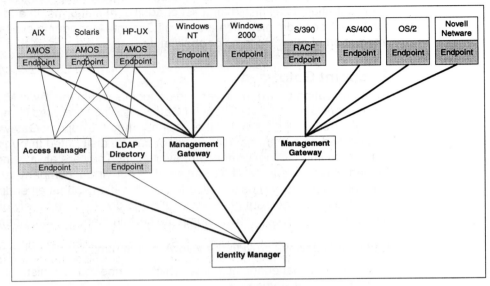

Figure 12-5   Supported platforms for Tivoli Identity Manager

Managed Node

A Tivoli Managed Node performs the same functions as the TMR server and also contains a database to manage endpoints in their environment.

For large remote locations, it is recommended to install a combination of Managed Node and Endpoint Gateway. For smaller remote locations, it will be sufficient to only install an Endpoint Gateway.

12.5.2 Identity Manager Web Interface

Tivoli Identity Manager contains a separate Web-based interface for easy-to-use access by users and administrators. It presents customized menus with access to individual functions depending on the user's security permissions.

The following functions are available for all users. They can be selected without any initial authentication:

► Request new account: Function is known as self-registration or subscription, and is available using the Identity Manager command line interface.

► Reset my password: This function is named "I forgot my password" on the Web interface and it uses a challenge response mechanism to identify a registered user without requiring the current user password. Users can configure their personal challenge/response question in their user attributes.

)wing functions are available for registered users. They can be selected
ial authentication with valid user ID and password:

1ge my password: This is a *self care function* and its execution does not
ire any further approval. This function does not work in case of lost,
)tten, or expired user passwords, or when the user account in the LDAP
try has been locked by an administrator.

ite my account: Self care function. Allows you to change certain
outes that belong to the user's account in the user registry and that are
d in the LDAP directory server. The security administrator can define the
f attributes that can be updated by users without relying on an
nistrator for approval.

)wing functions are available for authorized administrators. Only users
icient administrator permissions will be able to select and perform those
s. The predefined security roles AddUser, AdminChangePassword,
r, DeleteUser, ModifyUser, SecurityGroupMembership, and ViewUser
I to define fine-grained administrator permissions for the following
s:

1ge user authorizations: This task enables an administrator to delegate
)rity to other administrators for roles, such as approving (or rejecting)
ests, changing passwords, managing a user's roles for particular user
es, managing a user's roles for particular security group profiles, adding
s to user profiles or security group profiles, deleting users from user
es or security group profiles, and changing attributes of users in user
es or security group profiles.

1ge Security Membership: This function allows an administrator to add or
e users to security group profiles.

pending requests: This menu shows information about pending requests
llows an administrator to approve or reject pending requests.

t user's password: This function allows an administrator to change
ier user's password. It can be selected to either change the user's
non password or another user account password.

e user: This function allows an administrator to create a user by
ting a user profile for the new user and specifying user information.

1ge users: This function enables administrators to view, modify or delete
nformation for a single user.

e users: This function allows an administrator to delete one or more
 at once.

The following function, defined by the security role AdminTID, is only available for authorized security administrators:

► Edit Configuration: This menu allows an administrator to specify Tivoli Identity Manager configuration parameters.

The Identity Manager Web interface is split into two logical components: Identity Manager Servlet and Workflow Server. The Identity Manager Servlet handles all direct interaction with Web clients and the Workflow Server performs workflow management. Both components are described in the following sections.

Identity Manager Servlet

The Web-based interface has been implemented as a Java 2 Platform Enterprise Edition (J2EE) Web application using servlets and JSP technology and it requires a Web application server (IBM WebSphere Server) to run. New users can register themselves and request their initial user account using the command line interface or an individually customized graphical user interface (GUI). Registered users can login and will then see a customized menu to enter new requests and to view or manage outstanding requests. The customized menu will be dynamically generated and depends on the roles that are currently defined for the user. Users that have authorization to approve requests will see a menu item for that task. Tivoli Identity Manager uses information from the user registry to perform user authentication during login (to verify user credentials) and it makes requests to Tivoli Identity Manager Management Server to receive information about the user and his accounts, and about his roles and authorizations.

User Profiles are set up to allow authority to be delegated at a user profile level. Security Profiles are set up to implement the company security policy, and to create groups so that assigning resources can be delegated to the Adminstrator, and he can give access to resources by assigning users to security groups, as depicted in Figure 12-6 on page 303.

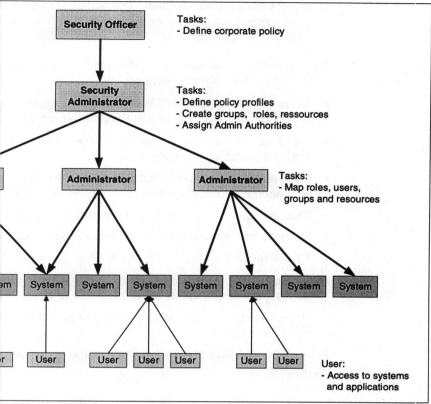

er and security administration

...y Manager Workflow Server

...ow engine has been integrated into the Web interface. This allows an
...trator to perform administrative tasks in a structured way and allows
...ment of certain business policies. Workflows can be customized to fit into
...pany's environment. Tivoli Identity Manager comes with predefined
...entations for the following three workflows:

...self-registration: The process in which an administrator initiates a new
...s registration. The workflow enables administrators to configure a set of
...overs that are notified in a specified order to approve or reject a pending
...tration.

...self-care: A feature that enables users to manage their own user data.
...workflow routes self-care requests to the proper administrators for
...oval.

► Approval: The process in which administrators, in a defined order, approve or reject pending user requests. The workflow enables administrators to route user requests to the proper approvers and to initiate mail notifications after request completion.

Each workflow consists of tasks that are to be executed in a certain order. Some examples for predefined tasks are:

► Send e-mail to approver: Used to inform approvers about new request. Each e-mail contains URL linking to the approval screen.

► Send e-mail to user: Used for notifications about completed requests or about status of pending requests.

► Start approval process: Each workflow may contain multiple approval steps and each approval step may generate e-mails sent to multiple approvers.

► Queue request: Add new request to workflow database.

► Remove request from queue: Remove request from workflow database.

► Check request status: Show status of a user request.

► Execute Tivoli User Administration command: Allows you to perform TUA commands and to update user attributes after successful request approval.

► Execute external command: Allows you to perform any customized task within a workflow.

Figure 12-7 on page 305 shows some of the tasks performed by the predefined workflows.

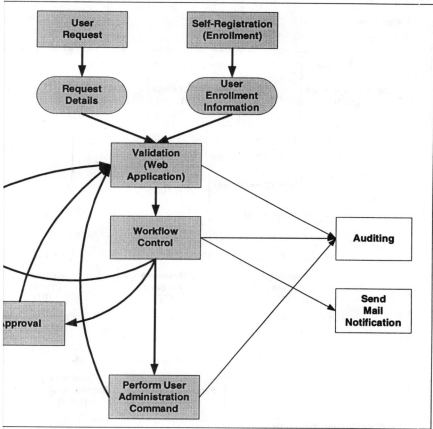

iistration workflow

ntity Manager Web interface uses other external components to store
nly information about outstanding requests for the Workflow Server is
ocally. All user information needed to authenticate during logins and all
ation information needed to build the customized menus is directly read
e directory server via LDAP. All updates within the user registry are
ed via the Tivoli Identity Manager Management Server via HTTPS and,
rds, those changes are distributed to the LDAP Directory under control of
ıtity Manager Management Server.

hnical implementation of workflows within Tivoli Identity Manager is
n Figure 12-8 on page 306.

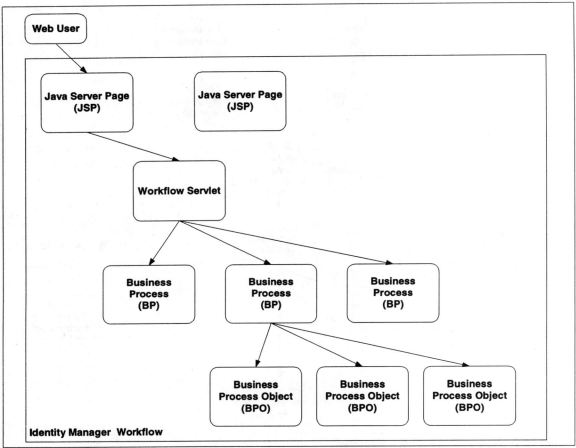

Figure 12-8   Technical workflow implementation with BPs and BPOs

The workflow server within Tivoli Identity Manager has been implemented as a Web application using Java servlet technology. Java-Server-Pages (JSP) on the Web server invoke the ID workflow servlet and interact with the Web users. Then the workflow servlet will use the user input to initiate new workflows and to continue pending workflows in a well-defined way.

Workflows are implemented using special Java applications. With Identity Manager, they are called Business Processes (BPs) and they are divided into individual tasks called Business Process Objects (BPOs). BPs can execute BPOs in a well-defined order and can make decisions based on their execution results. Splitting workflows into BPs and reusable BPOs is a structured approach and helps customize or create new workflows.

ed, workflows can be extended to contain external components by
j methods from external classes. This feature can be used to include
es that have already been implemented on other IT systems. As an
e, it is possible to use an existing approval process based on Lotus
Workflow with Tivoli Identity Manager without having to develop a new
ion for the same purpose.

unctions provided by the Identity Manager Web interface are
ented using workflows. Simple operations like Change My Password do
iire any additional notification or approval tasks. If the user is able to
a correct password during login, Change Password will directly update
r's password and will then present a status message on the Web
e.

The current version of Tivoli Identity Manager does not contain a
ow editor or workflow GUI. Modification of workflows and definition of
sks requires some general programming skills. For more advanced
nentations of workflows, it might be useful to either use an external
ow system like MQ Workflow or to start implementing a customized
n using advanced Java Programming Toolkits.

roli's stated intention that later versions of Tivoli Identity Manager will
different approach for their workflow implementation based on MQ
ow and they might integrate the Workflow Server into the Identity
er Management Server instead of its Web Interface. Such a solution
easily allow you to install multiple Identity Manager Web Interfaces.
l planning in that direction will make migration to the next version

anager Management Server

ntity Manager Management Server will be installed on the same system
with the Tivoli Management server (TMR server). It contains modules
Administration (TUA), Security Manager (TSM), the command line
e (CLI) and the new HTTPS interface (TUA Request Server).

oli User Administration Request Server (TUARS) accepts commands
Identity Manager Web interface via SSL sockets. The request is sent
XML format, and is parsed by TUARS. The response is also sent back
IL format. Because TUARS trusts requests from the Web interface and
s them without reevaluating permissions of the originating user or

administrator, it is important to protect all communication between TUARS and the Identity Manager Web interface. Attackers should not be able to communicate directly with the TUA Request Server or to send manipulated or unauthorized requests.

To satisfy those security requirements, TUARS can be configured to require SSL Version 3 client authentication and only accept requests from clients that use a known predefined PKI certificate. With this configuration all incoming connections from other clients will be rejected. The SSL Version 3 client authentication feature is needed when Tivoli Identity Manager is installed in an open Intranet environment without additional Intranet demilitarized zones (DMZs) to protect the communication path between the Identity Manager Web interface and the Identity Manager Management Server.

Tivoli Identity Manager provides detailed audit logging that enables security administrators to monitor user activity and document it in reports. All requests to the Tivoli User Administration Request Server, such as Delete User or Change My Password, are logged to the Tivoli User Administration log file. As a security precaution, requests are not processed when audit logging is enabled but the audit log cannot function, such as when there is insufficient disk space or permissions errors. This ensures that no actions are performed that are not logged.

Advanced access control for the IM Web interface

Most of the interactions with the functions above are used to carry sensitive user information. To satisfy basic security requirements concerning confidentiality and authentication for those operations, the Identity Manager Web interface can be configured to only accept connections via HTTPS and to ask for an user ID and password for authentication of registered users using forms-based authentication. If security is not an issue of concern in a certain environment, it can also be configured to accept regular HTTP connections without SSL protection.

When using Tivoli Identity Manager in a different network environment with more advanced security requirements, it is possible to combine it with a reverse proxy like Access Manager's WebSEAL. As a stand-alone solution, the current version of Tivoli Identity Manager only supports user/password authentication and a single Web Interface, but the combination with WebSEAL allows you to implement additional access control mechanisms. Such a combination is needed within large untrusted intranet environments or when using Tivoli Identity Manager to manage users for multiple enterprises, for example, for intranet users and for Internet users.

2-9 shows how to implement secure access to Tivoli Identity Manager's rface for Internet users and intranet users using WebSEAL. Instead of single Web interface accessible by both groups, this approach uses access points for both user groups. Both WebSEALs have their own ation settings and contain an SSL-Smart-Junction referring to the Identity r Web Interface.

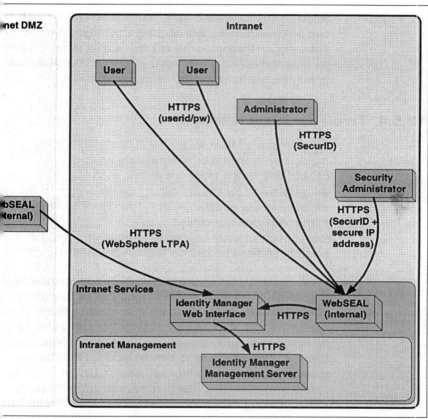

Identity Manager using WebSEAL

rnal WebSEAL in the Internet DMZ will only permit access from regular s defined by their group attributes, using an user ID and password. Any empt from administrators or any access to unauthorized URLs will be by WebSEAL.

The internal WebSEAL in the intranet will permit access from regular users, administrators, and from security administrators. It can be configured to require special authentication methods like RSA SecurID tokens or PKI certificates with SSL Version 3 client authentication for administrators. It might even be configured to restrict access for the security administrator so that only access to the critical Edit Configuration function is allowed from certain network locations, for example, from a protected network in the computing center.

Such an implementation with individual access points for different user groups can be used to eliminate security risks caused by misuse from untrusted networks. It eliminates the risk that stolen internal administrator passwords can be misused over the Internet to gain unauthorized access to the User Registry or to manipulate its contents, for example, by creation of new users.

12.5.4 Tivoli Security Manager

Tivoli Security Manager provides centralized security policy enforcement for multiple system platforms by managing access control. It extends security capabilities for the most commonly used platforms and provides a single point of administration for access control definitions on all those platforms. In addition to enforcement of access control rules, Tivoli Security Manager can also be used to manipulate other security policy aspects, such as the platform password policy, login policy, or audit configuration. It allows centrally managed deployment of security settings according to given business policies.

Tivoli Security Manager uses a role-based administration model, as shown in Figure 12-10 on page 311, to group lists of resources together and to provide defined access rights for users associated with that role. A role defines a list of resources and a set of access permissions to those resources. Roles can then be linked to groups of users, for example, depending on their current job function. Once this association is made, Tivoli Security Manager maps the resulting access rights for each user to the target platforms. This role-based model allows the granting of access to large numbers of resources in one step without having to change access rights for individual users or for individual systems.

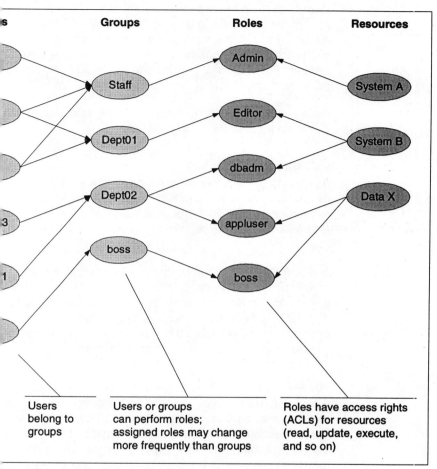

| | Groups | Roles | Resources |

Users
belong to
groups

Users or groups
can perform roles;
assigned roles may change
more frequently than groups

Roles have access rights
(ACLs) for resources
(read, update, execute,
and so on)

-10   Role-based authorization model

e system-independent and the resources may reside on many different
g systems. Changing access rights for a certain role results in changing
or resources on all systems associated with that role. Adding a resource
makes the access control determined for that resource apply to
e associated with that role. The process of combining systems and roles
subscription within the Tivoli Management Framework.

Role-based administration makes it possible to manage a large number of configurable options in a more efficient way. Once the roles have been defined maintenance is much lower than that required without a similar technology. The two functions of *population* and *distribution* are used for the management of profiles. Population of profiles allows you to discover security information from managed systems and distribution allows to update that information.

Here are some design guidelines for the selection of groups, roles and resources within an organization.

Groups

A group is responsible for a subset of the work done by the organization. To do its share of the work, a group needs specific access to selected system resources. In the Tivoli Security Manager role-based resource access model, groups are given the required access through assignment of one or more roles to the group.

A group can be any set of users within an organization. Example groups include divisions, departments, project teams, and job titles. After the initial definition of the security-relevant groups for the enterprise's organizational structure, the set of groups defined should only change when the organizational structure changes. However, the list of users that are members of a group changes as the people who make up the organization change.

Roles

A role defines the set of capabilities required to carry out a given job. After creating the required set of roles, roles only need to be added or removed when the job functions required for the enterprise's business activity change. A role's capabilities can be modified whenever the job function represented by the role requires new or different capabilities.

Roles can be nested, and a child role inherits capabilities from its parent. A child role can be configured to provide additional capabilities, remove certain capabilities, or both. The ability to inherit role capabilities simplifies the process of administering roles. A role can be defined to have a single parent from which it inherits its base capabilities. The inherited parent capabilities can be specialized in the following ways:

► New capabilities (resources and associated access permissions) can be defined in the child role.

► Inherited parent capabilities can be overridden to add capabilities to a resource defined in the parent role.

► Inherited parent capabilities can be overridden to subtract capabilities from a resource defined in the parent role.

n organization has been modeled as a set of groups and roles, security
stration can be performed almost exclusively at the organizational level.

urces

y resources are programs, files, systems, and similar objects in a
ted enterprise that need common access protection. They contain
ns of default access permissions, time-of-day restrictions on access, and
audit controls on each resource, to control and monitor when and in what
r resources are accessed.

e a variety of resources depend on the type of system being managed,
es are categorized by type and resource type. The set of resource types
supported are specific to the system or application type being managed.

ces are assigned to roles that correspond to job functions, thus enabling
sful execution of a given job. A resource definition can be a member of
an one role, thereby providing a means to group specific resources (and
onding access settings) based on business needs.

ity Profiles

rity management information is stored in *Security Profiles*. They contain
using system-independent formats so that they can be used within an
ise on different system types. The following types of records exist:

oup record contains user, group, and role membership lists. These lists
mapped at the system- and application-level to the membership
ionship between user IDs and groups. In addition, login and resource
ss audit policy and allowed login time policy can be set on a group
rd.

le record defines the set of capabilities required to carry out a given job
tion within the organization. Groups are given the necessary capabilities
ssignment of one or more roles to the group.

source record defines homogeneous collections of resource objects in the
rprise that can be accessed by users and groups via their role
gnments. The most common type of resource object is a file. Other types
sources are protected processes, trusted programs, terminals, network
ts, network servers, and surrogate users.

stem policy record provides the ability to define user- and
urce-related security policy rules that will be applied on a system-wide
s to all subscribed endpoints.

inistrator can choose how many and what combination of security profile
ypes a given security profile will contain. One security profile may contain
ole, and resource records, while another profile may contain only system

policy records. The exact combination of record types in a given security profile is influenced by the security requirements of the systems that subscribe to the profile manager that contains the security profile. For more information on planning security configurations, see the redbook *Tivoli Security Management Design Guide*, SG24-5101.

Using Tivoli Security Manager

Tivoli Security Manager allows you to perform the daily administration of security configurations without any expert administrators. But initial configuration of Tivoli Security Manager and the creation of effective security profiles for a list of systems and applications still requires assistance of an expert security administrator. Without solid security expertise and without extensive knowledge of applications the resulting security settings will either be ineffective or will be too strict, so applications might become unusable.

Here are some typical procedures implemented with Tivoli Security Manager:

▶ General procedures

- Define login time restrictions for users

- Define password and concurrent login policies

- Lock user after multiple login failures

▶ UNIX procedures

- Restrict root login capabilities (for example, only allow login as *root* from specific terminals or network addresses)

- Prevent root from administering UNIX users and groups

- Prevent root from accidentally deleting application files or system files

- Restrict access to files and directories (enforce read, write, and execute permissions on a per-user basis, for example, restrict access to audit and log files, or only allow specific programs to change a file)

- Protect UNIX processes from the `kill` command

- Protect su requests (switch user, for example, prevent users from switching to root or application administrator IDs)

- Restrict access to the `cron` and `at` commands

- Protect execution of privileged programs

- Block network connections (to block trojan horses or unwanted data transfer)

- Build a *Trusted Computing Base*; only allow changes to files and executables by authorized administrators, make it so that any unauthorized change leaves files and executables unusable

Perform consistent and secure auditing by monitoring access to files and executables

dows NT procedures

Specify access rights to a Windows NT resource

Specify auditing of a Windows NT resource

ecurity Manager provides the best value-add for UNIX platforms, where it dditional security modules to expand native UNIX security features. For vs systems, it does not implement any additional new security functions, ws you to manage security settings on many systems in a consistent and t way. Compared to other stand-alone security tools, the advantage of ecurity Manager is that it can be integrated into an existing management ment with common support for multiple platforms.

ecurity Manager should be used to harden systems running critical ss applications. It allows you to secure applications by controlling network to applications and by protecting key files and executables used by tions. It should not be considered the universal solution that automatically s any system running some unknown applications into a secure system. t solid knowledge about typical application behavior, it will be very difficult program to detect any types of unauthorized usage.

enting an advanced solution for user administration without increasing security aspects of the managed systems is not very useful, because ight be able to use security vulnerabilities to work around their sions and gain additional privileges, for example, users on UNIX systems e able to exploit vulnerabilities and gain superuser privileges instead of es associated with their given user IDs. Therefore, user administration always be combined with proper hardening of system security and al possibilities to enforce access rights associated with given user IDs ir desired permissions. Tivoli Security Manager helps to implement this d to make any user administration solution much more valuable.

User Administration and Tivoli Security Manager

lementation of Tivoli Security Manager and Tivoli User Administration independent of each other. If an organization has a requirement to UNIX access control, then they may only need to implement Security r. If the requirement is to centralize administration of user accounts, then er Administration may be required.

If both products are installed in the same Tivoli Management Region (TMR), then some integration features for easier management of user, group, role, and resource records are activated. For example, it becomes possible to add user accounts, managed through User Administration, to Tivoli Security Manager groups. This provides a form of workflow where the administrator adding a user account can also determine what resources the user gets access to, based on a security group.

When both products are installed, the typical usage would be a security administrator defining a policy in the Security Manager Roles, and an accounts administrator granting the correct access rights by security group placement of user accounts using User Administration.

Figure 12-11 on page 317 shows how policy information is implemented in Tivoli Identity Manager and how Tivoli Security Manager is able to utilize information managed via Tivoli User Administration.

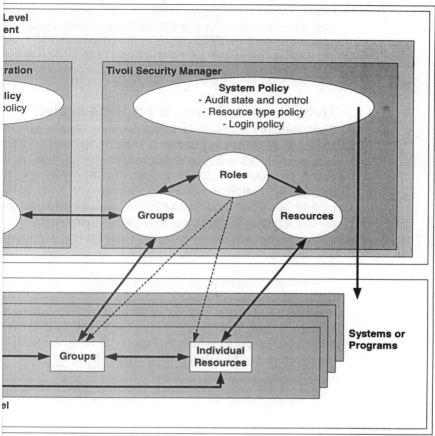

policy information for TUA and TSM

...ecurity Manager is very useful when installed as an additional option in
...ments where the Tivoli Management Framework and Tivoli User
...stration are already used. This provides the best added value without
...al overhead and allows you to strengthen the security level and to
... the configuration of the security settings. It allows you to combine
...e Distribution, Distributed Monitoring, Remote Control, User
...stration, and Security Management with a common approach and shared
...ositories.

Tivoli Security Manager for UNIX systems

Tivoli Security Manager for UNIX systems uses a component called Access Manager for Operating Systems (AMOS) to manage access control on UNIX systems. AMOS is a new development and replaces the earlier security product called Tivoli Access Control Facility (TACF), which was based on SeOS technology. AMOS shows a major increase in performance, and upgrade procedures from TACF to AMOS are available. AMOS extends security functions for UNIX systems and uses an external policy registry and an user registry to enforce access control decisions. Tivoli Identity Manager and Access Manager are used to maintain those registries.

The security engine of AMOS uses a multi-threaded design to avoid performance problems on multi-processor systems. It works as a UNIX kernel extension and does not require any kernel modifications or replacement of any of the UNIX system utilities. It is therefore possible to use AMOS even in combination with other UNIX security products. Figure 12-12 on page 319 shows the logical architecture of AMOS on a UNIX system.

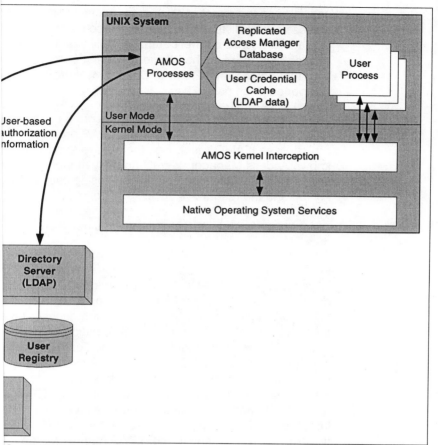

UNIX System

AMOS Processes

Replicated Access Manager Database

User Credential Cache (LDAP data)

User Process

Jser-based
authorization
nformation

User Mode
Kernel Mode

AMOS Kernel Interception

Native Operating System Services

Directory
Server
(LDAP)

User
Registry

S architecture on UNIX systems

rovides a layer of authorization policy enforcement in addition to that
by the native operating system. Administrators can define additional
tion policy definitions by applying fine-grained access controls that
r permit access to key system resources. Controls are based on user
jroup membership, the type of operation, time of the day or day of the
d the accessing application. An administrator can control access to
ile resources, login and network services, and changes of identity.
ntrols can also be used to manage the execution of administrative
es and to limit administrative capabilities on a per user basis. In addition
ization policy enforcement, AMOS provides mechanisms to verify
olicy and audit authorization decisions.

AMOS uses two external registries, which are centrally maintained, to control user access to protected resources. Access control definitions for resources (access control lists (ACLs) and resource records) are stored in Access Manager's access control database (policy registry) and are accessed via Access Manager's Authentication Server. For more information about Access Manager components, refer to Chapter 4, "Introduction to Access Manager components" on page 79.

The user definitions (user and group records) are stored in the directory server (user registry) and are accessed via LDAP protocol. When protected resources are accessed, AMOS first uses the user record to map the user's name to a known Access Manager user ID (Identity mapping) and then performs an authorization check based on the accessing user's identity, the time and day, the action, and the resource's access controls to determine if access is permitted or denied. It uses multiple attributes from the user's record to decide if the user account has been locked or if the user is not allowed to log in at a certain time or date.

For availability and performance reasons, data from both external registries is stored locally on the AMOS system and completion of the access control process does not depend on working network connections. A replica of Access Manager's access control database is stored locally on each AMOS system, and there is a procedure for automatic distribution of database updates. In case of updates, Access Manager Management Server will notify all registered AMOS systems and each AMOS system can then decide if and when they will retrieve the new access control database updates from Access Manager Management Server. In case of network connectivity interrupts, AMOS systems are able to retrieve outstanding updates after connectivity has been reestablished. Data from the LDAP user registry is cached locally after initial usage and does, in general, not require any further LDAP queries for the following operations by the same user. Contents in the credential cache will be refreshed after a configured holding time or upon manual request by the administrator.

The current release of AMOS may not address all scalability and
nance issues for certain environments. Because each AMOS system
replicate the complete contents of the Access Manager access control
se, performance problems may appear in case of frequent policy
s or within large environments with many systems or with many
ed resources. Each change to the access control database may cause
)S systems to start some activities and to download the most recent
s. The replication algorithm uses incremental updates and does not
that all systems always have to download the complete database with
)date.

al solution to address those problems would be to split management
s into smaller sized sub-domains or by applying access control
ns to well-structured resources.

rsions of AMOS may use a different algorithm for replication of the
Manager access control database and may be able to retrieve only a
subset of the access control database.

IOS uses Access Manager to enforce access control decisions, it needs
resources types to be protected and permission types to be enforced.

1 shows the types of system resources and individual system resources
e protected with AMOS.

System resources and corresponding AMOS resource types

e type	Resource type name	Description
m resources	File	
esources	NetIncoming	Incoming network connections, defined via remote host names, IP addresses, and/or IP ports
	NetOutgoing	Outgoing network connections, defined via remote host names, IP addresses, and/or IP ports
ources	Login/Terminal/Local	Login from local console
	Login/Terminal/Remote	Login over network
	Login/Holidays	Login during defined holiday period

Resource type	Resource type name	Description
Surrogate Resources	Surrogate	
Sudo Resources	Sudo	
Trusted Computing Base Resources	TCB/Login-Programs	
	TCB/Secure-Files	
	TCB/Secure-Programs	
	TCB/Impersonator-Programs	

AMOS provides the ability to define files on a system as being part of a trusted computing base. Files that are members of the Trusted Computing Base are monitored for changes in ownership, UNIX file permissions, creation and modification time stamps, presence or absence on a system, content of the file, and the device on which the file resides. These attributes are collectively referred to as the file's signature.

AMOS allows you to grant special AMOS privileges to programs by defining them in the Trusted Computing Base (TCB). If the integrity of a program defined in the TCB is compromised, it should no longer be trusted with special privileges. AMOS detects changes that compromise the integrity of a registered program. When a change is detected, AMOS records that the program is untrusted. AMOS will not allow an untrusted program to be executed until an administrator explicitly retrusts it.

Special privileges are granted to programs by defining them in one or more of the following classes of TCB resources:

► Secure-Files: Secure files are granted no special privileges. They are simply monitored for changes in their signature. AMOS defines some AMOS files as Secure-Files when initially configured.

► Secure-Programs: Many UNIX programs require UNIX privileges that are different from the UNIX permissions of the users who can run them. Such programs are marked with the set user ID or set group ID permissions and might include such commands as `su`, `mail`, or `telnet`.

► Login-Programs: UNIX systems have no specific action that can be classified as a login. AMOS detects a user's login from the execution of various surrogate operations by specific programs. The specific programs are defined by their membership in the Login-Programs class of TCB files. Only certain programs have been certified to work as Login-Programs in the AMOS environment. These are the programs that are involved in UNIX logins from

y attached terminals, graphical desktop environments, and common
ork protocols (FTP, RLOGIN, TELNET, REXEC, RSH).

rsonator-Programs: UNIX systems generally provide a mechanism (for
ple, cron) for users to schedule jobs to be executed as batch operations
they are not logged in to the system. Such programs typically run as the
ser and, when executing a task, change identity to the user who
duled the task. The initial AMOS configuration only lists cron in this class.

ne-Programs: A program might be integrated so tightly to a system that
rocess running that program was subject to authorization policy, as
ed by AMOS, the system would cease to function. You can mark such
ams as immune from all AMOS policy by making them a member of the
ne-Programs class of the TCB. Execution of immune programs is
ct to authorization as for any other program but, once running, the
am is immune to all AMOS authorization policy. This immunity includes
ng – no operations that a running immune program performs are
d.

nissions in Table 12-2 can be applied to certain AMOS resource types.

2 *AMOS permissions defined in the [OSSEAL] action group*

Description	AMOS resource type
Connect	NetIncoming and NetOutgoing
Change Directory	File
Surrogate	Surrogate
Kill Program	File
Login	Login
Create	File
Rename	File
Update Timestamp	File
Delete	File
List Directory	File
Change Ownership	File
Change Permission	File
Read	File
Write	File

Action	Description	AMOS resource type
x	Execute	File and Sudo

Tivoli Security Manager supports the following auditing functions:

► If access control policy is adequately set, then the focus of security auditing can change. Instead of checking every possible audit event for every type of policy violation (for example, root edited a sensitive file), auditing can concentrate on the real concerns. For example, policy states root has no access to the sensitive file; logging only successful attempts to modify the file produces much less data.

► Due to the native manipulation of system security engines, all audit features are intact and valid. Native tools for manipulating audit data can still be used. Audit policy can also be configured and dictated centrally using Tivoli Security Manager.

► Tivoli Security Manager has a number of reports configured through Tivoli Decision Support (currently a technology preview). These reports can highlight inconsistencies in policy across multiple targets.

► Tivoli Risk Manager can be used to correlate intrusion detection systems. In a future release of Tivoli Security Manager, security events might be sendable to Risk Manager for host-based intrusion detection correlation. In the current Tivoli Security Manager releases, numerous security events are already sent to TEC and these can be integrated with Risk Manager.

Note: AMOS can be used without the Tivoli Management Framework, but this affects central management of all AMOS systems. Without the Tivoli Management Framework, alternative procedures have to be used for installation and maintenance of AMOS systems. In any case, Tivoli Access Manager is needed to supply the access control databases for each system.

Tivoli Security Manager for Windows

Tivoli Security Manager for Windows NT or Windows 2000 systems uses native security capabilities and provides consistent management of those capabilities. It does not use an additional security package like AMOS on UNIX systems. The subsequent use of native security tools would reflect the configuration of data performed by Tivoli Security Manager.

It is likely that Tivoli Security Manager will outperform native Windows NT domain tools when it comes to simple access control administration, but the value of Tivoli Security Manager in this environment is in the integration with other Tivoli products (such as for event management) and the assurance that security is being applied consistently. This is especially useful in multi-domain environments

voli Security Manager does not require trust relationships between
to be established. Consistent policies across multiple domains can be
by sending the same (or similar) policy definition to each domain. This
y to access control policy, password policy and audit configuration.

wing list shows the resource types and their attribute types that can be
Tivoli Security Manager to build security policies for Windows 2000

tory

Access: Access to the object is explicitly denied.

ll Control: Full control of an object and its attributes, including the ability
manage access, permissions, and owner.

dify: All the privileges of Read, Write, Execute, and Delete.

ad: Can display files and subdirectories within a directory and view the
ributes.

rite: Can create subdirectories and files within the directory.

averse Folder/Execute File: Can access subdirectories of the directory.

st Folder/Read Data: Can list directory contents.

ad Attributes: Can read file attributes.

ad Extended Attributes: Can read extended file attributes.

eate Files/Write Data: Can create files in the directory.

eate Folder/Append Data: Can create subdirectories in the directory.

ite Attributes: Can change file attributes.

ite Extended Attributes: Can change extended file attributes.

lete Subfolders and Files: Can delete a directory and its files and
bdirectories, even if files are read only.

lete: Can delete a directory and its contents.

ad Permissions: Can read the contents of a directory.

ange Permissions: Can alter the access permissions of a directory.

ke Ownership: Can assign write ownership.

r files, the same attribute types can be defined as for directories

- Registry
  - Read: Can read the key, but cannot save changes to the key (corresponds to the combination of Query Value, Enumerate Subkeys, Notify, and Read Control).
  - Full Control: Grants full control of a key and its attributes, including managing access permissions and owner.
  - Delete: Can delete the key and its subkeys.
  - No Access: Access to the key is explicitly denied.
  - Take Ownership: Can change the ownership of a key.
  - Change Permissions: Can change permissions for a key.
  - Set Value: Can modify the current setting of a key.
  - Query Value: Can read the current setting of a key.
  - Create Subkey: Can add a subkey to a key.
  - Enumerate Subkeys: Can view a subkey tree under a key.
  - Notify: Can enable auditing of a key.
  - Create Link: Can link to this location within the registry.
  - Read Control: Can view security settings of a key.
- Printer
  - No Access: Access to the printer is explicitly denied.
  - Full Control: Full control of the printer and its documents, including pausing and resuming print jobs, changing print job priorities, and changing printer permissions.
  - Print Access: Can submit jobs to the printer and have full control of those jobs.
  - Manage Documents: Can manipulate print jobs belonging to any user (does not include printer configuration or printing to the device).
  - Read Permissions: Can read the permissions set for a printer and its documents.
  - Change Permissions: Can change access permissions for a printer and its documents.
  - Take Ownership: Can change ownership of a printer.
- Share
  - Read: Can display the files and subdirectories within a directory. The user can also view the owner, attributes, and permissions of the directory.

hange: Has the permissions provided by Read, and can also create, edit, d delete files and subdirectories.

ll Control: Has full control of a directory and its attributes, including the ility to manage file attributes, such as access permissions and owner.

Access: Access to the directory is explicitly denied.

tions demonstrate that fine-grained access control policies can be ted.

ecurity Manager for S/390

urity Manager for S/390 allows you to manage certain RACF tasks from ystem. Such a setup can be used to manage security settings (and user) consistently throughout a mixed mainframe, UNIX, and Windows ent. It might also allow you to delegate certain RACF administrative ch as password resets and access revocations to non-experts.

ailed description of the S/390 Security Manager Tivoli integration, refer lbook *The OS/390 Security Server Meets Tivoli: Managing RACF with urity Products*, SG24-5339.

ecurity Manager for Access Manager

urity Manager contains support to manage security information on an lanager Management Server without having to log onto Access This allows you to use Tivoli Identity Manager as the primary interface e identities, system and application security information for Security User Administration, and Access Manager. This reduces the number of faces needed by administrators and does not require an expert to e daily tasks of security management.

urity Manager defines an object in a Tivoli Management Region to a single installation of Access Manager. Once defined, the Access object can be used to populate security records from and distribute ecords to a Access Manager secure domain.

Part 4

anaging a
curity audit

we discuss the solution Tivoli offers in the security audit management
e overall security architecture. Audit information, which generally
ound managing intrusion and fraud, is mainly handled by Tivoli Risk
r Tivoli Intrusion Manager. These products handle a multitude of
aspects with all sorts of IT infrastructures and intrusion detection
d services, which are detailed throughout this part.

k Manager topology and astructure

ng into any specific customer scenario, we want to focus on a general ayout of an enterprise e-business IT infrastructure. Because a lot of the ts mentioned in this overview will be found in almost every installment, tion of these components into a centralized enterprise risk ent implementation will be very similar to ours.

Tivoli Risk Manager builds upon the Tivoli Framework infrastructure, line the general aspects of integration, while a more detailed Tivoli k overview with the necessary components can be found in .3, "Tivoli Framework architecture" on page 337. Based on the Tivoli k foundation, we will briefly describe all the available Tivoli Risk elements and how they fit together. Detailed information on each of be found in the product documentation.

13.1 From the front door to the backyard

The recently reported increase of cyberattacks in the press against e-businesses highlight the need for an integrated, multivendor approach to security management. New forms of cyberattacks constantly emerge, and security administrators must address the business risks arising from different increasing risks, such as:

► Virus threats

► Unauthorized access to Web servers

► Denial of service threats

► Network intrusion attacks

There are a number of ways to configure the IT infrastructure for an enterprise, depending on the size of the organization and on what you are trying to achieve. Basically, it is divided into three sections, as depicted in Figure 13-1.

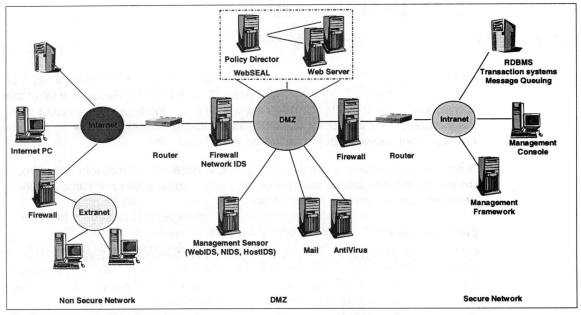

Figure 13-1   e-business topology

1. Non-secure network

   A public network that uses the Internet Protocol and the public telecommunication system to securely share business information or part of a operation with suppliers, vendors, partners, customers, or other businesses.

militarized zone (DMZ) is a computer host or small network that acts
eutral zone" between a company's private network and the outside
network. It prevents outside users from gaining direct access to a
that has company data. It is an optional and more secure approach to
all and effectively acts as a proxy server as well. Users of the public
k outside the company can only access resources in the DMZ.

network

cure network is a private network within an enterprise (also known as a
t). Typically, an intranet includes connections through one or more
y computers to the Internet.

et

m is only a "state of mind" in which the Internet is perceived as a way
usiness and connect with other companies, such as subcontractors or
ss partners. The intention is to establish secure connections from one
ny to the other by using the Internet as the network provider.

of components

3-1, we show a complex e-business scenario that might be found in
erprise environments. This section will briefly discuss the components
this infrastructure.

environment

erver environment includes different kinds of Web servers, Web
servers, and corresponding management and security technologies
ervers.

vers

ver provides informational content in the form of Web pages to Web
Web servers may contain pages about a company, product offerings,
iformation, or other static content. Web servers also offer some ways
g dynamic content and scripting capabilities. Due to security and
nt reasons, these areas are more and more delegated to specialized
ation servers.

Web application servers

Web application servers provide the business logic for an application program in a distributed network environment. These applications are mainly based on Java servlet or Enterprise Java Beans (EJB) technology. Web application servers provide access to valuable business data through Internet type browser based access models. They can be placed in the DMZ as well as in the intranet part of a IT infrastructure.

Access Manager WebSEAL integration

Access Manager is a robust policy management tool for e-business and distributed applications that takes care of authentication and authorization for accessing enterprise data. It includes:

► Access control for Web applications

► Authorization service and application programming interface (API) for legacy and distributed application integration based on C++ and Java2

► Access control for MQSeries based applications

► Highly available and performing Management Server infrastructure

More information on Access Manager can be found in Part 2, "Managing access control" on page 77.

13.2.2 Back-end data

The back-end data reflects the most valuable assets a company owns, not only in IT means.

Database systems

A database holds information that is organized, so that its contents can easily be accessed, managed, and updated. Databases contain aggregations of data records or files, such as sales transactions, product catalogs and inventories, and customer profiles. Typically, a database manager provides users the capabilities of controlling read/write access, specifying report generation, and analyzing usage. Databases and database managers are prevalent in large mainframe systems, but are also present in smaller distributed workstation and mid-range systems. Controlling access to these systems and protecting them against fraudulent action is most important.

...tion systems

...ion usually means a sequence of information exchange and related
... as database updating) that is treated as a unit for the purposes of
...a request and for ensuring database integrity. For a transaction to be
...and database changes to made permanent, a transaction has to be
...in its entirety.

...e queueing

...queueing is a method by which processes can asynchronously
...or pass data using an interface to a system-managed queue of
.... This queue is created by one process and used by multiple other
...that read and write messages to the queue.

...m connects many commercial systems in business today, and it works
...ntly of network disruptions, meaning that important data is always

...s a program, located at a network gateway, that protects the resources
...e network from users from other networks. Security policies
...ed at the network level, host level, and application level allow access
...horized users, applications, and systems.

...ise with an intranet that allows its workers access to the wider Internet
...rewall to prevent outsiders from accessing its own private data
...and for controlling what outside resources its own users have access

...a firewall examines each network packet to determine whether to
...oward its destination. A firewall also includes or works with a proxy
...makes network requests on behalf of workstation users.

...s often installed in a specially designated computer separate from the
...network so that no incoming request can get directly at private network

...mal attempt to access network resources through firewall devices has
...tored actively and carefully.

13.2.4 Router

A router is a device that determines the next network point to which a packet should be forwarded toward its destination. The router is connected to at least two networks and decides which way to send each information packet based on its current understanding of the state of the networks it is connected to. A router is located at any gateway (where one network meets another), and is often included as part of a network switch.

A router may create or maintain a table of the available routes and their conditions and use this information along with distance and cost algorithms to determine the best route for a given packet. Typically, a packet may travel through a number of network points with routers before arriving at its destination.

13.2.5 Intrusion Detection System

An Intrusion Detection System (IDS) is a type of security management system for computers (Host IDS), Web servers (Web IDS) and networks (Network IDS). An ID system gathers and analyzes information from various areas within a computer or a network to identify possible security breaches, which include both intrusions (attacks from outside the organization) and misuse (attacks from within the organization). An IDS uses *vulnerability assessment* (sometimes referred to as *scanning*), which is a technology developed to assess the security of a computer system or network.

Intrusion detection functions include:

► Monitoring and analyzing both user and system activities
► Analyzing system configurations and vulnerabilities
► Assessing system and file integrity
► Ability to recognize typical patterns of attacks
► Analysis of abnormal activity patterns
► Tracking user policy violations

ID systems are being developed in response to the increasing number of attacks on major sites and networks, including those of the Pentagon, the White House, NATO, and the U.S. Department of Defense. The safeguarding of security is becoming increasingly difficult, because the possible technologies of attack are becoming ever more sophisticated; at the same time, less technical ability is required for the novice attacker, because proven past methods are easily accessed through the Web.

r Intrusion Detection has been introduced with Tivoli Risk Manager. It
:tual access log files generated by a Web server to perform the
at detects the Web server attacks. Web IDS, which is deployed on
server, will monitor the log in real time using a knowledge based
) detect malicious access attempts.

anies use a multitude of Intrusion Detection Systems on a variety of
order to gain as much information as possible about malicious access
is very challenging to stay focused with the amount of alerts and false
oming in from all the ID systems.

atures are integrated with operating system management. This
a class of program that searches hard drive and floppy disks for any
otential viruses.

cture

nail is the exchange of computer-stored messages by
nication. It is one of the protocols included with the Transmission
tocol/Internet Protocol (TCP/IP). The most popular protocol for
nail is Simple Mail Transfer Protocol (SMTP); for receiving, it is Post
col Version 3 (POP3).

ework architecture

Vlanager adds enterprise risk management to the comprehensive list
e management solutions and third-party applications based on the
gement Framework. The Tivoli management architecture manages
of machines from a single server. Servers can interconnect to
ge multiple-domain networks.

nanagement architecture is based on a three-tier structure (see
on page 338) with four basic components: server, desktop, agent,
/.

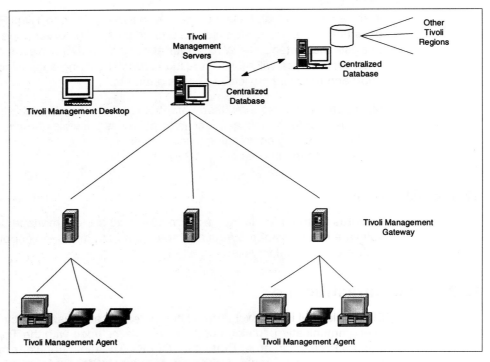

Figure 13-2   Tivoli management architecture

The Tivoli Management Framework provides a set of common services or features that are used by other Tivoli applications installed on top of the Tivoli Management Framework. These services include, but are not limited to, the following set:

► A task library, through which you can create tasks and execute them on multiple Tivoli resources.

► A scheduler that enables you to schedule all Tivoli operations, including the execution of tasks created in the Tivoli task library.

► An RDBMS Interface Module (RIM) that enables some Tivoli applications to write application-specific information to relational databases.

► A query facility that enables you to search and retrieve information from a relational database.

13.3.1 Tivoli Management Server

The Tivoli Management Region server (TMR server) includes the libraries, binaries, data files, and graphical user interface (GUI) needed to install and manage your Tivoli environment. The TMR server maintains an internal database that includes information about the managed objects, such as workstations, databases, and applications, and it coordinates all communication with Tivoli managed nodes. In addition, the endpoint manager is part of the TMR server and is responsible for endpoints. The server also performs all authentication and verification necessary to ensure the security of Tivoli data.

13.3.2 Tivoli Management Desktop

The management desktop enables the administrator to access the Tivoli management applications from any location in the network.

When you install the TMR server on a UNIX system, the Tivoli Management Desktop is automatically installed. When you install the server on a Windows NT system, you must install it separately.

13.3.3 Managed Node

A Tivoli *Managed Node* runs the same software that runs on a TMR server. Managed nodes maintain their own databases, which can be accessed by the TMR server. When managed nodes communicate directly with other managed nodes, they perform the same communication or security operations performed by the TMR server.

The difference between the TMR server and the managed node is that the TMR server database is global to the entire TMR, including all managed nodes. In contrast, the managed node database is local to the particular managed node. For management of the computer system that hosts the managed node, install an endpoint on that managed node.

13.3.4 Tivoli Endpoint

An endpoint is a PC or UNIX workstation running the Tivoli Management Agent. It enables one-touch management by quickly detecting changes within the environment and bringing them under Tivoli management. Each event source integrated into the management framework needs to be configured as an endpoint. Endpoints provide the framework services to Tivoli applications that run on the workstation or desktop. Adapters, which are described in Section 13.4.1, "Adapters" on page 348, use the endpoint to communicate alerts to the Tivoli event management platform.

13.3.5 Gateway

A gateway controls all communication with and o
single gateway can support communication with
gateway can launch methods on an endpoint or r
behalf.

A gateway is created on an existing managed node
provides access to the endpoint methods and provi
the TMR server that the endpoints occasionally req

13.3.6 Tivoli Management Desktop

The Tivoli Management Desktop, shown in Figure 1
interface (GUI). It presents an administrator's view (
From the Tivoli management desktop, resources an
accessed across the enterprise.

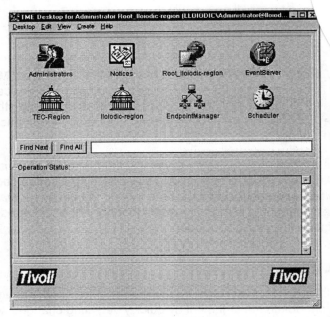

Figure 13-3   Tivoli Management Desktop

The Tivoli management desktop can display a variety of resources:

► Administrators

► Bulletin boards

- ► Policy regions
- ► Schedulers
- ► Generic collections
- ► Application-specific resources

13.3.7 Policies and policy regions

Policies and policy regions play a fundamental role in the Tivoli architecture. In the Tivoli environment, a policy is a set of rules applied to managed resources. A policy enables the administrator to control the default values of newly created resources (default policy) and maintain the guidelines when administrators modify or operate on resources (validation policy).

A specific rule in a policy is a policy method. A default policy method can supply a constant value or run a shell script or a program that generates a value, whereas a validation policy method typically runs a program or shell script to verify values supplied by the administrator. Administrators can define and maintain policies.

Policy regions are containers for managed resources that use the same set of policies (for example, a collection of desktops within a given administrative domain). Collectively, these desktops can be administered using permissions or roles that are assigned to administrators on the basis of policy regions. Policy regions can help organize the managed resources in the desktop and define and limit administrator access to these resources.

13.3.8 Centrally Managed Policies

Tivoli Risk Manager leverages policy regions, which enable security management staff to centrally manage policies and determine who is allowed to support which targets and in what manner. This can be done on the basis of skills (for example, antivirus administrators) or on the basis of geographical location (for example, New York branch analysts).

Tivoli Risk Manager offers policy-based delegation of authority, and IT management groups targets into policy regions. If a simple marketing department policy region contains four PCs, the antivirus administrator supporting the marketing department has authorization to access this policy region. A senior administrator can set up the policy region and delegate the support of the marketing department to a junior administrator. In this case, the defined policy may require antivirus signatures to be updated to all the desktops every week. The administrator uses a virus signature profile to implement the organization's antivirus update policy.

The policy regions in Tivoli Risk Manager provide granular access control and implement enterprise risk management in large organizations. Centrally managing policy makes the product scalable, because the complexity of management does not increase exponentially as the size of the network increases. Administrators are assigned roles on a region-by-region basis. Roles can help restrict the level of operations that an administrator can perform.

13.3.9 Tivoli Enterprise Console

Tivoli Enterprise Console (TEC) is a robust platform for centralized event management across the enterprise. Events generated from distributed event sources are stored in a relational database and managed by the Tivoli desktop console. System administrators use the Tivoli desktop console to manage events from applications, such as Tivoli Distributed Monitoring and Tivoli Security Manager, and manage events generated from third-party applications.

Tivoli Enterprise Console collects and integrates disparate management information into a common model for event processing and provides a central operations view. Types of event processing include event correlation, filtering, dropping duplicates, prioritizing, consolidating, closing self-correcting events, escalating events, and forwarding events. Tivoli Enterprise Console handles events from applications, databases, and systems and network devices.

When events are defined, Tivoli Enterprise Console rules can correlate events and define automated actions. Correlation automatically closes events related to resolved problems. An automated response capability enables problem resolution with no user intervention.

Security analysts can use Tivoli Risk Manager to quickly troubleshoot problems logged in to Tivoli Enterprise Console, such as monitoring open events, generating trouble tickets for problem resolution, or responding to serious events with actions. The new Tivoli Enterprise Console console panel in Figure 13-4 on page 343 shows a screenshot view of all open events.

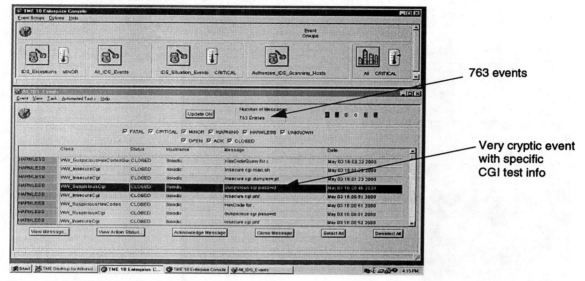

763 events

Very cryptic event
with specific
CGI test info

Figure 13-4   TEC console all open events

The TEC situation overview, as depicted in Figure 13-5, shows more precise
information after the correlation has been taking place.

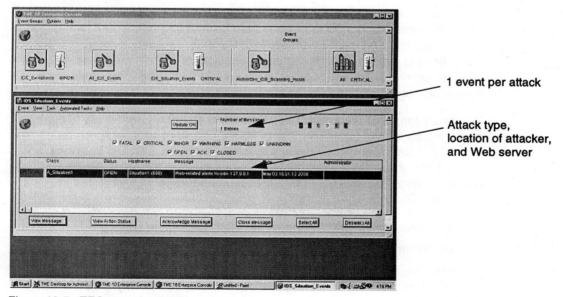

1 event per attack

Attack type,
location of attacker,
and Web server

Figure 13-5   TEC console situation overview

More details on the individual situation can also be obtained as shown in Figure 13-6.

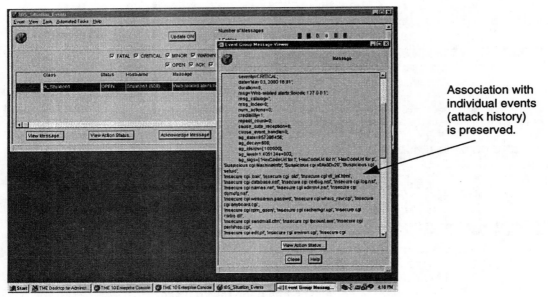

Association with individual events (attack history) is preserved.

Figure 13-6   TEC console individual event details

The newest release of Tivoli Enterprise Console adds significant performance enhancements with hundreds of events per second throughput and high-capacity event throttling. It enables extensive flexibility and scalability in large environments. No other event management system offers high-speed, logic-based reasoning and can centrally control and manage the intelligence with drag-and-drop interfaces.

Tivoli Risk Manager leverages Tivoli Enterprise Console capabilities to centrally managed enterprise intrusions. Alerts from a variety of sources, such as firewalls, routers, intrusion detection systems, antivirus, servers, desktops, and applications, are grouped centrally and managed from the Tivoli desktop console. Alerts from distinct event sources are aggregated and stored in Tivoli Enterprise Console event groups.

There are three main components in the Tivoli Enterprise Console:

► Event Sources

These are applications that gather information about resources throughout the IT environment. These applications typically run on any machine where availability is of concern. Once the information has been gathered, it is converted into an event and forwarded to the event server.

► Event Server

The event server is a group of cooperating processes that run on a single managed node within a TMR.

These processes cooperate with each other to receive events from various sources, perform various levels of processing on received events, and forward the events to the corresponding event consoles. The event server is the heart of TEC, as it provides the Prolog engine for applying rules to received events.

► Event Consoles

This is the user interface that an administrator uses to interact with the Enterprise Console. Each instance of an event console is configured to display logical groupings of events.

The administrator can perform actions to events displayed on the console, such as viewing the detail. Any changes made to an event from other consoles or the event server will be reflected on each console that has the event in its view.

13.3.10 Availability Intermediate Manager (AIM)

Tivoli Enterprise Console includes the AIM, a midlevel management server for Tivoli Enterprise Console events, to better control the environment and event management process. With the multitiered (n-tiered) capabilities of AIM, tremendous flexibility and scalability for the event stream result in better bandwidth utilization and more control over event flow, event storm protection, aggregation capabilities, and redundancy. The architectural scalability enables sophisticated filtering, routing, correlation, and automation to be performed anywhere in the event stream, as shown in Figure 13-7 on page 346.

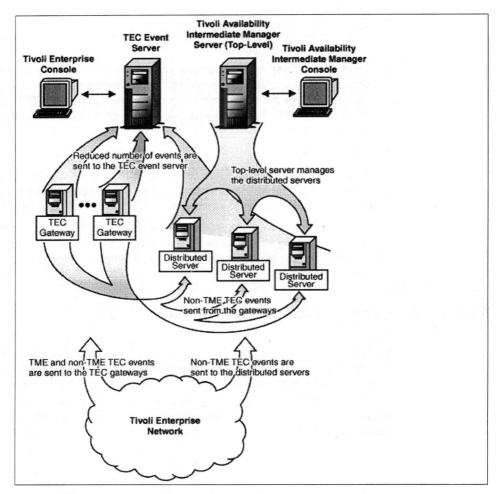

Figure 13-7   AIM topology

Additionally, AIM has an easy-to-use drag-and-drop GUI to create simple filters without any scripting and also has a critical management console to maintain and control a distributed intelligence environment. Figure 13-8 on page 347 shows the AIM console.

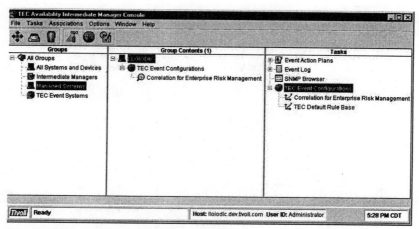

Figure 13-8   Tivoli Enterprise Console AIM

13.4 Risk Manager architecture

Tivoli Risk Manager is an add-on classic Tivoli Enterprise Console application that leverages the Tivoli Enterprise Console event management system to manage enterprise security threats. Figure 13-9 on page 348 describes the architecture that follows the Tivoli Enterprise Console guidelines for building Tivoli Enterprise Console adapters, Tivoli Enterprise Console rules, and Tivoli Enterprise Console tasks.

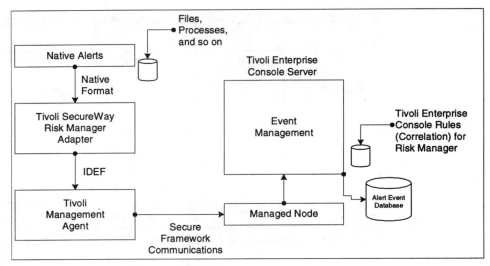

Figure 13-9   Risk Manager architecture

If you are familiar with the Tivoli Enterprise Console architecture, you will notice that Tivoli Risk Manager is a logically layered architecture that leverages Tivoli Enterprise Console components to implement enterprise risk management. Each of the managed technologies, such as firewalls, intrusion detection systems, routers, and hosts, has Tivoli Risk Manager-compliant adapters, rules, and (optionally) tasks that enable security analysts to manage their enterprise from a single control point.

13.4.1 Adapters

Adapters are software processes that monitor event sources and convert the events generated from event sources into a standardized format that can be securely forwarded to the Tivoli Enterprise Console Event Server using the Tivoli Framework. An event source is anything capable of generating a security alert, such as firewall log file alerts generated from network and host-based intrusion detection systems, syslog messages from UNIX, event logs generated from Microsoft Windows NT, and antivirus alerts generated by desktop virus software. Tivoli Risk Manager supports the Intrusion Detection Exchange Format (IDEF) standard - an Internet Engineering Task Force (IETF) draft - for alert sources to communicate event data to management systems. Standardizing on a common data format makes it easy for new event sources to leverage the distributed correlating, reporting, and decision support capabilities of Tivoli Risk Manager. New event sources can be easily integrated by the toolkit. Figure 13-10 on page 349 illustrates multiple event sources that use adapters to create IDEF-compliant messages.

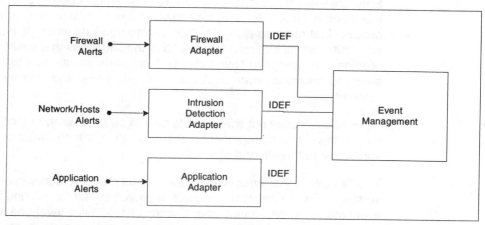

Figure 13-10   Adapters convert events and alerts into IDEF

13.4.2 Adapters and managed technologies

From a functional standpoint, adapters can be thought of as the "glue" that Tivoli Risk Manager uses to manage the technology components. Each managed technology requires an adapter. From a functional perspective, Tivoli Risk Manager supports three categories of managed technologies:

► Applications

► Systems

► Desktops

The applications category refers to applications, such as Web servers, firewalls, network intrusion detection systems, and custom and legacy applications, that are integrated using the toolkit. The systems category refers to UNIX and Windows NT servers, Cisco routers, and so on. The desktop category refers to managed desktop applications, such as virus tools.

13.4.3 Event management platform architecture

The event management platform is the set of event management services that provides the underlying infrastructure to manage the distributed alerts. The event management platform is built on flexibility, usability, and scalability. Flexibility refers to the ease with which new event sources can be integrated into the event management solution. New adapters can be easily built using IDEF and the toolkit. A scalable and highly performing event management platform ensures that security alerts can be filtered and correlated and that appropriate incident management and responses can be initiated in a timely fashion.

Enterprise event management is more than simply collecting and displaying events on a console for someone to view; it is a multifaceted, complex business process that requires analysis to determine how and where to filter, correlate, and route events and how to respond to the situations that event conditions represent in enterprise environments. It supports events from thousands of event sources - networks, servers, desktops, applications, and network management systems.

If the solution does not scale, alerts cannot be processed and correlated in real time. If the event management platform crashes, the organization is potentially vulnerable to threats and attacks.

The Tivoli Risk Manager event management platform is based on the new version of Tivoli Enterprise Console, a proven infrastructure and platform for event management. A new Java-based console helps level-one analysts watch consoles and also helps those who manage and maintain them. From a scalability perspective, a new AIM allows sophisticated filtering, routing, correlating, and automating to be performed anywhere in the event stream, so event management can scale to thousands of management nodes and adapt to business policies. AIM may be implemented virtually anywhere, as many as required, for tremendous flexibility and scalability. Its multitiered capabilities, tremendous flexibility, and scalability for the event stream result in better bandwidth utilization and more control over event flow, event storm protection, aggregation capabilities, and redundancy. With the new AIM, customers can easily process large volumes of events, re-route events based on any criteria, and duplicate event paths based on whatever policy has been established by the organization.

Event management enables all other IT processes, such as problem management and change management, and Tivoli Enterprise Console is uniquely suited to help IT organizations deliver flexible and scalable event management policies and processes. Tivoli Risk Manager exploits all the advanced capabilities of Tivoli Enterprise Console event management, and organizations quickly gain control of their environment and provide an integrated management of enterprise intrusions.

13.4.4 Correlation for enterprise risk management

Tivoli Risk Manager and the enterprise risk management correlation enable security analysts to establish relationships between multiple events and actions to run in response to the events, which clears the event condition and the event condition effects.

The distinction between rules and signatures causes confusion. Rules implement the logic needed to identify patterns of threats by correlating events from multiple sources. Signatures enlist misuse patterns that are used by intrusion detection systems to report events that match the signature criteria. New signatures need to be developed and updated for new attacks in a timely fashion; rules are independent of signatures and are updated during new product versions. Out-of-the-box rules are included for firewalls, intrusion detection systems, and routers. More details on the correlation engine can be found in the redbook *Tivoli SecureWay Risk Manager Correlating Enterprise Risk Management*, SG24-6021.

13.4.5 Decision Support for enterprise risk management

Decision Support is a critical aspect of enterprise risk management. Enterprises deploy sophisticated security systems with the overall objective of lowering the risks to enterprise business assets. Decision Support is an invaluable tool for companies to understand, interpret, and quantify the business risks arising from threats, attacks, and intrusions. Using the capabilities of the Tivoli Decision Support product, enterprise alerts are analyzed in real time. Through a comprehensive set of enterprise risk management guides, security analysts can quantify business risks through an analytical decision-making process and proactively implement security policies quickly to eliminate the security vulnerability or exposure. Tivoli Risk Manager leverages the Tivoli Decision Support product to provide decision support for firewalls, vulnerability assessments, virus management, and intrusion detection.

Tivoli Risk Manager enterprise risk management guides (also known as Tivoli Decision Support Discovery Guides) provide a ready-to-use view of the wealth of data by transforming the intrusion and virus alert data into easily accessible business-relevant information. Analytical Decision Support enables high-level data analysis to answer the following questions:

► Which systems are most susceptible to virus attacks?

► Are the system, network, and application usage consistent with enterprise security policies?

► Is there a correlation between unauthorized access and intrusion attempts?

This information is presented in a variety of graphical formats that can be viewed interactively (for example, slice, dice, drill down, or drill through) or posted on a URL.

Tivoli Decision Support Discovery Guides are available for a number of products, including Tivoli Enterprise Console, Tivoli Inventory, Tivoli NetView, Tivoli Service Desk, Tivoli Software Distribution, and Tivoli Distributed Monitoring, and they provide easily accessible IT business-relevant information.

13.5 The benefits of enterprise risk management

Risks are pervasive throughout the enterprise. Enterprise risk management lowers the overall risk to the enterprise by leveraging security intelligence across many different security products. There are four specific management disciplines to focus on:

► Firewall management

► Intrusion detection

► Risk assessment

► Virus management

13.5.1 Firewall management

Businesses today are deploying several firewalls to control access to their internal networks from the Internet and their extranet environment. Several resources manage firewalls and look at log files generated by firewalls containing a rich set of events crucial for enterprise risk management. Until now, security administrators had to manually sift through multiple firewall log files and look for intrusion data - an approach that is laborious, error-prone, and overwhelming to security administrators because of the sheer volume of log entries. The Tivoli Risk Manager Firewall Management feature enables customers to centrally manage their firewall log files. Tivoli Enterprise Console consolidates and monitors events from multiple firewalls. Customers can use Tivoli Enterprise Console as the centralized event management server to manage their firewall deployments. Tivoli Risk Manager monitors firewall log files in real time and forwards them to Tivoli Enterprise Console. Individual firewall alerts are grouped into event classes and archived in a relational database, making it easy for administrators to run various types of decision support queries using SQL.

Tivoli Risk Manager implements firewall rules that correlate and aggregate alerts issued by multiple firewalls and presents the alert information in an intuitive, easy-to-use, and manageable fashion. System administrators use the Tivoli desktop to manage firewall alerts, close open alerts, issue trouble tickets, and invoke predefined firewall tasks included with Tivoli Risk Manager. Role-based access control can be used to delegate specific firewall administration and management tasks to specific administrators.

For example, events from extranet and partner firewalls can be managed by one group, and Internet firewalls can be managed by a different group of administrators. Tivoli Risk Manager includes a number of tasks to automatically respond to firewall alerts, such as paging an administrator, invoking a firewall action to reset a TCP connection, or dynamically adding firewall filter rules to block networks or hosts from connecting to the enterprise.

Tivoli Risk Manager supports Check Point Firewall-1 and Cisco PIX Firewall. High-level toolkits are available to integrate other firewalls into Tivoli Risk Manager.

Managing Check Point FireWall-1

Tivoli Risk Manager supports Check Point Firewall-1 and the VPN-1 virtual private network. The firewall adapter for Check Point monitors the firewall log files on the Firewall-1 management station in real time, formats the log file events into IDEF, and forwards the events to the Tivoli Enterprise Console server through secure Framework communications.

Events from multiple Firewall-1 and VPN-1 deployments are aggregated and consolidated into an event group within Tivoli Enterprise Console. Firewall-1 alerts are grouped into event group categories, such as Firewall-1 communication messages, encryption engine messages, connection attempts, and critical alerts messages. Tivoli Plus modules for Check Point Firewall-1 allow customers to centrally manage and distribute VPN-1 and Firewall-1, such as new adapter versions and configuration data.

Managing Cisco PIX Firewall

Tivoli Risk Manager supports Cisco PIX Firewall. The firewall adapter for Cisco PIX Firewall monitors the firewall log files on the Cisco management station in real time, formats the log file events into IDEF, and forwards the events to the Tivoli Enterprise Console server using secure Framework communications. Events from multiple Cisco firewalls are aggregated and stored in a separate event group within Tivoli Enterprise Console.

13.5.2 Intrusion detection

Intrusion detection is an essential prerequisite to enterprise risk management. Customers are beginning to deploy several variants of intrusion detection systems:

► Network intrusion detection systems are being deployed to monitor unauthorized access and network-level intrusions.

► Host intrusion detection systems are being deployed to deal with host-level intrusions.

► Application-level intrusion detection is gaining popularity for detecting specific intrusions at the application level that are not detected by the network or host-level components. For example, Web servers are likely to have a real-time intrusion detection engine for HTTP (or HTTPS) application traffic.

Tivoli Risk Manager supports leading network intrusion detection solutions from Interactive Session Support (ISS) (network and host) and Cisco. It also provides an adapter for Tivoli's Network IDS and for Snort. In addition, Tivoli Risk Manager includes optional network and host-level intrusion detection and real-time application-level intrusion detection for Web servers.

Managing ISS RealSecure Network Engine

Tivoli Risk Manager supports both ISS RealSecure Network Intrusion Detection and the ISS RealSecure Host Intrusion Detection System. The RealSecure adapter monitors the log files generated by RealSecure in real time, formats the log file events into IDEF, and forwards the events to the Tivoli Enterprise Console server using secure Framework communications. Alerts from multiple RealSecure Intrusion Detection Systems are consolidated into an event group within Tivoli Enterprise Console and tagged with the appropriate criticality. System administrators can use the familiar and easy-to-use Tivoli desktop console to manage their diverse intrusion detection alerts with a single console rather than having to learn and use a new console for each intrusion detection system. More importantly, alerts from RealSecure are used by the Enterprise Intrusion Detection feature that enables system administrators to precisely identify patterns of threats, reduce false alarms, and manage their intrusions with a higher degree of assurance.

In addition to managing alerts, the Tivoli Plus module for RealSecure allows customers to centrally manage distribution and deployment of the intrusion detection engine from the Tivoli desktop console.

Managing Cisco SecureIDS

Tivoli Risk Manager supports the Cisco SecureIDS (formerly NetRanger) Network Intrusion Detection System. The Cisco SecureIDS adapter monitors the log files generated by RealSecure in real time, formats the log file events into IDEF, and forwards the events to the Tivoli Enterprise Console. Alerts from multiple Cisco SecureIDS Intrusion Detection Systems are consolidated in a separate event group within Tivoli Enterprise Console. System administrators can use the familiar and easy-to-use Tivoli desktop console to manage their diverse intrusion detection alerts with a single console rather than having to learn and use a new console for each intrusion detection system. More importantly, the Enterprise Intrusion Detection feature uses alerts from Cisco SecureIDS to help system administrators precisely identify patterns of threats, reduce false alarms, and manage intrusions with a higher degree of assurance using enterprise correlation.

13.5.3 Application intrusion detection management

As more applications are Web-enabled, the probability of attacks and intrusions on these applications increases. Web servers, Java applications, and databases must be secured and monitored to ensure their integrity and availability. Also, attacks increasingly use a secure transport, such as SSL, to render traditional network intrusion detection systems and firewalls incapable of defending against them. This opens up a new class of application-level intrusion detection systems that understand the application-level protocol and can monitor threats and intrusions on these applications.

Managing Web server intrusions using Web IDS

In today's e-business environment, protecting the Web infrastructure is one of the most serious challenges facing enterprises. Building a loyal customer base requires the Web infrastructure to be secure, highly available, and performant, and it must ensure the confidentiality, integrity, and privacy of customer transactions. High-profile denial of service attacks on Internet portal sites have shown how easily these threats can be carried out to destroy brand equity and cause a loss of customer confidence.

Tivoli Risk Manager includes an intrusion detection system feature called Web IDS. Web IDS is an essential component of enterprise risk management that enables organizations to monitor unauthorized intrusions and various forms of attacks on Web servers. Today, hackers use sophisticated tools that target URL-level attacks on public Web sites using HTTP or HTTPS (using HTTP over SSL). These type of attacks cannot be blocked by the firewall and frequently bypass monitoring by network intrusion detection tools. An application-level intrusion detection component, such as Web IDS, can detect these attacks and enable security administrators to implement incident management and containment.

Web IDS detects and manages attacks on a number of Web servers, including Netscape/iPlanet, Microsoft IIS, Domino, Apache, IBM HTTPS, and Tivoli Access Manager. By integrating with Tivoli Access Manager, organizations allow authorized access for their business constituents and ensure that unauthorized access attempts, attacks, and intrusions are monitored and responded to in real time.

Virus management

One of an IT manager's top concerns is protecting the enterprise from virus threats. Although many organizations have some type of antivirus solution deployed, many organizations are still susceptible to virus attacks, such as the ILOVEYOU virus.

Vulnerabilities remain because of a lack of ongoing virus management to ensure that all desktops and systems have the most recent virus software, that virus signature files are updated, and that desktops not complying with enterprise virus policies are identified and acted upon immediately.

Managing antivirus client alerts

Using the Tivoli Desktop feature in Tivoli Risk Manager, system administrators manage Norton AntiVirus and McAffee alerts. The adapters use the secure Framework communications to forward alerts from desktops to the Tivoli Enterprise Console server.

With Tivoli Risk Manager, security administrators can manage Symantec Norton AntiVirus and McAffee alerts from the Tivoli Enterprise Console. Examples of virus alerts include the following:

► Identify known viruses detected on different desktops

► Identify unknown viruses detected on different desktops

► Identify virus definitions that are out of date

► Identify virus-like activity

13.5.4 Managing host intrusions using Tivoli Host IDS

Tivoli Host IDS is a host-level intrusion detection system that manages host-level intrusions through-out the enterprise.

Managing alerts from UNIX servers

Frequently, the syslog facility within UNIX can be configured to log useful information on different subsystems within UNIX, such as the UNIX kernel, user processes, TCP/IP subsystem, and devices. The events recorded by syslog form an important basis for detecting intrusions on host systems. With the syslog facility, Tivoli Risk Manager includes a UNIX adapter that monitors intrusions on UNIX systems. Events are forwarded to the Tivoli Enterprise Console server by secure Framework communications, and they are correlated with events from other adapters according to Tivoli Risk Manager rules.

Managing Windows NT servers

The event log facility within Windows NT can be configured to log useful information on different subsystems within Windows NT, such as the operating system, user processes, remote access, applications, TCP/IP subsystem, and devices. The events recorded by the event log facility form an important basis for detecting intrusions on Windows NT and Windows 2000 servers. The event log facility in Tivoli Risk Manager includes a Windows NT adapter that monitors for intrusions on servers. Events are forwarded to the Tivoli Enterprise Console server by secure Framework communications, and they are correlated with events from other adapters according to Tivoli Risk Manager rules.

13.5.5 Risk assessment

Correlation for enterprise risk management is the industry's first solution that provides cross-product, cross-platform intrusion management and risk assessment capability. This unique feature of Tivoli Risk Manager provides a correlated view of enterprise intrusions and violations. For example, a business has deployed 50 intrusion detection systems (a combination of network-based, host-based, and application-based engines). Using Tivoli Enterprise Console rules, events from several intrusion detection engines go through a process of duplicate elimination, alert summarization, and distributed correlation to identify patterns of threats. Each pattern of attack is referred to as a situation. By classifying thousands of alerts into a few precise situations, security administrators can quickly gain invaluable insight into threats and attack patterns that are monitored by different intrusion detection engines.

Security analysts can use the correlation for enterprise risk management feature to:

▶ Reduce or eliminate false positives by correlating alerts from different sources. Correlation provides a higher degree of assurance in reported alert information and weeds out misleading false alarms.

▶ Identify attack patterns, single high-profile attacks, and distributed denial of service attacks. Attacks are classified into situations that enable administrators to quickly pinpoint attack patterns.

▶ Provide a summary view of intrusion data that enables administrators to comprehend the alert data in a meaningful way.

Situations

A situation is the result of applying the Tivoli Enterprise Console rules to correlate events received from the different event sources throughout the enterprise. Situations identify patterns of threats that provide invaluable insight into how the enterprise is being targeted.

Situation 1

Situation 1 identifies a single critical alert that involves a single attack host and a single target. Examples of Situation 1 alerts are an attack host trying to obtain a password file from a UNIX machine, or an attack host launching a PHF attack on a Web server. Situation 1 identifies these situations through correlation and immediately forwards these alerts to the security administrator with a high severity.

Situation 2

Situation 2 identifies patterns of attacks between two machines, patterns of attacks launched on a destination, or patterns of attacks originating from a single machine to a set of targets. For example, an attacker trying to probe for vulnerabilities on a machine by launching a series of probes will be immediately identified and alerted by the correlation engine. This type of situation is difficult to detect on a manual basis, and identifying this situation early helps a security analyst quickly respond to the intrusions and disable the attack.

Situation 3

Situation 3 identifies more complex situations, such as a pattern of attacks launched against specific destinations (for example, a distributed denial of service attack launched on a Web server or an e-mail server). Situation 3 addresses the distributed pattern of attacks that involve multiple sources and multiple destinations.

13.5.6 Tasks for enterprise risk management

Tivoli Risk Manager includes a variety of tasks to quickly resolve security problems, such as:

► Inhibit a connection to/from a specific IP address on the firewall

► Inhibit and close any existing connections to/from a specific IP address on the firewall

► Cancel a previously enabled action on the firewall

► Cancel all previously enabled actions on the firewall

► Terminate a user process on a server

► Suspend a user account on a server

► Scan or delete a virus on a desktop

13.5.7 The value of enterprise risk management

Finally, before we start going into the technical details with the next chapters, we want to summarize the basic Risk Manager values once again.

Modular deployment

Enterprise risk management offers flexibility for customers to pursue a modular approach to managing intrusions. For example, a customer interested in intrusion detection management can quickly leverage Tivoli Risk Manager to implement enterprise intrusion management as follows:

1. Install and configure a Tivoli Management Region (TMR) on one machine.

2. Install and configure Tivoli Enterprise Console.

3. Install and configure the Tivoli endpoint and the Tivoli Risk Manager adapters for the network intrusion systems that need to be managed using Tivoli Software Distribution (These steps have an estimated completion of three days, assuming five network intrusion systems need to be managed).

With the event management infrastructure in place, the power of an integrated risk management framework can now be demonstrated.

The steps required to integrate and manage additional servers, such as UNIX (50 UNIX servers) and Windows NT (100 Windows NT servers), are:

1. Distribute the Tivoli Management Agent and the Tivoli Host IDS (using the adapter profile) on the UNIX and Windows NT servers from the Tivoli desktop console

2. Create and distribute the appropriate host security configuration on all the managed servers from the Tivoli desktop console - configuration settings control the intrusions detected and alerted by the Tivoli Host IDS system

This illustrates the power of a scalable Framework across the enterprise. Customers can start with a small, manageable environment, such as managing intrusion detection systems or managing firewalls with a single TMR. With the risk management infrastructure in place, the solution can then be expanded to support managed technologies (using appropriate profile adapters), such as routers, Web servers, UNIX servers, and desktops.

Support for open standards

Tivoli Risk Manager actively promotes, supports, and contributes to the emerging open systems standards in the area of intrusion detection, including the following:

► The Common Vulnerabilities and Exposures (CVE)[1]

► The Intrusion Detection Exchange Format (IDEF)[2]

---

[1] www.cve.mitre.org

[2] www.ietf.org/html.charters/idwg-charter.html

The CVE list is a dictionary of standardized names for vulnerability and other information. CVE standardizes the names for all publicly known vulnerabilities and security exposures.

IDEF is a common intrusion data model specification that describes data formats that enable communication between intrusion detection systems and communication between intrusion detection systems and management systems.

Tivoli Risk Manager uses an IDEF-compliant protocol for communication with ID sensors. The IDEF standard integrates new security endpoints from multiple vendors into an enterprise risk management platform, such as Tivoli Risk Manager. An IDEF draft is available for review from the Intrusion Detection Working Group (IDWG) in the IETF.

Tivoli Risk Manager toolkit

Tivoli Risk Manager is built on top of Tivoli Enterprise Console, and it leverages the Tivoli Enterprise Console API for integration.

To integrate with Tivoli Risk Manager, an alert generator:

1. Sends IDEF-compliant events to the Tivoli server via an event generator
2. Provides response units to allow the administrator to react to attacks or resolve exposures
3. Provides a Tivoli-compliant mechanism to install and configure the event generators and response units

Conclusion

The knowledge economy is causing fundamental changes in enterprises as enterprises transform themselves to extend their traditional business models to the Web. Web companies are creating new ways of doing business on the Internet. All these changes are exciting but fraught with challenges, and companies must understand the challenge of being on the Internet. The open Internet environment combined with lack of security makes companies unwitting targets of intrusions, such as virus threats, denial of service attacks, and unauthorized access. These threats are real. In the Computer Security Institute's fifth annual Computer Crime and Security Survey[3], 85% of respondents detected computer viruses and 79% detected employee abuse of Internet access privileges. Companies can no longer deploy virus tools on all desktops or assume that virus threats can be mitigated. Managing virus policies, signatures, and compliance throughout the enterprise is crucial. A single user who does not comply with the virus policies becomes an unwitting participant in an *ILOVEYOU* virus threat that can bring down the company's e-mail system.

---

[3] Computer Security Institute, www.gocsi.com

Integrated management of security alerts, practices, and policies is imperative to mitigating enterprise risks. An enterprise risk management solution, such as Tivoli Risk Manager, enables security analysts to centrally manage their enterprise security and use intelligent correlation and decision support to quickly identify users, networks, or hot spots - such as critical systems - and fix vulnerabilities. The business implications are significant if the company's e-mail servers or Web servers go down or are compromised. Having a single point of control to deploy an enterprise risk management solution for security across the enterprise helps mitigate risk, ensures business continuity, and is a compelling return on investment strategy that companies cannot ignore.

Building a centralized security audit subsystem

As described in Chapter 2, "Method for Architecting Secure Solutions" on page 15, the purpose of the security audit subsystem is to address the data collection, analysis, and archival requirements of a computing solution to manage and measure the effectiveness of the security implementation. Security audit analysis and reporting includes real-time review and management of events as well as after-the-fact analysis to anticipate and take actions to maintain and improve the integrity and reliability of resources. Tivoli Risk Manager and Tivoli Intrusion Manager address both of these requirements. The Event Console and rules engine alert security managers to problems by correlating thousands of events into more specific situations to identify attacks. Decision support guides included with Risk Manager allow for the historical analysis of security events, enabling the security manager to understand vulnerabilities and initiate preventive actions.

This part of our redbook looks at another customer setup in order to describe the audit solution approach. The first scenario looks at a small medium business (SMB) enterprise, Nuts & Bolts, Inc., a manufacturing company. In Section 14.1, "Company profile" on page 364, we describe their current IT deployment, which includes a basic Web infrastructure (not necessarily e-commerce activity) and a few security products.

14.1 Company profile

Nuts & Bolts, Inc. is in the early stages of implementing an e-business infrastructure facing the Internet and the current information is distributed between two Web servers.

► Web server one

Web server one

The first Web server is designated for customers and interested parties. It is primarily for information retrieval, with product information and technical documents available for download.

► Web server two

The second Web server is designated for partners. It provides more detailed information about the products and allows partners to post forms and documents to the company.

Because both Web servers technically belong to different application project teams in the company and have been developed concurrently, they are based on different platforms: Netscape Enterprise Web Server and IBM HTTP server. Nuts & Bolts' overall environment is heterogeneous with multiple hardware and software platforms. There are two firewalls deployed: Cisco PIX and Check Point FireWall-1. They have setup one Internet demilitarized zone (DMZ), one production DMZ, and one intranet in one physical location. The employees are running Windows operating systems (Windows NT, Windows 98, and Windows 95) on their desktops. For a general overview of the initial network layout, see Figure 14-1 on page 365. The network operators have the responsibility for the firewalls and antivirus software. The security administration is handled by the application project teams.

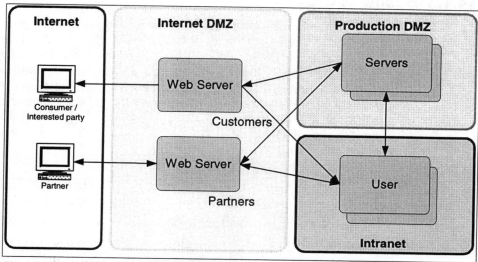

Figure 14-1   Initial IT architecture for Nuts & Bolts, Inc.

14.1.1 Security related problem

This company's infrastructure is very typical for small companies just starting with some Internet exposure. They have a small staff and limited technical expertise. In their current configuration, the company is unsure how to validate the security of its environment. They are aware of more tools in the marketplace, such as PKI or Intrusion Detection, but have no skills in house to attempt installation, and no overall security plan to convince their senior management to obtain the required resources.

14.1.2 Business requirements

At this stage, the CEO is looking for a way to validate the security of the network, and thus enhance customer and partner confidence. Having invested in a variety of security products (firewalls and routers), there is still a lack of comfort that the environment is secure. After a recent virus attack antivirus software was put in place, but his IT staff cannot assure him that people are using it. The IT staff is requesting more tools and the manpower and skills required to manage these products. The events recognized by the current security tools, such as invalid logons, attacks, or viruses, must be investigated and handled. With a small staff, it is difficult to handle all events, much less let the staff attend training or take vacation without constant pages and call ins. The CEO is concerned about the amount of investment required with no apparent way to measure the effectiveness.

14.1.3 Business design

To meet the needs of the business, the audit system (see Figure 14-2 for an overview) must look at the alerts from the security tools, be able to identify real threats and attacks, and define actions to be taken automatically or by manual intervention. Identifying real threats from the volumes of alerts generated by multiple security sensors will make the environment more secure and more manageable. Predefined actions will allow for quick and consistent handling of situations and increase the quality of service to users. The system must also be flexible enough to support additional tools and systems as they are implemented in the near future.

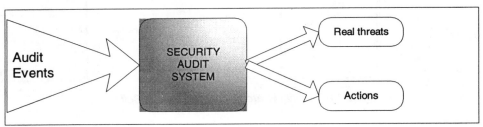

Figure 14-2   Audit flow structure

14.1.4 Security design objectives

The primary objective of the security audit subsystem is to enhance the security management function through the collection, analysis, and archiving security data generated by the security environment in both real-time and historical modes. The audit subsystem must be able to isolate real security alarms from the vast flow of security events and correlate events from several sources. The audit subsystem must also support the actual network structure, including firewalls, routers, and servers. A single control point to monitor, defend, and respond to attacks and intrusions is needed.

It is important to understand that the implementation of security tools does not eliminate the need for skilled security specialists. All tools must be configured to the specific system environment. The thresholds must be tweaked. Automated actions may vary by alert source or target. The desire is to make the security specialist more effective by delegating common tasks to operator level personnel or even automating responses to common situations.

14.2 Security audit subsystem

A security audit subsystem is responsible for capturing, analyzing, reporting, archiving, and retrieving records of events and conditions.

Figure 14-3 shows a use case model of a security audit function. The physical view shows the systems involved in the transaction. The component view depicts the information flow control function that will examine messages being sent and, based upon a set of rules, will allow valid messages to to flow. Invalid messages are stopped, and a record of the event is sent to the security audit function. The logical view breaks down the audit process into distinct functions.

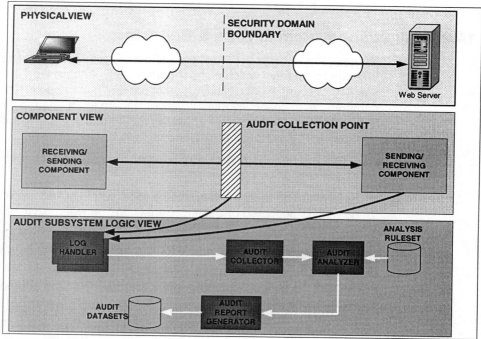

Figure 14-3   Audit subsystem

The log handler is usually a standard part of a component, for example, the system log file in an UNIX environment or the event log file on Windows NT. Most security products have a log handler function that generates events, such as a firewall violation attempt. Mostly, it routes them to a management console or stores them to a log file.

The audit handler converts or reformats the events from the generic log handler into a format usable to the audit subsystem.

The analysis engine receives events from the audit handler. It uses security rules based on an artificial intelligence engine and filters to correlate the events. This is the core function of the audit subsystem, and its effectiveness depends on the security rules.

The output of the analysis engine is sent to the alarm handler to perform two functions. First, to generate an alarm (if necessary) and route it to the correct application or device, and second, to store all records in a centralized database.

> **Note:** The analysis engine is an important part of the model; it receives events from several sources and correlates them. Security rules must be defined very carefully.

14.2.1 Audit subsystem at Nuts & Bolts, Inc.

To apply this subsystem within their IT infrastructure, Nuts & Bolts, Inc. would first need to identify which components in their configuration are generating security relevant events. Next, an audit handler has to be added to each of those components to collect events and forward them to an analyzer engine. In Figure 14-4 on page 369, we show the audit handlers in the customer's configuration. As shown, the components to be audited are:

► CISCO Router: To collect configuration change data, connection information, and exception or error events.

► Firewalls: The audit handler should allow you to collect information on flows as well as accepted or denied connections between parts of the network.

► Web servers: To summarize the activity of the Web server and to track down events like unsuccessful logins, configuration changes, long URL attacks, and so on.

► Servers: To collect access control exceptions from the operating systems and applications.

► Users: To gather data on viruses detected by antivirus software.

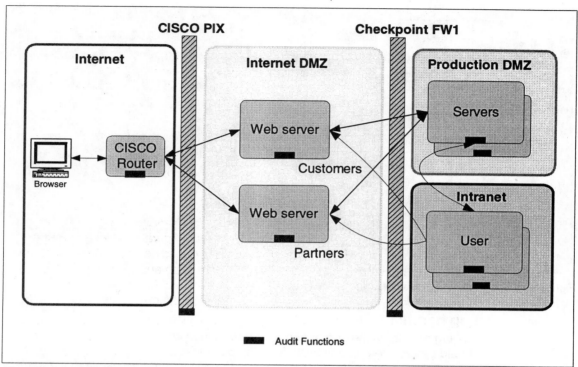

Figure 14-4   Audit functions

14.2.2 Risk Manager in the audit subsystem

As shown in Figure 14-5 on page 370, Risk Manager components can be mapped to the logical functions on the security audit subsystem.

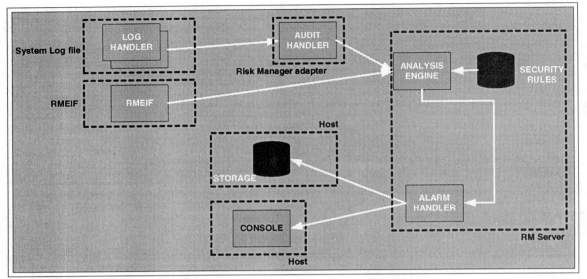

Figure 14-5   Logic view with Risk Manager components

Log handler

The log handler is the component that determines which events in a function should be reported. In a firewall, for example, the log handler could identify an unauthorized access attempt as an event to be reported and dispatch it. Other functions just store all events in a log, like the system log for an operating system. For these environments, Risk Manager provides *sensors* to read the logs and extract events for the audit subsystem. The sensors provided are for Web-based intrusion-detection, host-based intrusion detection, and network base. Each sensor uses the respective logs to detect attacks and suspicious activity.

Audit handler

The audit handler function is performed by Risk Manager *adapters*. The adapter takes the logs from the system and formats them in the correct way to be sent to the Risk Manager server. An important strength of the Risk Manager is the Event Integration Facility (EIF), a toolkit for building adapters using the application programming interface. In addition, existing adapters can be configured to invoke a summarization function that reduces high-volume floods of duplicate events into a relatively low-volume set of summarized events. This summarization reduces the volume of events sent to the Risk Manager server, greatly reducing network traffic.

Analysis engine

The Risk Manager adapters send events to the Tivoli Enterprise Console (TEC) event server. The TEC event server analyzes events and creates situations based on the class and destinations (target and source) of the events. Thousands of events can trigger the creation of a single situation. A situation is the result of applying the Risk Manager rules to correlate events received from the different event sources throughout the enterprise. Situations identify patterns of threats that provide invaluable insight into how the enterprise is being targeted.

Security rules

The Risk Manager rules and event format definitions are added to the TEC rules and definitions. These five rule files are the key to recognizing attack patterns and are the strength of Risk Manager:

► normalization.rls

This rules file is used to normalize information sent from different adapters and sensors. Specific information processed is the time of the event, the identity of the system sending the event (so the engine will recognize when a new sensor has spotted the problem), and the source and target destinations.

► sensorevent.rls

This rules file extracts information from the external raw events, searches for new patterns, and updates existing patterns that have been found. Three attributes are used as keys in searching for patterns: class category, destination host, and source host.

► situation.rls

This rules file analyzes all situation alerts (events). Situation events are queued for processing when they are first created and when they are periodically resubmitted for processing upon the triggering of a timer. Each situation is compared with existing situations to determine if the event is still relevant and if the event should be kept on the event console.

► timer.rls

This rules file catches, or executes, the triggering of various timers: Refresh, Cleanup, and Forward. The Refresh timer updates situations and resubmits them for analysis. The Cleanup timer checks for expired situations. The Forward timer sends situation data to another event server if Risk Manager is configured to do so.

► boot.rls

This rules file performs various startup functions. It is activated when a TEC_Start event is received. The boot.rls is the last rule set that is loaded because it is run only one time: when the TEC event server is started. If this rule set is loaded first, the unnecessary time will be spent on processing the boot.rls file for the event that is received

Alarm handler

The event server will send situations and events to the TEC console for display. The TEC event server, in addition to correlating events and generating situations, can initiate automated tasks in reaction to certain events or situations. This task will run a local script that could start some actions on the right hosts.

Storage

The Risk Manager event server stores events into a relational database. Risk Manager supports many third party databases, such as IBM DB2, Oracle, Sybase, or Microsoft SQL.

Console

The Risk Manager console can filter which situations and events are displayed by the priority of the events (all, warnings, critical, and fatal). The console of the audit subsystem is provided by TEC. You can arrange the event view by groups of events, by operators groups, filtering the view of the events and so on. Check out the different view described in Section 13.3.9, "Tivoli Enterprise Console" on page 342.

14.2.3 Integration of Risk Manager

As discussed in the previous chapters, the identity and access control components of our security architecture show how the consolidation and automation of functions provide effectiveness and efficiency in an overall solution. The same applies for the audit subsystem. Multiple security management consoles spread across multiple zones in the environment do not support a truly secure setup. To implement risk management at Nuts & Bolts, Inc., management functions should be grouped into a single zone. In Figure 14-6 on page 373, all management functions, including the Risk Manager event server, are placed within one zone.

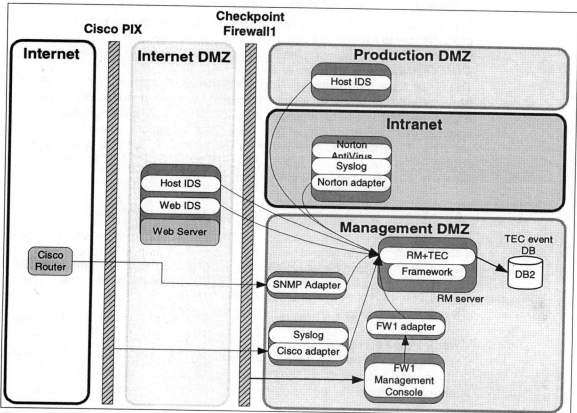

Figure 14-6   Risk Manager flows

Environment

The TEC server requires the Tivoli Framework as the underlying infrastructure. Nuts & Bolts, Inc. is currently running an environment without the Tivoli Management Environment (TME). In order to use Risk Manager, they have to install the Framework (included with Risk Manager) on the event server, which becomes the Tivoli Management Region server (TMR). All the adapters of Risk Manager are installed in a Non-TME mode. In this case, there is no need to set up the Tivoli environment all over the network (endpoints, managed nodes, gateways, and so on). TEC needs a relational database to store all the events sent by the components. Risk Manager does not come with a database. A DB2 database could be installed on the TMR server, but to increase performance, you should install the database on a dedicated host.

Communications with the Risk Manager server

In this section we discuss the different ways Risk Manager and the other products use to exchange audit data.

CISCO router

The Cisco router generates an Simple Network Management Protocol (SNMP) trap when the configuration changes or when there are unsuccessful logins. The SNMP event can be sent directly to a Windows or UNIX system, either an endpoint in a TME environment or a Tivoli SNMP adapter running on a non-TME machine. The Risk Manager adapter for Cisco Routers consists of files that configure the Tivoli SNMP adapter to capture and forward the Cisco router events to the event server for correlation.

> **Attention:** This feature needs to open port 162 on the firewalls

CISCO PIX

The adapter for Cisco Secure PIX Firewall resides on the host to which the Cisco Secure PIX Firewall sensor has been configured to send log messages. This host can be a UNIX or a Windows system. The Cisco PIX Firewall Syslog Server (PFSS) is required for logging to a Windows system host.

Check Point FIREWALL-1

The Check Point FireWall-1 sends its logs to a dedicated management console (data transfer is encrypted). The Risk Manager adapter uses the OPSEC interface to retrieve the log file stored on the FireWall-1 management console.

Web Intrusion Detection System (Web IDS)

The default configuration for Web IDS uses the Risk Manager EIF in order to send the Web IDS events to the Risk Manager server. You must customize the Risk Manager EIF to use the Web IDS format file in order to perform the proper mapping of Web IDS events into Risk Manager TEC events.

Host Intrusion Detection System (Host IDS)

The Risk Manager adapter for Host IDS maps events that are detected and logged by the Windows or UNIX system logs, into TEC events. The Risk Manager adapter for Host IDS uses the Tivoli log file adapter (syslogd) for UNIX systems or the Tivoli NT Event Log adapter for Windows systems to send events to the Risk Manager server.

Norton AntiVirus

Norton AntiVirus writes events in the Windows NT event log. The Tivoli NT Event Log adapter recognizes the virus-related events sent by Norton AntiVirus on Windows NT and maps them into Risk Manager events, which are then sent to the event server for correlation.

14.3 Expanding security monitoring

To enhance the security of Web environments, other security tools should be installed. For access control functions, a reverse proxy server solution like Tivoli Access Manager is recommended. In order to monitor network traffic (users, customers and partners), there is a need to use a network intrusion detection system like Tivoli Network IDS or Interactive Session Support RealSecure. Because most of the suspicious activity and threats still come from within the enterprise, a probe within the internal part of the network is essential as well. Both of these components can be easily integrated into the Risk Manager security audit subsystem

Web reverse proxy server

A Web reverse proxy server provides single point management of authentication and access control. Risk Manager comes with an adapter for Tivoli Access Manager's reverse proxy server, WebSEAL, in order to send alerts to the central Risk Manager server.

Intrusion detection

An Intrusion Detection System (IDS) is a scanning system designed for computers (Host IDS), Web servers (Web IDS) and networks (Network IDS). An IDS gathers and analyzes information from various areas within a computer or a network to identify possible security breaches, which include both intrusions (attacks from outside the organization) and misuse (attacks from within the organization). An IDS uses a vulnerability assessment (sometimes referred to as scanning), which is a technology developed to assess the security of a computer system or network. Intrusion detection functions include:

► Monitoring and analyzing both user and system activities

► Analyzing system configurations and vulnerabilities

► Assessing system and file integrity

► Ability to recognize patterns typical for attacks

► Analysis of abnormal activity patterns

Filter function

When the number of security products used within an enterprise increases, the number of single security events also increases. In this case, the audit subsystem needs to be able to filter events locally before they are sent to the Risk Manager server in order to improve overall throughput.

For this reason, Risk Manager provides a summarization engine. As shown in Figure 14-7, this feature allows you to locally filter events before they are sent to the Risk Manager server. The Risk Manager Observer (RMO) filter function is based on the RM EIF component and is installed with the adapter or sensor. The RMO summarizes events locally, so that there is less network traffic and reduced load on the Risk Manager server when it comes to a fast correlation process.

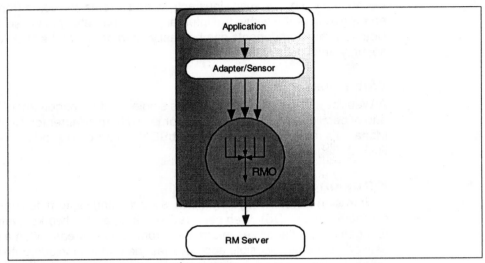

Figure 14-7   Local summarization engine

For more details about the RMEIF and the RMO function, please refer to the *Risk Manager 3.8 User's Guide*.

14.3.1 Tools supported

Risk Manager is shipped with adapters for some security tools, such as ISS RealSecure. Other products, like IBM Firewall 4.2.1, include the adapter for Risk Manager as part of their code.

Risk Manager also includes the Event Integration Facility (EIF) which provides an enhanced set of facilities for sending events to Risk Manager's TEC event server. These facilities include application programming interfaces (APIs) for C programs, a Perl interface for use with Perl scripts, and a command-line function.

Risk Manager supports the following kind of applications:

► Firewalls

► Web servers

► Intrusion detection systems

- ► Antivirus products
- ► Routers
- ► Operating Systems log file events
- ► RM EIF allows you to develop your own security applications and integrates them into the Risk Manager environment

For a complete list of products supported either by Risk Manager directly, through adapters shipped with the tool, or through the Tivoli Ready program, please see the actual Risk Manager information at:

`http://www.tivoli.com/products/index/secureway_risk_mgr/index.html`

14.4 Mapping the solution to the organization

The ability to delegate the audit functions within Risk Manager allows an organization to distribute responsibilities to different administrative people. Security administrators will have the responsibility for customizing the rules files and defining things like thresholds and categories whereas IT Operators only see basic security alerts and events. This functional delegation model should be applied according to the individual internal organization of the company; the purpose of this discussion is to describe the functional responsibilities.

Figure 14-8 on page 378 describes the organization and the role of each actor:

- ► Security Administrator

    He has to define the audit policies, for example, which system should be audited, what are the 'trusted' hosts, and so on. His job is also to configure the Risk Manager files and define values like thresholds, categories, adapters, and so on, to fit into the company profile and needs. Another administrator task is to document security instructions that describe situations and what actions should be taken for specific events, and to build automated scripts when it is possible. This is an ongoing task, as new threats are discovered and new tasks are needed to protect the network all the time.

- ► Operator

    He basically sits in front of the central console and receives the Security audit events. His job is to react accordingly and apply the procedures and documents written by the Security Administrator. He interacts with the System and/or Application Administrator to solve the problem; he could also interact with the users.

► Support

This function can be an external product's support, or the security Administrator himself. The major task of support is to assist the operator in the problem resolution by performing tasks he is not authorized to do.

This will ensure the continuity of security management without requiring the highest skilled administrators to perform the day to day management tasks. This helps the Security Administrator stay away from common tasks and lets him focus on upgrading his skills and therefore increase the security level and awareness of the overall company.

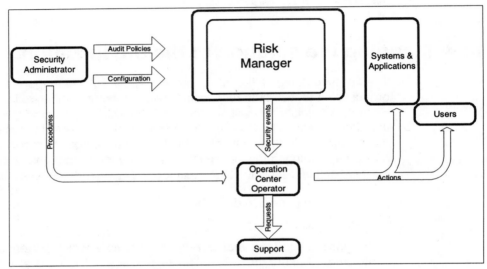

Figure 14-8   Organization flows

14.5 Intrusion Manager

For a smaller company with less than 20 servers to be managed, there is an entry level intrusion detection and vulnerability assessment product available. Tivoli Intrusion Manager provides many of the same functions as Risk Manager, but it is implemented as a single console environment.

This means that it does not rely on the Tivoli Management Framework and there is no hierarchical scaling capability. The central correlation engine and console functionality is implemented through the Availability Intermediate Manager (AIM), and multiple single Intrusion Manager environments cannot be linked together.

The ability to customize the rules engine or use the Tivoli Decision Support engine for analyzing your intrusion data is solely available to Risk Manager. So companies with the skills and complexity that requires modification of Risk Manager correlation rules would not be good candidates for Intrusion Manager.

However, all companies, even those with entry-level networks, still need protection for attacks. Intrusion Manager is a full-function system that provides that protection.

14.6 Summary

It is the function of the security audit subsystem to collect alerts from a variety of sensors, analyze them, identify real threats, and, if necessary, perform some automated actions. These actions can vary from displaying an alarm to executing a script to shutting down part of the network.

Tivoli Risk Manager provides a simple, easy-to-use enterprise console to monitor, view, and manage alerts across the enterprise. By correlating events from multiple security tools, Risk Manager is able to recognize attack patterns and escalate situations and events to the console. And because the events are routed to a single point of control (the management area), fewer resources are required. In addition, because the rules and actions have been defined by the administrator, lower level personnel can monitor the console and handle basic alerts.

In addition to the real-time handling of events, Risk Manager also has a powerful set of decision support reports for historical analysis to facilitate preventative measures.

Extending the centralized security audit subsystem

This chapter talks about expanding the security audit subsystem into a more complex environment. In addition to the real-time security management processes, the historical view of data collected by the audit subsystem, with tasks of data mining and analysis, is explored. These views allow IT management to understand the effectiveness of the security system, in order to identify areas of potential problems, and to take action for improved security.

15.1 Company profile

Nuts & Bolts, Inc. has been acquired by the large enterprise introduced in Chapter 11, "Basic management for identities" on page 259. After the merger, Nuts & Bolts, Inc. still maintains their own network, Web site, and applications, including e-commerce, but all connections external to their network will flow through the new corporate center. The challenge is how to integrate these entities into a secure corporate environment, with consistent security policies and management processes.

For this discussion, we focus on three locations, where each location maintains its own network (Web servers, servers, databases, and network sensors), as shown in Figure 15-1 on page 383. In each location, there is local administration available to supervise all the elements of the local environment, system, network, as well as security. Several types of firewalls (PIX, FW1, and IBM) and Interactive Session Support RealSecure network scanners are already installed.

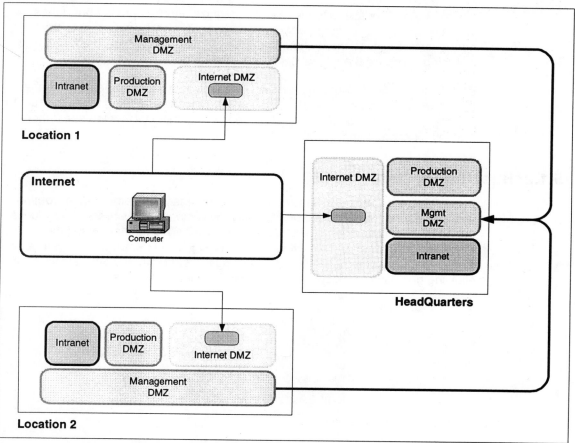

Figure 15-1   Network integration architecture

15.1.1 Business requirements

From the overall enterprise perspective, the goal is to have a consistent level of security across the business. The CEO wants to be assured that there will be no new exposures because they acquired some companies in order to expand the global reach of the enterprise.

As mentioned earlier, security is only as strong as the weakest link, and in this distributed environment, it is desirable to have local operators who can act quickly on threats.

At the headquarters location, the administrators need to see the security events coming from all locations to be able to recognize attacks across boundaries. There is an obvious concern about the number of events being sent to the headquarters site, so there should be a way to filter and reduce the number of incoming events to the consolidated administrators.

Beyond these day to day requirements, the CIO also wants to be assured that the environment is secure and that the proper actions are being taken to react to threats. He wants to be able to look at each organizational level to see if there are any local problems.

15.1.2 Business design

In each location, the complete set of audit functions is implemented for routine security monitoring. Because of the new requirements, this scenario introduces the concept of Data Mining, shown in Figure 15-2. This function helps the enterprise to understand the effectiveness of high level decisions and policies in greater detail by summarizing and analyzing the data in many different ways, allowing drill downs to identify individual component problems.

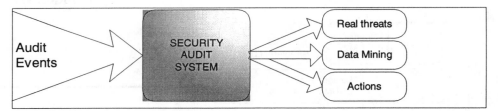

Figure 15-2   Enhanced audit flow structure

15.1.3 Security design objectives

The reduction of the number of events sent to the central management servers is very important, because you can easily overload the network with audit flow alone, which can be very heavy in the case of an ongoing attack (thousands of events per minute). The security audit product should provide a way to summarize similar events coming from the same source without attenuating the meaning of those events. In addition, local correlation could provide an even more meaningful event to be forwarded.

A data mining product is an essential tool in the security management system. The administrators must have the ability to build historical reports and to summarize suspicious activities (per day, per network, per location, and so on). A data mining tool provides the capability to be proactive and to have benchmarks to improve the global network security of the company. This tool should help the security administrators to prove the effectiveness of countermeasures taken.

Security administrators decide how to set up the security audit system and which actions are to be taken when a threat is discovered. The audit needs are not the same for each location, so the security audit product should provide the capability to distribute a general audit configuration to all sites and the flexibility to allow for independent customization of thresholds and actions.

15.1.4 Security audit subsystem

In this expanded enterprise view, all components of the security audit subsystem (log handler, audit handler, analysis engine, security rules, alarm handler, storage, and console) are implemented within each location of the company. Refer to Section 14.2, "Security audit subsystem" on page 367 for a detailed description of the components.

For the enterprise view, summarized alerts are sent to the headquarters security management zone for correlation with events from other locations. Data mining and analysis of raw data (all events from all locations) is performed at the headquarter level as well.

15.2 Risk Manager

The design of the Tivoli Management Environment (TME) is very scalable, making it very easy to implement Risk Manager in a larger enterprise. This section explains the layout for implementing the audit subsystem using Risk Manager.

15.2.1 The distributed environment

With multiple locations and an expanding set of security sensors, all the events cannot be sent to one Risk Manager server. Any one of the following situations could pose problems:

► The workload of the server will be so great that it cannot handle all the events in a reasonable time.

► The links between locations have a limited bandwidth, and are already partially loaded with production non-security events.

- Each location has its own particularity and administrator.

Risk Manager, TEC, and the TME Framework can be configured into a distributed environment that fits the structure of the enterprise:

- One Risk Manager server per location
- A global Risk Manager server that correlates all the pre-correlated situations and events passed from the location

This architectural approach, as shown in Figure 15-3, answers the workload concerns. Only correlated situations are sent to the central Risk Manager server instead of all the events.

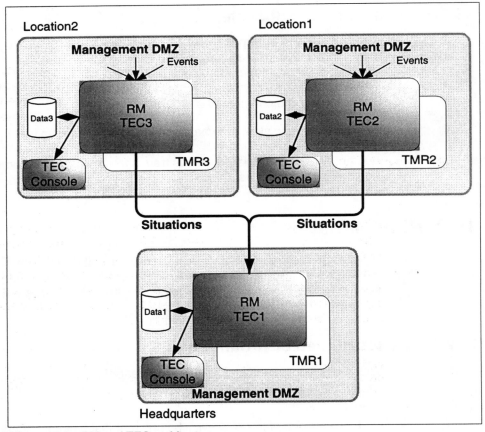

Figure 15-3   RM and TEC architecture

The Event Integration Facility (EIF) summarization capability can reduce the load of the local Risk Manager server in each location by only forwarding summarized events from the individual sensors and adapters. All location specific events are then correlated by the local Risk Manager server and stored locally within each location. After correlation, only situations are forwarded to the headquarter's Risk Manager server. The headquarter's server correlates these situations from the remote locations to recognize a distributed attack against the global enterprise. This is a good example of a case where individual policies can be the same, but the thresholds for correlation are different for headquarter and locations. Since the global Risk Manager server is only receiving situations, the thresholds would be much lower than on the remote servers receiving events.

This architecture gives you the ability to manage local security events and provided a high level correlation (situations correlation) for the headquarter administrator. The fact to correlate situations helps you detect an attack against all the locations.

Because all events are stored in a relational data base, standard SQL queries could be used to extract reports for Risk Manager events. The data mining capability however, which builds the event information into three dimensional cubes, provides analysis and reporting features beyond simple SQL.

15.3 Tivoli Decision Support

The Tivoli Decision Support (TDS) engine provides the capability to analyze and build data into three dimensional cubes. It also provides the interface for guides to run against those cubes. The guides are built upon best practices found in the particular disciplines being reviewed. The guides not only analyze the data and produce reports, but also offer best practice resolutions or proactive suggestions. Tivoli Decision Support aids analysis and decision making in an organization. In addition to Risk Manager, other Tivoli Decision Support Guides are available, such as Network Management, Support Center, Capacity Management, Event Management, and Software Distribution.

TDS enables the possibility of extracting data on a daily base so the data can be up-to-date. TDS handles the delivery and, more importantly, accessibility of the data. User access to information and the ability to share that information via printouts or files makes TDS an easy to use tool.

15.3.1 TDS and Risk Manager

The Tivoli Decision Support for Enterprise Risk Management component of Risk Manager provides aggregated, historical information about security events reported to the Risk Manager event console. You can use Tivoli Decision Support for Enterprise Risk Management to:

► Automate collection of security event data from the event database

► Answer questions about historical event rates, trends, peak volume, event types, and source of events

► Present historical information in multi-dimensional, graphical format

Tivoli Decision Support for Enterprise Risk Management works with all adapters. Information is presented using bar charts or text reports.

TDS retrieves data from Risk Manager servers using Open Database Connectivity (ODBC) connections. The architecture described in Figure 15-4 on page 389 shows one possible configuration. In this example, each location collects the event data and sends it to a centralized server.

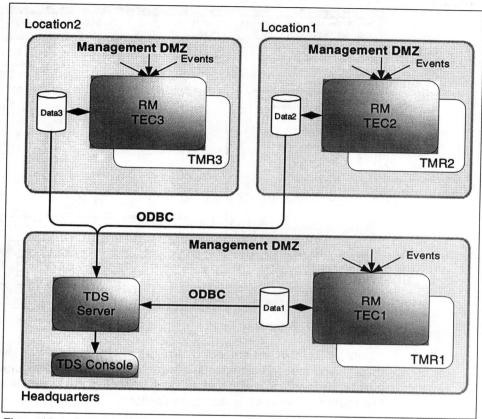

Figure 15-4   TDS architecture

15.3.2 TDS in the company architecture

The TDS architecture is built after the Risk Manager architecture, and all local events are stored in a local relational database. The central TDS server collects data from each location.

TDS can provide weekly or daily reports. In the following pages, we show some examples of TDS reports.

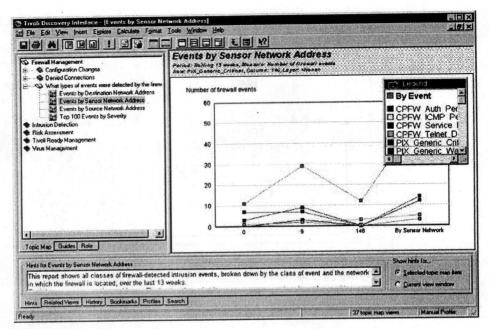

Figure 15-5   TDS Sensors report

Figure 15-5 shows the number of events send by sensor. This view is useful in determining the load of sensors in order to improve the configuration. Too many events per sensor is a sign that the configuration of the sensor is not optimized or that there are too much unauthorized actions.

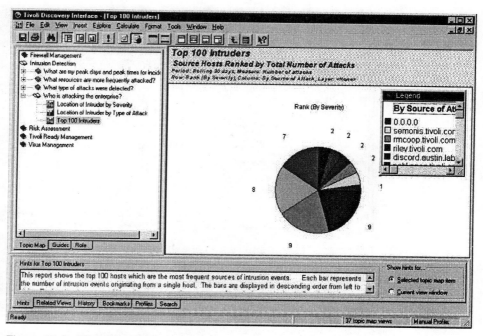

Figure 15-6   TDS Top 100 Intruders

Figure 15-6 helps show the most common sources of suspicious activities: an internal host, a partner, an isolated Internet user, and so on. This view provides a way to prove that somebody has tried to compromise your data or Web site using a particular host. These guides also provide the ability to 'drill down' to the event level that make up this picture.

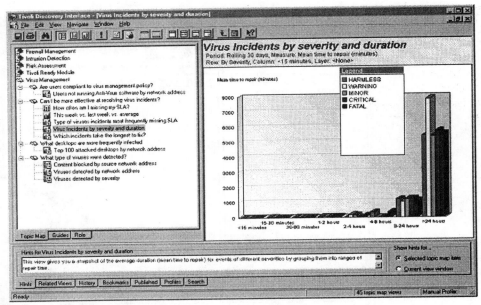

Figure 15-7   TDS antivirus report

The antivirus analysis Figure 15-7 helps security administrators identify users not conforming to company virus protection guidelines, as well as those systems most frequently plagued by viruses. As with the other guides, best practice recommendations are provided for proactive measures.

TDS provides a multitude of other views. You can also filter the reports to provide separate views for the individual companies or partners in your enterprise. Reports can be built for each location and for the entire company. Tivoli Decision Support provides a Web publishing feature, which gives you the ability to produce reports and allow users to review the reports for only their environment with a Web browser.

15.3.3 Mapping the solution to the organization

The architecture depicted in Figure 15-8 on page 393 provides good help to everybody involved in organizing the security effort.

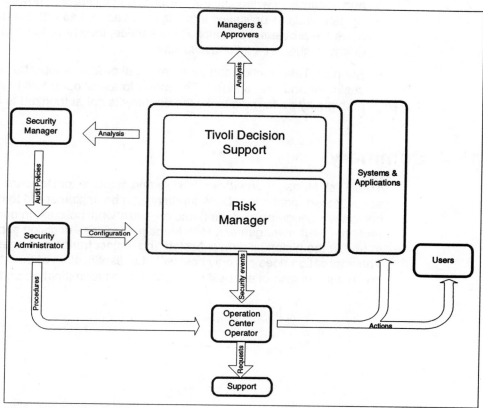

Figure 15-8   Organization flow

► Managers: They consult the reports coming from Tivoli Decision Support and it helps them to supervise the activities on the network.

► Security Manager or Security Officer: Responsible for defining the audit policies (what, when, and how). To refine these policies, the manager can use Tivoli Decision Support to figure out the strengths and weaknesses of the overall implementation.

► Security Administrator: Physically configures the Risk Manager files (thresholds, categories, adapters and so on) to implement the audit policies defined by the Security Manager or Security Officer. Another administrator task is to document instructions that describe situations, what actions should be taken for specific events, and to build automated scripts when it is possible. This is an ongoing task as new threats are discovered and new tasks are needed to protect the network.

► Operators: An operator sits in front of the console when receiving security audit events. Their job is to react to situations by executing the procedures and documents written by the Security Administrator. They interact with the System and/or Application administrators as well as with the users in order to solve the problem. For continuity of service, they have to be organized in teams to support a 24x7 availability.

► Support: This function can be an external product support or internal customer and user support. The aim is to assist operators to solve the problem by performing tasks the operator is not authorized to do on his own.

15.4 Summary

Tivoli Risk Manager provides a flexible and scalable tool for consolidating security alert monitoring. Configurations can be implemented to meet a company's geographic, staffing and organizational policies. In addition to real-time alert management, Risk Manager provides decision support capability to review the historical data collected and project trends and potential issues. The application does not only help with the identification of threats and security breaches, but also offers best practices actions for mitigation and remedy.

Part 5

Using MASS in business scenarios

In this part, we discuss how to apply the Method for Architecting Secure Solutions (MASS) to specific business scenarios in order to define an overall enterprise security architecture.

Global MASS - an example

In our final chapter, we present a practical example of applying the Method for Architecting Secure Solutions (MASS) within an e-business IT infrastructure.

As described in Chapter 2, "Method for Architecting Secure Solutions" on page 15, MASS will work with standard components to represent the security solution in a formal way. MASS will start from a high level view, based on the business requirements, and end with a detailed (but still non-product or technical related) view. This chapter discuses the four steps of this process.

16.1 Business view

In this view, we are focusing on the elements that are defined by the company's business needs: the customers, as well as the internal staff, have to work on the ordering system. The customer is located in an area that is totally *uncontrolled* by the company while the internal employees are working on the company intranet. This section of the network is controlled and its access is *restricted*. The ordering system is located in the most *secured* part of the network.

Despite several levels of *access control,* a flow needs to be established and controlled between the three components that all belong to the same *community* performing e-business transactions.

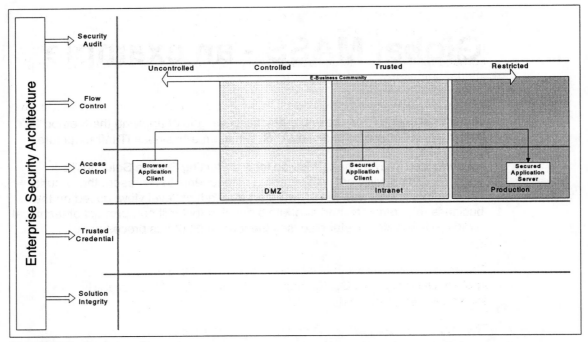

Figure 16-1   Business view

The view depicted in Figure 16-1 integrates all the aspects of the solution described before. In the next step, we describe all the components necessary to achieve the security solution in a more detailed way.

16.2 Logical view

The logical view is now applying some security concepts to the previous one, such as:

▶ Different level of network security

▶ Portals

▶ SSO

Two new areas will also be introduced:

▶ Auditing

▶ Integrity

Although the customers, the employees and the ordering system are part of the same community, they are obviously not directly connected. They belong to areas that are not offering the same level of trust. The e-business community is composed of (sub)communities with different levels of trust and the equivalent security measures.

The *external community* is the least trusted and controlled one, and the systems that are located in this community are uncontrolled. In order for these systems to become part of the overall e-business community they will have to verify their identities by using specific authentication mechanisms, that is, user authentication within the Web application.

The *managed communities* are considered controlled because there are at least basic control mechanisms in place to monitor access in this area. Any system located in this community can be considered an 'authorized system' located on the intranet.

The *closed community* contains critical systems where a high level of control is applied. Dynamic Host Configuration Protocol (DHCP) is, for example, not allowed in this community.

The customers are part of the external community. Because this system is not considered trusted, the communication channel must be secured and the user authenticated. This will be done within the controlled area, which is a demilitarized zone (DMZ) between the uncontrolled area and the restricted area. A new component has to be added in order to deliver the necessary functionality: a Web portal working as an interface between the remote system and the internal secured ordering system.

It is obvious that, due to the nature of the information exchanged, the data integrity must be preserved. Also, auditing functions are needed to supervise the external/internal communication in order to log all transactions within the ordering system. A single sign-on system is needed to propagate user authentication and credential information from one system to the other.

The different components are shown in Figure 16-2.

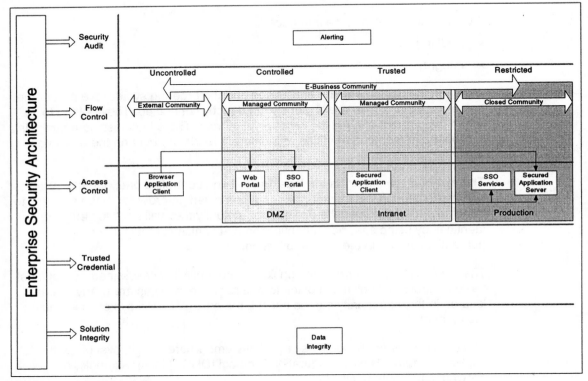

Figure 16-2   Logical view

16.3 Detailed view

We have introduced the basics of the functions that we are using, such as SSO, Web portal, data integrity, and so on. This section describes them in more detail and Figure 16-3 on page 401 draws the picture.

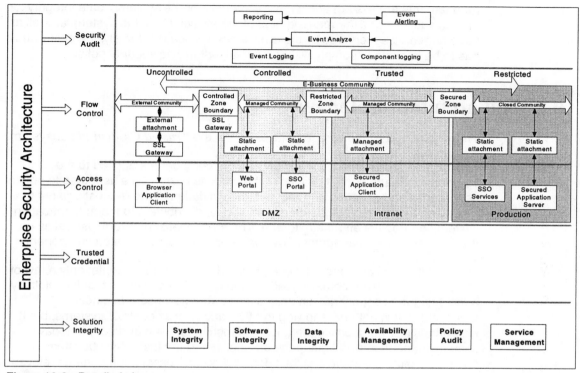

Figure 16-3   Detailed view

The access and flow control section are now dealing with the need to interface the various areas with their different levels of trust. Therefor the *boundary components* are added. These components can be implemented as a firewall or network segregation function. Another function of a boundary component is the SSL terminator that is located between the uncontrolled and the controlled community.

The *security audit* subsystem is collecting two specific types of elements: the *event logging* receives life events from active devices/applications and the *component logging* gets information from sources, such as other log files or active network scanners, and so on. This will result into the delivery of reports and alerting and/or reactions.

Another level of detail is added in terms of attachment type. This describes the actual type of connectivity, mainly if it is static or managed (for example, dynamic IP addressing, when using DHCP services for intranet systems).

In terms of solution integrity, all the components are described by now. The basic requirements are system and software integrity for the systems, data integrity for the transactions and the management of the availability of the system, as well as the other services required by the e-business application. Finally, the policy audit has to be in place to comply with the overall enterprise security policy.

16.4 Full architectural view

We have added all the components except in the *Trusted Credential* subsystem.

This section represents the workflow and the components applied to the credential management. It describes the process flow when a user tries to obtain new access authorization: the request, the validation of the request against the rules, and the creation of the credential and its distribution to the authentication systems/end-points and their storage. The credential subsystem also relies on the corporate user management system represented as a related component.

This architectural approach is representing a very simple example; only a few of the components were actually used. However, it already shows that it is globally addressing the security design objectives of an enterprise e-business architecture. It is not only showing the flow and access controls systems, but it also brings into perspective the auditing function that is mandatory in today's security infrastructures. Adding the credential and the integrity subsystem into one global picture lets the architect depict all the necessary components relevant to an overall enterprise security architecture, as shown in Figure 16-4 on page 403.

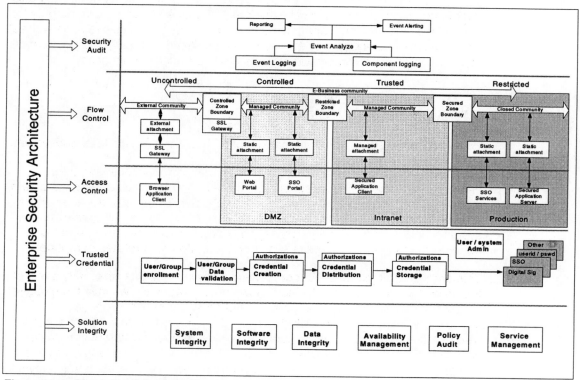

Figure 16-4   The full architectural view

Part 6

Appendixes

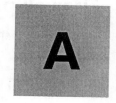

Additional product information

This appendix provides additional product information for firewalls, PKI, and virus protection software that were not discussed in Chapter 3, "IT infrastructure topologies and components" on page 49.

This appendix contains information on the following:

- ► Firewalls
  - – Cisco PIX
  - – Symantec Enterprise Firewall
  - – Check Point VPN-1/FireWall-1
- ► PKI environments
  - – iPlanet Certificate Management System
  - – RSA Keon
  - – Verisign
- ► Antivirus packages
  - – Norton AntiVirus
  - – Panda Global Virus Insurance
  - – Trend AntiVirus

Firewall packages

Firewalls are part of the security architecture of a network. They protect resources from other networks and individuals by controlling access to the network and enforcing a security policy that can be tailored to suit the needs of the enterprise. There are many firewalls available for purchase today. This section will only touch upon three: Cisco PIX, Symantec Enterprise Firewall (formerly Axent Technologies Raptor Firewall) and Check Point Software's Check Point Firewall-1.

Cisco PIX

The Cisco PIX Firewall solution is an integrated hardware/software appliance that uses a version of the Cisco IOS and offers good performance. The product line is available for almost any size operation or enterprise. Cisco's PIX firewalls provide the latest in security technology, ranging from stateful inspection, IPSec, L2TP/PPTP based VPNs, content filtering, and integrated intrusion detection.

The center of the PIX firewall family is an Adaptive Security Algorithm (ASA), which maintains secure perimeters between networks controlled by the firewall. The ASA design creates session flows based on source and destination TCP sequence numbers, port numbers, and additional TCP flags. Some models of Cisco PIX firewalls will allow you to create multiple demilitarized zones (DMZs) for your network by adding additional interface cards.

Cisco PIX firewalls provide a scalable and secure architecture. They also offer reliability by leveraging integrated stateful fail-over capabilities that can allow network traffic to automatically be sent to a hot standby in the event of a failure, supported by maintaining the concurrent connections via automated state synchronization between the primary and the secondary. PIX also provides Network Address Translation (NAT) and Port Address Translation (PAT) to concealed IP addresses of internal networks and to expand network address space for internal networks.

For more information on this and other Cisco products, visit:

`http://www.cisco.com`

Symantec Enterprise Firewall

Symantec Enterprise Firewall (formerly Axent Technologies Raptor Firewall) is a full featured security software package that will allow you to protect your network from outside threats. Enterprise Firewall is fairly easy to install and configure. It includes such features as content filtering, Out of Brand Authentication, Windows NT Domain Authentication, and RSA SecureID or CryptoCard. Combined with the optional packages, Symantec Enterprise VPN (formerly PowerVPN) and personal firewall, Symantec Enterprise Firewall can also extend the corporate perimeter to provide secure, low-cost connectivity for remote offices and telecommuters.

Symantec Enterprise Firewall minimizes your network's vulnerabilities and delivers full-featured security, offering control of information entering and leaving the enterprise but still providing partners and customers with secure access to resources. Its support for user authentication methods such as Radius, Digital Certificates, LDAP, and NT domain authentication, gives administrators the flexibility to use existing security policies. Symantec Enterprise Firewall offers a choice of hardware- or software-based solutions as well as integrated Web and Usenet content filtering.

Developed for the Windows NT/2000 and Solaris platforms, Enterprise Firewall allows administrators to manage security policies from a central console. Enterprise Firewall can be utilized as a basic communication mechanism with network devices, deployed with a DMZ or with a DMZ and multiple firewalls. With the proper licensing, you may deploy Enterprise Firewall wherever you perceive a weakness in your network.

For more information visit the Symantec Web site at `http://www.symantec.com`.

Check Point Software's Check Point FireWall-1

Check Point FireWall-1 is a full featured enterprise security product that has a modular and scalable architecture. This component approach allows you to design and implement security as your business needs change and to manage those changes from a central point. Like the preceding products, authentication, console management, security policy implementation, and LDAP are core components. However, with the addition of the many optional modules available, you may expand the breadth of the base product.

FireWall-1 software is designed to run on Windows NT, Sun Solaris, Red Hat Linux, HP-UX, and IBM AIX.

FireWall-1 supported hardware platforms include Check Point VPN-1 Appliances, ODS SecurCom 8000 family, Alcatel (Xylan) switches, Nortel ARN - ASN - BN System 5000 routers, and Nortel Connectivity switches. FireWall-1 is designed to integrate with the following network interfaces: ATM, Ethernet, Fast Ethernet, FDDI, and Token Ring.

For much more detailed information concerning FireWall-1 and its various component packages, visit Check Point Software's Web site at:

`http://www.checkpoint.com`

PKI

X.509 Public Key Infrastructure (PKI) is an Internet Official Protocol Standard that is, in simple terms, a digital ID. It is used to verify that a message or document was authored by a certain person, and that it was not altered or modified by anyone else. Digital IDs are a standard way to establish proof of identity using a variety of protocols. They certify that a document was signed by a person with a certain public key when opened by the recipient that holds the private key. It does not matter if someone else holds the original public key, because it is of no value in decrypting the document.

The discussion regarding how this is achieved is lengthy and beyond the scope of this redbook. More detailed information may be found in the redbook *Deploying a Public Key Infrastructure,* SG24-5512 or *RFC2459 Internet X.509 Public Key Infrastructure* at `http://www.ietf.org/rfc.html`.

iPlanet/Netscape Certificate Management System

iPlanet™ Certificate Management System delivers a PKI solution that enables an organization to deploy and manage its own certificate authority. iPlanet Certificate Management System offers easy integration with existing systems and business processes, comprehensive support for controlled networks and certificate-enabled applications, enhanced deployment and policy control, and a highly scalable and extensible architecture that supports large e-commerce deployments. iPlanet Certificate Management System may be extended through integration with third-party products and can be further customized using published application programming interfaces (APIs) for authentication, policy modules, and custom extensions.

Features Overview

- Provides a complete solution to issue, renew, suspend, revoke, and manage X.509v3 certificates

- Provides high scalability and performance to support millions of users

- Enables fast deployment and easy management through integration of iPlanet Directory Server

- Offers extensibility and easy integration through published APIs

- Provides interoperability with leading third party VPN, router, smartcard, token, and other PKI solutions

For additional information, visit iPlanet's Web site at:

`http://www.iplanet.com/products`

RSA Keon

RSA offers a family of PKI products for e-business that alone or together offer the ability to manage digital certificates.

▶ RSA Keon Certificate Authority

RSA Keon Certificate Authority software issues, manages, and validates digital certificates. The software includes secure administration, enrollment, and directory and logging servers, as well as a Simple Certificate Enrollment Protocol (SCEP) server that provides automatic enrollment for issuing certificates to SCEP-compliant Virtual Private Network (VPN) devices. RSA Keon Certificate Authority software also features a powerful signing engine for digitally signing end-user certificates and system events, as well as an integrated data repository for storing certificates, system data, and certificate status information.

▶ Registration Authority

RSA Keon Registration Authority (RA) software works with the Certificate Authority (CA) to streamline the enrollment process for handling large volumes of end-user certificate requests. It verifies the credentials of certificate requests and provides certificates to the requestor. The RSA Keon RA software enables organizations to set up either remote or local stand-alone enrollment centers for large user implementations at distributed geographic locations, thereby allowing the organization to scale its certificate management system while moving the approval process closer to the users.

▶ Key Recovery Module

The RSA Keon Key Recovery Module (KRM) software, an optional component of the RSA Keon CA software, provides a way to securely archive and recover private encryption keys of users. It combines reliable and secure long-term encryption key-pair storage with straightforward, secure user enrollment.

For more information, see:

http://www.rsasecurity.com/products/keon/index.html

VeriSign

Offers several different options for PKI as well as other services that are out sourced.

OnSite Managed Trust Service

VeriSign OnSite is a fully integrated PKI managed service designed to secure intranet, extranet, Virtual Private Network (VPN), and e-commerce applications by providing maximum flexibility, performance, and scalability with the highest availability and security.

The OnSite service allows you to establish a customized PKI and Certificate Authority (CA) system for issuing digital certificates throughout your enterprise. Unlike software-only solutions or building your own PKI, the OnSite managed service lets you leverage the knowledge at VeriSign without adding additional tasks to your internal staff. With OnSite, you control certificate issuance and management while VeriSign provides a backbone of certificate processing services.

For more information, see the Web site:

`http://www.verisign.com/products/pki/index.html`

Antivirus software

Why include antivirus software in a discussion of security architectures? Viruses are a breach of your system, can result in lost man hours, down time and, ultimately, lost revenue. One of the top ten tips for protecting your online assets should include the distribution and use of antivirus software.

Packages available today are easy to install and have an effective update mechanism.

Norton AntiVirus by Symantec

One of the world's leading antivirus solutions delivers advanced virus detection and elimination software to businesses of all sizes. This multiplatform solution provides easy-to-use, customizable, install-and-forget protection that begins guarding your workstations, servers, and gateways as soon as it is installed.

Safety first

Rare or previously unknown viruses do not have to be fatal. During installation, Norton AntiVirus/IBM® Solution Suite provides a generic disinfection feature, a patent-pending technology that records information about your files for later use in disinfection. If a file is infected with a rare or previously unknown virus, generic disinfection attempts to use the recorded information to reconstruct the original uninfected file. If the reconstruction exactly matches the original file, the file will be safely disinfected.

Automatic updates

With an average of 10 to 15 new viruses discovered every day, it is critical to keep your virus protection current. LiveUpdate enables automatic retrieval of new virus definitions from Symantec up to once a week. Run your first Live Update session during installation and schedule future sessions to run automatically, helping ensure that your network is always protected against the latest virus threats without interrupting network activity.

Efficient performance

Exclusive Scan Caching technology provides fast scanning time and low bandwidth consumption. Once a file has been scanned and found to be virus-free, it will not be scanned again until changes are made, greatly improving day-to-day server performance. Norton AntiVirus scans all files in real-time as they are accessed or copied to and from the server. You can save even more time by scheduling automatic scans at regular intervals.

Quarantine infected files

Norton AntiVirus Quarantine technology provides a safe zone on a Quarantine server where you can isolate infected files and attachments for repair when network activity is lower. This quarantine area helps ensure that your other files stay clean and that you do not accidentally send infected files to anyone else. Quarantines, virus scans and removal can be managed from any location using a Web browser.

Product Highlights

▶ Detects and removes known, previously unknown and unidentified viruses

▶ Works in the background to provide continuous, automatic protection

▶ Provides broad coverage of clients, servers, and gateways

▶ Detects and disinfects most in-the-wild viruses

▶ Analyzes viruses byte-for-byte before disinfection

▶ Offers the same look-and-feel across multiple platforms

▶ Automates and centralizes administration

▶ Virtually eliminates false alarms

▶ Delivers automated, server-based updates of the AntiVirus products

For more information, see the Web site http://www.symantec.com/product/.

Panda Software Global Virus Insurance

Global Virus Insurance is an easy to use and effective package, which includes the Panda Administrator. Global Virus Insurance offers protection for NT Servers, Exchange Servers, Novell Servers, and all workstation platforms, such as Windows 98, Windows 95, Windows NT Workstations, Windows 3.1x, MS-DOS and OS/2.

Centralized deployment across all workstations, servers, and e-mail platforms is simplified with technology that scans at the Winsock and TCP/IP level. One signature file fits all platforms. Panda Software's Virus Signature Database can be updated every day and the package can be configured to download the update automatically. When the download is complete, Panda Administrator automatically sends the update out to all workstations. This feature ensures that the updates actually get done on all the workstations.

Product features

► Daily, automatic, intelligent updates of the Virus Signature Database.

► Automatic distribution of updates to all workstations on your network.

► Scans and disinfects the FTP, NNTP, POP3, and SMTP Internet protocols at the Winsock level.

► Offers scanning and disinfection for ALL the most widely used e-mail clients in the market, both MAPI and/or POP3. Also integrates into Exchange and Notes/Domino GroupWare environments.

► Is the only antivirus product that offers scanning and disinfection in the BODY of e-mail messages, both in Rich Text Format (RTF) and HTML formatted e-mail messages. Panda also scans and disinfects OLE embedded objects and nested messages, as many levels as needed.

► Performs e-mail scanning while in memory, as opposed to copying files to temporary drives, disinfecting them with the desktop antivirus, and re-attaching them to e-mail messages.

► Free 24 hour S.O.S. Virus service.

► Centralized antivirus management for the corporate and enterprise infrastructure, with end-to-end protection for the widely used operating system platforms.

► MAPI-Compliant antivirus that scans and disinfects the Message Transfer Agent (MTA) Connectors, such as the Internet Mail Connector and the X.400 Connectors.

For more information, refer to the Web site:

`http://www.pandasecurity.com/gviinfo.htm`

Trend Antivirus Solutions

Trend Micro, Inc. is a leader in network antivirus and Internet security software and services over a large variety of packages for your enterprise. Its solutions protects the flow of information on PCs, file servers, e-mail servers and at the Internet gateway, providing a complete, centrally-controlled VirusWall for enterprise networks. With an innovative and technology-driven focus, Trend Micro has migrated antivirus applications from the desktop to the network server and the Internet gateway. Utilizing ease of installation and use, multi-platform support and strong central management tools.

For a complete set of product descriptions and management tools, please visit:

`http://www.antivirus.com/products/`

Additional resources and information

For more information on virus related issues or antivirus products, visit these Web sites:

- ► CNET Networks: `http://www.cnet.com`
- ► Ziff-Davis Press: `http://www.zdnet.com`
- ► Consumer Information Organization: `http://Anti-Virus.com`
- ► CarnegieMellon Software Engineering Institute: `http://www.cert.org`
- ► Computer Security Resource Center: `http://csrc.ncsl.nist.gov`

Single Sign-On - a contrarian view

The purpose of this appendix is to outline some of the issues associated with achieving Single Sign-On (SSO) in a real enterprise environment. Many organizations embark on these efforts without having thoroughly considered the issues and, more importantly, the costs and benefits. We hope that this discussion will help better understand the issues and the implications of an SSO solution. The content of this appendix is the work of Keys Botzum, a Senior Consulting I/T Specialist in the IBM Software Services, WebSphere Practice. For updates on the original whitepaper and other material published by the author, please visit http://www.transarc.ibm.com/~keys.

Introduction

Single Sign-On (SSO) is the holy grail of many organizations. Broadly, by achieving SSO, users will log in once to an SSO domain and then never be challenged again while accessing multiple secured resources. The Open Group defines SSO as:

> *Single Sign-On (SSO) is a mechanism whereby a single action of user authentication and authorization can permit a user to access all computers and systems where that user has access permission, without the need to enter multiple passwords.*[1]

Originally, this was to be achieved by developing all applications and tools to use a common security infrastructure and avoid the current situation of heterogeneous security infrastructures. This includes a common format for representing authentication information or credentials. This approach implies a number of valuable benefits:

► For end users

- Only one authentication mechanism to remember. For password-based authentication, this means users only have to remember one password.

- If using passwords, users only have to update one password and follow one set of password rules.

- A single sign-on for each user into the SSO domain, typically only once per day.

► For I/T operations

- A single common registry of user information (possibly replicated).

- A single common way to manage user information.

- A single common security infrastructure.

► Security advantages

- A common secure infrastructure leveraged enterprise wide that can be carefully managed and secured.

- Depending on the security approach taken, secure delegation of credentials is possible. This will enable end-to-end security, possibly across application and system boundaries.

- Easier to manage and protect common registry.

- Easier to verify user security information and update when necessary rather than tracking down all operational systems. This is particularly valuable when users move to new roles with different access levels.

---

[1] Taken from the security section of the Open Group Web site (http://www.opengroup.org/security/topics.htm)

- Can enforce common enterprise wide password and security policies.
- Users less likely to write down passwords since they only have to remember one.

The problem

Creating a common enterprise security infrastructure to replace a heterogeneous infrastructure is, without question, the best technical approach. This has been and is being attempted with technologies like the OSF Distributed Computing Environment (DCE), Kerberos, and with PKI based systems, but few, if any, enterprises have actually achieved this.

Unfortunately, the task of changing all existing applications to use a common security infrastructure is very difficult. This has been further hampered by the lack of consensus as to what should be the common security infrastructure. Today we have many proprietary security systems, as well as several competing security standards and pseudo-standards: Kerberos, DCE, Microsoft's Active Directory and related technologies, PKI, and so on. Of course, these technologies do not interoperate seamlessly. As a result, these proprietary and standards based solutions, while very appropriate, cannot be applied to every system. For example, until recently[2], WebSphere Application Server could not recognize authentication information from systems other than itself. Organizations that had some proprietary Web based authentication system found that they were problematic with WebSphere Application Server. Problems like these occur over and over again across an enterprise as organizations buy products without fully considering the implications.

The Proxy-SSO "Solution"

Since moving all applications to a single common security infrastructure is extraordinarily difficult, many enterprises attempt to create the illusion (for end users) of one common security infrastructure through the use of a number of SSO products that support some mechanism to authenticate to existing legacy systems without user intervention. Throughout this document I will refer to this as proxy-SSO to distinguish this from *true* SSO achieved by creating a common security infrastructure. These products typically use some proprietary authentication mechanism and then reauthenticate transparently to multiple underlying systems via the user interfaces to those systems. This involves some

---

[2] WebSphere Application Server now (as of WebSphere Application Server 3.5.3 and later) supports a feature known as Trusted Associations that allows the WebSphere Application Server security infrastructure to recognize (via custom coding) credentials from other security systems when provided to Web based applications. The Lightweight Third-Party Authentication (LTPA) cookie provides another means of forwarding user's credentials.

form of scripting engine that drives the interaction with each underlying system's authentication challenge. The scripting engine simulates a user logging in like normal so the underlying systems do not need to be changed. A proxy-SSO database stores all combinations of user names, passwords, and systems.

The solution is difficult, expensive, and incomplete

The task of configuring a proxy-SSO system for a typical large enterprise with numerous existing systems is staggering, as custom scripts must be developed for every possible user authentication interaction. For the UNIX operating system utilities, we have ftp, telnet, rsh, and rlogin. Add to this list the utilities for other operating systems, custom applications, and Web sites, and the number is enormous. In addition, once the scripts are created, they must be maintained. As the underlying systems change their interfaces, the scripts will require changes. This results in an ongoing maintenance cost that is rarely considered. The scripting also hides the "front-door" to an application from the end users and thus might bypass important information such as security warnings that are displayed on the login page.

A central proxy-SSO database of user name and password mappings must also be created and maintained. This database must follow all password restriction and invalidation rules for all enterprise systems. It must be updated whenever underlying passwords are changed, or it must be the only system that changes passwords (creating yet another scripting task for each enterprise system). This does not even address systems that use other authentication mechanisms, such as certificates, challenge-response, SecureID cards, and so on.

Here is a summary of the costs of proxy-SSO:

► Initial costs

- Product purchase.

- Customization of product for existing systems. This usually involves creating custom scripts to drive the legacy systems. This is a large work effort.

- Loading existing user information into the proxy-SSO solution and deploying to users.

► Ongoing costs

- The usual software upgrade costs.

- Another registry to maintain. This system must be highly available.

- Password management by users. When passwords expire in the various legacy systems, users must update the legacy system and the SSO system. Since users are no longer familiar with the login procedure for the legacy systems, they may not even know their passwords. This may make it impossible for users to change their own passwords without assistance.

- Script maintenance. As the legacy system user interfaces change, the scripts will have to change. It is important to understand how much effort will be required to do this.

Of course, many of these costs can be controlled by carefully designing the underlying applications to work with a script-based proxy-SSO solution, but this largely defeats the main tenant of these proxy-SSO solutions: no need to modify "legacy" systems.

On the benefit side, the proxy-SSO solution saves users the trouble of typing in their user name and password to several different systems several times per day and remembering all of these user name and password combinations. While this is certainly an issue, it is not clear how much real benefit this provides to the organization. The most troublesome aspect of multiple authentication systems is probably remembering the number of passwords, not the actual authentication effort. This point will be revisited later. Of course, in very high cost situations, such as call centers, these benefits are significant and can probably justify the cost of a SSO solution. In other, more routine environments, the benefit is far less clear.

From a security perspective, the results are mixed. The enterprise still has multiple incompatible security infrastructures and now has one more security product and one more user registry (another point of attack). On the positive side, if the proxy-SSO solution can manage the changing of user passwords in all legacy systems transparently, then users will no longer have difficulty remembering passwords and will no longer write them down.

In summary, proxy-SSO solutions tend to provide limited benefit to end users while not addressing most of the operational and security costs of a heterogeneous security infrastructure and introduce new operational costs.

The Web

Recently, efforts to achieve fully general SSO have largely died out. Now, however, a newer form of limited SSO is becoming popular: Web based SSO. In this space, there are products that authenticate users using some mechanism and then create credentials that can be used by downstream Web applications for authorization. This is the perfect insertion point of a Policy Director based Web portal that can provide true Web SSO to all back-end Web application spaces.

Unfortunately, as in the non-Web space, changing all existing Web systems is difficult. Thus, people are again embarking on proxy-SSO solutions for the Web. It is believed that this is simpler because Web applications have just one interface: the Web browser. However, while a single user interface simplifies the problem, it does not mean that all Web applications authenticate the same way. There are many different ways of asking a user to authenticate. Even in a simple Web based application, the proxy-SSO scripting engine must be able to traverse an arbitrary Web application and enter input just as if the user had done so. This problem, while significantly simpler than enterprise proxy-SSO, is still difficult in general.

To script a Web interaction around a password based authentication system, the following issues must be considered:

► The initial request to the target site must be rerouted to the proxy-SSO server that will then retarget the request appropriately.

► Basic authentication is trivial, because the challenge protocol is well defined and easy to intercept.

► Form based authentication presents the following unique problems:

– The login page must be loaded and parsed in order to extract the needed hidden fields and find the action and target servlet.

– Forms may ask additional questions beyond user name and password.

– There may be more than one action on the form.

– Sites may use elaborate Java Script to challenge the user and/or encrypt the user's authentication information before sending it back to the server.

– Browser's are notoriously lenient in their presentation of illegal HTML. The proxy-SSO solution needs to work with illegal HTML that is browser displayable to avoid forcing changes to existing sites.

► Traversing a Web site to simulate a user login interaction requires addressing these issues:

– Some sites present informative messages to users before the login process starts. Bypassing these messages, particularly if they are security warnings, is problematic.

– Cookies sent before the post-login welcome page of the target application must be preserved.

– Sites that detect the browser type and make decisions before or during the login process must be handled. This information must be passed through from the browser by the proxy-SSO solution.

- Sites may create dynamic URL strings during and before the login process with encoded information in the URL (for example, http://www.abc.com/index.html?session=12345).

- Sites may pop up additional browser panels during the login process

► Proxy server (in the Web proxy server sense) solutions must address these additional issues:

- URLs embedded in the responses must be rewritten to point to the proxy. Embedded URLs may be absolute (for example, http://www.abc.com/app/page.html), server root relative (for example, /app/page.html), or page relative (for example, page.html).

- URLs embedded in Java Script must be rewritten. For some systems, this may be impossible if the URLs are computed on the client. Even if not, this requires parsing the entire response stream looking for particular characters. This will affect performance.

- Cookies sent back by the site must have the Domain and Path values rewritten to point to the proxy so the browser will not discard them.

- Multiple sites, when combined under a single proxy, may reference resources that conflict with each other. URLs and cookie names may no longer be unique.

It is worth noting that some applications that appear to be Web applications are so sufficiently complex that they are really full-fledged applications. Many "Web" applications use plug-ins, extensive Java Script, and Java applets to create a fuller user experience. These types of applications may not be addressable via the techniques described above.

One should not forget that Web application user interfaces change rapidly and this will affect scripts that depend on the existing interface. It should be obvious, that while the Web solution simplifies the client interaction problems, it is hardly trivial. Finally, the other operational issues (heterogeneous infrastructure, multiple, registries, password maintenance, and so on) associated with a proxy-SSO solution remain.

An alternative approach

We have spent quite a bit of time discussing the weaknesses of the proxy-SSO approaches. Now it is time to look at the problem more closely and try to determine an approach that achieves as many of the benefits of "true" SSO as possible without creating new operational problems.

Looking back at the benefits of SSO from "Introduction" on page 418, we can see that most of the benefits derive from the single registry. Here is the list again, this time with items that are the direct result of a common registry *emphasized*:

► For end users

- Only one authentication mechanism to remember. *For password-based authentication, this means users only have to remember one password.*

- *If using passwords, users only have to update one password and follow one set of password rules.*

- A single sign-on for each user into the SSO domain, typically only once per day.

► For IT operations

- *A single common registry of user information (possibly replicated).*

- *A single common way to manage user information.*

- A single common security infrastructure.

► Security advantages

- A common secure infrastructure leveraged enterprise wide that can be carefully managed and secured.

- Depending on the security approach taken, secure delegation of credentials is possible. This will enable end-to-end security, possibly across application and system boundaries.

- *Easier to manage and protect common registry.*

- *Easier to verify user security information and update when necessary rather than tracking down all operational systems. This is particularly valuable when users move to new roles with different access levels.*

- *Can enforce common enterprise wide password and security policies.*

- *Users less likely to write down passwords because they only have to remember one.*

Interestingly, from a business perspective, the emphasized items are the ones with the greatest cost benefit. While a complete solution is most desirable, this comes remarkably close. It is especially worth noting that while end users get most of the benefits of SSO with a single registry, an organization can also significantly reduce the operational cost of registry maintenance simply by consolidating to single registry. For the end user, they must authenticate multiple times per day using the same user name and password, which, while irritating, is not a significant cost.

It is also worth noting that a proxy-SSO solution can be built on top of a common registry solution. This will greatly simplify the proxy-SSO problem and result in a better overall infrastructure. However, it is not clear if this is worth the additional cost given the limited benefit.

Of course, there is no panacea. Using a common registry requires that all existing applications be migrated to use this new registry and some organization must manage this critical business system. While not trivial, this cost will be leveraged across numerous applications that no longer have to manage a user registry.

The best registry to choose is one that supports Lightweight Directory Access Protocol (LDAP). There are a number of LDAP server products that can be purchased. Additionally, most security products and middleware products that support secure access can use an LDAP directory for authentication. Once an enterprise embarks on this effort, they may find that many applications can switch easily to LDAP simply by reconfiguring the middleware that they use. For example, Netscape Enterprise Server, Apache, IBM's HTTP Server, AIX, Solaris, and WebSphere Application Server already support LDAP out of the box. Additionally, Microsoft's Active Directory can provide LDAP services to other clients.

How to select an LDAP directory product is beyond the scope of this redbook. As with any enterprise class product, you should examine vendor support, scalability, performance, replication, fault tolerance, extensibility, security, tools, and features. In particular, you will want to consider password management features, such as account lockout and strength rules. These are not part of the LDAP standard, so they will be vendor specific.

For applications that use custom developed security registries, change will be required. This fact alone should raise concerns. If an application team develops the registry, how does the enterprise security team know that the registry is well designed and well managed?

Fortunately, LDAP application programming interfaces (APIs) are available for many programming languages, including C/C++, Java, and Perl. The APIs are quite trivial to use because of their simplicity, so conversion of existing applications is feasible. While it is not realistic to believe that all applications can be converted, it is reasonable to expect that future applications will use a common registry. Additionally, most PKI based systems require a registry for user information and LDAP is widely supported. Because many organizations are moving toward PKI anyway, this can be viewed as a stepping-stone toward a full PKI-based security infrastructure. Existing applications can be converted to use the LDAP registry as appropriate, based on cost and benefit. Over time, this will greatly improve the situation without introducing a large and complex system that will require ongoing maintenance without significantly improving the situation. For those considering an SSO solution, now is the time to act. With each passing day, more and more incompatible systems are being deployed in your enterprise.

Conclusion

The appendix has discussed two approaches to SSO: a homogenous infrastructure and proxy-SSO. The costs and benefits of these approaches have been discussed. A practical alternative to SSO involving a common registry has also been discussed.

We hope that you now more fully understand the issues, costs, and benefits surrounding SSO solutions. You have to look at your own organization and carefully consider the costs and benefits in order to derive a true and accurate picture. This will require careful analysis and experimentation by highly skilled people. Should you then decide to go forward with a proxy-SSO solution, you will at least understand the task that lies before you.

Related publications

The publications listed in this section are considered particularly suitable for a more detailed discussion of the topics covered in this redbook.

IBM Redbooks

For information on ordering these publications, see "How to get IBM Redbooks" on page 430.

- ▶ *All About Tivoli Management Agents*, SG24-5134
- ▶ *Deploying a Public Key Infrastructure,* SG24-5512
- ▶ *Extending Network Management Through Firewalls*, SG24-6229
- ▶ *HACMP Enhanced Scalability Handbook,* SG24-5328
- ▶ *e-business Risk Management with Tivoli Risk Manager*, SG24-6036
- ▶ *IBM WebSphere V4.0 Advanced Edition Security*, SG24-6520
- ▶ *The OS/390 Security Server Meets Tivoli: Managing RACF with Tivoli Security Products*, SG24-5339
- ▶ *Tivoli Enterprise Management Across Firewalls*, SG24-5510
- ▶ *Tivoli SecureWay Risk Manager Correlating Enterprise Risk Management*, SG24-6021
- ▶ *Tivoli Security Management Design Guide*, SG24-5101

Other resources

These publications are also relevant as further information sources:

- ▶ *Tivoli SecureWay Policy Director WebSEAL Administration Guide Version 3.8.0*, GC32-0684
- ▶ Keys Botzum, Single Sign-On - A contrarian view, IBM whitepaper. For more resource information see http://www.transarc.ibm.com/~keys.
- ▶ Lloyd and Galambos, *"Technical Reference Architectures,"* IBM Systems Journal 38, No. 1, 51–75 (1999), G321-0134
- ▶ Rechtin, *Systems Architecting: Creating and Building Complex Systems*, Prentice Hall, 1991, ISBN 0138803455

- Schneider, *Trust in Cyberspace*, National Academy Press,1999, ISBN 0309065585

These publications are packaged with their corresponding software and cannot be purchased separately:

- *Access Manager Version 3.9 Base Administration Guide*
- *Access Manager WebSEAL Administration Guide*
- *Risk Manager 3.8 User's Guide*
- *Tivoli Access Manager Administration API Developer Reference*
- *Tivoli Access Manager for WebSphere Application Server User Guide Version 3.9*

Referenced Web sites

These Web sites are also relevant as further information sources:

- This RiskServer site is intended to act as a launchpad for information security and security review needs. It covers a variety of solutions and topics, including security risk analysis, information security policies, ISO 17799 (BS7799), business continuity, and data protection legislation.

  http://www.riskserver.co.uk/

- Home page of the Common Criteria, which represents the outcome of a series of efforts to develop criteria for evaluation of IT security that are broadly useful within the international community.

  http://www.commoncriteria.org

- Anti-Virus.com home page

  http://Anti-Virus.com

- CERT Coordination Center home page

  http://www.cert.org

- Check Point home page

  http://www.checkpoint.com

- Cisco Systems home page

  http://www.cisco.com

- CNET.com home page

  http://www.cnet.com

- ► IBM alphaWorks Web page

  `http://www.alphaworks.ibm.com`

- ► IBM Security Software Web page

  `http://www.ibm.com/software/security`

- ► IBM WebSphere Application Server home page

  `http://www.ibm.com./software/webservers/appserv/`

- ► IBM WebSphere Edge Server home page

  `http://www.ibm.com/software/webservers/edgeserver/`

- ► iPlanet home page

  `http://www.iplanet.com/products`

- ► Lotus Domino R5 Application Server Web page

  `http://www.lotus.com/home.nsf/welcome/dominoapplicationserver`

- ► National Institute of Standards and Technology Computer Security Resource Center home page

  `http://csrc.ncsl.nist.gov`

- ► Open Group Security Forum Web page

  `http://www.opengroup.org/security/topics.htm`

- ► Panda Security home page

  `http://www.pandasecurity.com/gviinfo.htm`

- ► RFC home page

  `http://www.ietf.org/rfc.html`

- ► RSA Keon Web page

  `http://www.rsasecurity.com/products/keon/index.html`

- ► Symantec home page

  `http://www.symantec.com`

- ► Symantec product home page

  `http://www.symantec.com/product/`

- ► Tivoli Public Key Infrastructure Web page

  `http://www.tivoli.com/products/index/secureway_public_key/index.html`

- ► Tivoli Risk Manager Web page

  `http://www.tivoli.com/products/index/secureway_risk_mgr/index.html`

- ► Tivoli User Administration Web page

  `http://www.tivoli.com/products/index/user_admin`

- ► Trend Micro product home page

  `http://www.antivirus.com/products/`

- ► VeriSign home page

  `http://www.verisign.com/products/pki/index.html`

- ► WebSphere Application Server - Software Prerequisites Web page

  `http://www-3.ibm.com/software/webservers/appserv/doc/v35/idx_aas.htm`

- ► WebSphere Application Server - Supported prerequisites and APIs Web page

  `http://www-3.ibm.com/software/webservers/appserv/doc/v40/prereqs/ae_v402.htm`

- ► ZDNET.com home page

  `http://www.zdnet.com`

How to get IBM Redbooks

Search for additional Redbooks or Redpieces, view, download, or order hardcopy from the Redbooks Web site:

   `ibm.com/redbooks`

Also download additional materials (code samples or diskette/CD-ROM images) from this Redbooks site.

Redpieces are Redbooks in progress; not all Redbooks become Redpieces and sometimes just a few chapters will be published this way. The intent is to get the information out much quicker than the formal publishing process allows.

IBM Redbooks collections

Redbooks are also available on CD-ROMs. Click the CD-ROMs button on the Redbooks Web site for information about all the CD-ROMs offered, as well as updates and formats.

Glossary

ActiveX   ActiveX is the name Microsoft has given to a set of "strategic" object-oriented programming technologies and tools. The main technology is the Component Object Model (COM). Used in a network with a directory and additional support, COM becomes the Distributed Component Object Model (DCOM). The main thing that you create when writing a program to run in the ActiveX environment is a component, which is a self-sufficient program that can be run anywhere in your ActiveX network (currently a network consisting of Windows and Macintosh systems). This component is known as an ActiveX control. ActiveX is Microsoft's answer to the Java technology from Sun Microsystems. An ActiveX control is roughly equivalent to a Java applet.

BS7799   British Standard 7799, a document describing enterprise security.

CA   A Certificate Authority is an authority in a network that issues and manages security credentials and public keys for message encryption. As part of a public key infrastructure (PKI), a CA checks with a Registration Authority (RA) to verify information provided by the requestor of a digital certificate. If the RA verifies the requestor's information, the CA can then issue a certificate.

CORBA   Common Object Request Broker Architecture is an architecture and specification for creating, distributing, and managing distributed program objects in a network. It allows programs at different locations and developed by different vendors to communicate in a network through an "interface broker." CORBA was developed by a consortium of vendors through the Object Management Group, which currently includes over 500 member companies. Both the International Organization for Standardization (ISO) and X/Open have sanctioned CORBA as the standard architecture for distributed objects (which are also known as components). CORBA 3 is the latest level.

CTCPEC   Canadian Trusted Computer Product Evaluation Criteria published by the Canadian government.

DMZ   A DMZ (demilitarized zone) is an area of your network that separates it from other areas of the network, including the Internet.

EJB   Enterprise JavaBeans is an architecture for setting up program components, written in the Java programming language, that run in the server parts of a computer network that uses the client/server model. Enterprise Java Beans is built on the JavaBeans technology for distributing program components to clients in a network. Enterprise Java Beans offers enterprises the advantage of being able to control change at the server rather than having to update each individual computer with a client whenever a new program component is changed or added. EJB components have the advantage of being reusable in multiple applications. To deploy an EJB Bean or component, it must be part of a specific application, which is called a container.

ITSEC   Information Technology Security Evaluation Criteria, published by the European Commission.

J2EE   Java 2 Platform Enterprise Edition is a Java platform designed for the mainframe-scale computing typical of large enterprises. Sun Microsystems, together with industry partners such as IBM, designed J2EE to simplify application development in a thin client tiered environment.

JDBC   Java Database Connectivity is an application program interface (API) specification for connecting programs written in Java to the data in popular database. The application program interface lets you encode access request statements in structured query language (SQL) that are then passed to the program that manages the database. It returns the results through a similar interface. JDBC is very similar to the SQL Access Group's Open Database Connectivity (ODBC) and, with a small "bridge" program, you can use the JDBC interface to access databases through the ODBC interface.

JNDI   Java Naming and Directory Interface enables Java platform-based applications to access multiple naming and directory services. Part of the Java Enterprise application programming interface (API) set, JNDI makes it possible for developers to create portable applications that are enabled for a number of different naming and directory services, including file systems, directory services, such as Lightweight Directory Access Protocol (LDAP), Novell Directory Services, and Network Information System (NIS), and distributed object systems, such as the Common Object Request Broker Architecture (CORBA), Java Remote Method Invocation (RMI), and Enterprise JavaBeans (EJB).

JSP   Java Server Page is a technology for controlling the content or appearance of Web pages through the use of servlets, small programs that are specified in the Web page and run on the Web server to modify the Web page before it is sent to the user who requested it.

LDAP Lightweight Directory Access Protocol is a software protocol for enabling anyone to locate organizations, individuals, and other resources, such as files and devices, in a network, whether on the public Internet or on a corporate intranet. LDAP is a "lightweight" (smaller amount of code) version of Directory Access Protocol (DAP), which is part of X.500, a standard for directory services in a network.

LTPA Lightweight Third Party Authentication implements an authentication protocol that uses a trusted third-party Lightweight Directory Access Protocol (LDAP) server. LTPA causes a search to be performed against the LDAP directory. LTPA supports both the basic and certificate challenge type.

MASS Method for Architecting Secure Solutions

NIS Network Information System is a network naming and administration system for smaller networks that was developed by Sun Microsystems. NIS+ is a later version that provides additional security and other facilities. Using NIS, each host client or server computer in the system has knowledge about the entire system. A user at any host can get access to files or applications on any host in the network with a single user identification and password. NIS is similar to the Internet's domain name system (DNS) but somewhat simpler and designed for a smaller network. It is intended for use on local area networks.

OPSEC Open Platform for Security Check Point initiative to provide a common architecture for integrating security solutions.

OSI Open Systems Interconnection is a standard description or "reference model" for how messages should be transmitted between any two points in a telecommunication network. Its purpose is to guide product implementors so that their products will consistently work with other products. The reference model defines seven layers of functions that take place at each end of a communication. Although OSI is not always strictly adhered to in terms of keeping related functions together in a well-defined layer, many if not most products involved in telecommunication make an attempt to describe themselves in relation to the OSI model. It is also valuable as a single reference view of communication that furnishes everyone a common ground for education and discussion.

PKI A public key infrastructure enables users of a basically unsecure public network such as the Internet, to securely and privately exchange data and money through the use of a public and a private cryptographic key pair that is obtained and shared through a trusted authority.

RA A Registration Authority is an authority in a network that verifies user requests for a digital certificate and tells the certificate authority (CA) to issue it. RAs are part of a public key infrastructure (PKI), a networked system that enables companies and users to exchange information and money safely and securely. The digital certificate contains a public key that is used to encrypt and decrypt messages and digital signatures.

SOAP Simple Object Access Protocol is a way for a program running in one kind of operating system to communicate with a program in the same or another kind of an operating system by using the HTTP Protocol and XML as the mechanisms for information exchange.

SSL The Secure Sockets Layer is a commonly-used protocol for managing the security of a message transmission on the Internet. SSL has recently been succeeded by Transport Layer Security (TLS), which is based on SSL.

UDDI Universal Description, Discovery, and Integration is an XML-based registry for businesses worldwide to list themselves on the Internet. Its ultimate goal is to streamline online transactions by enabling companies to find one another on the Web and make their systems interoperable for e-commerce.

WAP Wireless Application Protocol is a specification for a set of communication protocols to standardize the way that wireless devices, such as cellular telephones and radio transceivers, can be used for Internet access, including e-mail, the World Wide Web, newsgroups, and Internet Relay Chat (IRC). While Internet access has been possible in the past, different manufacturers have used different technologies. In the future, devices and service systems that use WAP will be able to interoperate.

WML Wireless Markup Language, formerly called HDML (Handheld Devices Markup Languages), is a language that allows the text portions of Web pages to be presented on cellular telephones and personal digital assistants (PDAs) via wireless access. WML is part of the Wireless Application Protocol (WAP) that is being proposed by several vendors to standards bodies.

WSDL The Web Services Description Language is an XML-based language used to describe the services a business offers and to provide a way for individuals and other businesses to access those services electronically. WSDL is the cornerstone of the Universal Description, Discovery, and Integration (UDDI) initiative spearheaded by Microsoft, IBM, and Ariba.

XML eXtensible Markup Language is a flexible way to create common information formats and share both the format and the data on the World Wide Web, intranets, and elsewhere. For example, computer makers might agree on a standard or common way to describe the information about a computer product (processor speed, memory size, and so forth) and then describe the product information format with XML. Such a standard way of describing data would enable a user to send an intelligent agent (a program) to each computer maker's Web site, gather data, and then make a valid comparison. XML can be used by any individual or group of individuals or companies that wants to share information in a consistent way.

XSL eXtensible Stylesheet Language is a language for creating a style sheet that describes how data sent over the Web using the eXtensible Markup Language (XML) is to be presented to the user.

Abbreviations and acronyms

AAT	Application Assembly Tool
ACL	Access Control List
ADDS	Architecture, Development, and Deployment Support
ADS	Microsoft Active Directory
AIM	Availability Intermediate Manager
AM	Access Manager
AM/BI	Access Manager for Business Integration
AMOS	Access Manager for Operating Systems
AMWAS	Tivoli Access Manager for WebSphere Application Server
anzAPI	Authorization Application Programming Interface
API	Application Programming Interface
ASA	Adaptive Security Algorithm
BA	Basic Authentication
BEA WLS	BEA WebLogic Server
BP	Business Processes
BPO	Business Process Object
CA	Certificate Authority
CAS	Collaborative Application Server
CC	Common Criteria
CDAS	Cross Domain Authentication Service
CDMF	Cross Domain Mapping Framework
CDSA	Common Data Security Architecture
CDSSO	Cross Domain Single Sign-On
CICS	Customer Information Control System
CLI	Command Line Interface
COM	Common Object Model
CORBA	Common Object Request Broker Architecture
CTCPEC	Canadian Trusted Computer Product Evaluation Criteria
CVE	Common Vulnerabilities and Exposures
DAP	Directory Access Protocol
DB2	Database 2
DCE	Distributed Computing Environment
DCOM	Distributed Common Object Model
DECS	Domino Enterprise Connection Services
DHCP	Dynamic Host Configuration Protocol
DMZ	Demilitarized Zone
DNS	Domain Name Server
DOM	Document Object Model
DTD	Document Type Definition
EAR	Enterprise Archive File
EAS	External Authorization Service
EIF	Event Integration Facility
EJB	Enterprise Java Beans
EPAC	Extended Privilege Attribute Certificate
EPAC	Extended Privilege Attribute Certificate
ESMTP	Extended Simple Mail Transfer Protocol

EWG	IBM Everyplace Wireless Gateway	**JNDI**	Java Naming and Directory Interface
FTP	File Transfer Protocol	**JSP**	Java Server Page
GRE	Generic Routing Encapsulation	**LDAP**	Lightweight Directory Access Protocol
GUI	Graphical User Interface	**LTPA**	Lightweight Third-Party Authentication
HDML	Handheld Devices Markup Language	**MAC**	Message Authentication Code
HTTP	Hypertext Transfer Protocol	**MAS**	Master Authentication Server
HTTPS	Secure Hypertext Transfer Protocol	**MASS**	Methodology for Architecting Secure Solutions
IBM	International Business Machines Corporation	**MIME**	Multipurpose Internet Mail Extensions
IDE	Integrated Development Environment	**MPA**	Multiplexing Proxy Agent
		MTA	Message Transfer Agent
IDEF	Intrusion Detection Exchange Format	**NAT**	Network Address Translation
IDS	Intrusion Detection System	**ND**	Network Dispatcher
IDWG	Intrusion Detection Working Group	**NIS**	Networked Information System
IETF	Internet Engineering Task Force	**NTP**	Network Time Protocol
IMAP4	Internet Message Access Protocol Version 4	**OCSP**	Online Certificate Status Protocol
IP	Internet Protocol	**ODB**	Object Database
ISO	International Organization for Standardization	**ODBC**	Open Database Connectivity
		OPSEC	Open Platform for Security Checkpoint
ISS	Interactive Session Support	**OSI**	Open Systems Interconnection
ITSEC	Information Technology Security Evaluation Criteria	**PAM**	Plug-in Authentication Module
ITSO	International Technical Support Organization	**PAT**	Port Address Translation
		PDA	Personal Digital Assistant
J2EE	Java 2 Platform Enterprise Edition	**PII**	Personally Identifiable Information
JAR	Java Archive	**PKI**	Public Key Infrastructure
JASS	Java Authentication and Authorization Services	**PKIX**	Public Key Infrastructure X.509
JDBC	Java Database Connectivity	**POC**	Proof of Concept
JMS	Java Message Service	**POP**	Protected Object Policy

POP3	Post Office Protocol Version 3	TGSO	Tivoli Global Sign-On
QoS	Quality of Service	TIM	Tivoli Identity Manager
RA	Registration Authority	TLS	Transport Layer Security
RACF	Resource Access Control Facility	TME	Tivoli Managed Environment
RDBMS	Relational Database Management System	TMF	Tivoli Management Framework
RMI	Java Remote Method Invocation	TMR	Tivoli Managed Region
		TOE	Target of Evaluation
RMO	Risk Manager Observer	TPKI	Tivoli Public Key Infrastructure
RPC	Remote Procedure Call	TSF	TOE Security Functions
S/MIME	Secure Multipurpose Internet Mail Extensions	TSM	Tivoli Security Manager
SLA	Service Level Agreement	TUA	Tivoli User Administration
SMB	Small Medium Business	TUARS	Tivoli User Administration Request Server
SMP	Symmetric Multi-Processor		
SMS	Short Messaging Services	UDDI	Universal Description, Discovery, and Integration
SMTP	Simple Mail Transfer Protocol	VPN	Virtual Private Network
SNMP	Simple Network Management Protocol	W3C	World Wide Web Consortium
SOAP	Simple Object Access Protocol	WAP	Wireless Application Protocol
		WAR	Windows Archive
SQL	Structured Query Language	WML	Wireless Markup Language
SSL	Secure Socket Layer	WPM	Access Manager Web Portal Manager
SSO	Single Sing-On		
TACF	Tivoli Access Control Facility	WSDL	Web Service Description Language
TAI	Trust Association Interceptor	WTE	Web Traffic Express
TAME	Tivoli Access Manager for e-business	XML	eXtensible Markup Language
		XSL	eXtensible Style Language
TAR	Token Authenticator		
TCB	Trusted Computer Base		
TCP	Transmission Control Protocol		
TCP/IP	Transmission Control Protocol/Internet Protocol		
TCSEC	Trusted Computer System Security Evaluation Criteria		
TDS	Tivoli Decision Support		
TEC	Tivoli Enterprise Console		

Index

Numerics

4758
IBM PCI Cryptographic Coprocessor 75

A

access control 4, 19, 20, 23, 32, 37, 43, 53, 92, 158, 288
access control mechanisms 29
access control monitoring 29
access control subsystem 115
  security design objectives 148
Access Manager 106, 295, 334
  ... for BEA WebLogic Server 105
  ... for Business Integration 101, 252
  ... for Operating Systems 103
  ... for WebSphere Application Server 104, 221
  access control 92
  Access Manager for Operating Systems 318
  ACL 84
  architecture 125
  authentication 93
  authorization 320
  authorization database 84, 86, 92, 106
  authorization service 80, 85, 92, 106
  availability 159
  aznAPI 106, 219
  bridging 240
  CDAS 186
  CDMF 244
  CDSSO 243
  communication 126
  component deployment 123
  components for CDSSO and e-Community 232
  Cross Domain Authentication Service 108
  Cross Domain Mapping Framework 109
  Cross Domain Single Sign-On 243
  delegation 87
  distributed communication 238
  e-Community single sign-on 95, 246
  EPAC 81
  extended attributes 85
  External Authorization Service 107
  hardening 141
  identity 80
  Immune-Programs 323
  Impersonator-Programs 323
  interfaces 106
  J2EE 210
  JAAS 210, 211
  junction 91
  LDAP configuration 168
  Login-Programs 322
  LTPA 211, 217
  Management Console 86
  Master Authentication Server 247
  pdadmin 81, 86, 106
  PDPermission 211, 220
  permission types 321
  permissions 323
  physical component layout 139
  Plug-in for Edge Server 97
  Plug-on Authentication Modules 184
  Policy Server 81, 86, 120, 126, 235
  Policy Server availability 169
  POP 84
  protected object policy 84, 106
  protected object space 84, 91, 106, 169
  query_contents 92
  reverse proxy 91
  scalability 170
  Secure-Files 322
  Secure-Programs 322
  security policy 125
  single sign-on 91, 95, 114, 118, 148, 212, 242
  SSL 238
  TGSO junction 212
  trust 180
  Trust Association Interceptor 211, 213
  user registry 80, 81, 120, 127
  virtual hosting 97
  VPN 239
  Web Portal Manager 81, 86
  Web Server plug-in 98
  WebSEAL 111
Access Manager Policy Server
  availability 169
  failure 161

Access Policy Evaluator 115
account management 272
accountability 55
ACL 84, 164, 169
ActiveX 63, 431
adapters 339
administration 55
AMOS 103
analysis of security audit data 26
anonymity 32
antivirus 337, 355, 412
Application Offload 69, 70
application-level intrusion detection 353, 355
architectural decision 40
asset classification 6
asset protection 55
assurance 55
audit 23, 25, 37, 43, 114, 118, 140, 158
Audit Generator 115
audit subsystem 363, 367, 381, 385
    security design objectives 366, 384
auditing 289
authentication 19, 20, 29, 32, 93, 108, 114, 148, 178, 181, 184, 187, 288
    fingerprint 278
    flexibility 175
    smartcard 278
    step-up 175
    strength 175
    WebSEAL 94
authorization 55, 114
authorization database 84, 86, 92, 106
authorization mechanisms 29
Authorization Server
    scalability 171
Authorization Server availability 166
authorization service 80, 85, 92, 106
availability 55, 157, 159, 162, 165
    Access Manager Policy Server 169
    Authorization Server 166
    user registry 167
    Web Portal Manager 169
    Web server 165
    WebSEAL 163
Availability Intermediate Manager 345
Axent Technologies Raptor Firewall 408
aznAPI 106, 205, 211, 219, 221
    Java 2 security model 106

B

basic authentication 185
BEA WebLogic Server
    Access Manager for ... 105
    Custom Realm 105
Binding Enabler 115
blade 79
British Standard 7799 3
BS7799 3
business continuity 4
business process flow 32
Business Process Objects 306
business requirements 147, 365, 383
    access control application integration 202
    access control subsystem 147
    audit subsystem 365, 383
    CDSSO 228
    credential subsystem 263
    e-Community 228
    identity and credential subsystem 287
    WebSEAL 117, 175

C

CA 75, 410, 411, 431
Caching Proxy 70
CDAS 108
CDSA 75
CDSSO 243
certificate 44, 185, 310
Certificate Authority 75, 410, 411, 431
Check Point FireWall-1 353, 374, 409
Cisco Local Director 163
Cisco NetRanger 354
Cisco PIX Firewall 353, 374, 408
Cisco router 374
Cisco SecureIDS 354
collection of security audit data 26
Common Criteria 15, 20, 23, 53
Common Object Request Broker Architecture 431
communication 20
compliance 5
component access 20
component architecture 46
computer management 6
confidentiality 101
container-based authorization 221
Content Distribution Framework 69, 70
content filtering 408

controlled zone 54
CORBA 63, 431, 432
correlation 342, 350, 357
    local 384
Credential Validator 115
credentials 53
credentials life cycle 32
Cross Domain Authentication Service 108
Cross Domain Mapping Framework 109
Cross Domain Single Sign-On 243
cryptographic 32
cryptographic support 20
cryptography 28, 29, 31
Custom Realm 105
CVE 360

D

data confidentiality 19
data integrity 19
data mining 384, 385
decision support 351
declarative security 207
default policies 276
delegation 87, 176, 178, 183, 190, 341
denial of service 355
deployment descriptor 207, 221, 223
design objectives 35, 37, 53
    authentication 175
    identities and credentials 288
    mapping to security subsystems 36
    WebSEAL 118, 175
DHCP 140
digital certificate 44
DMZ 55, 112, 124, 333
DNS 139
Domain Name Service 139
Domino 71
dynamic business entitlements 184
dynamic roles engine 104

E

e-business patterns 55
e-Community single sign-on 95, 246
Edge Server 64, 163
EJB 62, 162, 220, 432
    role-based security 207
EJBContext 210
electronic commerce 34

encryption 101
endpoint 272, 339
enforcement mechanisms 29
Enterprise Archive files 206
Enterprise Java Beans 62, 162, 432
environmental security 5
EPAC 81
Error Handler 115
event console 345
Event Integration Facility 370, 376, 387
event log 348, 356
event management 349
event server 345
event sources 344
Everyplace Wireless Gateway 189
extended attributes 85
eXtensible Markup Language 434
eXtensible Stylesheet Language 61, 434
External Authorization Service 107
external zone 54
extranet 333

F

failure 160
failure recovery 27
fault tolerance 27
fingerprint authentication 278
firewall 72, 335, 408
    filters 132, 135
firewall management
    Check Point FireWall-1 353
    Cisco PIX Firewall 353
firewall risk management 352
flow control 23, 30, 37, 43, 53
forms-based login 185
fraud 53
FTP 141
functional design 44

G

gateway 340
Generic Routing Encapsulation 67
Global Sign-On 278
GSKit5 95

H

hacker attack 117

hardware security modules 28
Host IDS 374
    event log 356
    syslog 356
host intrusion detection 353, 356
hosting service 133
HTTP Proxy 73
HTTP variables 197

I

IBM 4758 PCI Cryptographic Coprocessor 75
IBM MQSeries 252
IBM SecureWay Firewall 72
IDEF 360
IDEF message 348
identification 20, 29, 32
identity 80
identity and credentials 23, 32, 37, 43, 44
Identity Manager 283, 294
    audit 308
    Management Server 302, 305, 307
    Request Server 307
    self care 294, 301
    self registration 294
    servlet 302
    Web interface 300
    Web interface authentication 308
    WebSEAL and IM 308
    workflow 294
    workflow server 303
Immune-Programs 323
Impersonator-Programs 323
integrity 102, 288
Interactive Session Support 66
intrusion detection 353, 408
intrusion detection system 336
    Web IDS 337
Intrusion Manager 363
iPlanet™ Certificate Management System 410
IPSec 73, 408
ISO 17799 4
ISS RealSecure 354
IT security architecture 19
ITSEC 432

J

J2EE 62, 221, 432
    Access Manager 210

declarative security 207
deployment descriptor 207, 223
EJBContext 210
programmatic security 210, 221
J2EE 1.2 206
JAAS 106, 210, 211, 220
Java 2 security model 106
Java Authentication and Authorization Services
106, 210
Java Database Connectivity 432
Java Naming and Directory Interface 432
Java Server Pages 61, 89, 162, 432
JavaBeans 61
JDBC 61, 432
JNDI 63, 432
JSP 162, 432
junction 57, 91, 117, 121, 130, 163, 165, 183
    mutually authenticated 216
    stateful junction 165

K

Key Recovery Module 411
KRM 411

L

LDAP 62, 71, 425, 432, 433
    availability 236
liability 8
Lightweight Directory Access Protocol 425, 433
Lightweight Third Party Authentication 433
Load Balancing 69, 70
Login-Programs 322
Lotus Domino 71, 199
LTPA 70, 97, 198, 211, 217, 433

M

managed node 339
Management Console 86
Management Desktop 339, 340
MASS 15, 53
    access control 23, 37, 43
    architectural decision 40
    audit 23, 25, 37, 43
    component architecture 46
    flow control 23, 30, 37, 43
    functional design 44
    identity and credentials 23, 32, 37, 43, 44

solution integrity   23, 27, 37
solution model   40
subsystems   24
use case   41
Master Authentication Server   247
message encryption   101
message queueing   335
Method for Architecting Secure Solutions   15, 53
MPA   189
MQSeries   101, 252
Multiplexing Proxy Agent   189

N
Network Address Translation   73
network architecture   51
network configuration   123
Network Dispatcher   66
network intrusion detection   353, 354
network management   6
network security   123
nonrepudiation   19
NTP   140

O
OCSP   187
ODBC   432
Online Certificate Status Protocol   187
Open Systems Interconnection   433
OSI   433
OSI security services   19

P
Panda Global Virus Insurance   414
password   193
PD3.7 differences
    Java 2 security model   106
pdadmin   81, 86, 106
PDPermission   211, 220
performance   162
persistence   63
Personally Identifiable Information   104
personnel security   5
physical security   5
PII   104
PKI   44, 74, 102, 433
PKIX   75, 410
pkmscdsso   243

pkmsvouchfor   247
Plug-in for Edge Server   97
plug-ins   132
Plug-on Authentication Modules   184
policy
    corporate   8, 55
    security   114
Policy Director   79, 227
policy region   341
Policy Server   81, 120, 126
POP   84, 106, 169
port restrictions for WebSEAL   153
practices   10, 263
privacy   20, 53, 104
Privacy Manager   104
procedures   10
programmatic security   210, 221
prolog engine   345
protected object policy   84, 106
protected object space   84, 91, 106, 164, 169
protection of security audit data   26
protocol switching   56
proxy-SSO   419
pseudonymity   32
Public Key Infrastructure   74, 433

Q
Quality of Service   69, 70
query_contents   92
quotas   28

R
RA   75, 411, 433
Raptor Firewall   408
recovery   27
Redbooks Web site   430
    Contact us   xxiii
Registration Authority   75, 411, 433
Request Server   307
resource manager   204, 206
resource utilization   20
restricted zone   54
reverse proxy   91, 119, 132, 177, 293
risk assessments   293
Risk Manager   324, 363, 385
    adapter   347, 348, 349, 370
    analysis engine   371
    application-level intrusion detection   353, 355

architecture 347
audit handler 370
correlation 350, 357
correlation thresholds 387
data mining 384, 385
Event Integration Facility 370, 376, 387
event log 348
event management 349
firewall management 352
Host IDS 374
host intrusion detection 353, 356
IDEF message 348
intrusion detection 353
local correlation 384
log handler 370
network intrusion detection 353, 354
rules 371
sensor 370
Situations 358
summarization engine 376
syslog 348
toolkit 360
topology 331
Web IDS 337, 355, 374
WebSEAL adapter 375
risk mitigation 6, 293
role-based security 207
router 336
RSA Keon 411
RSA SecureID token 408
RSA SecurID token 186, 310

S

S/MIME 71
scalability 157, 170
Authorization Server 171
user registry 172
Web server 171
WebSEAL 170
secrets 32
Secure Sockets Layer 434
Secure-Files 322
Secure-Programs 322
SecurID token 186, 310
security architecture 19, 34
security audit 20
security audit data 26
security cost 117

security design objectives 35, 37, 53, 148, 264, 288, 366, 384
security functions
management 20
protection 20
security management 118
Security Manager 103, 283, 294, 295, 310
Access Manager for Operating Systems 318
auditing 324
group 312
procedures for UNIX and NT 314
resource 313
role 312
role-based administration 310
Security Profiles 313
subscription 311
Windows resource types 325
security organization 6
security policy 6, 114, 117, 125, 271, 286
security subsystems mapping to design objectives 36
security zones 293
sendmail 141
Service Level Agreement 264
servlet 61
session cookie 183
Simple Object Access Protocol 434
single point of failure 159
single sign-on 70, 91, 93, 95, 114, 118, 148, 184, 190, 198, 212, 242, 417
proxy-SSO 419
Situations 358
smart card 75
smartcard authentication 278
SOAP 62, 434
SOCKS 73
solution architecture 40
solution integrity 23, 27, 37
solution model 40
spoofing 72
SSL 126, 238, 434
SSL hardware acceleration 95
stateful inspection 408
stateful junction 165
stateful packet filtering 119
step-up authentication 175
subsystems 24
Symantec Enterprise Firewall 408
syslog 348, 356

T

TACF 318
TGSO junction 191, 195, 212
TGSO password 193
time services 28, 140
time synchronization 140
Tivoli Access Manager 295
Tivoli Decision Support 298, 351, 387
Tivoli Endpoint 298, 339
Tivoli Endpoint Gateways 299
Tivoli Enterprise Console 298, 342, 354, 357, 371
  correlation 342
  event console 345
  event server 345
  event sources 344
Tivoli Global Sign-On 278
Tivoli Intrusion Manager 378
Tivoli Managed Node 300, 339
Tivoli Management Desktop 339, 340
Tivoli management environment 385
Tivoli Management Framework 272, 295, 297, 337
Tivoli Management Gateway 340
Tivoli Management Region 339
Tivoli Management Server 298
Tivoli PKI 75
Tivoli Policy Director 79, 227
Tivoli policy region 341
Tivoli Risk Manager 324
Tivoli Security Manager 103, 295, 310
Tivoli User Administration 274, 295
TMR server 339
transaction system 335
transactions 32
Trend Micro Antivirus 415
trust 180
Trust Association Interceptor 211, 213
Trusted Computing Base 322
trusted credentials 53
trusted path 20
trusted zone 54

U

UDDI 62, 434
uncontrolled zone 54
Universal Description, Discovery, and Integration 434
use case 41
  access control 115

  audit 367
User Administration 283, 294, 295
  account management 272
  default policies 276
  endpoint 272
  introduction 274
  security policy 271
  validation policies 275
user data protection 20
user registry 80, 81, 120, 127
  availability 167
  failure 161
  scalability 172

V

validation policies 275
VeriSign OnSite 412
virtual hosting 70, 94, 97
Virtual Private Networks 73
virus management 355
VPN 73, 239, 408, 411

W

WAP 189, 434
Web application server 334
Web IDS 337, 355, 374
Web Portal Manager 81, 86, 130, 161
  availability 169
  Java Server Pages 89
Web server 160, 165, 333
  intrusion detection 355
  scalability 171
Web Services Description Language 434
Web Traffic Express 66, 67
WebSEAL 57, 111
  access control 92
  ACL 164
  adapter for Risk Manager 375
  adding a new WebSEAL 170
  authentication 93, 94, 108, 114, 181, 184, 187
  availability 163
  business requirements 117, 175
  CDMF 244
  components for CDSSO and e-Community 233
  Cross Domain Single Sign-On 243
  delegation 183, 190
  design objectives 118, 175
  e-Community single sign-on 246

failure   160
hardening   141
Identity Manager uses ...   308
junction   91, 117, 121, 130, 163, 165, 183
LTPA   211, 217
LTPA authentication   198
Master Authentication Server   247
mutually authenticated junction   216
network configuration   123
pkmscdsso   243
pkmsvouchfor   247
port restrictions   153
principles   118
query_contents   92
replication   94
reverse proxy   119
scalability   170
single sign-on   93, 198, 212
SSL hardware acceleration   95
TGSO junction   191, 195, 212
trust   180
Trust Association Interceptor   213
webseald.conf   164, 170
WebSphere
    Access Manager for ...   104, 221
    Application Server   59, 89, 206
    deployment descriptor   207
    Edge Server   64, 97, 163
    Enterprise Archive files   206
    Everyplace Suite   97, 189
    Transcoding Publisher   69
    Trust Association Interceptor   213
Wireless Application Protocol   434
Wireless Markup Language   62, 434
WML   62, 434
WSDL   62, 434
WTE   66

X
X.500   433
X.509   71, 74, 185, 410
XML   61, 62, 434
XSL   61, 434